Hegel

'An impressive achievement . . . I have no doubt students will find it very useful, and that it will be widely adopted as a teaching text: it covers the right topics to the right level; it engages with a wide range of Hegel's works; it is critical, while also being sympathetic.'
Robert Stern, Sheffield University, UK

'. . . the best available account in the English language of the whole sweep of Hegel's philosophy. It will be a valuable resource for students encountering Hegel for the first time.'
Sean Sayers, University of Kent, UK

'A very clear introduction . . . its greatest strengths consist in its clarity and its ability to contextualize Hegel's philosophy . . . masterfully done – the presentation is clear and engaging.'
Paul Redding, University of Sydney, Australia

Routledge Philosophers

Edited by Brian Leiter
University of Texas, Austin

Routledge Philosophers is a major series of introductions to the great Western philosophers. Each book places a major philosopher or thinker in historical context, explains and assesses their key arguments, and considers their legacy. Additional features include a chronology of major dates and events, chapter summaries, annotated suggestions for further reading and a glossary of technical terms.

An ideal starting point for those new to philosophy, they are also essential reading for those interested in the subject at any level.

Hobbes	A. P. Martinich
Leibniz	Nicholas Jolley
Locke	E. J. Lowe
Hegel	Frederick Beiser
Rousseau	Nicholas Dent
Schopenhauer	Julian Young
Freud	Jonathan Lear

Forthcoming:

Spinoza	Michael Della Rocca
Hume	Don Garrett
Kant	Paul Guyer
Fichte and Schelling	Sebastian Gardner
Husserl	David Woodruff Smith
Rawls	Samuel Freeman

Frederick Beiser

Hegel

Routledge
Taylor & Francis Group

NEW YORK AND LONDON

First published 2005 in the USA and Canada
by Routledge
711 Third Avenue, New York, NY 10017 (8th Floor)

Simultaneously published in the UK
by Routledge
2 Park Square, Milton Park, Abingdon, Oxon, OX14 4RN

Routledge is an imprint of the Taylor & Francis Group, an informa business

© 2005 Frederick Beiser

Typeset in Joanna MT and DIN by
RefineCatch Ltd, Bungay, Suffolk

Library of Congress Cataloging in Publication Data
Beiser, Frederick C., 1949–
  Hegel / Frederick Beiser. — 1st ed.
    p. cm.—(Routledge philosophers)
  Includes bibliographical references and index.
  ISBN 0–415–31207–8 (hardback : alk. paper) — ISBN 0–415–31208–6 (pbk. : alk. paper)
  1. Hegel, Georg Wilhelm Friedrich, 1770–1831. I. Title. II. Series.
  B2948.B43 2005
  193—dc22   2004020256

British Library Cataloguing in Publication Data
A catalog record for this book is available from the British Library

ISBN10: 0–415–31207–8 (hbk)
ISBN10: 0–415–31208–6 (pbk)

ISBN13: 978–0–415–31207–3 (hbk)
ISBN13: 978–0–415–31208–0 (pbk)

To my Hegel students: past, present and future

The main purpose of this book is to provide a comprehensive introduction to Hegel's philosophy, one that covers, as far as possible in a confined space, every major aspect of his thought. Although I hope it can be read with profit by Hegel scholars, it has been written primarily with a first-time reader in mind. I do not consider, therefore, some of the usual problems of Hegel scholarship, such as the detailed transitions of the dialectic or the interrelations between different parts of the system. Although these are important issues, they should not have priority in an introduction where the primary goal is to provide an overview of Hegel's philosophy.

Since my chief aim is introductory, my focus has been thematic rather than textual. I want the student to know the main themes of Hegel's philosophy rather than the content of specific texts. With the exception of Chapter Seven, I have not engaged in sustained exegesis or commentary. There are many good commentaries on Hegel's *Phenomenology*, *Logic* and *Philosophy of Right*, to which the reader is referred in the Bibliography. The chief reason for the exegetical foray in Chapter Seven will be apparent to every Hegel scholar and student. The 'Lordship and Bondage' chapter of the *Phenomenology* is central to Hegel's entire project, yet its meaning has been much disputed. It is likely that every student, sooner or later, will have to read this famous chapter. A close reading of it is therefore a necessity, even for an introduction. It was entirely appropriate when Alexander Kojève entitled his famous commentary on this chapter *Introduction to the Reading of Hegel*.

Although I have striven for comprehensive coverage, limitations of space have made it impossible for me to treat important aspects of Hegel's philosophy. Much more needs to be said about Hegel's *Science of Logic*, not least because of its foundational role in Hegel's system. I do not accept the current criticisms of Hegel's logic, and believe that it should be restored into its central place in Hegel's system; but, for reasons of space, I have had to limit myself to rebutting a few misunderstandings and to sketching its dialectical method (pp. 163–9). I have also done scant justice to Hegel's *Naturphilosophie*, which is crucial for his entire philosophy, especially his attempt to justify the organic concept of the world. Finally, Hegel's epistemology deserves much more attention; doing it full justice, however, would have unduly lengthened an already long introduction. For this reason, an earlier chapter on Hegel's reaction to the *Grundsatzkritik* and meta-critical campaign of the 1790s was dropped.

This book is the product of three decades of reflection on Hegel and his contemporaries. I first began to study Hegel in the early 1970s at Oxford, the dawn of the Hegel renaissance in the Anglophone world. My study of Hegel first came from an interest in the intellectual sources of Marxism, but gradually evolved into a general fascination for classical German philosophy. I wrote my Oxford DPhil on the origins of Hegel's *Phenomenology* under the supervision of Charles Taylor, a model *Doktorvater*, to whom I have many debts. I shelved my plans to write a detailed commentary on the *Phenomenology* when I first learned of Henry Harris's similar project, which finally bore such marvelous fruit in *Hegel's Ladder*.

All the material for this book is new, written especially for this series. An early version of Chapter Seven appeared in my 1980 DPhil. dissertation, 'The Spirit of the Phenomenology', but it has been revised heavily since then. Some of the material in Chapters One and Three has appeared in my *The Romantic Imperative: The Concept of Early German Romanticism* (Cambridge, MA: Harvard University Press, 2003). Some work on Chapters Eight and Nine, and the epilogue, began as an article on Hegel's political philosophy, which was due to appear in 1994 in the *Cambridge History of Nineteenth-Century Political Thought*, though this volume has still not appeared. Much of the material for the book was the content for a lecture course on Hegel given at Harvard in the spring of 2002.

I have now taught Hegel at six universities – Syracuse, Indiana, Harvard, Yale, Penn and Wisconsin – and I still struggle with the daunting pedagogical challenges. My students, both graduate and undergraduate, have been unfailingly enthusiastic, diligent and longsuffering fellow climbers in the attempt to conquer the Hegelian Matterhorn. My debts to their many objections, suggestions, doubts and queries over the years are immense. So to them this book is dedicated.

Finally, I am especially grateful to Robert Stern for his detailed reading of the entire manuscript.

Frederick Beiser
Syracuse, New York
10 July 2003

Abbreviations

PHILOSOPHERS OTHER THAN HEGEL
Hardenburg

HKA   *Novalis Schriften, Kritische Ausgabe*, ed. Richard Samuel, Hans Joachim Mahl and Gerhard Schulz (Stuttgart: Kohl Hammer, 1960–88), 5 vols.

Kant

Unless otherwise noted, all references to Kant are to the Akademie edition, *Gesammelte Schriften*, ed. Preußischen Akademie der Wissenschaften (Berlin: de Gruyter, 1902 *et seq.*). The page numbers of this edition appear in the margin of most English translations.

GMS   *Foundations of the Metaphysics of Morals* (*Grundlegung zur Metaphysik der Sitten*).

KpV   *Critique of Practical Reason* (*Kritik der praktischen Vernunft*).

KrV   *Critique of Pure Reason* (*Kritik der reinen Vernunft*). Cited according to the first and second editions, 'A' and 'B' respectively.

KU   *Critique of Judgment* (*Kritik der Urteilskraft*).

TP   'On the Common Saying: This May Be True in Theory but It Does Not Apply in Practice' (*'Ueber den Gemeinspruch: Das mag in der Theorie richtig sein, taugt aber nicht für die Praxis'*).

Marx–Engels

MEGA *Marx–Engels Gesamtausgabe*, ed. Institut für Marxismus–Leninismus (Berlin: Dietz, 1982).

Schiller

NA   *Werke, Nationalausgabe,* ed. Benno von Wiese *et al.* (Weimar: Böhlau, 1943).

Schlegel

KA   *Kritische Friedrich Schlegel Ausgabe,* ed. E. Behler (Paderborn: Schöningh, 1958 *et seq.*).

Schleiermacher

KGA   *Kritische Gesamtausgabe,* ed. H. Birkner *et al.* (Berlin: de Gruyter, 1980 *et seq.*).

HEGEL

BF   *Berner Fragmente,* in *Werke* I, pp. 9–104.
        The *Berne Fragments* in *Three Essays 1793–1795,* ed. and trans. Peter Fuss and John Dobbins (Notre Dame, IN: University of Notre Dame Press, 1984), pp. 59–103. Cited according to the marginal Nohl pagination.

Briefe *Briefe von und an Hegel,* ed. Johannes Hoffmeister (Hamburg: Meiner, 1969), 5 vols.

BS   *Hegel: The Letters,* trans. Clark Butler and Christiane Seiler (Bloomington: Indiana University Press, 1984).

D   *Differenzschrift,* or *Differenz des Fichteschen und Schellingschen Systems der Philosophie,* in *Werke* II, pp. 9–140.
        The *Difference between Fichte's and Schelling's System of Philosophy,* trans. H.S. Harris and Walter Cerf (Albany: SUNY Press, 1977).

EPW   *Enzyklopädie der philosophischen Wissenschaften* in *Werke* (1830), vols 8–10. Cited by paragraph number (§). Additions are indicated by an A, remarks by an R. The *Encyclopedia Logic, Part I of the Encyclopedia of Philosophical Sciences,* trans. T.F. Geraets, W.A. Suchting and H.S. Harris (Indianapolis: Hackett, 1991).
        Hegel's Philosophy of Nature, Part Two of the Encyclopedia of Philosophical

Sciences (1830), trans. A.V. Miller (Oxford: Oxford University Press, 1970).

Hegel's Philosophy of Mind, Part Three of the Encyclopedia of Philosophical Sciences (1830), trans. A.V. Miller (Oxford: Oxford University Press, 1971).

ER   *Über die englische Reformbill, in Werkausgabe XI,* 83–130.
'The English Reform Bill', in *Hegel's Political Writings,* ed. Z.A. Pelczynski, trans. T.M. Knox (Oxford: Clarendon Press, 1964), pp. 295–330.

GC   *Der Geist des Christentums und sein Schicksal, in Werke I,* 274–418.
The Spirit of Christianity and its Fate, trans. T.M. Knox, in *Hegel's Early Theological Writings* (Philadelphia: University of Pennsylvania Press, 1948). Cited according to Nohl pagination.

GP   *Vorlesungen über die Geschichte der Philosophie, in Werke XVIII, XIX and XX.*
Lectures on the History of Philosophy, trans. E.S. Haldane (Lincoln: University of Nebraska Press, 1995), 3 vols.

GuW   *Glauben und Wissen oder Reflexionsphilosophie der Subjektivität in der Vollständigkeit ihrer Formen als Kantische, Jacobische und Fichtesche Philosophie, in Werke II,* 287–434.
Faith and Knowledge, trans. Walter Cerf and H.S. Harris (Albany: SUNY Press, 1977).

GW   *Gesammelte Werke,* ed. Rheinisch–Westfälischen Akademie der Wissenschaften (Hamburg: Meiner, 1989 *et seq.*).

H   *Philosophie des Rechts. Die Vorlesung von 1819/20 in einer Nachschrift,* ed. Dieter Henrich (Frankfurt: Suhrkamp, 1983). Cited by page number.

N   *Hegels theologische Jugendschriften,* ed. Herman Nohl (Tübingen: Mohr, 1907).

P   *Die Positivität der christlichen Religion (1795/1796), in Werke I,* 190–229.
The Positivity of the Christian Religion, in *Early Theological Writings* (Philadelphia: University of Pennsylvania Press,

1971), trans. T.M. Knox. Cited according to the Nohl pagination.

PG   *Phänomenologie des Geistes*, ed. Johannes Hoffmeister (Hamburg: Meiner, 1952).

    Phenomenology of Spirit, trans. A.V. Miller (Oxford: Oxford University Press, 1977). References are to the paragraph number, indicated by '¶'.

PR   *Grundlinien der Philosophie des Rechts* (1821), in *Werke* VII. Cited by paragraph number (§). Additions are indicated by an A, remarks by an R.

    Elements of the Philosophy of Right, ed. Allen Wood, trans. H.B. Nisbet (Cambridge: Cambridge University Press, 1992). Cited by paragraph number (§).

TE   'Religion ist eine . . .', in *Werke* I, 9–44.

    The Tübingen Essay in Three Essays 1793–1795, ed. and trans. Peter Fuss and John Dobbins (Notre Dame: University of Notre Dame Press, 1984), pp. 30–59. Cited according to the Nohl pagination.

VBG   *Vorlesungen über die Beweise vom Dasein Gottes*, ed. Georg Lasson (Hamburg: Meiner, 1966).

VG   *Die Vernunft in der Geschichte*, ed. J. Hoffmeister (Hamburg: Meiner, 1955).

    Lectures on the Philosophy of World History: Introduction, trans. H.B. Nisbet (Cambridge: Cambridge University Press, 1975).

VD   *Die Verfassung Deutschlands*, in *Werke* I.

    'The German Constitution', in *Hegel's Political Writings*, trans. T.M. Knox (Oxford: Clarendon Press, 1964).

VNS   *Vorlesungen über Naturrecht und Staatswissenschaft. Heidelberg 1817/18. Nachgeschrieben von P. Wannenmann*, ed. C. Becker et al. (Hamburg: Meiner, 1983). Cited by paragraph number (§).

VPR   *Vorlesungen über die Philosophie der Religion*, ed. Walter Jaeschke (Hamburg: Meiner, 1983). Volumes 3–5 of *Ausgewählte Nachschriften und Manuskripte*. Cited by volume and page number.

Lectures on the Philosophy of Religion, ed. Peter C. Hodgson (Berkeley: University of California Press, 1984–5), 3 vols.

VRP   Vorlesungen über Rechtsphilosophie, ed. K.-H. Ilting (Stuttgart: Frommann, 1974), 3 vols. Student lecture notes from Hegel's lectures 1818–19 (C.G. Homeyer), 1821–2, 1822–3 (K.G. von Griesheim), 1831 (D.F. Strauss). Cited by volume and page number.

VSP   Verhaltnis des Skeptizismus zur Philosophie in W II, pp. 213–72. 'Relation of Skepticism to Philosophy', in Between Kant and Hegel, ed. George di Giovanni and H.S. Harris (Albany: SUNY Press, 1985).

VVL   Verhandlungen in der Versammlung der Landstände des Königsreichs Württemberg im Jahr 1815 und 1816. W IV, pp. 462–597.
Proceedings of the Estates Assembly in the Kingdom of Württemberg, in Hegel's Political Writings, ed. Z.A. Pelczynski, trans. T.M. Knox (Oxford: Clarendon Press, 1964), pp. 246–94.

W   Werke in zwanzig Bänden. Werkausgabe, ed. Eva Moldenhauer and Karl Michel (Frankfurt: Suhrkamp, 1970).

WBN   Wissenschaftliche Behandlungsarten des Naturrechts, in Werke II, pp. 434–532.

WL   Wissenschaft der Logik, ed. Georg Lasson (Hamburg: Meiner, 1971).

1770	Hegel is born in Stuttgart, August 27. Hölderlin is born Lauffen am Neckar, March 20.
1775	Schelling is born in Württemberg, January 27.
1776	Hegel begins to attend the Stuttgart *Gymnasium*.
1781	Publication of Kant's *Critique of Pure Reason*.
1785	Publication of Kant's *Groundwork for the Metaphysics of Morals*. Hegel begins to write a diary.
1788	September: Hegel leaves the *Gymnasium*. October: he begins study in the *Tübinger Stift*. He shares a room with Schelling and Hölderlin.
1789	July 14: Storming of the Bastille in Paris.
1790	Hegel receives M.A. Kant publishes his *Critique of Judgment*.
1793	Hegel becomes house tutor in Berne. Louis XVI guillotined. Hegel writes *Tübingen Essay*.
1794	Publication of Fichte's *Foundation of the Science of Knowledge*.
1795	Hegel begins to write *Positivity of the Christian Religion*
1797	Hegel moves to Frankfurt am Main to be house tutor with the wine merchant Gogal. Hegel begins discussions with Hölderlin. Hegel writes *Fragments on Religion and Love*.
1799	Hegel writes *The Spirit of Christianity and its Fate*.
1800	Hegel writes his *System Fragment*.
1801	Hegel moves to Jena in January. He becomes *Privatdozent*. Publication of first substantial philosophical writing, *Difference between Fichte's and Schelling's System of Philosophy*.

1802–03	Hegel collaborates with Schelling on the *Critical Journal of Philosophy*. He writes 'Faith and Knowledge', 'Relation of Skepticism to Philosophy', 'On Natural Law'.
1805	Hegel appointed Extraordinary Professor.
1806	Hegel completes *Phenomenology of Spirit*. Napoleon defeats Prussian troops at the Battle of Jena.
1807	Hegel moves to Bamberg to be editor of a local newspaper.
1808	Hegel moves to Nuremberg to be rector of a *Gymnasium*.
1811	Hegel marries Marie von Tucher.
1812	Publication of Volume I of *Science of Logic*.
1813	Publication of Volume II of *Science of Logic*.
1815	Defeat of Napoleon at Waterloo.
1816	Publication of Volume III of *Science of Logic*. Hegel becomes Professor of Philosophy at University of Heidelberg.
1817	Publication of First Edition of *Encyclopedia of Philosophical Sciences*.
1818	Hegel becomes Professor of Philosophy at the University of Berlin.
1819	Karlsbad Decrees, which impose censorship and surveillance of universities.
1820	Publication of *Philosophy of Right*.
1821	Hegel lectures for the first time on *Philosophy of Religion*.
1822	Hegel travels to Rhineland and the Low Countries.
1824	Hegel travels to Prague and Vienna.
1827	Hegel travels to Paris. He visits Goethe on way home. Publication of second edition of *Encyclopedia of Philosophical Sciences*.
1830	Hegel is Rector of the University of Berlin. Publication of third edition of *Encyclopedia of Philosophical Sciences*.
1831	Hegel dies of cholera in Berlin, December 24.

A QUESTION OF RELEVANCE

Why read Hegel? It is a good question, one no Hegel scholar should shirk. After all, the burden of proof lies heavily on his or her shoulders. For Hegel's texts are not exactly exciting or enticing. Notoriously, they are written in some of the worst prose in the history of philosophy. Their language is dense, obscure and impenetrable. Reading Hegel is often a trying and exhausting experience, the intellectual equivalent of chewing gravel. 'And for what?' a prospective student might well ask. To avoid such an ordeal, he or she will be tempted to invoke the maxim of one of Hegel's old enemies whenever he lost patience with a tiresome book: 'Life is short!'[1]

The question is all the more pressing when we ask what Hegel has to say to us today in our post-modern age. In the beginning of the last century Franz Rosenzweig, one of the greatest Hegel scholars, declared that he lived in an age *post Hegel mortuum*.[2] Rosenzweig's statement seems as true now as it was then. Our age seems to have outgrown Hegel. We have lost the feeling for religion, 'the taste for the absolute', which was the inspiration for Hegel's metaphysics. After two world wars, the gulags and the Holocaust, we have lost faith in progress, though this faith is the cornerstone of Hegel's philosophy of history. We live in such a specialized and pluralistic age that no one expects to see the restoration of wholeness, the recovery of unity with ourselves, others and nature; but these were the grand ideals behind Hegel's philosophy.

When we consider all these points it seems we have no choice but to accept Rosenzweig's verdict. Hegel, it seems, has little to say to our age, which has moved beyond him. So the question is all the more imperative: Why read Hegel?

Part of the answer, of course, is that even if Hegel is dead, he was still enormously influential, so much so that he is still deeply interwoven into our culture today. If we are to understand that culture, we have to comprehend its origins, which means that, eventually but inevitably, we have to come to terms with Hegel. It is a remarkable fact that virtually every major philosophical movement of the twentieth century – existentialism, Marxism, pragmatism, phenomenology and analytic philosophy – grew out of reaction against Hegel. The concepts, arguments and problems of these movements will remain forever alien and arcane to us until we understand what they grew out of and what they reacted against. So here we have at least one good reason to read Hegel: to understand the roots of our own culture.

We might well question, however, whether Hegel is really that dead after all. In some respects he is more alive than ever. Since the Hegel renaissance of the 1970s, Hegel has become an established figure in the history of philosophy. The dissertations, books and articles on every aspect of his philosopy have increased exponentially since then. It is a striking fact that Hegel's star seems to be steadily rising just as those of his most vocal critics (e.g. Popper and Russell) have been steadily sinking. The reason for the Hegel renaissance lies to some degree in an overdue recognition of Hegel's historical importance. Many of those who studied Hegel did so to uncover the roots of Marxism, which had a great flowering in the 1960s. But there were then, as there are now, more philosophical reasons for Hegel's revival. In the 1970s and 1980s Hegel became, at least in the Anglophone world, the rallying figure for the reaction against analytic philosophy. To study Hegel was to protest against the narrow scholasticism of analytic philosophy and to embrace 'continental philosophy'. Ironically, Hegel was as important for the philosophical counterculture of the 1970s and 1980s as he was for the cultural mainstream in late nineteenth-century England and America.

Nowadays the cultural war between continental and analytic philosophy has lost much of its original meaning. But it is striking that the interest in Hegel remains as strong as ever. Hegel has now been adopted by some prominent philosophers in the analytic tradition, who study him not for historical but philosophical reasons.[3] They recognize they share some of the same problems as Hegel, and that he has something interesting to say about them. How is it possible to avoid the extremes of conventionalism and foundationalism in epistemology? How is it possible to combine realism with a social epistemology? How is it possible to synthesize the freedoms of liberalism with the ideals of community? How is it possible to adopt the insights of historicism and not lapse into relativism? How is it possible to avoid dualism and materialism in the philosophy of mind? All these questions are very much on the contemporary agenda; but they were crucial issues for Hegel too. It is no accident that many philosophers now see Hegel as the chief antidote and alternative to many outworn and problematic positions, such as Cartesian subjectivism, naive realism, extreme liberalism and mental-physical dualism, or reductivist materialism. So here is another reason for reading Hegel: he still remains, despite his damnable obscurity, an interesting interlocuter to contemporary philosophical discussions.

A QUESTION OF METHOD

Assuming that we should read Hegel, the question remains how we should do so. There are two possible approaches. We can treat him as if he were a virtual contemporary, as a participant in present conversations. In that case we could analyze his arguments and clarify his ideas to show how they are relevant to our contemporary concerns. Or, we can treat him as an historical figure, as a contributor to past conversations. In this case we study him in his historical context, trace the development of his doctrines, and attempt to reconstruct him in his historical integrity and individuality. The first approach has been characteristic of many recent analytic interpretations of Hegel; the second approach has been characteristic of many older hermeneutical studies, especially the work of Rudolf Haym, Wilhelm Dilthey and Theodor Haering.

Both approaches have their rewards and pitfalls. The danger of the analytic approach is anachronism. We make Hegel alive and relevant, a useful contributor to our concerns; but that is only because we put our views into his mouth. What we learn from Hegel is then only what we have read into him. With good reason this approach has been caricatured as 'the ventriloquist's conception of the history of philosophy'.[4] On the other hand, the trouble with the hermeneutical approach is antiquarianism. Although we are more likely to concern ourselves with the philosophy of a real historical being, it is of less interest and relevance to us because his ideas and problems are so specific to his age. What we are left with, it seems, is like an historical portrait from a museum.

So how do we avoid both anachronism and antiquarianism? This is the eternal dilemma of all history of philosophy. We could attempt an eclectic strategy. We could take the analytic approach and be careful not to confuse our contemporary reconstruction with historical reality; or we could take the hermeneutical approach and be selective about those aspects of the historical Hegel that are relevant to our contemporary concerns. But, either way, we seem to compromise what is of value in each approach. For, unfortunately, there is a discrepancy between the real historical Hegel and the contemporary relevant Hegel. The more we make Hegel relevant to our contemporary concerns, the less he will be like the real historical thinker; and the more we reconstitute Hegel in his historical individuality, the less he will be relevant to our contemporary concerns. In any case, an eclectic strategy approach is easier to devise than execute. For who among the analytic interpreters has a precise historical knowledge of Hegel, so that he or she knows how to avoid anachronism? And who among the hermentical interpreters has a thorough knowledge of contemporary philosophy, so that he or she can escape antiquarianism? Alas, what we know about Hegel is the result of our method; it is not as if we can choose the right method based on what we already know.

In the face of this predicament the philosophical historian has to make his or her choice. There can be pragmatic reasons for a decision, but there is no right or wrong when each method has its strengths and weaknesses. Contrary to the current preference for the analytic approach, the present study adopts the older hermeneutical method. It does so for two reasons. First, many recent analytic studies of Hegel have lapsed into anachronism, and indeed to such an excessive degree that their reconstructed relevant Hegel has virtually no resemblance to the actual historical Hegel. Rather than frankly admitting the distance between these Hegels, they virtually confuse the two, as if the real Hegel were the analytic thinker of their dreams. Second, contemporary Hegel scholars, especially those in the Anglophone tradition, have failed to individuate Hegel. They assume that certain ideas are characteristic of Hegel that were really commonplaces of an entire generation. We are told that Hegel's absolute idealism, his attempt to wed communitarianism and liberalism, to synthesize Spinoza's naturalism and Fichte's idealism, were original and unique to him; but these projects were really part of the legacy of early romanticism. If, however, we cannot individuate Hegel – if we cannot state precisely how his views differ from some of his major contemporaries – can we be said to understand him? Especially when these differences were often so crucial to him?

The most pressing need of Hegel scholarship today is to individuate him, to determine what was his precise relation to his contemporaries. This need will become more apparent when scholars recognize the full import of the latest research on early romanticism. This research, undertaken by Dieter Henrich, Manfred Frank, Violetta Waibel, Michael Franz, Marcelo Stamm, and many others in Germany, has greatly illuminated the philosophical depths of early romanticism. Until we can situate Hegel within that movement – showing precisely what he inherits from it and where he takes issue with it – we cannot claim to have an adequate understanding of his philosophy.

The anachronism of analytic studies is especially apparent from the many recent non-metaphysical interpretations of Hegel. These studies attempt to rehabilitate Hegel – to make him viable in the light of contemporary concerns – by reading the metaphysics out of his philosophy. If Hegel were a metaphysician, these scholars argue, then his philosophy would be doomed to obsolescence. Hence Hegel's philosophy has been read as virtually everything but a metaphysics: as a theory of categories, as social epistemology, as neo-Kantian idealism, as cultural history, and as proto-hermeneutics. What all these studies have in common is the belief that Hegel's philosophy is in its essential purport or spirit non-metaphysics. This can mean either of two things: that his metaphysics is irreducible but unimportant, so that the rest of his philosophy can be perfectly understood without it; or that his metaphysics, when properly understood, is really reducible to a theory of categories, social epistemology, neo-Kantian idealism, and so on. No one would have protested more stridently against such interpretations, however, than Hegel himself, who regarded metaphysics as the foundation of philosophy, and as the basis of each part of his system. To understand Hegel in his individuality and integrity demands first and foremost restoring metaphysics to its central role in his thinking. For this reason virtually every chapter of this study will stress how metaphysics is fundamental to each part of Hegel's system. We shall find that metaphysics plays a pivotal role in Hegel's social and political philosophy, his philosophy of history and aesthetics.

Those who advocate non-metaphysical interpretations might protest that to read the metaphysics back into Hegel is to make him obsolete to our own non-metaphysical age. It is precisely here, however, that Hegel challenges us to rethink our own philosophical presuppositions and values. For most of the contemporary objections against Hegel's metaphysics, it must be said, simply beg the question against him, coming from perspectives that he had already questioned. In Hegel's view, any form of positivism about metaphysics was simply bad philosophy because it involved, but failed to reflect upon, a metaphysics of its own. Rather than helping to combat such positivism, contemporary Hegel scholarship has simply bowed to it, betraying one of the most valuable aspects of Hegel's legacy.

BRIEF BIOGRAPHY

In 1844 Karl Rosenkranz, Hegel's first biographer, wrote that 'The history of a philosopher is the history of his thinking, the history of the formation of his system'.[5] Rosenkranz claimed that this maxim was especially true of Hegel. His life was the story of his academic career. Hegel did not have the love affair of an Abelard, the political intrigues of a Bacon, the religious dramas of a Spinoza. Some biographers would question Rosenkranz's dictum, which does seem drastically reductionist. A close examination of Hegel's life shows that it too had its own personal dramas and scandals, such as bouts of melancholy, an illegitimate son by his *Putzfrau*, a desperate struggle to earn a living. Still, Rosenkranz had a point. For Hegel himself gave little importance to his own individuality and he defined himself by his devotion to philosophy. No doubt, his passions and obsessions would fill a volume the size of Rousseau's *Confessions*. But the problem is that Hegel himself did not regard them as noteworthy. True to Rosenkranz's dictum, Hegel's life divides rather neatly, with a few lapses and aberrations, into the stages of an academic career.

1   Stuttgart (August 1770–September 1788)

Hegel was born in Stuttgart on 27 August 1770, the eldest son of a middle-class family. His father was a minor civil servant in the

Duchy of Württemberg. The duchy was a Protestant enclave sur-
rounded by Catholic territories. Several generations of Hegels had
been ministers in the Protestant Church, and Hegel's mother, who
died when he was only 11, probably envisaged a career in the
clergy for her son. From his earliest years Hegel developed a strong
sense of his religious identity. Though he did not become an
orthodox Lutheran in belief or habit, his Protestant heritage is still
fundamental for understanding his thought. He embraced some of
its basic values, imbibed some of its intellectual traditions.[6]

After receiving his first Latin lessons from his mother, Hegel
attended a Latin school from the ages of 5 to 7. He was then sent to
the *Gymnasium illustre* in Stuttgart, which he attended for the next
eleven years (1777–88). Rosenkranz astutely summarizes his education there by saying that it 'belonged entirely to the Enlightenment with respect to principle, and entirely to classical antiquity
with respect to curriculum'.[7] Hegel's teachers imparted to him the
values of the Enlightenment; and the curriculum consisted mainly
in the Greek and Latin classics. His education was governed by the
belief that classical Greece and Rome are the highest models of
civilization.[8] This belief would sometimes clash with Hegel's
Protestant education, leaving him, as so many before him, with
the perennial problem of reconciling Christianity with ancient
paganism.

2   Tübingen (October 1788–October 1793)

After graduating from the *Gymnasium*, Hegel went to the *Tübinger
Stift*, a seminary to train Protestant clerics for the Duchy of
Württemberg. It is a commonplace that Hegel's training in the *Stift*
biassed him toward religion and made him a covert theologian; but
the evidence does not support this: Hegel never intended to be a
minister, and he had a profound distaste for the study of orthodox
theology.[9] He probably entered the *Stift* only because it allowed him
to receive his education at state expense. Like many of his fellow
students, Hegel had a deep aversion to the basic values of the

Stift, which seemed to represent all the vices of the *ancien régime*: religious orthodoxy, princely despotism and aristocratic nepotism.[10] He was highly critical of the reactionary theology of some of his professors, who attempted to use Kant's doctrine of practical faith to buttress traditional dogmas.

Although Hegel was not happy at the Stift, he formed two friendships there that were to have the greatest importance for himself, and indeed the history of German philosophy. In autumn 1788 he met Friedrich Hölderlin, who became one of Germany's greatest lyric poets; and in the autumn of 1790 he met Schelling, who became one of Germany's leading philosophers and later Hegel's rival. In the Stift the three became close friends, and for a while even shared a room together. Schelling and Hölderlin, who were more advanced in their philosophical education than Hegel, soon became important influences upon him.

For the first two years in the Stift, Hegel studied for the degree of *Magister*. His courses for this degree were mainly philosophical, and included logic, metaphysics, moral philosophy, natural law, ontology and cosmology.[11] In his second term, the Summer Semester of 1789, Hegel took a course on empirical psychology, in which he studied for the first time Kant's *Critique of Pure Reason*.[12] For the next three years Hegel had to qualify for the ministry, and so his curriculum became essentially theological. He had to take courses on ecclesiastical history, dogmatics, moral theology and the gospels.[13] Apart from the official curriculum, Hegel read, on his own or with friends, some of the latest philosophical literature. He read Plato, Schiller, F.H. Jacobi, Rousseau and Voltaire. His favorite author was Rousseau. Though Hegel had already read Kant, it is noteworthy that he did not join a club to discuss his ideas. It was probably due to the influence of Schelling and Hölderlin that he later came to appreciate fully the import of Kant's philosophy.[14]

The most important event of the Tübingen years was the French Revolution. Hegel, Schelling and Hölderlin celebrated the events across the Rhine as the dawn of a new era. They read French newspapers, sang the *Marseillaise*, and formed a political club to discuss the events and read revolutionary literature. According to legend, on one fine Sunday morning in 1790 Hegel, Schelling and Hölderlin went out to a meadow in Tübingen and planted a liberty tree. While this story is probably false, it at least represents what the three would have liked to have done. Hegel was known as one of the most ardent spokesmen for liberty and equality in the Stift.[15] His sympathy for the Revolution lasted his entire life. Even in his final years he toasted Bastille Day, admired Napoleon, and condemned the Restoration.

The surviving writings of the Tübingen period are only four sermons and several short fragments.[16] Of these fragments the largest and most important is the so-called *Tübingen Essay*, the fragment '*Religion ist eine der wichtigsten Angelegenheiten . . .*'.[17] This fragment sets the agenda for much of Hegel's early development. True to his republican politics, Hegel's main concern is to outline a civic religion. In the republican tradition of Machiavelli, Montesquieu and Rousseau, Hegel believed that the chief source of republican virtue and patriotism came from religion.

3 Berne (October 1793–December 1796)

After passing his *Konsistorialexamen* in September 1793, Hegel got a job as a *Hofmeister*, a private tutor, to the Berne patrician family of Hauptmann Friedrich von Steiger. Although the job left him free time to pursue his own studies, Hegel felt lonely and isolated in Berne. He wished to be with Hölderlin and Schelling, closer to the exciting intellectual activity now taking place in Weimar and Jena.

In Berne Hegel read a lot, wrote much, but published nothing. Still, he had hopes for a literary career. Like many young men of literary ambition in the 1790s, he saw himself as a *Volkslehrer*, a teacher of the people, in the tradition of the *Aufklärung* or German Enlightenment. His aim was to enlighten the public, to fight superstition, oppression and despotism. There was a political objective behind such an education: to prepare people for the high civic ideals of a republic. True to the ideal of a *Volkslehrer* Hegel explicitly and self-consciously forswore the goal of becoming a professional philosopher, a *Doktor der Weltweisheit* at a university. He wanted to popularize and apply the principles of Kant's philosophy, not investigate their foundations.

True to his ideal, Hegel continued to occupy himself with his project for a civil religion. This concern is most evident in a series of sketches known as the *Berne Fragments*.[18] These fragments are notable for their many sharp criticisms of orthodox Christianity. Hegel's search for a civil religion eventually led him to write the one complete fragment of his early years, his 1795 *Life of Jesus*.

Hegel's main writing during the Berne years, a work constantly revised but never finished, was his so-called *Positivity Essay*.[19] The main aim of this essay is to explain how Christianity, whose gospel consists in moral autonomy, degenerated into a positive religion, i.e. a religion commanded by civil authority. To answer this question, Hegel delves into the fundamental issue of alienation, of why people abandon their own freedom. His analysis of this issue anticipates Feuerbach and Marx, and his later account of the 'Unhappy Consciousness' in the *Phenomenology*.

The Berne years were especially formative for Hegel's political thought. He read the Scottish political economists; and he studied closely at first hand the affairs of the Berne aristocracy, whose nepotism appalled him. True to his republican beliefs and his mission as a *Volkslehrer*, he decided to expose the despotism of the Bernese by translating a pamplet by J.J. Cart, *Lettres confidentielles*, which attacked the Bernese aristocracy for depriving the people of the '*pays de Vaud*' of their native liberties. The pamphlet, published anonymously with Hegel's notes and introduction, was his first publication.[20] More important for the development of Hegel's political views in the Berne years was his sketch of a liberal political philosophy in some sections of the *Positivity Essay*. Here Hegel argues that the state has the duty to protect my rights, among which are freedom of speech and conscience as well as security of person and property. Such liberalism did not jibe well with Hegel's ideal of a civil religion. This tension raised a broader issue of central importance for Hegel's mature political philosophy: How is it possible to reconcile communitarian ideals with liberal principles?[21]

4 Frankfurt (January 1797–January 1800)

Later in 1796, thanks to the efforts of Hölderlin, Hegel got a post in Frankfurt as a *Hofmeister* to the family of a rich wine merchant, Johann Gogel. Hölderlin had been in Frankfurt since early 1796, and Hegel rejoiced at the prospect of joining him there. In Frankfurt Hegel recovered his spirits, and was happier with his circumstances. Rather than attempting to save humanity as a *Volkserzieher*, he became more reconciled with his world. He took part in social life, going to balls, concerts and operas. Living close to Hölderlin, he had constant conversations about philosophy, politics and poetry.

During the Frankfurt years, Hegel's thinking about religion and politics underwent a dramatic reversal. In the Berne years Hegel interpreted and criticized religion from the standpoint of the Enlightenment; in the Frankfurt years, however, he defended religion against such criticism and re-interpreted it in more mystical terms. While in Berne Hegel believed he could reform the world according to the principles of reason, in Frankfurt he criticized such idealism and preached reconciliation with history.

The first manuscripts of the Frankfurt period, the *Sketches on Religion and Love*, which Hegel probably wrote in the summer of 1797, reveal the radical change in Hegel's thinking. These sketches are attempts to define the distinctive nature of religion, what separates it from metaphysics and morality. Rather than identifying religion with morality, as Hegel had done in Berne, Hegel now finds the essence of religion in the mystical experience of love where subject and object become perfectly identical. The main writing of the Frankfurt years was Hegel's large manuscript *The Spirit of Christianity and its Fate*. In many respects, this manuscript is the birthplace of Hegel's mature philosophy. It is here that Hegel first formulates, if only in *nuce*, his idea of spirit, his concept of dialectic, his theme of reconciliation, and his organic vision of the world.

The reversal of the Frankfurt years was in large measure the result of Hegel's appropriation of early Jena romanticism, of which Hölderlin was an essential contributor and participant. In fundamental respects, Hegel's thinking adopts the substance of early romanticism: an organic concept of nature, an ethic of love, an appreciation of religious mysticism. Most significantly, he even disputes the Enlightenment principle of the sovereignty of reason, the power of reason to criticize religious belief. Hegel will never depart from the content or substance of the romantic legacy; his main departure from it will be only in terms of its form, in how to demonstrate this substance.

5   Jena (January 1801–March 1807)

After receiving a modest inheritance upon the death of his father, Hegel decided to attempt to realize his hopes for an academic career. He joined his friend Schelling in Jena in January 1801. When Hegel arrived 'the literary frenzy' of Jena had already died down, most of its leading lights (Reinhold, Fichte) having left years ago. Hegel became a *Privatdozent*, his income entirely dependent on student fees; he never achieved there his ambition of becoming a salaried professor.

Hegel's resolve to become a university professor marked a significant shift in his intellectual ambitions. He ceased to regard himself as a *Volkserzieher* who would simply apply philosophical principles to the world; he now saw himself as a philosopher in his own right, devoted to the development of his own system. The reasons for this shift seem to be twofold. First, as a result of political developments, Hegel had lost much of his earlier idealism (see pp. 214–16). Second, he also realized that the Kantian principles he intended to apply were problematic or suspect.

Hegel's debut in Jena was his first philosophical publication, his so-called *Differenzschrift*. True to title, this tract explains the basic differences between the systems of Schelling and Fichte; it also defends the thesis that Schelling's philosophy is superior to Fichte's. With this thesis Hegel at once ended the old alliance between Fichte and Schelling and forged a new one with Schelling. The Differenzschrift is Hegel's manifesto for absolute or 'objective idealism', a critique of the 'subjective idealism' of Kant and Fichte.

The formation of the Schelling–Hegel alliance led to their joint editorship of a common journal, the Critical Journal of Philosophy. Some of Hegel's most important early works are essays from the Journal. They include Faith and Knowledge, Scientific Treatment of Natural Right and the Relation of Skepticism to Philosophy. The Journal lasted only a few issues, beginning in January 1802 and ending in spring 1803. The Schelling–Hegel alliance dissolved when Schelling left Jena in the spring of 1803. It is a mistake to think that Hegel was simply Schelling's disciple, his 'stout warrior' or 'spear carrier'. This ignores too many basic facts: that Hegel developed the outline of his metaphysics before his arrival in Jena; that Schelling's own metaphysics underwent crucial changes from 1801 to 1803 due to Hegel's influence; and that even in the Differenzschrift and Critical Journal Hegel does not hesitate to express views at odds with Schelling's.

Throughout the Jena years Hegel struggled, without success, to formulate his own system of philosophy. His lectures were often preliminary accounts of parts of the system.[22] These lectures concerned logic and metaphysics, the philosophy of nature, and the philosophy of spirit. There are many surviving drafts of these lectures, the so-called Systementwürfe of 1803/4, 1804/5 and 1805/6.[23]

After Schelling's departure from Jena, Hegel became more critical of his old colleague. In his 1804/5 Winter Semester lectures he began to criticize Schelling's views openly and to rethink the foundation of his metaphysics. He rejected Schelling's attempt to base absolute idealism upon an intellectual intuition and developed instead the idea of a science to lead ordinary consciousness up to the standpoint of philosophy. This line of thought eventually culminated in the *Phenomenology of Spirit*, Hegel's self-described 'journey of self-discovery', the beginnings of his mature philosophy.

6   Bamberg (March 1807–November 1808)

After failing to find a salaried professorship in Jena, Hegel became in March 1807 the editor of a small town paper, the *Bamberger Zeitung*. Hegel was successful at his job, which gave him a nice salary and social status. His newspaper supported the Napoleonic reforms of the Bavarian government, then an ally of the French. Although this job did not fulfil Hegel's academic aspirations, it did suit his political ideals. Hegel held that the Napoleonic reforms could succeed only if they found broader-based support among the people; a newspaper was the perfect means to create that support.

7   Nuremberg (November 1808–October 1816)

In November 1808, through the mediation of his friend I.H. Niethammer, the Bavarian minister of education, Hegel became the rector of the *Ägidien-Gymnasium* in Nuremberg. Here too Hegel proved very successful, both as administrator and teacher. It is noteworthy, however, that he judged the attempt to introduce philosophy into the *Gymnasium* a failure. In September 1811 Hegel married Marie von Tucher, daughter of a Nuremberg patrician family. Despite his busy life as a rector, Hegel managed to find time to finish his *Science of Logic*, which he had begun in Jena. He published the first volume in 1812, the second in 1813, and the third in 1816.

8   Heidelberg (October 1816–October 1818)

In October 1816 Hegel finally achieved his academic ideal, becoming a professor of philosophy at the University of Heidelberg. When Hegel arrived at Heidelberg, however, the literary scene had already disappeared, just as happened in Jena; he was disappointed by some professors' hostility toward philosophy and by the students' purely vocational attitude toward learning. In Heidelberg Hegel gave his first lectures on aesthetics; his 1817/18 lectures on political philosophy there became the basis for his later *Philosophy of Right*. The most important publication of the Heidelberg years was Hegel's *Encyclopedia of the Philosophical Sciences*, a three-volume work, the first exposition of the whole system.

9   Berlin (October 1818–November 1831)

In December 1817 the Prussian minister of education, Karl Altenstein, wrote Hegel to offer him the chair of philosophy, once taken by Fichte, at the new University of Berlin. Altenstein wanted Hegel chiefly because he knew him to be sympathetic to the goals of the Prussian Reform Movement, which had begun in 1807 under the leadership of Baron von Stein. This movement hoped to realize the ideals of the French Revolution by gradual reforms from above. Its ideals were a new constitution ensuring fundamental rights for all citizens, freedom of trade, abolition of feudal privileges, and more local self-government. Hegel was greatly attracted to Berlin chiefly because he shared the ideals of the Reform Movement. Prussia laid great importance upon its new university for the regeneration of Prussian cultural life. In Berlin Hegel knew he would finally find himself in the center of a lively cultural scene, and in a position to have some influence on Prussia's cultural and political affairs.

Shortly after Hegel's arrival in Berlin, however, the Reform Movement suffered a serious setback. In 1819 the Prussian government under Friedrich Wilhelm III, fearing radical conspiracies, revoked its plans to introduce a new constitution. It then endorsed the repressive Karlsbad Decrees, which introduced censorship and strict measures against 'demagogues'. Suspected of subversive activity, some of Hegel's students were banished or imprisoned; Hegel himself was under police surveillance for some time. Although Hegel endorsed the goals of the Reform Movement, and although he was despised by reactionary circles within the Prussian court, many of his liberal contemporaries suspected him of collusion with the reactionary government. Since he enjoyed the support of Altenstein, and since he had supported the dismissal of two liberal professors, whom he had viciously attacked in the preface of the *Philosophy of Right*, Hegel seemed to many to endorse a reactionary politics. This was the beginning of one of the oldest Hegel legends: that he was a spokesman for the Prussian restoration.

It was in Berlin that Hegel acquired fame and influence. Although by all accounts Hegel was a poor university lecturer – he stuttered, moved rigidly, gasped for breath, and tirelessly repeated '*Also*' – his many lectures gained a wide following. On several occasions he held lectures on aesthetics, the history of philosophy, the philosophy of religion, and the philosophy of history. Though Hegel himself never published these lectures, they were recorded by his students, who put them in the first edition of his collected works.

Due to his position and success, Hegel finally found time and means to travel. An avid tourist, he made trips to Prague, Vienna, Brussels and Paris. Though he gave many lectures, Hegel published little during the Berlin years. In 1826 he founded a leading journal, *Jahrbücher für wissenschaftliche Kritik*, for which he wrote several review articles; he published two new editions of the *Encyclopedia* (1827, 1830); and he began to rework his *Logic*, volume I of which appeared in 1832.

Hegel died suddenly in Berlin on 14 November 1831, according to legend from cholera, but probably from a stomach ailment or gastrointestinal disease. The funeral was a massive procession of Berlin notables and his students. According to his wish, he was buried next to Fichte in the Dorothea cemetery in Berlin.

Part One
Early Ideals and Context

One

THE TWILIGHT OF THE ENLIGHTENMENT

The 1790s in Germany, the decade when Hegel and the romantic generation came of age, was a time of extraordinary intellectual upheaval and ferment. This has been the view of most historians; but even contemporaries saw their decade in these terms. Thus, K.L. Reinhold, a prominent philosopher and shrewd observer of the *Zeitgeist*, wrote in 1790:

> The most conspicuous and characteristic feature of our age is the convulsion of all hitherto familiar systems, theories, and manners of thinking, a convulsion the breadth and depth of which the history of the human mind can show no example.[1]

The main source of this cultural cataclysm was a crisis in the *Aufklärung*, the German Enlightenment. The *Aufklärung* had dominated German intellectual life for most of the eighteenth century; but now its days were numbered. What had seemed so certain at the dawn of the century now seemed doubtful at its dusk. The crisis could not fail to affect Hegel and the young romantics, who had grown up under the tutelage of the *Aufklärung*. Athough they would later rebel against it, they were still deeply in its debt. They were all, so to speak, *Kinder der Aufklärung*.

The crisis of the *Aufklärung* affected no one more than Hegel. For what so deeply separates him from other thinkers of the romantic generation is his attempt, beginning in his mid-Jena years (1803–6), to preserve the legacy of the *Aufklärung* against the criticisms of his contemporaries. Hegel too was very critical of the Enlightenment, subjecting it to almost scornful treatment in one notable chapter of his *Phenomenology of Spirit*.[2] Yet there were aspects of the Enlightenment legacy that he never abandoned, and which he grew to appreciate the more they were imperilled. Chief among these was the Enlightenment faith in the authority of reason. Hegel's mature philosophy was first and foremost an attempt to rescue and rehabilitate the authority of reason after all the criticisms of the *Aufklärung* in the 1790s. Its aim was both to accommodate and surpass these criticisms, to preserve their rightful claims and to cancel their exaggerated pretensions. Hegel's grand achievement was to synthesize the *Aufklärung* with some of the currents of romanticism, creating a romanticized rationalism or a rationalized romanticism.

So, to understand Hegel's philosophy, we first need to know something about the crisis of the *Aufklärung* in the 1790s. It was this crisis – the attack upon the authority of reason by the critics of the *Aufklärung* – that posed the fundamental challenge for Hegel's philosophy.

How, in a few words, are we to characterize the Enlightenment? Aptly, the Enlightenment had often been called 'the age of reason' or 'the age of criticism', not only by historians but also by contemporaries themselves. Here is the definition that Kant himself gave to his age in the preface to the first edition of his *Critique of Pure Reason*:

> Our age is, to a preeminent degree, the age of criticism, and to criticism everything must submit. Religion through its sanctity, and the state through its majesty, may seek to exempt themselves from it. But then they arouse just suspicion against themselves, and cannot claim the sincere respect which reason gives only to that which sustains the test of free and open examination.
>
> (A xii)

The Enlightenment was the age of reason because it made reason into its highest authority, its final court of appeal, in all intellectual questions. Its central and characteristic principle is what we might call the *sovereignty of reason*. This principle means that there is no source of intellectual authority higher than reason. Neither scripture, nor divine inspiration, nor ecclesiastical and civil tradition have the authority of reason. While reason judges the legitimacy of all these sources of authority, none of them stands in judgment of it.

Paradoxically, the crisis of the Enlightenment arose from within, and indeed from its most cherished principle. The problem is that this principle is self-reflexive. If reason must subject *all* beliefs to criticism, it must also subject its own tribunal to criticism. To exempt its tribunal from scrutiny would be nothing less than 'dogmatism', accepting beliefs on authority, which is the very opposite of reason. The criticism of reason therefore inevitably became the *meta*-criticism of reason. If the Enlightenment was the age of criticism, the 1790s were the age of meta-criticism. All the doubts about the authority of reason, which are so often said to be characteristic of our '*post-modern*' age, were already apparent in late eighteenth-century Germany.

When the critics of the *Aufklärung* began to examine the tribunal of criticism itself, they quickly found that its legitimacy rested on several questionable assumptions. All these assumptions came under intense scrutiny in the 1790s. Anti-foundationalism, the pantheism controversy, nihilism, the rise of historicism, and the theory–practice dispute – these were the crucial developments in undermining faith in reason and in provoking the crisis of the Enlightenment. Hegel's philosophy directly grew out of his response to these developments. Each therefore deserves closer examination.

ANTI-FOUNDATIONALISM

The Enlightenment faith in the authority of reason rested first and foremost on the possibility of providing a firm foundation for knowledge. The alternative to a firm foundation seemed to be the abyss of skepticism. The search for a foundation appears in both the empiricist and the rationalist traditions of the Enlightenment. While the empiricist tradition discovered that foundation in the simple ideas of experience, the rationalist tradition sought it in self-evident first principles. Despite their opposing ideas about where to place it, both shared a belief in the possibility, and indeed necessity, of some foundation.

Starting in the early 1790s in Jena, a host of young thinkers began to criticize foundationalism, and more specifically the attempt of Reinhold and Fichte to base Kant's critical philosophy on self-evident first principles. Because it focussed on the possibility of these first principles or *Grundsätze*, their critique of foundationalism has sometimes been called the *Grundsatzkritik*. In the forefront of this critique were some leading students of Reinhold and Fichte, among them Johann Benjamin Erhard, Immanuel Niethammer, Carl Immanuel Diez, Friedrich Carl Forberg, Carl Christian Schmid, A.W. Rehberg, Friedrich Heinrich Weißhuhn, and Paul Johann Feuerbach. Of no less importance for the critique were some of the young romantics, Hölderlin, Friedrich Schlegel, and Novalis.[3]

Although Hegel arrived in Jena only in 1800, after the *Grundsatzkritik* had subsided, he knew well its central tenets and basic criticisms, which had an important and under-appreciated influence on the development of his own methodology.[4] Hegel's rejection of first principles, his emphasis on systematicity, and his mistrust of the mathematical method in philosophy, were only some of the more obvious effects of the *Grundsatzkritik*. Yet Hegel was as much challenged by the *Grundsatzkritik* as influenced by it. He could not accept its fundamental anti-foundationalist conclusion: that the *philosophia prima* is only an ideal, a goal for the infinite striving of enquiry.

It is difficult to summarize the richness and complexity of the *Grundsatzkritik*, a development lasting nearly a decade and involving many thinkers. Here we can only hint at some of the main lines of its criticism, some of the basic reasons for its doubts about the possibility of beginning philosophy with self-evident first principles. (1) The first principle would have to be analytic (of the form 'A is A') or synthetic (of the form 'A is B'). If it were analytic, it would be trivial and without consequences; if it were synthetic, it would be deniable and so subject to skeptical doubt. (2) It is impossible to justify a first principle by appeal to immediate experience, some self-evident intellectual intuition, because it is always possible for someone else to appeal to a contrary intuition. (3) The first principle cannot be merely formal, a law of logic, because that is not sufficient to determine material truth; but if it has some content, it must be very general to encompass the great variety of truths subsumed under it; and such generality is insufficient to derive the specific truths of experience. (4) Even if the first principle were sufficient to derive an entire system, it would not follow that it is true; we can determine its material truth only by consulting experience itself. But experience too is no final arbiter: we can conceptualize, systematize or interpret the same facts in incompatible ways. (5) Reinhold and Fichte have confused Kant's distinction between mathematical and philosophical method. The mathematical method is synthetic: it begins with self-evident principles and constructs its objects in intuition; the philosophical method is analytic: it begins with concepts given in ordinary discourse and only then arrives at its general principles.

As a result of these criticisms, thinkers like Niethammer, Novalis, Schmid, Schlegel and Feuerbach attempted to return to a more Kantian position. They insisted that first principles, and the system of reason, would have to be conceived only as regulative ideals, as goals that we can approach but never attain through an infinite striving. For this reason, the main result of the *Grundsatzkritik* has been called a 're-Kantianization' of epistemology.[5]

THE PANTHEISM CONTROVERSY

Crucial to the Enlightenment faith in the authority of reason was its belief in a natural religion and morality. The *Aufklärer* and *philosophes* held that natural reason alone – independent of revelation – had the power to demonstrate all our fundamental moral and religious beliefs. A natural religion or morality would be one established according to reason alone, such that it held for everyone alike, simply as an intelligent being. Only if reason had such a power would it be possible to dispense with competing forms of intellectual authority, such as the Bible, ecclesiastical tradition and inspiration.

In the late 1780s, the Enlightenment faith in natural religion and morality came under attack in the most dramatic and spectacular manner in the famous 'pantheism controversy' between F.H. Jacobi and Mendelssohn.[6] In his 1786 *Letters on the Doctrine of Spinoza* Jacobi argued that reason – if it is only thorough, honest and consistent – does not support but undermines morality and religion. It is fair to say that Jacobi's sensational attack on reason had a more powerful impact on his age than Kant's sober criticisms in the first Critique.

The core of Jacobi's attack on reason rests on his identification of rationalism with a complete scientific naturalism, and more specifically with the mechanistic paradigm of explanation. Jacobi saw Spinoza as the paragon of this new scientific naturalism, because Spinoza had banished final causes and held that everything in nature happens according to mechanical laws. The fundamental principle of Spinoza's philosophy, Jacobi argued, is nothing less than the principle of sufficient reason. Spinoza is to be praised because he, unlike Leibniz and Wolff, had the courage to take this principle to its ultimate conclusion: a complete scientific naturalism. This principle means that there must be a sufficient reason for any event, such that given that reason, the event must occur and cannot be otherwise. If this principle holds without exception, Jacobi reasoned, then there cannot be (1) a first cause of the universe, a God who freely creates it, and (2) freedom, the power of doing otherwise. For Jacobi, the first result means that Spinozism leads to atheism, the second implies that it ends in fatalism. By identifying Spinoza's rationalism with his naturalism rather than with his geometric method, Jacobi succeeded in reviving at once both the relevance and the danger of Spinozism. If Spinoza's geometric method had fallen victim to Kant's criticisms, his naturalism seemed to be confirmed by the progress of the sciences.

The net effect of Jacobi's attack was to challenge the Enlightenment with a dramatic dilemma: either a rational atheism and fatalism or an irrational leap of faith, a *salto mortale*. There was no middle path: a rational justification for our most important moral and religious beliefs. In sum, Jacobi was saying that the search for a natural morality and religion is futile.

Like so many thinkers of his generation, Hegel was deeply disturbed by Jacobi's challenge to the Enlightenment. On several occasions, he devoted much space and energy to discussing Jacobi's critique of reason.[7] Indeed, he regarded Jacobi's critique as more important than Kant's (EPW §62R). The chief purpose of Hegel's philosophy was to find a middle path between the horns of Jacobi's dilemma. Hegel wanted to reestablish rationalism, to provide it with the means to justify our most important moral and religious beliefs; but he wanted to do so without relapsing into the problematic rationalism of the past, whether that was Spinoza's naturalism, Kantian-Fichtean idealism or the old Leibnizian–Wolffian dogmatism.

THE BIRTH OF NIHILISM

It was already in the early 1800s that nihilism, 'that most uncanny of guests',[8] came knocking at the door. This specter first raised its ugly head during the discussion of Kant's philosophy in the late 1780s. In 1787 the mystical hermit J.H. Obereit, friend of Fichte, Goethe and Schelling, had insinuated in a series of polemical writings that Kant's philosophy, and indeed all rationalism, is guilty of 'nihilism'.[9] Kant's philosophy was the epitome of rationalism, Obereit argued, because it had taken criticism to its ultimate limits; yet it had limited all knowledge to appearances, which are really only representations in us. Nihilism was Obereit's term for the doctrine that we cannot know anything beyond our consciousness, so that our ultimate values and beliefs have no rational basis. Nowhere was the horror of nihilism expressed with more power and passion than in the extraordinary anonymous work *Nightwatches – By Bonaventura* (1804). Its hero, an asylum inmate, preaches the gospel of nothingness, basing his black moods and psychotic ravings on the doctrine of recent philosophy that 'everything is only in ourselves and outside us there is nothing real'.[10] His despair culminates in his belief that all values and beliefs ultimately collapse into the abyss of nothingness.

It was above all Jacobi who made nihilism such a disturbing issue for German philosophy in the early 1800s. After his first assault on reason in the late 1780s, Jacobi pressed home his attack in the late 1790s, now making Kant's and Fichte's philosophy his main target. In his 1799 *Letter to Fichte* he argued that rationalism must end in a complete 'egoism' or solipsism, or what he called 'nihilism' (*Nihilismus*). According to Jacobi, the nihilist is someone who doubts the existence of everything: the external world, other minds, God, and even his own self. The nihilist follows his reason to the bitter skeptical end, doubting the existence of anything outside the immediate contents of his own mind. The transcendental idealism of Kant and Fichte ends in this abyss, Jacobi argues, because its paradigm of knowledge is that we know only what we create or what we produce according to the laws of our activity. We are then forced to admit that we know either ourselves or nothing.

Again, Jacobi's polemic proved remarkably successful in disturbing his contemporaries. He made nihilism the inevitable result of Kant's philosophy, and indeed the entire 'way of ideas' of modern philosophy. In Jacobi's usage, the term 'nihilism' already had the connotation later associated with it in the nineteenth century: the Christian's despair that life is meaningless because there is no God, providence or immortality. But Jacobi gave the problem of nihilism a much deeper dimension by connecting it with the classical challenge of skepticism, with the skeptic's thesis that we have no reason to believe in the existence of everything beyond our own passing impressions. He read Hume's closing statement in the first book of the *Treatise of Human Nature* as the confession of a nihilist. With Jacobi, then, the problem of nihilism is not only a moral crisis of the Christian's lack of faith; it involves the fundamental skeptical challenge to all our beliefs. It was in this form that Hegel first confronted the problem. We shall see in Chapter Six how he addressed it in the famous 'Lordship and Bondage' chapter of the *Phenomenology*.

THE RISE OF HISTORICISM

The Enlightenment faith in the universality and impartiality of reason was badly shaken by the rise of historicism in the late 1770s and 1780s. The leading thinkers behind the growth of historicism in Germany were J.G. Hamann, Justus Möser and J.G. Herder.[11] Their views about history grew out of their reaction against the historiography of the Enlightenment, and more specifically the tendency of the *Aufklärer* to judge the past according to their contemporary moral principles. They made two chief criticisms against such historiography: first, it abstracts from context; and, second, it judges past cultures in terms of its own.

What, more precisely, was historicism? Although the term 'historicism' has acquired many different meanings, we need here only to focus on its meaning in the late 1790s and early 1800s. We can best summarize that meaning in three methodological points. (1) *History*. Everything in the social and political world has a history. All laws, institutions, beliefs and practices are subject to change, and each is the result of a specific historical development. Hence nothing in the social and political world is eternal. (2) *Context*. We should examine all human beliefs, practices and institutions in their historical context, showing how they arose of necessity from their specific economic, social, legal, cultural and geographic conditions. We must see them as parts and products of a wider whole. (3) *Organicism*. Society is an organism, an indivisible whole, whose politics, religion, morality and legal system are inextricably intertwined.

Like all organisms, it undergoes a process of development, having a birth, a childhood, maturity and decline.

To appreciate the challenge of historicism, we only have to consider the consequences of these methodological principles for the Enlightenment faith in reason. The *philosophes* and *Aufklärer* regarded the principles of reason as universal and impartial, as holding for people in all times and places simply as intelligent beings. But the historicist warns us that these principles are only *apparently* universal and eternal. Once we place them in their context and see how they arose in history, they show themselves to be the product of a specific culture at a specific time; they express only the self-consciousness of their age. In believing in the universality of certain principles the *philosophes* and *Aufklärer* suffer from amnesia. They fail to see the origin of their principles, the conditions under which they arose, and so they generalize the ideals of their own age as if they were the ideals of all mankind.

The danger of historicism for the Enlightenment therefore came from its implicit relativism. The historicist views all values as equally legitimate, as the necessary response of a people to specific circumstances. Since that response is necessary, we should not presume to judge it, for that just falsely presupposes that we could have done something better in the same circumstances. All putative universal values are ultimately ethnocentric, invalid generalizations beyond our own specific time and place. There is no such thing as an ideal system of laws suitable for all people and valid for all times and places; the proper constitution for a people depends on its specific circumstances and history.

Hegel was both influenced and challenged by historicism. Some of his early writings reveal how he had absorbed its fundamental tenets. Hegel is often given credit for introducing historicism into philosophy, for making it integral to epistemology.[12] It is very important to see, however, that, for all his historicism, Hegel refused to accept its relativist consequences. One of the main aims of his political philosophy, as we shall soon see, was to reestablish the natural law tradition while still doing justice to historicism (pp. 208–9).

THE THEORY–PRACTICE DEBATE

Nothing more shook the Enlightenment faith in reason than that grand cataclysmic event of 14 July 1789 and its aftermath: the French Revolution. To many people, the French Revolution seemed to be the apotheosis of the Enlightenment. All of society and the state were to be reconstructed according to rational principles, and all historical institutions and laws were to be swept away if they failed to pass the test of reason. It was the great promise of Enlightenment that if we only follow reason in social and political life there will be heaven on earth.

Rather than heaven, there was hell. The more the *philosophes* tried to force a rational constitution upon France, the more it slid into bloodshed, chaos and terror. All the constitutions of reason were like so many assignats: their value was only on paper. What had gone wrong? Some critics contended that reason is inherently anarchic. If everyone follows their reason, always questioning their superiors, there will be no authority at all. Each individual will judge differently. Society and the state will be like the first days of the French revolutionary army, when enlisted men had the right to question the orders of their officers. Other critics stressed that there was an insurmountable gap between theory and practice. Assuming that reason can determine the fundamental principles of the state, people still do not *act* according to them. They are moved more by passion (the September massacres), self-interest (the speculators) or tradition (the Vendée revolt).

Some of these criticisms of the Enlightenment were voiced in a famous controversy that took place in the 1790s in Germany, the so-called 'theory–practice' debate. The focus of the debate was Kant's moral and political philosophy, which had attracted the ire of conservative critics because it seemed to provide a rationale for Jacobin policies in France. Kant seemed to have the same unbounded faith in the practical powers of reason as the Jacobins. In the *Critique of Practical Reason* Kant had argued that reason is practical in two senses: first, it provides a sufficient justification for the principles of our actions; and, second, it provides a sufficient incentive or motive for moral action. In his famous 'Theory–Practice' essay Kant had pushed his argument further, contending that reason is also practical in the political sphere. He contended that reason has the power to determine not only the general principles of morality but also the specific principles of the state. From his categorical imperative he derived a constitution consisting in the principles of liberty and equality, much like those already established in revolutionary France. Against Hobbes and Machiavelli, he argued that these moral principles are also binding in politics.

There were several replies to Kant's essay, the most important by Justus Möser, Friedrich Gentz and A.W. Rehberg.[13] They argued three points. (1) Even if reason were a sufficient foundation for our moral obligations, it still cannot provide a basis for the state. The principles of morality are simply too general, compatible with all kinds of different social and political arrangements. The only way to determine the specific principles of the state, the proper constitution of a people, is to consider its history and traditions. (2) Even if it could provide *specific* principles of the state, reason still could not provide a sufficient incentive or motive for action. The main motives for human action were not reason but tradition, imagination and passion. (3) If he is to remain in power and to uphold law and order, it is impossible for a statesman to act on the principles of reason; for in doing so he would simply make himself vulnerable to others who are not so scrupulous.

The theory–practice debate revealed two antithetical positions about the role of reason in politics. Kant and Fichte stood for a left-wing rationalism. They argued that practice should follow theory in politics because the principles of morality, which are determined by pure reason, are also binding in politics. Their critics represented a right-wing empiricism. They maintained that theory should follow practice in politics because the principles of reason are too formal to have any bearing on constitution or policy, and that to determine what to do in politics we need to consult experience, 'the accumulated wisdom of our ancestors'.

We will see later how Hegel's own political philosophy grew out of his attempt to find a middle path between the rationalists and empiricists in the theory-practice debate (pp. 220–3).

Two

Early Ideals

THE ROMANTIC LEGACY

To introduce Hegel it is not sufficient to consider the problems he faced; it is also necessary to know the ideals he wanted to achieve. What were Hegel's basic values? How did he think philosophy should help us to achieve them? These questions are the most important that we can ask about any philosopher, especially Hegel. We cannot understand his philosophy if we interpret it simply in technical terms, as if it were only a set of arguments, a series of deductions, or a systematic structure; for we still need to ask the more basic question: What were all these arguments, these deductions, and this system for? Although Hegel sometimes writes as if philosophy were an end in itself, serving no higher goal than contemplation, a consideration of his intellectual development shows that he became a philosopher to serve moral, political and religious ends.

Hegel's early ideals grew out of early German romanticism, the period sometimes called *Frühromantik*.[1] This intellectual movement flourished from 1797 to 1802 in Jena and Berlin. Among its leading lights were Friedrich Schlegel, Friedrich von Hardenberg (Novalis), Friedrich Wilhelm Joseph Schelling, Friedrich Daniel Schleiermacher, Ludwig Tieck and, though somewhat on its fringes, Hölderlin. The romantic circle would hold meetings at the literary salons of Rahel Levin and Henriette Herz in Berlin, and at the household of A.W. Schlegel in Jena. Though Hegel never attended these meetings, and though he came to Jena only after its 'literary frenzy' had faded, he was still greatly influenced by the romantics. The crucial channels of influence were his close friends, Schelling and Hölderlin. Some of Hegel's Frankfurt writings, especially the 1797/8 *Sketches on Religion and Love* and the 1797–9 *Spirit of Christianity*, are typical of the romantic spirit.

Although the importance of the romantic legacy seems obvious, it has lately become unpopular even to associate Hegel with romanticism. Walter Kaufmann, Shlomo Avineri and Georg Lukács, to name a few, have argued strenuously against any conflation of Hegel with the romantics, even in his early years.[2] There is an important element of truth to this. Hegel came into his own only in his later Jena years (1804–7) when he reacted against some of the central ideas of the romantic circle. The preface to the *Phenomenology* is his *Abschiedsbrief*, his settling of accounts with the romantics. We can see some of these critical tendencies even in the early fragments, so it would be a mistake to see Hegel as a romantic pure and simple even in his Frankfurt years.

Nevertheless, it is also a mistake to treat Hegel as a figure apart, as if we can understand him without the romantics, or as if he were fundamentally opposed to them. This would be anachronistic for the early Hegel; but it would also be inaccurate about the later Hegel, who never entirely freed himself from romantic influence. His distinguishing features are still within a common genus. What seems to be a difference in quality is very often only one of quantity or emphasis. It is indeed a very common mistake of Hegel scholarship to regard ideas as distinctly Hegelian that are in fact common to the whole romantic generation. Hegel's absolute idealism, his organic conception of nature, his critique of liberalism, his communitarian ideals, his vitalized Spinozism, his concept of dialectic, his attempt to synthesize communitarianism and liberalism – all these ideas are sometimes seen as uniquely Hegelian; but they were part of the common romantic legacy.

Hegel scholars have often been led astray by Hegel's own polemics. They accept these polemics as infallible, as if what Hegel says about his differences with the romantics had to be true simply because Hegel knew himself best. But sometimes the polemics distance Hegel from the romantics only at the cost of obscuring or disguising his own affinity with them. When, for example, in the preface to the *Phenomenology* Hegel states that his own view is that the absolute is not only substance but also subject, Hegel scholars take this as a distinguishing feature of Hegel's philosophy over Schelling's and the romantics. But what Hegel claimed as his own project – the attempt to combine substance and subject, Spinoza and Fichte – was a common enterprise of the romantic generation.[3]

The reason many scholars have separated Hegel from the romantic generation is that they have a very anachronistic conception of *Frühromantik* that virtually equates it with the later more reactionary tendencies of *Spätromantik*. Their conception of Hegel's intellectual context rests upon a neglect of the early philosophical works of the romantics, the unpublished fragments of Schleiermacher, Novalis, Friedrich Schlegel and Hölderlin, most of which have been accessible in critical editions only in the last fifty years. A careful study of these fragments is a fundamental desideratum of Hegel studies; it alone will allow us to locate him historically and to determine his individuality.

THE HIGHEST GOOD

To know Hegel's fundamental values, it is necessary to go back to a classical but neglected question of ethics: What is the highest good? This question concerns the ultimate values in life, and indeed the purpose of life itself. Aristotle had explicitly defined the concept in Book I of the *Nicomachean Ethics*.[4] He argued that the highest good has two fundamental components: finality and completeness. The highest good is *final* in the sense that it is always an end and never a means; and it is *complete* in the sense that it cannot be made better by the addition of any other good. Although Aristotle's question had been central to ancient and medieval ethics, it had lost much of its importance in the early modern era. Locke and Hobbes had belittled it, claiming that what is good is simply relative to the desires of the agent.[5] But the question never disappeared in German philosophy. It was always implicit in the Protestant tradition as the question 'What is the vocation of man [die Bestimmung des Menschen]?' With the revival of classical learning in mid-eighteenth-century Germany, the question took on a whole new lease of life. It was an important issue for the early romantic generation, especially for Friedrich Schlegel, Schleiermacher and Hegel himself.[6]

We can formulate the highest good of Hegel and the young romantic generation in a single phrase, one they would often use and constantly imply: unity of life (Einheit des Lebens). The highest good, the end of life, consists in achieving unity, wholeness or harmony in all aspects of our being. This unity holds on three levels: with oneself, with others, and with nature. The main threat to such unity consists in division (Entzweiung) or alienation (Entfremdung). Though the self should live in unity with itself, others and nature, it finds itself divided from itself and from them. Its goal is to overcome these divisions and achieve unity, so that it is again 'at home in the world' (in die Welt zu Hause).

The ultimate source for this ideal of the unity of life was classical antiquity, and more specifically the works of Plato and Aristotle.[7] One crucial fact about Hegel, Hölderlin, Schelling, Friedrich Schlegel, and Schleiermacher is that, from an early age, they were enthusiastic students of the Greek classics, all of which they read in the original. In the Tübinger Stift Hegel, Hölderlin and Schelling formed a reading club that often read Plato. Rosenkranz informs us of how Hegel had mastered Aristotle's Nicomachean Ethics by the age of 18.[8]

The ideal of unity is present in Plato and Aristotle in many ways. First, Plato's and Aristotle's ideal of human excellence requires that the self be a whole, a harmony of reason and passion. Second, Plato and Aristotle insisted that the polis be an organism, where the whole cares for each part and each part lives for the whole. While they notoriously differed over how much diversity there should be in the state, both held that the ideal state should be an organic unity, having a single religion, art, morality, education and language for all citizens. Third, Plato and Aristotle understood nature in organic terms, as 'a single visible living being'.[9] In all these respects Plato and Aristotle presented the sharpest contrast with the modern worldview, whose self is divided into soul and body, whose state is a contract between self-interested parties, and whose concept of nature is mechanical. It was the great achievement of Hegel and the romantic generation to have reaffirmed the classical ideal of unity against the modern worldview.

The young Hegel and the romantics had a very idealistic conception of ancient Greek life. Their paradigm for unity of life was that of fifth-century Athens. They had their own theory about the ancient Greek: that he lived in harmony with himself, with others and with nature. We scarcely need to bother about the historical accuracy of such a fanciful theory: it is a myth whose value entirely lies in what it tells us about the Germans rather than the ancient Greeks. The romantic conception of Greek life came from several sources: from Rousseau, Wieland, Herder and Schiller. But its ultimate source was that Homer of German myth, 'the divine' J.J. Winckelmann. It was Winckelmann who taught the Germans that Greek culture was an aesthetic whole. Winckelmann's constant refrain that Greek life was 'natural' stemmed from his political conviction that the Greeks were a free people who could express their humanity. The political message behind Winckelmann's classicism was never lost on a public weary of absolutism: we could all become Greeks if we were only free.

We can have a more definite idea of Hegel's early ideals only if we consider each aspect of his highest good: unity with oneself, others and nature. This requires having a basic idea of romantic ethics, politics and religion.

ETHICAL IDEALS

Romantic ethics has its source in the classical ideal of self-realization or excellence. The romantic ideal was articulated by Friedrich Schlegel, Novalis, Schleiermacher and Hölderlin. But the ideal had a long history before them, and was part of the legacy of German humanism. It is also found in Schiller, Herder, Wieland, Goethe, and Wilhelm von Humboldt.

The romantic ideal of excellence, of unity with oneself, consists of three basic components: (1) *totality*, that a person should develop *all* his or her characteristic human powers, (2) *unity*, that these powers be formed into a whole or unity, and (3) *individuality*, that this whole or unity should be individual or unique, characteristic of the person alone.

The demand for totality means that we should overcome all one-sidedness, that we should not neglect any side of our being, because we are as human in our sensibility as in our reason. The demand for unity means that we should form all these powers into a single organic whole. The romantics would sometimes formulate the demand for unity in aesthetic terms. They insisted that we should make our lives into novels. Like all works of art, they should show unity in multiplicity, where the unity must be spontaneous, deriving from within rather than being imposed from without. The demand for individuality means that each person should develop not only those powers characteristic of humanity in general, but also those distinctive of her or his individuality; each work of art should be unique, expressive of the individual alone.

The romantic ethic of self-realization has to be conceived in contrast against its two main alternatives: the utilitarianism of Bentham and Helvetius, which defined the highest good as happiness and happiness in terms of pleasure; and the ethics of duty of Kant and Fichte, which made the highest end in life the performance of moral duties. The romantics rejected utilitarianism because it sees human beings as passive consumers of pleasure and neglects the active development of characteristic human powers. They objected to the Kantian–Fichtean ethic because it divides human beings into reason and sensibility and develops rationality at the expense of sensibility.

To achieve unity with oneself, the romantics, true to name, laid the greatest importance on the experience of love. They were greatly inspired by Plato's *Phaedrus* and *Symposium* where love unites the two sides of the soul, reason and need. They saw an ethics of love as indeed superior to an ethics of duty. Love supersedes duty because in acting from love we do our duty from rather than *contrary to* inclination. Although we act from self-interest in love, the self no longer separates its essential interests from others; rather, the self finds itself in others; it becomes what it is only through others, which it perceives as equal to and independent of itself.

This ethic of love appears in Friedrich Schlegel, Schleiermacher, Novalis and Hölderlin. Its father was Schiller, who had suggested it in his *Philosophical Letters* and *Grace and Dignity*.[10] Perhaps its most enthusiastic exponent was Hegel himself. In his *Spirit of Christianity* he argued that love should be the fundamental principle of ethics, and that only love could overcome the dualisms of Kant's ethics. In some early Frankfurt fragments he had developed a whole metaphysics of love, maintaining that the unity of subject and object, the identity of the self with the universe, is attained only through the experience of love.

Although Hegel had great debts to the romantic ethic, he would later distance himself from it in two respects. First, Hegel did not lay the same high value on individuality. For Hegel, to be an individual means to have a specific place or role within society and the state.[11] Hegel would later criticize Friedrich Schlegel's concept of 'divine egoism' for its perverse and presumptuous separation of the individual from the social world. Second, despite his initial enthusiasm, Hegel abandoned the ethic of love. He began to realize that the feelings and inclinations of love are insufficiently universal to serve as the basis of moral and political life. I love my parents, my siblings, and my friends, perhaps, but not my compatriots, still less humanity in general. Hegel already knew this in the Frankfurt years; but he drew the full consequences from it only in his Jena years; by the time of the *Philosophy of Right* he had confined love to the ethical life of the family.[12]

POLITICAL IDEAL

The romantic ideal of unity with others is their concept of the organic state. The model for their organic state was the ancient republics of Greece and Rome. The romantic republic consists in (1) the right to participate in public affairs, to elect rulers and to determine public policy, (2) the freedom of its individual members, i.e. rights for equal protection of their property, freedom of speech and press, and (3) care of the state for the education and development of its citizens.

The romantic republic was, in part, a reaction against 'the machine state' of enlightened absolutism, where the command of the prince would set all wheels in motion If everything in enlightened absolutism was done for the people, it was never done by the people. Contrary to the machine state, the organic state would develop from the participation of its citizens. The romantic republic was also a reaction against the atomistic state of liberalism, which was held together by a contract between self-interested individuals. The romantics rejected this state as an attempt to square the circle: if agents act always on their self-interest, they will disobey the laws whenever they can avoid punishment, so that the only remedy would be total tyranny.

In the late 1790s and early 1800s the romantic ideal of the organic state underwent some transformation as a result of the course of the French Revolution. In response to the anarchism and chronic instability in France, Hegel and the romantics began to qualify their original classical ideals. They stressed the importance of historical continuity, the role of independent groups within the state, the value of a mixed constitution, and the importance of a central ruler (the monarch). The organic state became more historical, more pluralistic and more centralized. In all these respects it lost its classical inspiration. It is not surprising that in the early 1800s we find Hegel, Schlegel and Novalis looking back to the Middle Ages rather than classical antiquity. Nevertheless, it is fair to say that the organic state never lost its democratic element, its constitutionalism and its belief in fundamental rights. This is true of Novalis, Schlegel, Schleiermacher until at least 1801; it remained true of Hegel throughout his life.

Although the romantics' ideal state was inspired by classical Greece and Rome, there is one respect in which it was, from the very beginning, modern. This was the romantics' insistence on freedom of the individual. The romantics wanted to have not only the classical freedom of democratic participation, but also the modern freedom of the rights of man. They knew all too well that the ancient republics did not value tolerance and individual freedom. They also realized that it was impossible to go back in history and to revive the ancient republics or the medieval constitution. Their ideal was to achieve a synthesis of the ancient ideal of community with the modern ideal of freedom. This was not a unique Hegelian ambition but the common goal of all romantic political thought.

RELIGIOUS IDEAL

If we place the romantic ideal of the highest good in general historical perspective, it immediately becomes apparent that it is entirely immanent or this-worldly. The romantics held that the highest good is to be attained in this life, not in a world beyond it. If we achieve unity with ourselves, others and nature in this life, we have achieved the purpose of life, which serves no end beyond itself. The romantic conception of the highest good is therefore the negation of the classical Christian conception, according to which the highest good consists in eternal salvation. In Book XIX of the *City of God* Augustine had argued that the classical Aristotelian ideal of the highest good could not be realized in this life, which is only a vale of death, disease and distress. Famously, Augustine saw life on earth as a pilgrimage, a rite of passage, to an eternal destination. Self-consciously, firmly, and passionately, Hegel and the romantics broke with the Augustinian tradition. It is indeed noteworthy that Hegel, along with Hölderlin and Schleiermacher, explicitly denied personal immortality and excoriated the entire ethic of salvation based on it. From his early Berne manuscripts to his 1831 lectures on the philosophy of religion Hegel attacked the ethic of salvation for its self-centered concern for the fate of the soul.[13]

True to his immanent ideal of the highest good, Hegel believed that the meaning of life could and should be achieved in the community alone. We find satisfaction and purpose in our lives, he argued, when, like the ancient Roman and Greek, we contribute to the common good and help to create its laws. The ancient Greeks found immortality and meaning in their lives by living for the *polis*, which was a whole greater than themselves, and which they knew would survive them; they had no concern for their individual salvation, for the fate of their soul after death. In Hegel's view, the Christian ethic of personal salvation was only a cry of desperation, a feeble *Ersatz*, after the loss of community. This ethic arose in the first place only because of the decline of the ancient republics. When people lost their freedom to govern themselves, they could no longer find meaning by participating in communal life; and so, out of despair, they sought the source of meaning in a world beyond the earth.

Hegel and the romantics were stalwart opponents not only of the Christian ideal of the highest good but also of the traditional forms of Christian theology. They abhorred both theism and deism. The source of their animus against theism was essentially political: theism had been part of the ideology of the *ancien régime*, a pillar of the old alliance of throne and altar. Because of the legacy of enlightened criticism, they also had little faith in the Bible, the mainstay of theism. The source of their antipathy to deism was more cultural: it had been a powerful force in alienating the self from nature.

Because the deist still clung to the old dogma of a supernatural soul, he placed the self outside nature, which he saw as nothing more than a gloomy machine. Since God existed in a supernatural realm and had abandoned nature after its creation, the natural realm lost its divine significance.

Although their ideal of the highest good was entirely immanent, and although they were opposed to traditional forms of theology, Hegel and the romantics were still religious. Their conception of the divine, like their conception of the highest good, was entirely immanent. They held on to the traditional concepts of the infinite – the *ens realissimum*, that of which nothing greater can be conceived – but they interpreted them in immanent terms to be the universe as a whole. Only such an immanent conception of the divine, they believed, would overcome the self's alienation from nature. The self would identify itself with nature only if it were a mode of the single infinite substance, a part of the universal whole.

The most important forebear and model for this immanent conception of the infinite was, of course, Spinoza, whose doctrines underwent a dramatic renaissance in Germany as a result of the pantheism controversy. Growing up in the 1790s, the young romantics were inevitably drawn into the vortex of this dispute. Their notebooks give more than ample evidence of their study of, and sympathy for, Spinozism. For them, Spinoza was 'der Gott betrunkene Mensch' (the man drunk with God).[14] To write 'Hen kai pan' – 'Eins und Alles' (one and all) – in Stammbücher became something of a fashion. Famously, in his *Speeches on Religion* Schleiermacher asks us to make an offering to 'the holy rejected Spinoza'.[15]

What did Hegel and the young romantics get from Spinoza? What they saw in him was first and foremost his attempt to rationalize religion. Spinoza's famous dictum *deus sive natura*, his identification of God with the infinitude of nature, seemed to resolve the conflict between reason and faith that had preoccupied philosophers and theologians throughout the Enlightenment. Spinoza's dictum divinized nature as much as it naturalized the divine, and so it seemed to make a religion out of science, a science out of religion. If God were the same as 'the one and all' – if the divine were the creative force of nature, the dynamic unity behind all its laws – then there would be no reason to oppose reason and faith. Instead, the objects of religion and science would be one and the same. The case for Spinozism seemed only strengthened by the weakness of its traditional rivals, theism and deism, which, by the end of the eighteenth century, were on their last legs. Theism not only rested its case on miracles, which were hard to square with science, but it also suffered greatly from the new biblical criticism. For its part, deism had simply collapsed under the relentless barrage of Hume's and Kant's criticism of the traditional proofs of God's existence. Only Spinoza's pantheism did not seem in danger of such obsolescence. The reality of Spinoza's God was as palpable as that of nature itself. Rather than being a mysterious spirit, like the God of traditional theism, or an irrelevant abstraction, like the God of deism, Spinoza's God is the whole of nature, and so equally present within everyone alike. Since we are all modes of the single infinite substance, we only have to reflect upon ourselves to find the divine within us.

It is important to see that the romantic attraction to Spinoza was not only religious but also political. To understand these political factors, it is worthwhile to keep in mind a famous remark of Heinrich Heine: that pantheism had always been the secret religion of Germany, the faith of its cultural underground.[16] Heine knew whereof he spoke. Since the end of the seventeenth century in Germany, Spinoza had become the patron saint of radical Protestants, of all those discontented reformers who accused Luther of selling out to the princes and betraying his two grand ideals: religious liberty and the priesthood of all believers. These radicals embraced Spinoza for a variety of reasons, all of them perfectly Protestant. They saw Spinoza's separation of church and state as a guarantee of religious liberty; they embraced his critique of the Bible because it freed Lutheranism from its biblicism, its deadening emphasis upon the letter as a rule of faith; and they loved his pantheism because it seemed to justify the equality and priesthood of all believers. After all, if God is infinitely present within everyone alike, we are all equal; and then there is no need for a priest or spiritual authority to mediate our relationship with God. Of course, Spinoza was a Jew, at least by background; but for these radical Protestants, who were ecumenical to the bone, that was all the more reason to embrace him. What could better show their universalist credentials? And, in any case, did Spinoza not live with the brethren at Rijnsberg? Was the affinity in doctrine that accidental after all?

Despite constant persecution, the flames of religious radicalism in Germany never died out; and clandestine editions of the *Ethica* and *Tractatus* never ceased to circulate. The radical ideals lived on well into the eighteenth century, when they found their foremost exponents in writers like Gottfried Arnold, Conrad Dippel, Johann Edelmann, and finally Lessing and Herder. When the romantics embraced Spinozism in the late 1790s they were – somewhat unwittingly – carrying on the tradition of the radical reformers. The Spinoza revival of the 1790s was nothing less than the last great manifestation of the radical reformation. Its finest literary and philosophical expression was Schleiermacher's *Speeches*.

Eventually, Hegel too was taken up by the wave of enthusiasm for Spinoza. In his writings during the Berne period (1793–6) he seems almost immune to it. He endorses Kant's idea of moral faith, according to which belief in a supernatural God is justified on moral grounds. But he abandoned this doctrine in his Frankfurt years and developed instead an immanent conception of God. In his 1801 *Differenzschrift* Hegel defended Schelling's Spinozism (see pp. 58–9). Although Hegel rightly resisted any conflation of his absolute idealism with Spinozism, he never ceased to regard Spinoza's philosophy as the foundation for modern philosophy and religion. In his *History of Philosophy* he wrote of Spinoza's substance: 'When one begins to philosophize one must be first a Spinozist.

The soul must bathe itself in the aether of this single substance, in which everything one has held dear is submerged.'[17]

Although the romantic ideal of unity of life is beautiful, it also seems unattainable. It seems romantic in the popular sense of that term: an unrealistic dream. The classical ideals of Hegel and the romantic generation came into sharp conflict with modern reality. While the classical ideals demanded unity, modern society seemed to create division, and on every level: division within oneself, with others and with nature. For Hegel and the young romantics, the fundamental challenge was how to legitimate their ideal of unity of life in face of the growing divisions of modern life. The need for philosophy arose, as Hegel famously put it, from division (*Entzweiung*) (D II 20/89).

Each ideal of unity seemed to be undermined by some aspect of modern life. The ideal of unity with oneself was threatened by the growing division of labor, the need for each individual to specialize and devote himself to a narrow task. The more production became rationalized or efficient, the more he would have to cultivate specific skills and talents. Rather than realizing all their powers, people could develop only one narrow side of themselves. Acutely aware of this problem, the romantics agreed with Schiller's famous lament:

> Always chained to a single little fragment of the whole, man himself develops into only a fragment; always in his ear the monotonous sound of the wheel that he turns, he never develops the harmony of his being; and instead of putting the stamp of humanity upon his nature he becomes nothing more than the imprint of his business or science.[18]

(NA XX, 323)

Of course, in classical culture the division of labor had not been such a danger. This was not only because of the lack of technology, but also because of the entrenched institution of slavery. Free from the realm of economic necessity, the citizens of the Greek and Roman republics had more time and energy to spend on civic affairs. But slavery was not acceptable to the modern world; and so the claims of the economic world became inescapable. The problem for Hegel and the young romantics was how to achieve the classical ideal of excellence without the classical institution of slavery. This seemed all but unattainable when modern forms of production and exchange seemed only to enslave everyone.

The ideal of unity with others also faced grave dangers in the modern world. The fundamental trends of modern civil society seemed to be toward atomism and anomie, the decomposition of society and the state into a multitude of separate individuals who sought only their self-interest. Rather than joining together for the common good, individuals were forced to compete in the market place. There was no hope for participation in the community of a republic because of the sheer size and scale of the modern state, its increasing centralization and bureaucratization. The modern individual saw the state as a hostile and alien being, whose purpose was to dominate and control him. These atomistic trends of civil society were clearly perceived in Germany toward the close of the eighteenth century. Writers complained about the decline of the village community and parish from growing urbanization, and they deplored unemployment among urban masses.[19]

Finally, the ideal of unity with nature also seemed unattainable. The ancients would identify themselves with nature, because they saw it as a living whole of which they were a part. But the whole realm of nature had become disenchanted through the growth of modern science and technology. Rather than seeing nature as an object of contemplation, as a realm of beauty, mystery and magic, the technologist gave it only an instrumental value. He was engaged in a struggle against nature, which he wanted to dominate and control by a machine. Since nature is only a machine, it can be controlled to serve us.

How, then, was it possible to achieve unity in life if modern society only creates divisions? For Hegel, and the young romantic generation, that was the crucial issue of the age. It seemed as if the grand romantic ideals were obsolete as soon as they were formulated, that they were only a cry of protest against the inevitable 'forces of progress'. It was the task of philosophy to show the legitimacy of their ideals, to establish the possibility, indeed the necessity, of wholeness despite the divisions of modern life. It was necessary first of all to do battle against *Reflexionsphilosophie*, which seemed to legitimate all the divisions of modern life. It was necessary to show – against Descartes, Kant and Fichte – that the world is not divided into subject and object, mind and body, self and other. The young Hegel believed that doing battle against dualism and showing the possibility of wholeness was the task of one special field of philosophy: metaphysics.[20] It is to that metaphysics that we must now turn.

Part Two
Metaphysics

Three

Absolute Idealism

THE QUESTION OF METAPHYSICS

Any interpretation of Hegel's philosophy must begin with his metaphysics. Hegel accepted the traditional account of metaphysics as the foundational discipline of philosophy. Like Descartes and Aristotle, he saw metaphysics as the root of the tree of knowledge, whose sap gave life to every branch and leaf. We cannot pretend to give the specific sciences a foundation independent of metaphysics, Hegel argued, because they presuppose answers to fundamental metaphysical questions. If we attempt to escape these questions, he warned, we really only beg them.[1] Hence Hegel made metaphysics the foundation of his own philosophy. He began the mature exposition of his system with logic; but he saw logic as an essentially metaphysical discipline, whose task is to determine the nature of being in itself, not merely formal laws of inference (EPW §24).

But if Hegel's metaphysics is important, it is also controversial. Probably the most disputed question in Hegel scholarship concerns the status of his metaphysics. Much traditional scholarship has put forward a straightforward metaphysical interpretation of Hegel's thought, stressing the central role religion plays in it.[2] According to this interpretation, Hegel's philosophy was an attempt to justify through reason some fundamental Christian beliefs, such as the existence of God, providence, and the trinity. More recently, however, many scholars have advocated non-metaphysical approaches to Hegel's philosophy. They have read it as a theory of categories, a neo-Kantian epistemology, a proto-hermeneutics, a social epistemology, or as an anti-Christian humanism.[3] What motivates all these non-metaphysical readings is the conviction that if Hegel's philosophy is a metaphysics, it is doomed to obsolescence, given that Kant and many others have shown metaphysics to be a bankrupt enterprise.

What are we to make of this dispute? Of course, everything depends on the precise sense of 'metaphysics', a term with many meanings. The sense in question here is that defined by Kant in the *Critique of Pure Reason*: metaphysics is the attempt to gain knowledge of the unconditioned through pure reason (KrV B7, 378–88, 395). Kant understands the unconditioned as whatever completes a series of conditions: the final cause, the last unit of analysis, the ultimate subject of predication. He explains that there are three fundamental ideas of metaphysics corresponding to three basic concepts of the unconditioned: God, freedom and immortality (B 395). It was in this sense that Kant had censured metaphysics in the *Critique*. If reason attempts to go beyond the limits of experience to know the unconditioned, he argued, it lapses of necessity into all kinds of fallacies: the 'paralogisms', 'amphibolies' and 'antinomies' so ruthlessly exposed in the Transcendental Dialectic. Hence Kant declared that metaphysics, understood as the attempt to know the unconditioned through pure reason, is impossible.

If metaphysics is understood in this sense, it is possible to see truth on both sides of the dispute. Strong evidence for the traditional interpretation comes from Hegel's many statements about the religious purpose and subject matter of philosophy. In his *Differenzschrift* he states that the task of philosophy is to know the absolute (II, 25/93). In his *Encyclopedia* he declares that the subject matter of philosophy is God and God alone (VIII, 41, §1). And in his lectures on the philosophy of religion he affirms that philosophy and religion share one and the same object: the absolute or God (VPR I, 33/I 116). He even equates philosophy with theology, describing philosophy as a form of worship since it is devoted to a proof of God's existence and a determination of his nature (VPR I,

3/I, 84). Since Hegel thinks that philosophy attempts to know God through reason, and since he understands God to be infinite or unconditioned, it follows that his philosophy is a metaphysics, and indeed in roughly the Kantian sense; for it attempts to acquire knowledge of the unconditioned through pure reason.

It would be incorrect, however, to conclude from these statements that Hegel's philosophy is a metaphysics in *exactly* the sense proscribed by Kant. Kant saw metaphysics as speculation about *transcendent* entities, as a priori reasoning about objects lying beyond the sphere of experience. In this sense Hegel cannot be a metaphysician at all, and for a very simple and compelling reason: he denied the existence of the transcendent, the purely noumenal or supernatural. If metaphysics consists in speculation about such a realm, then Hegel would be the first to condemn it as a pseudo-science. It is necessary to stress that Hegel's own concept of the infinite or unconditioned is entirely immanent: the infinite does not exist beyond the finite world but only within it.

There is indeed much truth behind the non-metaphysical interpretations. These scholars rightly emphasize Hegel's rejection of traditional metaphysics, his endorsement of Kant's critique of Leibnizian–Wolffian rationalism, and his purely immanent conception of philosophy. On the other hand, these points do not imply that Hegel was not a metaphysician at all. If Hegel abjured metaphysics as a science of the transcendent, he still pursued it as a science of the immanent. Whether the unconditioned is beyond this world or the world as a whole, it still remains the unconditioned. For Hegel, the problem with traditional metaphysics is not that it attempted to know the infinite, but that it had a *false interpretation* of the infinite as something transcending the finite world of ordinary experience. It is indeed striking that Hegel commended the old rationalism precisely because it assumed that thinking could grasp reality in itself, and in this respect he even held that it stood on a higher level than Kant's critical philosophy (EPW §28).

The chief problem with the non-metaphysical interpretation is that it presents us with a false dilemma: either Hegel is a dogmatic metaphysician or not really a metaphysician at all. The crucial assumption behind the dilemma is a very narrow notion of metaphysics as speculation about transcendent entities. It is of the first importance to see, however, that Hegel did not share this notion of metaphysics, and that he wanted to avoid just this dilemma. In a post-Kantian age he was keenly aware of the need to provide a new rationale for metaphysics. It was the central challenge of his philosophical career to provide a critical foundation for metaphysics, to base it upon a method that would satisfy the demands of the Kantian critique of knowledge. This method is his famous dialectic, which we will examine later in Chapter Six.

Regarding the precise status of Hegel's metaphysics, it is necessary to walk a fine line, a middle path between inflationary and deflationary, or exorbitant and reductionist readings. While inflationary or exorbitant readings make the absolute into a super-entity, deflationary or reductionist readings reduce it to nothing more than abstract or pious talk about particular things. Whereas the inflationary reading makes Hegel a Platonist who believes in the existence of abstract entities, the deflationary reading makes him into a nominalist who reduces everything universal down to the particular. That neither reading is correct is apparent from a basic distinction stressed by Hegel himself – a distinction fundamental to his entire philosophy though often ignored by commentators (VG 37, 81, 87/34, 69, 74). This is the ancient Aristotelian distinction between what is first in order of explanation and what is first in order of being.[4] According to Hegel, the universal is first in order of explanation, the particular first in order of existence. The universal is first in order of explanation because, to determine what a thing is, it is necessary to ascribe universals to it; we define the essence or nature of a thing through its properties, each of which is universal. The particular is first in order of existence, however, because to exist is to be determinate, to be some individual thing. To say that the universal is prior to the particular does not mean, therefore, that it is a cause prior in time to the particular; rather, it is only to say that it is the reason or purpose of the thing. This reason or purpose does not exist as such prior to the thing but comes into existence only through it, embodying itself through the complete and full development of the thing.

This crucial distinction provides the middle path between inflationary and deflationary readings of Hegel's metaphysics. Both readings confuse this distinction. The inflationary readings think that logical priority also involves ontological priority, and so they hypostasize the idea as if it *exists* in itself, prior to its embodiment in the physical and historical world. But this would be to say that the universal could exist apart from and prior to the particular, a doctrine that Hegel expressly and emphatically denies (VG 85/72; EPW §24A, VIII, 82). The deflationary readings assume that Hegel's insistence on ontological priority commits him to denying logical priority, as if the idea were nothing more than the sum of the particular things in which it exists. The first reading makes Hegel into a Platonist who thinks that universals exist beyond the historical and natural world; and the second reading makes him into a nominalist who thinks that the meanings of universals are explicable entirely in terms of the individuals to which they refer. But Hegel is first and foremost an Aristotelian: he thinks that universals exist only in things, even though their meaning is not reducible only to them.

In Chapter Six we will again examine the question of Hegel's metaphysics, which ultimately involves the role of religion in his thought.

WHAT IS THE ABSOLUTE?

Hegel's metaphysics is often summarized and labelled with the phrase '*absolute idealism*'. It is striking, however, that Hegel himself rarely uses it. This is only in keeping with his general dislike of abstract slogans and phrases. Understandably, Hegel feared having his philosophy reduced down to a single phrase. He held that a philosophical term had its precise meaning only in its systematic context, and that apart from it there was no end to arbitrary associations. The phrase 'absolute idealism' really came into fashion only in the later half of the nineteenth century when it was used to describe the philosophy of the British and American idealists.

It would be wrong to conclude, however, that the term is anachronistic or inaccurate. It was in general currency by the late 1790s; it seems that the first to use it was Friedrich Schlegel.[5] It was later adopted by Schelling, who used it on several occasions to define his own position.[6] It is indeed significant that Schelling applied the term in works he co-authored with Hegel, and to designate the very philosophy he and Hegel defended in the early 1800s. For all his dislike of general phrases, Hegel himself did not disown the term. According to student lecture notes, he used the term at least thrice to describe his own position.[7] In his own published work he sometimes used the term 'idealism' *simpliciter* to define his philosophy.[8]

Given that 'absolute idealism' is neither inaccurate nor anachronistic, what does it mean? We must begin with its adjective 'absolute'. Absolute idealism is first and foremost an idealism about the absolute. But what is the absolute? This term, so resonant for the entire nineteenth century, has almost entirely lost its meaning for us.

'The absolute' (*das Absolute*) is Hegel's technical term for the subject matter of philosophy. He writes in the *Differenzschrift* that the task of philosophy is to know the absolute (II, 25/93). He seems to regard 'God' as a synonym, or more popular religious expression, for the same.[9] In his lectures on the philosophy of religion, for example, he explains that philosophy and religion share one and the same object: the absolute or God (VPR I, 33/I, 116). Despite its importance, Hegel is singularly unhelpful in providing an explanation of what he means by the absolute. Although he said that his *Logic* was nothing more than a series of definitions of the absolute (WL I, 59), he never gave a simple working definition of the term, a preliminary account of what these definitions were definitions of.

Fortunately, some of Hegel's predecessors and contemporaries did provide definitions, which set the context for Hegel's own usage. According to Kant, the term 'absolute' is utterly ambiguous (KrV B 380–1). In one sense it designates what is valid of a thing 'considered in itself and thus internally', and so apart from its relations to other things; in another sense it signifies what is true of a thing in every respect or relation. Hegel's usage is remarkable for joining both these senses: when fully considered in itself or internally, his absolute includes all relations within itself.

Another definition is provided by Hegel's onetime collaborator, Schelling. According to Schelling, the absolute is 'that which is in itself and through itself', or 'that whose existence is not determined through some other thing'.[10] Hence Schelling sometimes calls the absolute 'the in-itself' (das An-sich). Schelling's phrasing is reminiscent of Spinoza's definition of substance in the Ethics: 'That which is in itself, and is conceived through itself; in other words, that of which a conception can be formed independently of any other conception' (Part I, def. 7). The affinity with Spinoza is no accident, since, during his Jena years, Schelling had become a virtual convert to Spinoza. The allusion to Spinoza's definition of substance is all the more evident when Schelling calls his absolute 'substance' (die Substanz).[11]

There can be little doubt that Hegel shared Schelling's definition, and that he too saw the absolute in Spinozist terms. To be sure, Hegel sharply criticized Spinoza's concept of the absolute (see pp. 91–5), and even in his Jena years these differences are already nascent. Still, Hegel saw Spinoza's definition of substance as the basis or starting point for all philosophy. Hence, in the Differenzschrift he sometimes refers to the absolute as substance (II, 10, 49/80, 116), and in his History of Philosophy he said that one must first bathe in the aether of Spinoza's substance before beginning to philosophize (XX 165; III, 257).

In making substance the fundamental object of metaphysics, Schelling and Hegel were, like Spinoza before them, going back to the Aristotelian tradition.[12] In his *Metaphysics* Aristotle had made substance the primary object of first philosophy. He defined his 'science of first principles' as the study of being as being, and more specifically as the study of those things that exist in a primary sense, those upon which all other things depend in order to be. Since substance alone is the basis of all other forms of being, first philosophy would have to be primarily a theory of substance.[13]

Although Hegel states that the absolute or God is the goal and subject matter of philosophy, he does not think that philosophy should begin by proving its existence, still less that it should presuppose its existence. Famously, he insists that the absolute should be the *result*, not the *starting point*, of doing philosophy (PG 21/¶20). It is only *after* his investigation that the philosopher understands that his object has been all along the absolute or God. In this regard Hegel's metaphysics differs from traditional theology, which from the very beginning makes God its subject matter.

With what then does philosophy begin? With a very simple question, the fundamental question behind all metaphysics: What is reality in itself? What is the thing itself, apart from its relations to other things? In both his *Phenomenology* and *Logic* Hegel begins with this question. The *Phenomenology* begins when consciousness asks itself what is its object, the object in itself (*das An-sich* or *Ansichselbstsein*); all the stages of its development can be understood as progressively more specific or concrete answers to this question. The *Logic* too begins with the concept of pure being (*reines Seyn*), being as it is apart from any determinations that we attribute to it. For Hegel, this is another formulation for substance, for reality in itself, reality apart from the specific determinations that relate it to something else. Indeed, in the *Encyclopedia* version of his logic he is explicit that pure being is the proper characterization of Spinoza's substance (§86; VIII, 183).

This account of the method of philosophy was first developed jointly by Schelling and Hegel in their Jena years. They held that it is the task of reason to know something in itself, apart from its relation to other things.[14] Reason must grasp each thing as if it were the entire world, and as if nothing else existed outside it.[15] This means that reason should strip away from the thing its properties or distinctive form, the determinations by which it differs from all other things, since these properties or determinations constitute its relations to other things. Once we remove all the distinguishing properties of the thing we see the entire universe within it, for all things are the same without distinguishing properties. This method of considering a thing in itself by abstracting from its distinguishing properties Schelling and Hegel called construction. Although Hegel would later abandon the method, he would still adhere to its underlying task: to grasp the thing itself.

SUBJECT–OBJECT IDENTITY

Now that we have examined the meaning of the absolute, we have a better idea of the subject matter of absolute idealism. But we still have none about the doctrine itself. Unfortunately, Hegel is again not very helpful. He provides no working definition of the phrase or preliminary account of its meaning. The few occasions where he uses it already presuppose some established general meaning.

One important clue is offered by Schelling, who, during his collaboration with Hegel, defined the term explicitly on two occasions. According to Schelling, absolute idealism is the doctrine that the ideal and the real, the subjective and objective, are one and the same in the absolute.[16] In other words, it is the doctrine that the absolute consists in subject–object identity. As it stands, Schelling's definition could not pass for Hegel's own, given that, already in the Jena years, Hegel differed significantly from Schelling regarding the nature of the absolute. As early as his *Differenzschrift* he declared that the absolute is not only subject–object identity but the identity of subject–object identity and subject–object non-identity (II, 96/156). Nevertheless, it would be a mistake to disregard Schelling's definition entirely. For Hegel does agree with Schelling that subject–object identity is one important moment of the absolute; furthermore, he tells us explicitly in the preface to the *Differenzschrift* that the principle of subject–object identity expresses the very spirit of 'authentic idealism' (II, 9–10/79–80). It was indeed Hegel's purpose in the *Differenzschrift* to defend Schelling's interpretation of this principle against Kant's and Fichte's.

So, to understand the meaning of Hegel's absolute idealism, we must determine what Schelling and Hegel mean by 'the principle of subject–object identity'. But now it seems that we have only replaced one slogan with another, making the obscure more obscure, for the principle of subject–object identity is one of the most dense and difficult in all German idealism. The principle has no single univocal meaning, its precise meaning depending on its specific context. We must be very careful, therefore, to distinguish Hegel's understanding of this principle from that of his contemporaries.

One apparent hint about its meaning comes from the preface to the *Differenzschrift* where Hegel states that Kant has expressed the principle of subject–object identity in his transcendental deduction of the categories.[17] 'In the principle of the deduction of the categories', Hegel writes, 'Kant's philosophy is authentic idealism . . .' (II, 9/79). Here Hegel is referring to Kant's principle of the unity of apperception, which states that I can have representations only if I can be aware of them. In the *Critique of Pure Reason* Kant made this principle the basis for his 'transcendental deduction', i.e. his attempt to show that the categories (the most basic concepts by which we understand the world) must apply to experience. The precise role of this principle in Kant's deduction has been the subject of endless controversy, which need not concern us now. The crucial question is whether Hegel's concept of subject–object identity should be understood according to Kant's principle. It is striking that Fichte uses the term 'subject–object identity' to describe the act of self-knowledge involved in Kant's principle. Since Hegel

uses the same term, it would seem that he too has a Kantian interpretation of this principle.

It is important, however, not to be misled by this verbal similarity. Despite its initial plausibility, the Kantian interpretation cannot
withstand closer textual scrutiny. Immediately after praising Kant's
deduction in the *Differenzschrift*, Hegel expressly states that Kant has
imperfectly understood the principle of subject–object identity. He
complains of Kant's interpretation: '. . . on what a subordinate stage
it grasps the principle of subject–object identity' (II, 10/81).
Throughout the *Differenzschrift* Hegel criticizes Kant's principle of the
unity of apperception because it is only formal and subjective:
formal, since it is mere self-awareness of representations, regardless
of the content of the representations themselves; and *subjective*, since
the identity takes place only in the subject, amounting to nothing
more than its self-awareness. Hegel charges Kant with having a
subjective concept of reason, according to which reason is something
imposed on the world by the activity of the subject, where the
world prior to this activity is an unknowable thing-in-itself.

The Kantian reading of the principle of subject–object identity
also ignores Schelling's and Hegel's explicit critique of it in their
Jena writings. Schelling and Hegel argue that the Kantian–Fichtean
reading of the principle of subject–object identity ultimately ends
in solipsism, the doctrine that I know only the immediate contents
of my own mind.[18] Since the transcendental subject knows only
what it creates, it is caught inside the circle of its own consciousness; and since it cannot create the entire world, the reality outside
it will be an unknowable thing-in-itself. Hence, during their Jena
years, Schelling and Hegel spurn rather than embrace Kant's interpretation of the principle of subject–object identity.

The prototype for Hegel's reading of the principle of subject–
object identity came not from the Kantian–Fichtean tradition but
its very antithesis: Spinozism. For Schelling and Hegel around
1801, the principle of subject–object identity essentially func-
tioned as a declaration of their monism. It served as a statement of

protest against all forms of dualism, whether Kantian, Fichtean or Cartesian. Schelling and Hegel greatly admired Spinoza for his monism, for showing how to overcome dualism when Kant, Fichte and Jacobi had only reinstated it. True to Spinoza, their principle of subject–object identity essentially means that the subjective and the objective, the intellectual and the empirical, the ideal and the real – however one formulates the opposition – are not distinct substances but simply different aspects, properties or attributes of one and the same substance. The principle follows immediately from the Spinozist proposition that there is only one substance, of which everything else is either a mode or an attribute.[19] If this is the case, then the subjective and objective cannot be two things but must be only modes or attributes of one and the same thing.

Though he never used the term, Spinoza himself had developed something like a principle of subject–object identity. In Part Two of the *Ethics* he argued that the mental and physical are simply different attributes of one and the same substance.[20] The order and connection of ideas is one and the same as the order and connection of things, Spinoza wrote, because both the mental and the physical are ultimately only different aspects of one and the same thing. That Hegel wanted to give his principle of subject–object identity this Spinozist meaning there cannot be any doubt. On two occasions in the *Differenzschrift* he refers approvingly to Spinoza's propositions (II, 10, 106/80, 166).

But here again it seems that we are offering only an explanation *obscurum per obscurius*. For Spinoza's doctrine is one of the most impenetrable in his philosophy. A large part of its difficulty comes from Spinoza's notoriously equivocal definition of an attribute: 'that which the intellect perceives as constituting the essence of substance'.[21] The definition is a masterpiece of ambiguity. Are the attributes essentially subjective, simply different ways in which the intellect perceives, explains or understands substance? Or are they objective, different manifestations, appearances or forms of substance? Or are they somehow both?

Fortunately, though, we need not dwell on the precise meaning of Spinoza's doctrine. The only question for us now is how Hegel understood it or the meaning he gave to it. In his *Differenzschrift* Hegel explains the precise meaning he wants to give to Spinoza's principle. He insists that the difference between the subjective and objective must be not only ideal but also real, i.e. it must be not only one in perspective but also one in the object itself. This means that the subjective and the objective are distinct appearances, embodiments or manifestations of the absolute. On several occasions he stresses that philosophy needs to explain the distinction between the subjective and the objective of ordinary experience. That the subject is distinct from the object – that the object is given and produces representations independent of our will and imagination – is a fact of ordinary experience. Philosophy should not dismiss this appearance as an illusion, Hegel insists, but it should explain it and show its necessity.[22]

It is precisely on these grounds that Hegel departs from Schelling, insisting that the absolute is not only identity but also the identity of identity and non-identity. If philosophy is to explain the opposition between subject and object in ordinary experience, then it must somehow show how the single universal substance, in which the subject and object are the same, divides itself and produces a distinction between subject and object. The philosopher faces an intrinsically difficult task: he must both surmount and explain the necessity of the subject–object dualism. It was precisely the failure of Spinoza, Hegel argues, that he could not explain the origin of finitude.[23] We shall later consider how Hegel attempted to explain the origin of finitude and the dualism of subject–object identity (see pp. 92–5).

THE MEANING OF 'IDEALISM'

We have now seen that Hegel's absolute idealism is essentially a monistic doctrine. It is important to see, however, that it is so in two very different senses. First, in the *anti-dualist* sense that it denies there is any substantial distinction between the subjective and objective, the ideal and real, the mental and physical, and affirms instead that they are distinct attributes or appearances of one and the same substance. Second, in the *anti-pluralistic* sense that it denies there are many substances and affirms instead that there is only one substance. The anti-dualist sense need not imply the anti-pluralist sense, because even if the subjective and objective are aspects of a single substance it is still possible that there are many such substances. But Schelling and Hegel also affirmed the stronger form of monism. They endorsed Spinoza's argument that there could be one, and only one, being that has an independent essence. If there were two substances, then they would have to be conceived in relation to one another, at least in the negative sense that one is essentially *not* the other; in that case both substances would have a dependent essence.

What, though, does this radical monistic doctrine have to do with idealism? The answer is not obvious since, *prima facie*, there is no necessary connection between monism and idealism, in either the ancient Platonic or the modern Berkeleyian sense. After all, some monists are not idealists; for example, Spinoza and Schopenhauer.

Hegel states that absolute idealism is the doctrine that things are appearances of 'the universal, divine idea' (EPW §24A). It is tempting to read this as a form of Platonic idealism, as if the idea were Plato's form or archetype. Absolute idealism would then be a form of idealistic monism or monistic idealism, according to which everything is an appearance of a single absolute idea. So when Hegel says with Spinoza that everything is a mode or attribute of the single universal substance he also means with Plato that it is an appearance or manifestation of the single universal idea.

This reading comes close to Hegel's meaning; but not close enough. For Hegel identifies the idea not with Plato's archetype but with Aristotle's formal–final cause. Hegel saw Aristotle, not Plato, as the proper founder of absolute idealism: 'Aristotle superseded Plato in speculative depth, since he knew the most solidly grounded speculation [or] idealism ...' (XIX, 133/II, 119). Following Aristotle's critique of Plato, Hegel thinks that universals do not exist as such but only *en re*, in particular things.[24] As forms inherent in things, as concrete universals, universals are, in Aristotle's language, the *formal–final* causes of things. The formal cause consists in the essence or nature of a thing, what makes it the thing that it is; and the final cause is the purpose the object attempts to realize, the goal of its development. The two senses of causality are joined in Hegel, as in Aristotle, because the purpose of a thing is to realize its essence or to develop its inherent form. Like Kant, Hegel calls the formal-final cause the 'concept' (*Begriff*) of a thing.[25]

If we keep in mind Hegel's Aristotelian concept of the idea, then his idealism has a fundamentally teleological meaning. To state that everything is an appearance of the idea now means that it strives to realize the absolute idea, or that everything acts for an end, which is the absolute idea. Such was Hegel's Aristotelian transformation of Spinoza's monism: the single universal substance now becomes the single absolute idea, the formal–final cause of all things. Since he despised teleology, Spinoza would have turned over in his grave.

This teleological dimension of Hegel's absolute idealism appears very explicitly in the introduction to his lectures on world history. Here Hegel states that the fundamental thesis of philosophy is that reason governs the world, a thesis he identifies with the old teaching of Anaxagoras that the world is ruled by '*nous*' (VG 28/27). To say that the world is governed by reason, he then explains, means that it has an ultimate purpose (VG 50/44). This means that whatever happens does so of necessity, but not merely in the sense that there are prior causes acting upon it in time but also in the sense that they must realize some end. What this end is we will determine later (pp. 266–7).

The teleological aspect also becomes clear from his implied distinction between 'subjective' and 'objective' idealism.[26] According to this distinction, the subjective idealist holds that the rationality of the world, its conformity to law, has its source in the creative activity of the subject; its fundamental principle is Kant's doctrine that we know a priori of objects only what we create or produce in them. The subjective idealist therefore holds that the world is rational only to the extent that we create or make it so; and to the extent that we cannot create or make it, the world is an unknowable thing-in-itself, an irrational surd. The objective idealist, however, holds that the rationality of the world is not something imposed on the world by the subject but something that inheres in the object itself, its concept or formal–final cause. Objective idealism is therefore another phrase for Hegel's doctrine that reason governs the world, an equation Hegel explicitly confirms when he writes: 'To say that there is reason in the world is what is meant by the expression "objective thought" ' (EPW §24).

Hegel's concept of objective idealism, and his Aristotelian concept of the idea, show that he does not limit the idea to the realm of subjectivity, as if it were the content or intention of some mind. On several occasions in his lectures on world history he is at pains to stress that the reason that governs the world should not be understood to mean a self-conscious subject or a spirit (VG 29, 37, 81/ 28, 34, 69). The purpose that governs the world is only its inherent form or structure, and it does not necessarily imply the intention of some agent.

Understood as the thesis that everything is an appearance of the idea, absolute idealism is compatible with realism, i.e. the doctrine that objects exist apart from and prior to consciousness. The appearances of the idea might be material objects as well as self-conscious subjects, and indeed the whole realm of nature prior to the development of humanity. Hegel assumes throughout his *Naturphilosophie* that nature exists apart from and prior to human consciousness, and that the development of humanity presupposes and only arises from the prior development of the organic powers of nature.

Hegel's absolute idealism is also compatible with naturalism. If naturalism is the general thesis that everything in nature happens according to laws, then absolute idealism sanctions naturalism, because it holds that everything that happens in nature happens of necessity. It is also compatible with the more specific thesis that everything in nature conforms to *mechanical* laws, i.e. laws where the cause of any event is some prior event in time. Hegel does not deny the mechanism of nature because he regards its workings as the necessary means for the realization of ends. Absolute idealism is incompatible only with a naturalism that claims everything is explicable *only* according to mechanical laws. The proper antithesis of absolute idealism is therefore neither realism nor naturalism but a radical or narrow mechanism that claims to be the only paradigm of explanation.

According to Hegel's absolute idealism, then, the whole dispute between materialism and idealism is misconceived. The absolute idea is neither subjective nor objective because it is the form or structure that inheres equally in both. We cannot reduce the subject down to the object, as if it were only material, and neither can we reduce the object down to the subject, as if it were only ideal. Both the subjective and objective are equally real, and the opposition between them is apparent from our everyday experience; it is indeed a necessary condition for the self-realization of the absolute that it divides itself into the subjective and objective (as we shall see, pp. 93–5). Nevertheless, this opposition does not diminish the identity or unity of the absolute, because as the formal and final cause, as the intelligible principle of all things, it can be either subjective or objective.

Although Hegel insists that the absolute idea realizes itself in the realm both of subjectivity and of objectivity, there is still a sense in which his absolute idealism gives pride of place to subjectivity over objectivity. It is one of Hegel's fundamental criticisms of Spinoza that he did not sufficiently honor subjectivity and recognize its status over nature; he made subjectivity one attribute of substance, an attribute having the same status as matter, and indeed only one of an infinite number of attributes. For Hegel, however, subjectivity is the highest manifestation, organization and development of the absolute. The absolute fully realizes itself only in the realm of history, and most of all in the domain of culture, i.e. in art, religion and philosophy. Hegel restores to Spinoza's monism the idea of a great chain of being, a hierarchy of natural forms, which begins with matter, develops progressively through minerals, vegetables and animals, and finally culminates in humanity itself. The absolute is therefore better realized in the realm of subjectivity than objectivity. Although the absolute could indeed *exist* apart from and prior to subjectivity, it still could not *fully realize* or *develop* its nature without subjectivity. Nature without subjectivity could indeed exist, but it would be like the sapling that never grew into a mighty oak.

The important role of subjectivity in Hegel's idealism, combined with his statement that the absolute must be conceived as subject as well as substance, has been one of the main sources of a very popular, but ultimately mistaken, reading of his absolute idealism. According to this reading, Hegel's absolute idealism is a form of cosmic subjectivism or supersubjectivism. It is essentially the doctrine that the absolute is spirit, the divine universal subject, and that this subject creates the entire world. This interpretation makes Hegel's idealism a form of subjective idealism, though of a higher-order and more metaphysical kind. The subject is no longer finite (i.e. empirical and individual) but infinite (i.e. rational and universal). This infinite self would not be simply the Kantian transcendental subject, which is purely formal; rather, it would be the Kantian transcendental subject with all restrictions removed, i.e. one that is not individuated and that has the power to create the content as well as the form of experience. Although the material world exists independent of the finite subject, it does not exist independent of the infinite subject, who has posited the whole realm of nature through its infinite activity.

There are several problems with this reading. First, Hegel thinks that even if we eliminate the restrictions on the transcendental subject – even if we remove the thing-in-itself and the given content of experience – we still have *subjective* idealism because the forms of

thinking are true only for the subject and not of the world itself
(EPW §42A3, 45A). Second, Hegel maintains that the opposition
between the subjective and objective has no meaning within the
absolute idea, so that it cannot be regarded as exclusively subjective
or objective (EPW §24A1). Third, Hegel maintains that the subjectivity of the absolute is only its *final stage* of organization and development; it is only the result, not the beginning. In the beginning,
considered in itself, the absolute is not subject but substance.

THE SYNTHESIS OF IDEALISM AND REALISM, FREEDOM AND NECESSITY

It should be clear by now that one purpose of Hegel's absolute
idealism is to transcend the stalemate between idealism and naturalism. Absolute idealism would somehow preserve the merits, and
negate the flaws, of these limited standpoints. Both were conceived
as one-sided abstractions, false of the whole but true of one of its
parts. But what, more precisely, were these standpoints? And how,
more concretely, were they to be synthesized?

For Hegel, and the entire romantic generation of the 1790s, the
standpoint of realism or 'dogmatism' represented the philosophy
of Spinoza; and the standpoint of idealism or 'criticism' represented the philosophy of Fichte. Fichte had declared that these are
the only two possible positions, and he demanded that one choose
between them. But his ultimatum was rejected by Hegel and the
romantic generation, who saw merits in both standpoints. The
great strength of Fichte's idealism was its concept of radical freedom, the right and power of the self to create itself and its entire
world. Fichte's concept of the self-positing ego – that the self is
only what it makes of itself – was irresistibly attractive to the generation of the 1790s, who wanted to break down all the limits of the
traditional order and to create a new heaven and earth. The great
virtue of Spinoza's naturalism is that it saw the divine in nature and
not as a supernatural heaven existing beyond it. Spinoza's naturalism
seemed to reconcile the demands of science and faith by naturalizing

the divine and divinizing nature. Given the strengths of both positions, it was the ideal of the entire romantic generation to
synthesize Fichte's freedom and Spinoza's naturalism.

But this ideal seems to be a mere dream, requiring a squaring of
the circle. The problem is that Fichte's concept of freedom and
Spinoza's naturalism seem utterly irreconcilable, just as Fichte had
insisted. According to Fichte's concept, freedom consists in the
power of the self to make itself whatever it chooses to be; the self
has no nature prior to its own choices. The self has the power of
choice, the capacity to do one action or the other, completely
independent of prior causes. Fichte realized that we do not now
have such radical freedom, and that most of our character is determined by external causes in nature; he still insisted, however, that
such freedom should be an ideal or goal for action. The self should
strive to gain more control over nature, so that its entire character
depends on nothing but its own free activity. Such a radical concept
of freedom is undermined, in two respects, by Spinoza's naturalism. First, Spinoza's naturalism is deterministic. According to
Spinoza, God acts from the necessity of his own nature alone, and
cannot do otherwise any more than a triangle can have its three
angles be less than 180 degrees; since all human thoughts and
actions are simply modes of the divine nature, they too must be
necessary. What I think or do will be simply what God thinks and
does through me; someone cannot act otherwise any more than the
eternal divine nature can change. Second, Spinoza's naturalism is
also quietistic, undermining any motivation to change the world.
For Spinoza, the essence of God is perfect and eternal: and since
everything expresses or manifests the essence of God, everything
should be perfect and eternal. Why, then, bother to change things?
Despite Spinoza's own radical politics, his metaphysics seemed to
undercut motivation for social and political change, or at least to
offer consolation to those who could not change it. For Fichte,
though, philosophy should end in a call for action: the world is not
rational yet we should strive to make it so. What the dogmatist

hypostasized – a self in harmony with its world – Fichte wanted to make into the goal of action.

The hopelessness of trying to wed Fichte's idealism with Spinoza's naturalism becomes all the more apparent when we consider Hegel's critique of Fichte. Like all the romantics, Hegel had been sharply critical of Fichte's dualism, his distinction between the noumenal or intelligible realm of freedom and the phenomenal or sensible realm of necessity. This dualism seemed to eternalize the alienation between the self and nature, making it impossible for them ever to become one. But there was good reason behind the Fichtean dualism. Like Kant, Fichte had been forced to postulate such a dualism to ensure the possibility of freedom. His reasoning seemed inescapable: since freedom involves choice, the power to do otherwise, and since everything in nature is determined, such that it is necessary and cannot be otherwise, freedom is possible only if it is taken outside the sphere of nature entirely and placed in an intellectual or noumenal realm. For Hegel and the romantics, dualism was not the solution but the problem. However, this made the problem of freedom all the more urgent. How is freedom possible in Spinoza's monistic and naturalistic world?

Hegel's answer to this question lay, in part, with his idealist reinterpretation of Spinoza. Since his absolute idealism restored subjectivity as the purpose and pinnacle of nature, Hegel reinstated one aspect of Fichte's idealism. In one sense Fichte was right after all: the self should be the first principle. Fichte was indeed correct in placing self-consciousness at the center of all things, as the basis to explain nature, for self-consciousness is the purpose of nature, the highest degree of organization and development of all its living powers. Where Fichte went astray, however, was in interpreting the final cause as the first cause. He had wrongly assumed that the ego is the fundamental ontological principle of nature when it is really only its purpose or end. The first cause is nothing less than Spinoza's substance, which does indeed act from the necessity of its own nature alone.

Hegel's absolute idealism also gave human agency a much greater role in the cosmos than anything imagined by Spinoza. Spinoza had made man into a mode of the single divine substance. Since substance has an independent essence and existence, and since a mode has a dependent essence and existence, man depends on God but not God on man. God has an eternal, complete and self-sufficient existence, which remains the same despite the activity of man. For Hegel, however, God depends on human beings as much as they depend on God. For it is only through human activity and self-awareness that the divine finally realizes itself. If there were no human self-awareness and activity, the divine nature would still exist, to be sure, yet it would remain imperfect, potential, inchoate and indeterminate. It is only through our activity, then, that we perfect, complete and realize the divine, so that human activity is divine itself. By giving such a greater role to human agency, Hegel believed he could do some justice to Fichte's activism. Since it is only through our activity that the divine realizes itself, we have good reason to act, and indeed a divine mission. In acting we help to realize the essence of God himself.

These aspects of absolute idealism soften the sting of Spinoza's determinism; but they do not remove it. Even if the self is the height of creation, and even if its acts realize the divine nature, it is still the case that the divine acts from the necessity of its own nature alone, so that all acts of the self will be necessary too. It is precisely in this regard that Hegel makes his most important move in reconciling Fichte and Spinoza: re-interpreting the concept of freedom itself. In his lectures on world history Hegel often uses Fichte's language in describing freedom. He states that the self is self-positing, and that it is what it makes of itself (VG 55. 58/48, 50). Yet, despite the apparent similarity of language, Hegel's underlying concept is very different from Fichte's.[27] Contrary to Fichte, Hegel thinks that freedom involves necessity, and he accepts Spinoza's definition of freedom in the *Ethica*: 'That thing is called free that exists from the necessity of its own nature alone and is determined into action by itself alone' (Part I, def. 7).[28] Both Fichte and Hegel see freedom in terms of self-determination; but their concepts are similar in name only. Self-determination in Hegel means that (1) I have a specific essence or nature, and that (2) it is natural and necessary for it to be realized. Fichte denies both these points, because (1) his self is only what it posits itself to be, having no pre-existing essence or nature, and (2) it can choose between different courses of action.

The question arises, however, how any finite agent or human being can be free in Spinoza's sense. Spinoza's concept of freedom seems to apply only to God, because he alone acts from the necessity of his own nature. All finite modes of the single infinite substance are determined into action by other finite modes, and so on *ad infinitum*. Ultimately, Hegel adopts the same solution to this problem as Spinoza: I am free in so far as I am really identical with the whole universe; I realize this freedom only in so far as I become aware of this identity through philosophy, what Spinoza calls the intellectual love of God. The same concept resurfaces in Hegel through his concept of reconciliation, which teaches the self to accept the necessity of the world in so far as he finds his identity in it.

It should be clear that Hegel's concept of freedom implies a form of compatibilism, the doctrine that the claims of freedom and determinism can be made compatible. Hegel upholds the fundamental dictum of all compatibilism: to say that the self is free does not mean that its acts are undetermined; my willing to do something does not exclude, but indeed implies, that I have been determined to will it. In adopting such compatibilism Hegel believed that he could avoid the need to postulate any form of dualism to save freedom. Even if all my actions were part of the natural order and could not be otherwise, I was still free in doing them as long as I wanted to do so. We will later investigate some of the problems of this compatibilism (pp. 263–6).

THE MYTH OF PANLOGICISM?

One of the fundamental issues of Hegel's absolute idealism concerns the status of contingency. Some scholars maintain that Hegel's position commits him to 'panlogicism', i.e. the doctrine that everything happens of necessity according to reason. Others hold, however, that Hegel fully recognizes the reality of contingency, and that he is indeed one of the first modern philosophers to argue for the necessity of contingency.[29] For these scholars, the panlogicist interpretation is best consigned to the dustbin of intellectual history as one of the Hegel myths and legends.[30]

Both interpretations have a point. The panlogicists have a strong case, insufficiently appreciated by their critics. Their interpretation follows from two premises, both of them indisputable. First, Hegel holds that the absolute is *causi sui*, existing from the necessity of its own nature alone. Second, Hegel also maintains that the absolute is all reality, having nothing outside itself to limit it. Both premises entail that everything exists by the necessity of the divine nature. If, *per contra*, we introduce something contingent into Hegel's system, it would have to be outside the absolute, which would limit it and make it finite. Hegel therefore seems to be as committed to panlogicism as Spinoza, who holds that everything exists of necessity in the single infinite substance.

The advocates of contingency also have a point. Hegel insists that philosophy must explain the finite world; and he holds that one of the central characteristics of finitude is contingency, the fact that something could be or not be. If, therefore, philosophy is to explain the finite world, it must establish the necessity of contingency. Indeed, Hegel regards Spinoza's failure to explain finitude as the main flaw of his system. Hegel would be guilty of just such failure, though, if he could not explain the reality of contingency itself.

It is important to see that it would not satisfy Hegel to limit contingency to appearances in the *subjective* sense, i.e. what appears to, and exists only for, the finite understanding. When Hegel insists that philosophy explain finitude he means appearance in the stronger *objective* sense, where it signifies the manifestation, expression or embodiment of the idea, whether it is perceived by the finite intellect or not. It was one of Hegel's main criticisms of Schelling that he had limited finitude to appearances in the subjective sense; because he could not explain it on the basis of the absolute, he ended, like Spinoza, condemning finitude as an illusion.

The question remains, however, whether Hegel can explain the reality of contingency in the stronger objective sense. It is precisely here that absolute idealism faces its most intractable problem. We shall soon see how Hegel faced this difficulty in the case of the particularity and difference of the finite world (pp. 94–5). He will show that particularity and difference arise of necessity from the self-differentiation of absolute life. But contingency eludes easy explanation in these terms. Although the metaphor of life makes it possible to understand how the universal becomes particular, and how the one becomes the many, it cannot explain how the necessary becomes contingent. There is a straightforward contradiction here: what happens of necessity cannot be otherwise; but the contingent can be otherwise. It was on these grounds that the late Schelling attacked Hegel's system, which, he argued, conflated the realms of essence and existence. While the realm of essence is necessary, that of existence is irreducibly contingent, a surd for all thought.[31]

The problem deepens, however, as soon as we explore what an explanation of contingency would mean. Such an explanation would have to show the necessity of contingency. But this could mean either of two things. First, that the specific content of the contingent is really necessary, so that only the *appearance* of contingency is necessary. Second, that it is necessary that there is contingency, so that the specific content of the contingent is *not* really necessary. The first possibility gives contingency only a subjective status, and so does not really explain its objective appearance. The second possibility gives the contingent objective status; but it also limits the absolute, because there is something that exists outside it. In general, if we argue that the absolute needs something not itself to become itself, then we must again admit that the absolute is finite after all.

It must be said that Hegel's defenders do not admit the depth of this problem. Some content themselves with pointing out that Hegel recognizes the necessity of contingency. But this is only to state a desideratum. It leaves both the problem of how contingency comes from necessity, and of how the realm of contingency, once it is admitted, does not limit the absolute. Others point out that Hegel holds that only the general features of reality are necessary, admitting that its particular features are contingent.[32] But this interpretation introduces a dualism between form and content into Hegel's system; and it too accepts a reality outside the absolute. Still others point out that contingency is an essential moment of the dialectic, because one constantly discovers that the necessity of each lower stage depends on a higher stage, which is contingent itself.[33] Although this is an accurate account of the dialectic, it still does not give an *objective* contingency, because the contingency holds only for the consciousness or level of reflection going through the dialectic. The philosopher, who sees things from the perspective of the whole, should know that everything happens of necessity.

Critics of the 'myth' of panlogicism often argue that it was never Hegel's intention to deduce the realm of the contingent. There is indeed strong evidence for this. Famously, Hegel had refused to derive Herr Krug's pen;[34] and in his *Philosophy of Nature* he stressed that philosophy cannot explain the multiplicity and variety of nature (§250). But this evidence is beside the point. It is perfectly possible for Hegel to be a panlogicist and to admit the limits of philosophical deduction. For these limits concern only the capacity of the philosopher to comprehend or reconstruct absolute necessity, which still exists whether he can reconstruct it or not. We must distinguish between what the philosopher could do in principle, were he infinitely wise, and what he can do in practice, given the limits of the finite human intellect.

The difficulties of contingency are especially apparent in Hegel's notorious difficulties in deriving nature from his logic. In the final section of the *Encyclopedia Logic* Hegel argues that the idea 'decides' (*sich entschliesst*) to 'dismiss' nature out of itself (*aus sich zu entlassen*) (§244). There are two problems here. First, the idea should reveal nature from the necessity of its own nature, so that it cannot 'decide' or 'resolve' to do so. Second, the content of the logic is formal and abstract, and so it cannot derive the concrete content of nature. To be sure, the category of the idea, which ends the *Logic*, is a much richer category than that of being, with which it begins; but the idea is still only a *logical* category, having only other logical categories within itself. The identity of the idea with nature is therefore only an identity *in thought*, still leaving the contingent realm of nature outside itself. If the idea has any other content in itself, it is only because it has illegitimately presupposed it.

In the end, the problem of contingency presents Hegel with a dilemma. The realm of contingency must be inside or outside the system. If it is inside the system, then contingency has only a subjective status, so that there is no explanation of real contingency. If, however, it is outside the system, it has an objective status; but it then limits the absolute and introduces a dualism between form and content.

Four

The Organic Worldview

THE ORGANIC DIMENSION

One of the first impressions Hegel's writings make on any reader is their ubiquitous organic metaphors. This is indeed one of the most important clues for a proper understanding of Hegel's entire philosophy. For all Hegel's thinking essentially proceeds from an organic vision of the world, a view of the universe as a single vast living organism. Hegel saw the absolute as the 'one and all', the *Hen Pai Kan*, of the pantheistic tradition. But, like Herder, Schiller, Schelling and Hölderlin, he understood this structure in dynamic, indeed organic, terms. The absolute develops in the same manner as all living things: it begins from inchoate unity; it differentiates itself into separate functions; and it returns into itself by re-integrating these functions into a single whole.

A reductionist or non-metaphysical reading of Hegel would attempt to limit his organic metaphysics to one part of his mature system, to his *Naturphilosophie*, Part II of the system of the *Encyclopedia of Philosophical Sciences*. But this is a mistake. For the organic view of the world appears throughout Hegel's system. It plays a fundamental role in his logic, ethics, politics and aesthetics. Hegel understood all these fields in essentially organic terms. The predominance of the organic concept in Hegel's system derives not least from his naturalism: since everything is a part of nature, and since nature is an organism, everything must be shown to be part of the organism of nature.

The significance of the organic view is evident from some of

Hegel's central and characteristic concepts, such as the unity of opposites, dialectic, and identity-in-difference. All these concepts grew directly out of his organic concept of nature, and presuppose its triadic schema of organic development, according to which organic growth consists in three moments: unity, difference and unity-in-difference. The oxymoronic aspect of these concepts derives from the thesis that organic development is essentially a movement between opposites: unity and difference, potentiality and actuality, inner and outer, essence and appearance.

Not only Hegel's central ideas, but also his basic vocabulary, are organic. The term 'in itself' (*an sich*) means not only something by itself, apart from its relations to other things, but also something potential, undeveloped and inchoate. The term 'for itself' (*für sich*) means not only something self-conscious, but also something that acts for ends and that has become organized and developed. The pivotal term 'concept' (*Begriff*) means the purpose and the essence of a thing, its formal–final cause.

Hegel's organicism also plays a central role in his absolute idealism. Both fundamental aspects of absolute idealism – its monism and idealism – ultimately presuppose organicism. Monism (in the anti-dualistic sense) is based upon the organicist thesis that the mental and physical, the ideal and real, are only different stages of development or degrees of organization of a single living force. Idealism rests upon the organicist doctrine that everything in nature and history conforms to a purpose or an end.

The purpose of Hegel's *Science of Logic* is indeed to develop a *logic of life*, a way of thinking to understand life. The main challenge to such a logic was the old mechanistic paradigm of nature, which Kant and Jacobi elevated into the very paradigm of rationality. There were two reasons why that paradigm made it impossible to understand life. First, a living being is *self*-generating and *self*-organizing; but a mechanism explains an event only by another acting upon it. Second, a living being is an indivisible unity, a *totum* where the whole precedes its parts; but mechanism understood everything analytically, as a *compositum* where the parts precede the whole. The task of Hegel's logic was to provide a method to understand living beings as self-generating and self-organizing, a method to conceive them as indivisible wholes.

THE RISE OF ORGANICISM

To the modern reader, Hegel's organic concept of the world is bound to appear quaint and poetic. It seems to hark back to a more anthropomorphic view of the world, the ancient Greek idea that the world is a *macroanthropos*. It also seems to be very speculative and metaphysical, the result of making bold analogies and wild generalizations that go beyond empirical evidence. Indeed, for just this reason, some scholars downplay or deprecate Hegel's organicism, which they regard as illegitimate metaphysics. If Hegel's philosophy is to have any abiding value, they reason, we must extract its rational core from its mystical shell, which consists in its *Naturphilosophie* and organicism.[1]

It is important to see, however, that this attitude toward Hegel's organic concept is question-begging and anachronistic. It not only ignores the state of the natural sciences in the late eighteenth century, but also presupposes a sharp distinction between philosophy and science, which Hegel, and many others in his age, would have questioned. Thinkers in the late eighteenth century knew no sharp distinction between empirical science and speculative *Naturphilosophie*. To them, the organic concept of nature of *Naturphilosophie* seemed to be the best scientific worldview, the only theory to explain the facts. It seemed confirmed by all the latest empirical research into living matter, electricity, magnetism and chemistry. By the beginning of the nineteenth century, the organic concept had virtually become 'normal science', gaining widespread recognition among most natural philosophers. Hegel's own *Naturphilosophie* was typical, and indeed a late development.

The organic concept of the world grew out of a reaction against mechanism, which had dominated physics since the beginning of the seventeenth century. Starting in the late seventeenth century, mechanism had come under increasing criticism, so much so that by the end of the eighteenth century it was in crisis. To understand why organicism seemed so attractive to Hegel and his generation, it is necessary to examine the precise meaning of its antithesis, mechanism, and the reasons for its eventual demise.

The founder of mechanism was Descartes, who laid down its basic principles in his *Principia philosophiae* (1644). The main point behind his principles was to make nature formulable in precise mathematical laws. Mechanism can be reduced down to a few fundamental principles, all of which more or less serve the purpose of mathematization.

(1) *The essence of matter*. The nature of matter consists in extension, that is, the occupation of space, or having a certain length, breadth and depth. If matter is only *res extensa*, then it is measurable and calculable.

(2) *Inertness*. Because matter does nothing more than occupy space, it is inert or static, changing its place only if something acts upon it. Matter therefore obeys the *law of inertia*, remaining in its state of rest or motion unless something else acts upon it.

(3) *Impact*. For one body to act on another is for that body to have an impact upon it, to push the other thing. Impact is measured in terms of how much space a body moves in a given amount of time when some other body hits against it.

(4) *Efficient causality*. Mechanism states that the paradigm of causal explanation involves *efficient* causality, i.e. causes are events prior in time, where these events consist in one body having an impact on another. In other words, to explain an event is to show how prior events impact upon it. There is no need to resort to *formal* or *final* causes, where the formal cause is the essential structure of the thing, and the final cause is its purpose. Hence the physicist considers *how* things happen, not *why* they happen; he or she banishes teleology because it seems to involve theology, a reference to providence, which falls outside his or her purview.

(5) *Atomism*. The mechanical paradigm of explanation went hand-in-hand with atomism. According to atomism, matter consists in indivisible and extended particles, which are separated by empty spaces. All fundamental forces, such as gravity, electricity and magnetism, are explained by the interrelations between these atoms. According to George-Louis Le Sage (1724–1803), one of the great champions of mechanism, chemical affinity is due to the compatibility between the size and shape of atoms; gravity is due to the motions of atoms in a fluid; and magnetism is due to the special affinity between atoms.

Although mechanism was the dominant paradigm of explanation from the seventeenth century, it had never been without problems. Toward the close of the eighteenth century, when Hegel and the romantic generation came of age, these problems accumulated and intensified, so that mechanism faced a crisis. Its sources were various.

(1) *Attraction*. The mechanical model of explanation always had difficulty in explaining the attractive force of Newtonian gravity, which seems to imply action at a distance. If one body acts upon the other through distance, there is no impact, no one body pushing against another. The attempt to explain action at a distance through the presence of subtle fluids failed to find experimental confirmation.

(2) *Magnetism and electricity*. The many discoveries in magnetism and electricity in the late eighteenth century seemed only to compound the problems with the explanation of gravity. It was difficult to explain magnetism and electricity through the action of subtle fluids or media; and their action seemed to consist in attractive and repulsive forces just like gravity. Hence if mechanism could not explain the attractive force of gravity it could no more explain electricity and magnetism.

(3) *Chemistry*. The new chemistry seemed to suggest that bodies consisted of electrical and magnetic forces. If this were so, then mechanism could no more explain the forces of the macrocosm than the forces of the microcosm.

(4) *Epigenesis.* Toward the close of the eighteenth century the theory of preformation, which postulated the existence of preformed organisms in embryos, had been discredited by the experiments of Caspar Wolff and Johann Friedrich Blumenbach. Preformation had been allied with mechanism because, once preformed, the growth of the organism seemed to require nothing more than external causes. The decline in preformation went hand-in-hand with the rise of the theory of epigenesis, according to which organisms develop from the inchoate to the organized by virtue of their own power alone. Contrary to mechanism, this seemed to mean that an organism has the power to act independently of the operation of external causes.

(5) *Human sciences.* All these difficulties of mechanism in explaining the physical and organic were only compounded when it came to the sciences of man. In attempting to explain human action, mechanism confronted an insurmountable problem. Since it was necessary to explain events by impact, and since impact is measurable only in terms of the degree of change of place in a specific time, it seemed impossible to explain the action of the mind on the body or of the body on the mind. For mental events are not locatable in space; they do not have an identifiable location and do not change place. If we adopt only a mechanical model of explanation, we have only two options regarding the human sciences: either we admit that the mind falls outside nature, so that it is inexplicable and mysterious; or we stress that it falls within nature, so that the mind turns out to be really only a complicated machine. In other words, we are either dualists or materialists. But if dualism limits naturalism, materialism seems to deny the *sui generis* characteristics of the mind. There is no third option: no naturalistic explanation of human action that does justice to its distinctive qualities and yet upholds the continuity and unity of nature.

As a result of this crisis, the organic worldview seemed enormously appealing to a whole generation of thinkers at the close of the eighteenth century. The great attraction of the organic paradigm is that it seemed to uphold the unity and continuity of nature by explaining both the mental and the physical according to a single paradigm. It seemed to realize that long-sought ideal of all science since the seventeenth century: a non-reductivistic yet naturalistic explanation of life and the mind. The organic paradigm is non-reductivistic since it explains events holistically, by showing how they play a necessary role in a whole. The organic paradigm is also naturalistic, partly because it does not postulate occult forces, and partly because it understands all events according to laws, where these laws are holistic rather than mechanistic, determining the relationship of a part to a whole rather than simply the relationship between events within time.

Central to the holism of the organic paradigm was a conception of matter antithetical to mechanism. According to the organic conception, the essence of matter consists not in dead extension but in power or force, which expresses itself as motion. It is the very essence of these forces to act or to realize themselves, and so to move; if they are not acting it is only because of some countervailing force acting against them. Matter consists in the interplay between attractive force and repulsive force; and the various kinds of matter derive from the different ratios between these forces.

The father of this alternative conception was Leibniz, whose physics was explicitly revived by Herder and Schelling toward the close of the eighteenth century. According to Leibniz, the essence of matter consists not in extension but in living force (*vis viva*). Reviving a concept of Aristotle and the scholastic tradition, Leibniz maintained that living force is an *entelechy*, the power of a body to realize its inherent form. We must measure this power, Leibniz maintained, not in terms of extension − the *quantity of motion* (the velocity times the size of an object) − but in dynamic terms − the *quantity of effect* (how much can be produced by its activity). To many of his late eighteenth-century successors, Leibniz's conception of living force seemed to offer a means of bridging the gap between the subjective and objective, the mental and physical. Living force has none of the reductivistic implications of dead extension. The subjective or mental will be simply the highest degree of organization and development of living force, whereas the objective or physical will be simply its lowest degree of organization and development. In other words, mind was living force internalized, the body living force externalized. While Leibniz himself was proud to be the inventor of the pre-established harmony, which seemed to commit him to dualism, his eighteenth-century heirs latched on to the apparent anti-dualistic implications of his conception of living force. Ironically, Leibniz, the arch-dogmatist whom Kant had only recently interred, was resurrected as the father of *Naturphilosophie*.

CLASSICAL AND CHRISTIAN ORIGINS

Although the origins of Hegel's organic worldview were deeply interwoven with the developments of natural philosophy, its initial inspiration seems to have been classical, and indeed Platonic. In their early days in the *Tübinger Stift* Schelling, Hegel and Hölderlin were enthusiastic students of Plato, and one of their favorite texts was the *Timaeus*.[2] There they found the root metaphor behind organicism: that the world is 'a single visible living being', 'a living being that contains within itself all living beings' (30d, 33b). According to this conception, all of nature should be conceived on analogy with a human being, so that it is a *macroanthropos*.

Hegel first sketched his organic metaphysics in several writings from his Frankfurt period: the 1797 fragments on love, passages from the 1798 *Spirit of Christianity*, and finally in the 1800 *System-fragment*.[3] In formulating this worldview, Hegel followed in the footsteps of others. Schiller had given it a poetic, indeed rhapsodic, exposition in his 1786 *Philosophical Letters* (NA XX, 107–29); and Herder expounded it in dialogue form in his 1787 *God, Some Conversations* (*Sämtliche Werke* XVI, 403–572). The theory was given more solid empirical backing by C.F. Kielmeyer in his influential 1793 lecture *On the Relations among Organic Powers*.[4] The same organic view appears later in the 1790s in the fragments of Friedrich Schlegel,

Hölderlin and Novalis. Schelling gave the most systematic account of it in his 1799 *On the World Soul*.[5]

Although all these sources were important in determining the context of Hegel's thinking, the immediate origin of his organic concept seems to have been more religious than philosophical. When he introduces his concept in *The Spirit of Christianity* he does so in the context of discussing the infinite or divine life. His source of inspiration seems to have been the gospel of John, especially the passage he cites from John 1 (1–4): 'In the beginning was the word, and the word was with God . . . What has come into being in him was life, and the life was the light of the people.'[6] Hegel seems to have latched on to the organic concept for at least two reasons. First, it provided him with an explanation for the trinity: just as the parts of an organism are organisms themselves, so each person of the trinity is a distinct person.[7] Second, it overcame the alienation between individual and nature: if the universe is an organism, the individual is inseparable from it just as it is inseparable from the individual.

When Hegel first stated his organic view he stressed its mystical dimension. He insisted that the infinite organic whole cannot be expressed in discursive terms, that its life lies beyond all forms of conception and demonstration.[8] For most of his Frankfurt years Hegel was still in the grip of the common romantic doctrine that all forms of discursive thought are finite and therefore inadequate for the infinite. We are aware of the infinite, he held, only through the experience of love, where we feel our oneness with others and all living things. Hegel further argued that the infinite, the universe as a whole, could be only an object of faith, where faith consisted not simply in belief but also in the feeling for the divine life permeating all things. The only role of philosophy would be to criticize the forms of finitude to make room for faith.[9]

By late 1800, however, Hegel had reversed his attitude toward conceptual discourse. Where he had once stressed its limitations he now asserted its necessity. What had once been an object of faith now became an object of reason. Mystical experience had to be put in some discursive form. In his 2 November 1800, letter to Schelling, written near the end of his Frankfurt years and shortly before his departure for Jena, Hegel himself noted this important change in his thinking:

> In my intellectual development, which began from the subordinate needs of human beings, I was driven to science [i.e. philosophy], and I had to transform the ideal of my youth into the form of reflection, into a system; I ask myself now . . . how to find my return to intervention in the life of men.[10]

'The ideal of his youth' was Hegel's organic vision of the world, his concept of infinite life, which would reconcile the individual with the universe. 'The form of reflection' is Hegel's term for discursive thinking, for the concepts, judgments and syllogisms of reason. In this case the specific form of reflection would have to be a system, for only a system would do justice to an organic view of the world where all the parts form an indivisible whole.

This shift in Hegel's thinking also becomes apparent from another revealing fragment written around 1800, which was probably a draft of the introduction of his *Verfassungschrift*.[11] This fragment shows that Hegel now realizes his holistic ideals are better served by metaphysics than mysticism. Hence he describes the need of the present age for philosophy, and more specifically for a metaphysics. The task of this metaphysics will be to make explicit and self-conscious the implicit and subconscious ideal of the people: the longing for a more holistic life that overcomes all the oppositions of contemporary culture. This metaphysics will take the form of a system, because only a system will be adequate to the totality of life. Such a system will give each of the older forms of life their due by preserving them as necessary parts of the whole; but it will also destroy their false claims to universality by revealing their inner contradictions. In a few lines Hegel sketches, if only *in nuce*, his later idea of a dialectic: an immanent critique of forms of life that shows their contradictions in attempting to represent the idea of the whole, but their validity as only one part of the whole.

THE SPINOZA LEGACY

Hegel's search for a rational foundation for his organic vision of the world took place in several domains: metaphysics, epistemology, and the natural sciences. In the realm of metaphysics he saw his organic vision as the only means of explaining the fundamental conundrum of monism: the relation between the one and many. In the field of epistemology he held that it is the only means to solve the outstanding dualisms of Kant's and Fichte's idealism. And in the field of natural sciences he saw it as the only means of overcoming the persistent problems of mechanism. We should now consider Hegel's metaphysical arguments for organicism; in later sections we will examine his epistemological arguments (pp. 100–7).

In the realm of metaphysics Hegel's search for a rational foundation for his organic vision finally forced him to come to terms with Spinozism. Hegel's acquaintance with Spinoza goes back to his earliest years in the *Tübinger Stift*. It was probably then that he read Jacobi's *Letters on the Doctrine of Spinoza*.[12] But it is striking how much Hegel seemed to have forgotten Spinoza during his Berne and Frankfurt years. He then saw Kant's doctrine of practical faith as the proper form of a rational religion.[13] Only in his Frankfurt years did he abandon this dour and rickety Kantian doctrine for the mystical pantheism of *The Spirit of Christianity and its Fate*. But even in this work there is little trace of Spinozism. Hegel turned fully to Spinoza only in his early Jena years during his collaboration with Schelling, who had been especially inspired by Spinoza, and who, even during his Fichtean phase, declared himself to be a Spinozist. But Hegel's turning toward Spinozism was not simply the result of Schelling's influence. It fitted hand-in-glove with his own intention to find some rational foundation for his organic vision. After all, there were some deep affinities between Spinoza's doctrines and Hegel's mystical pantheism; Hegel could only have admired Spinoza's monism, his immanent religion, and his intellectual love of God. It was indeed Spinoza who had first attempted to find a rational foundation and technical vocabulary for such doctrines. It is no accident, then, that we find Hegel's first metaphysical writings in the Jena years replete with Spinozist vocabulary and full of sympathetic references to Spinoza.

Yet, for all his sympathy and affinity with Spinoza, there were other respects in which Hegel was deeply at odds with him and had to settle scores with him. Hegel could never proclaim, as Schelling once did, 'I have become a Spinozist!' (Ich bin Spinozist geworden!). If Spinoza's single universal substance was the starting point of philosophy, it could never be its goal or conclusion. For Hegel, there were profound problems with Spinozism. For one thing, there was its geometric method, its method of beginning with axioms and definitions and then rigorously reasoning from them. As a student of Kant's Critique, Hegel saw the geometric method as a defunct remnant of the older rationalism, whose fallacies had been so ruthlessly exposed in the Transcendental Dialectic. 'No philosophical beginning could look worse than to begin with a definition, as Spinoza does', Hegel wrote in his Differenzschrift (II 37/105). This was already an implicit warning to Schelling, whose Presentation of My System had taken Spinoza's geometric method as its model. For another thing, Spinoza was an arch-mechanist; his model of explanation, and his concept of matter, were taken directly from Descartes. Like Descartes, Spinoza held that the essence of matter is extension; and he saw the model of explanation as efficient causality, where the cause of an event is a prior event. In the Appendix to Part I of the Ethics Spinoza had explicitly rejected the older teleological model of explanation as anthropocentric. In the end, then, Spinoza's single universal substance was in fact nothing more than a giant machine. Nothing could be further removed, then, from Hegel's organic vision of the world.

Hence Spinoza's philosophy was as much a challenge as it was a support for Hegel's organic metaphysics. The failure of Spinoza's method, and his radical mechanism, made it necessary for Hegel to develop a new foundation for his organic vision. But Spinoza's system presented not only a challenge but also an opportunity. For there was a fundamental weakness to Spinoza's philosophy, a serious deficiency that Hegel exploited to the advantage of his own organic worldview. This was the ancient conundrum of the one and the many, or how the world of difference and multiplicity ever originates from primal unity. Spinoza did not solve this ancient problem but only reinstated it, making its solution all the more imperative. This becomes clear from a brief look at Spinoza's *Ethics*.

According to Spinoza, all individual things exist in God (*Ethica*, Pt I, Prop. 15), and are only modifications of his attributes (Pt I, Prop. 25). But everything that follows from some attribute of God must be infinite and eternal (Pt I, Prop. 21). This raises the question: how is there anything finite and in time? This problem becomes all the more apparent when Spinoza attempts to explain the actions of finite things. He maintains that their cause is an attribute not of God but of some other finite things *in so far as they are a modification* of some attribute. If the cause were the attribute itself, which is eternal and infinite, then the effect would be eternal and infinite too. Hence the cause cannot be the attribute itself but only some other finite thing that is a modification of the attribute (Pt I, Prop. 28). But this still leaves the question: How do these modifications of attributes arise? If everything exists in God, and if God is infinite and eternal, then everything should be infinite and eternal. But then why does the finite world exist? In the end Spinoza could do nothing more than relegate the whole temporal world to the realm of the imagination.[14]

The problem of the relationship between the infinite and the finite in Spinoza can be put more neatly and simply in the form of a dilemma: the infinite and finite must be, and yet cannot be, united. On the one hand, the infinite and finite *cannot be* united because they have opposing characteristics. The infinite is eternal, indivisible and unlimited; the finite is temporal, divisible and limited. Hence if we were to join them in a single substance, that substance would be self-contradictory; it would be *per impossibile* both eternal and temporal, indivisible and divisible, unlimited and limited. On the other hand, however, the infinite and finite *must be* united because if the infinite excludes the finite, it cannot be all reality; it loses its infinite status because it becomes limited by something outside itself, namely the finite. It is the very nature of the infinite to be that of which nothing greater can be conceived; but this means that the infinite must somehow include the finite within itself, because if it is left outside itself it becomes limited by it or conceivable only in contrast against it.

This dilemma was one of the fundamental problems faced by Schelling during his Jena years, the years of his collaboration with Hegel. It is clear that his own reflections on this problem were greatly encouraged by Hegel,[15] though there was never any final agreement between them. It was indeed Schelling's failure to solve this problem that eventually led to Hegel's break with Schelling after his departure from Jena. At first, in his 1801 *Presentation of My System* Schelling argued that the absolute is pure identity, complete undifferentiated unity, and that it excludes any difference or opposition within itself or between things (§§16, 23). He insisted that it was fallacy to assume that the absolute 'goes outside itself', as if it could somehow posit the finite and temporal world opposed to its infinite and eternal nature (§§14, 30). Partly due to Hegel's prodding, however, Schelling soon flinched from such an uncompromising position, and reformulated his views in his 1802 *Further Presentation* and *Bruno*. Here he argued that the absolute should include finite things within itself; yet this modification of his position was more nominal than real since he insisted that finite things could be within the absolute only in so far as they are identical with one another, or only in so far as they are stripped of their distinguishing properties (*Sämtliche Werke* IV, 393, 408). In his 1804 *Philosophie und Religion* Schelling virtually abandoned the attempt to explain the origin of finitude (*Sämtliche Werke* IV, 42). The infinite contains only the possibility of the finite; and the reality of the finite comes only from a fall or leap from the infinite. The absolute is not the ground of this fall, which lies in original sin and therefore in the arbitrary action of the finite itself. The fall cannot be explained; it is just an arbitrary and spontaneous action that defies all conceptual reconstruction.

For Hegel, Schelling's theory of the fall was simply an admission of failure, a recognition of the breakdown of the philosophy of identity.[16] Hegel's solution to this dilemma was nothing less than his organic vision of the world. If the absolute were to be conceived as life, then it must include finitude and difference within itself for the simple reason that organic development consists in self-differentiation. Life is a process by which an inchoate unity becomes more determinate, complex and organized; it is the movement from unity to difference, and from difference to unity within difference. As Hegel puts the point in his *Differenzschrift*:

> To cancel established oppositions is the sole interest of reason. But this interest does not mean that it is opposed to opposition and limitation in general; for necessary opposition is *one* factor of life, which forms itself by eternally opposing itself, and in the highest liveliness totality is possible only through restoration from the deepest fission.
>
> (II 21–2/91)

If Spinoza's single universal substance were now conceived as an organism, it would have to be understood not as something eternally static but as something eternally moving and in development. Spinoza's substance could still be retained as one moment of the truth, yet only as one moment. It would be the single universal organism in so far as it is something inchoate, formless and undeveloped. Of course, Spinoza would only have dismissed such a suggestion, for this transformation of his single substance meant nothing less than returning to the standpoint of teleology, against which he had fought with such passion and energy. Yet, for Hegel, there was no choice but to transform Spinoza's substance into a living organism, since by this means alone is it possible to escape the snares of the ancient problem of the origin of finitude.

THE KANTIAN LEGACY AND CHALLENGE

Prima facie Hegel's concept of the organic is a mere metaphor, something derived entirely from classical and Christian literature. But it is crucial to see that the concept has a much more precise and technical meaning. That meaning was laid down by Kant with his analysis of the concept of a 'natural purpose' (*Naturzweck*) in sections §§64–5 of the *Critique of Judgment* (V 373–4). In §55R of the *Encyclopedia* Hegel himself paid handsome tribute to his debts to Kant in this regard. But Hegel's debts to Kant were both positive and negative. If Kant provided a clear technical meaning for the concept of the organic, he also challenged Hegel by laying down severe regulative constraints upon the use of this concept.

In sections §§64–5 of the *Critique of Judgment* Kant maintains that there are two defining characteristics of a natural purpose. First, the idea of the whole precedes all its parts in the sense that it determines the identity of each of them. Second, the parts are reciprocally cause and effect of one another. Kant argued that the first characteristic alone is not sufficient to define a natural purpose, since it is found too in works of art, which are also produced according to a plan, an idea of the whole. It is also necessary to add the second characteristic, which means that an organism, unlike a work of art, is *self*-generating and *self*-organizing. In both respects, Kant argued, an organism is unlike matter. In matter the parts precede the whole and make them possible; and it is not self-generating or self-organizing because it acts only when acted upon by some external force.

To understand the organic concept of nature it is of the first importance to dwell on the full meaning of Kant's first requirement. For Kant, an organic whole is not only irreducible to its parts, as if it were only something more than them; it is also the *source* or *foundation* of its parts because the idea of the whole determines the identity of each of its parts. In sections §§76–8 of the *Critique of Judgment* Kant elaborated this point by his distinction between an analytic and a synthetic universal, the analogue of the traditional scholastic distinction between a *compositum* and a *totum*.[17] In an analytic universal or *compositum* the parts precede the whole and each has its identity apart from it; in a synthetic universal or *totum* the whole precedes the parts and makes each of them possible. For an analytic universal there is a distinction between possibility and reality because there is no reason the universal applies to anything; for a synthetic universal there is no such distinction because the universal is self-realizing. When Hegel and the romantics write about the organic concept of nature they have in mind a *totum* or synthetic universal. Kant's distinction was the ancestor of Hegel's own later distinction between an abstract and a concrete universal.

Alone Kant's concept of a natural purpose is still not sufficient to explain the organic concept of nature. Although it determines the structure of each organism, it does not take the added – and very large – step that the entire cosmos is a natural purpose. Here again, though, Kant anticipated Hegel and the romantics. In §67 of the *Critique of Judgment* Kant had suggested that we can generalize the idea of an organism so that it applies to nature as a whole. Once we conceive of things having final causes, we can go further, so that each organism becomes part of a wider organism and belongs to 'a system of purposes' (V 378, 380–1). This system of purposes comprises the idea of a 'universal organism' or a 'system of ends'.

Setting another precedent for Hegel and the romantics, Kant had argued in the *Critique of Judgment* that his idea of a universal organism is irreducible to mechanical principles. Famously, he declared that there could not be a Newton for a single blade of grass (V 400). The apparent design of nature, its order and harmony, appears contingent with respect to the laws of nature, Kant argued, because we cannot see how it could arise purely through mechanical means

(§61; V 360). In two fundamental respects Kant argued that the concept of an organism went beyond mechanism. First, an organism is self-generating and self-organizing; but mechanism explains an event only by another acting upon it. Second, an organism is an indivisible unity, a *totum* where the whole precedes its parts; but mechanism understood everything analytically, as a *compositum* where the parts precede the whole.

Kant had further attracted his romantic contemporaries to the idea of a universal organism by suggesting in the *Critique of Judgment* that it could bridge his dualisms between the ideal and real, the noumenal and phenomenal, which had been such a stumbling block for the critical philosophy. In the *Critique of Pure Reason* (1781) and *Critique of Practical Reason* (1788) Kant had resolved the conflict between freedom and necessity by assigning each to a distinct ontological domain: freedom belongs to a noumenal or intelligible realm where people act according to rational principles; and necessity is the hallmark of the phenomenal or empirical realm of nature, where everything acts according to mechanical laws of cause and effect. While this seemed to save the claims of both freedom and necessity by giving them a distinct jurisdiction, it also posed a problem of how to explain the interaction between such distinct realms. If the noumenal is intelligible, active and non-temporal, and if the phenomenal is sensible, passive and temporal, how do these realms interact with one another? In the *Critique of Judgment* Kant postulated the idea of a universal organism to address this dualism. There would be no mysterious harmony between the noumenal and phenomenal if the entire realm of nature were created according to the design of a divine understanding. The concept of a natural purpose seemed to provide an even closer connection between the ideal and real because the purpose of the organism, its formal or ideal element, is *inherent* in its matter, the material or real element. The purpose is not external to the matter, imposed upon it from outside, as an artist fashions a lump of clay, but it is internal to the matter, the source of all its activity.

Regarding the meaning of the organic, its irreducibility to mechanism, and its importance in overcoming dualism, there was the closest agreement between Kant and Hegel. It was for all these reasons that Hegel declared in *Encyclopedia* §55R that Kant had expressed all the defining characteristics of the idea. Yet, despite all their agreement, there was still the most fundamental point of friction between them. Namely, Hegel affirmed, and Kant denied, that we have reason to assume that nature really *is* an organism. Throughout the *Critique of Judgment* Kant had argued that the idea of an organism has only a *regulative* status, i.e. it has only a heuristic value in guiding enquiry into nature, so that we have the right to proceed only *as if* nature were an organism. However, this principle has no *constitutive* status, i.e. we have no right to assume that nature really *is* an organism.

Why did Kant insist on imposing regulative constraints on the idea of a natural purpose? Why did he hold that the human understanding is limited to a mechanical understanding of nature? Kant had three basic arguments.

Kant's first argument, which appears chiefly in his early essay on teleology,[18] is essentially skeptical. It states that we have no means of knowing whether objects in nature, such as vegetables and animals, are really purposive; in other words, we have no *criterion* to determine whether such objects are really organisms rather than just very complex machines. According to Kant, we understand the power to act from purposes only from our own human experience when we create something according to our will, where the will consists in 'the power to produce something according to an idea' (VIII 181). If, therefore, something cannot act according to ideas, we have no right to assume that it has the power to act for ends. Hence the concept of a being that acts purposively yet does not have a will is 'completely fictitious and empty' (*völlig erdichtet und leer*) (181). In drawing such a conclusion Kant is not saying that the concept is completely *meaningless* – in that case it could hardly have even a regulative status – but that it has no *reference*. His point is simply that we only *know of* purposiveness in the cases of beings that act with will and understanding, and that we cannot therefore make verifiable claims about the purposiveness of beings that do not have will and understanding. In a nutshell, Kant's argument is that intentionality – in the sense of conscious end- or goal-directed action – is the *criterion* of purposiveness.

Kant's second argument, which occurs in §68 of the *Critique of Judgment*, consists in a simple application of the central principle of the critical philosophy, what Kant calls the principle behind its 'new method of thought'.[19] According to this principle, which Kant explicitly restates at §68, 'we have complete insight only into that which we can make ourselves and according to our own concepts' (V 384). This principle means that organisms are incomprehensible to us, Kant argues, because we do not have it within our means to create or produce them. We can indeed create some material thing, just as nature can produce one, and we do so through some combination of efficient causes. But we have no power to produce the infinitely complex structure of an organism. Hence if we know only what we can produce, and if we cannot produce organisms, it follows that we cannot know organisms.

Kant's third argument is directed against hylozoism or vital materialism, the doctrine that matter consists in *vis viva* or living force. Kant's argument against hylozoism proceeds from his analysis of matter in the *Metaphysical Foundations of Natural Science*. According to Kant's second law of mechanics, the law of inertia, every change in matter must have an *external* cause, i.e. it persists in rest or motion, in the same direction and with the same speed, unless there is some external cause to make it change its direction and speed (IV 543). This principle states, therefore, that changes in matter cannot be *internal*, or that matter has no *intrinsic* grounds of determination. This means, Kant contends, that matter is essentially *lifeless*. For life is the faculty of a substance to act from an *internal* principle, its power to change *itself*. Kant vehemently insists that the very possibility of natural science rests upon fully recognizing these implications of the law of inertia, damning hylozoism as nothing less than 'the death of all philosophy of nature' (*der Tod aller Naturphilosophie*).

On the basis of all these arguments Kant concludes that the concept of an organism or a natural purpose has only a regulative status. To avoid some common misunderstandings, it is important to see precisely what this doctrine means. Except for the most radical version of vital materialism, Kant is not saying that this concept is only a fiction, as if it were false that there are organisms in nature. Rather, he is saying that this concept has only a problematic status. In other words, we have no evidence or reason to assume the existence or non-existence of organisms; while it is indeed possible that there are organisms or natural purposes, it is also possible that there are none at all and that they are really only complicated machines. It is important to see that, as a critical philosopher whose only goal is to determine the limits of our cognitive powers, Kant neither affirms nor denies the *sui generis* status of organisms, and he neither affirms nor denies the impossibility of mechanism. He states explicitly at §71 of the third *Critique*: 'We are quite unable to prove that organized natural products cannot be produced through the mechanism of nature' (V 388). When Kant denies the possibility of a complete mechanical explanation of organisms, when he famously proclaims that there will never be a Newton to explain the growth of a single blade of grass, he does so not because he thinks that organisms *are* extra-mechanical – for that too would be a dogmatic claim to knowledge – but because he thinks that it is a *necessary limitation of the human understanding* that we cannot fully understand an organism mechanically, and that we must resort to teleology to make them comprehensible.

REPLY TO KANT

It was these Kantian arguments that posed such a challenge to Hegel and the whole generation of *Naturphilosophen* in the 1790s. To vindicate their organic concept of nature – to establish its constitutive validity – they would have to show the need to overcome

Kant's regulative restraints. How did Hegel and the *Naturphilosophen* respond to Kant's arguments?

Their first strategy was to distance themselves from traditional Christian teleology with all its indefensible metaphysical assumptions. They insisted that they did not wish to retain or revive the old *extrinsic* teleology, according to which the purposes of nature had been imposed upon it by God during the creation. This old teleology was essentially anthropocentric, holding that natural things were created by God to serve the purposes of human beings. God had created cork trees, for example, so that their bark could serve as stoppers in wine bottles. Hegel and the *Naturphilosophen* stressed that their teleology was completely *intrinsic*, limited to the ends observable within nature itself. According to their view, nature is an end in itself, and it has no higher purpose beyond itself.

While this strategy purges teleology of some questionable metaphysics, it still has little purchase against Kant's main arguments. Although Kant sometimes wrote as if the concept of the objective purposiveness of nature inevitably led to a physico-theology (§75; V 398–9), the thrust of his arguments was directed against the concept of a *natural purpose* (*Naturzweck*), the idea that nature alone was self-generating and self-organizing. Hence his target was indeed the central doctrine of Hegel and the *Naturphilosophen*: an intrinsic teleology.

Limiting the question to the realm of nature itself, Hegel and the *Naturphilosophen* still counter that the concept of a natural purpose involves none of the other questionable assumptions Kant had attributed to it. First of all, Hegel insists that this concept does not involve intentionality, the attribution of will or self-conscious agency to a living thing. To state that a natural object serves a purpose is not to hold that there is some intention behind its creation, still less that there is some concealed intention within the object itself. Rather, all that it means is that the object serves a function, that it plays an essential role in the structure of the organism. Secondly, Hegel and the *Naturphilosophen* also contest that the idea of living matter entails that there is some kind of soul or spirit within matter itself, directing and organizing its growth. It is important to see that, like Kant, they were opposed to animism and vitalism, i.e. a doctrine that attributes some supernatural force or agency to organic growth. They too wanted to avoid the dilemma of materialism versus vitalism. While materialism was too reductivist, denying the *sui generis* structure of organisms, vitalism was too obscurantist, appealing to some occult force or supernatural agency.[20]

All this makes it seem as if there is really no dispute after all. Kant is denying the attribution of purposiveness to objects in nature only in a very strong sense, one that implies the existence of intentionality or spiritual powers in nature, whereas Hegel and the *Naturphilosophen* are affirming it in a weaker sense, one that has no such implications. By denying that the idea of a natural purpose implies providence, intentionality or spiritual powers, some of the *Naturphilosophen* assumed they could bring the claims of teleology within the realm of experience itself. To them, it seemed possible to observe the self-generation and self-organization of a living thing. To understand their confidence about the empirical proof of organization, it is essential to consider the state of late eighteenth-century physiology.[21]

By the late eighteenth century, the theory of preformation, which held that organisms were already preformed in the embryo, had been discredited because it could not account for some basic facts, such as hybrids and regeneration. J.F. Blumenbach and Caspar Wolff argued that they had strong empirical evidence for the theory of epigenesis, according to which an organism began from an inchoate mass and gradually organized itself. It seemed to be a datum of observation, therefore, that living matter organizes itself. Hence, in his famous dispute with Albrecht Haller, Wolff contended that his theory of epigenesis rested not upon the inference that what could not be observed (namely, a preformed embryo) did not exist but upon the simple observation of what did exist.

Wolff held that he could simply see the structure of the embryo developing under the microscope, and those who denied its epigenesis were simply refusing to look through it.[22] To those who align Kant with the cause of natural science, it is important to keep in mind that his regulative doctrine found little or no support among late eighteenth- and early nineteenth-century physiologists. They treated organic concepts not as regulative fictions but as constitutive truths, which referred to active forces in nature.[23] When Wolff and Blumenbach claimed to observe epigenesis they were simply expressing this crucial assumption.

It is unlikely, however, that Kant would have been impressed by these appeals to observation and experiment. Hegel and the *Naturphilosophen* held that empirical evidence for both organic unity and self-organization is sufficient for the attribution of purposiveness to nature. But Kant denies this very point. He maintains that even if something in our experience shows both organic unity and self-organization, that still does not warrant the inference of the existence of natural purposes. Why not? Because, for all we know, the thing might still be acting strictly from mechanical causes. Again, Kant was quite explicit and emphatic about this point: 'We are quite unable to prove that organized natural products cannot be produced through the mechanism of nature' (§71; V 388). The attribution of purposes to nature implied that there is some other form of causality not strictly reducible to mechanism; but no amount of experience was sufficient to prove its existence. Ultimately, then, Kant was too much of a skeptic to be easily convinced by the empirical evidence in favor of organicism.

It is important to see, however, that Kant's skepticism was not decisive. For it was not on the empirical plane that Hegel and the *Naturphilosophen* attempted to meet the Kantian challenge. The more important battle took place on the tougher terrain of epistemology.

IN DEFENSE OF *NATURPHILOSOPHIE*

Hegel's concern to defend his organic worldview around 1800 made him turn toward Schelling's *Naturphilosophie*. Forming an alliance with Schelling suited Hegel's own agenda, because Schelling had already defended an organic concept of nature in his 1798 tract *On the World Soul*. Although Hegel forged his own organic concept of nature independent of Schelling, he still had much to learn from his old friend from the *Tübinger Stift*. It was Schelling who was so well versed in all the latest developments of the natural sciences, and who had already formulated some of the technical arguments necessary to justify organicism. But, around 1800, Schelling was in urgent need of aid to defend his *Naturphilosophie*. He was on the verge of breaking his old alliance with Fichte, who had sharply criticized the possibility of a *Naturphilosophie*. Hence one of Hegel's first acts as an ally of Schelling was to defend the necessity of a *Naturphilosophie* in his *Differenzschrift*.

Hegel's argument in behalf of *Naturphilosophie* in the *Differenzschrift* was essentially a defense of its organic concept of nature. His central thesis is that only the organic concept can overcome the persistent dualism between the subjective and objective that still vitiates Kant's and Fichte's idealism. According to Hegel, Kant and Fichte had not overcome the dualism of the Cartesian legacy but only reinstated it in new terms. Kant's and Fichte's idealism remained caught in a dualism between the transcendental and the empirical, the analogue of Descartes's dualism between the *res cogitans* and *res extensa*. The Kantian transcendental ego is the source of the form of experience, while its empirical content remains simply given. If the form of experience arises from the active transcendental ego, which is beyond space and time, its content is simply given and passively received within space and time. Fichte had taken an important step toward overcoming Kant's dualism, Hegel acknowledged, because he insisted upon a principle of subject–object identity, according to which the transcendental ego would create the entire content of its experience. Nevertheless, Fichte had still not succeeded in removing dualism, Hegel argued, because his principle of subject-object identity is only a goal, a regulative ideal, that the ego could forever approach, but never attain, in a process of infinite striving. The goal of subject–object identity contrasted sharply with the reality of a dualism between subject and object in ordinary experience. These dualisms can be overcome, Hegel maintains, only if we accept an organic concept of nature according to which the subjective and the objective are only different degrees of organization and development of a single living force. This means reinterpreting the principle of subject–object identity, so that it refers not to the activity of the knowing subject but to the living force within nature itself. This force is both subjective and objective since the realms of matter and self-consciousness are simply stages of its development.

The dense and obscure argument of Hegel's *Differenzschrift* gains much in purpose, meaning and cogency if we place it more in its original context. In his characteristically cumbrous prose Hegel was defending and elaborating an earlier argument of Schelling's, which appears in its most compelling form in the introduction to his 1797 *Ideas toward a Philosophy of Nature*. The heart of Schelling's argument is that only the organic concept of nature can resolve the outstanding *aporia* of transcendental philosophy. Schelling begins his argument with the basic question 'What problems must a philosophy of nature resolve?' It is striking that he answers by referring to the basic problem of transcendental philosophy: 'How a world outside us, how nature, and with it experience, is possible?' (*Sämtliche Werke* II, 15). Schelling makes it perfectly explicit, therefore, that *Naturphilosophie* has a *transcendental* task: its basic objective is to solve the problem of knowledge. The solution to this problem is especially difficult, Schelling explains, because all knowledge requires some form of correspondence or connection between the subjective and the objective, the ideal and the real, or the transcendental and the empirical. Such a connection or correspondence seems impossible, however, because these realms appear to be completely heterogeneous. To explain the possibility of knowledge, then, it is necessary to unite these realms, to forge a bridge between them. Schelling then argues at length that this problem cannot be resolved from conventional Kantian premises (II 16, 25–6). He contends that the orthodox Kantian distinction between the form and matter of experience simply reinstates the dualism that gave rise to the problem in the first place. The Kantians cannot bridge the gulf between these realms, because they make so sharp a distinction between the form and the matter of experience that they cannot explain how their interaction occurs. They simply state that the forms are imposed upon this matter, though they offer no explanation of how that is possible.

Schelling's solution to the persistent Kantian dualisms is nothing less than his organic concept of nature. If nature is an organism, he argues, then it follows that there is no distinction in kind but only one of degree between the mental and the physical, the subjective and the objective, the ideal and the real. They are then simply different degrees of organization and development of a single living force, which is found everywhere within nature. These apparent opposites can then be viewed as interdependent. The mental is simply the highest degree of organization and development of the living powers of the body; and the body is only the lowest degree of organization and development of the living powers of the mind. According to the organic concept of nature, as Schelling puts it, 'Nature should be visible spirit, and spirit [should be] invisible nature' (II, 56).

Schelling's and Hegel's response to the Kantian regulative constraints is that they undermine the fundamental aim of transcendental philosophy itself: to explain the possibility of knowledge. Since we need to overcome dualism to explain the possibility of knowledge, to grant only regulative status to the solution to that dualism means that we have no final explanation for the possibility of knowledge itself. We have no choice but to give the idea of an organism constitutive status; for only under the assumption that *there is* an organism is it possible to explain the *actual interaction* between the subjective and the objective, the ideal and the real, the noumenal and the phenomenal. To assign the concept a purely regulative status simply left the mystery of their actual interaction. Hence, for these reasons, Schelling and Hegel think that the concept of an organism had its own transcendental deduction: it is nothing less than a necessary condition of possible experience.

We will have to leave aside here the large question of the general merits of Schelling's and Hegel's argument. Clearly, the organic concept of nature is very bold and speculative, standing in much need of further argument. The only point to be stressed here is that it is question-begging to dismiss the organic concept of nature as an illegitimate metaphysics and to stress the need for philosophy to remain within the limits of epistemology. This was the old neo-Kantian criticism of *Naturphilosophie*, which still finds its defenders today.[24] But the neo-Kantian criticism is dogmatic itself, for Schelling and Hegel are questioning its underlying premise: the self-sufficient status of epistemology, its power to solve its fundamental problem through its own resources. The heart of their argument is that the *aporia* of the critical philosophy are resolvable only by going beyond the Kantian limits and postulating the constitutive status of some of the ideas of reason.

MYTHS ABOUT *NATURPHILOSOPHIE*

Hegel's attempt to justify his organic worldview in the 1800s drove him into the realm of the empirical sciences. In his early Jena years Hegel would often lecture on *Naturphilosophie*, which was to be an integral part of his forthcoming system of philosophy. In an introduction we have no space for a detailed consideration of the doctrines and deductions of Hegel's *Naturphilosophie*. All that we can do here is correct some common misconceptions.

Hegel's *Naturphilosophie* has often been dismissed as the worst aspect of his metaphysics. Rather than engaging in observation and experiment, it seems to indulge in a priori theorizing about nature and to force facts into a preconceived mould. As a result of this flawed method – so the objection goes – Hegel made some fantastic blunders: he opposed the theory of evolution; he disparaged Newton's theory of motion in favor of Kepler's; he retained Aristotle's theory of the four elements; and he demonstrated the necessity of four planets around the sun. On these grounds, since the early nineteenth century, Hegel's *Naturphilosophie* had been held up as a perfect example of how *not* to pursue the study of nature. Not surprisingly, therefore, some contemporary Hegel scholars avoid Hegel's *Naturphilosophie* because it seems to doom his philosophy to obsolescence.[25]

There can be no question that Hegel did make some blunders, and that he was guilty of forcing facts into preconceived molds, contrary to his own methodological guidelines. Still, these points concern more the results and practice of *Naturphilosophie* than the enterprise itself. To avoid some crude neo-Kantian misconceptions about that enterprise, it is necessary to make a few points in Hegel's behalf.

First, Hegel never held that the conceptual method of *Naturphilosophie* should be a replacement for observation and experiment; he understood it as a method for *organizing* and *systematizing* the results of the empirical sciences, so that it presupposed their concrete results (EPW §§246, 250R). This does not mean that these results were to be developed according to the principles Hegel had already laid down in his *Science of Logic*; for Hegel insisted that each science develop according to the inherent logic of its subject matter, and that its principles should derive solely from this inherent logic. To apply presupposed principles from another discipline would be formalism, which he strongly condemned.

Second, although Hegel insisted that *Naturphilosophie*, as the thinking consideration of nature, is distinct from observation and experiment, he never accepted any fundamental distinction in kind between philosophy and empirical science. Rather, he insisted that philosophical doctrines had to be true to experience and that they ultimately had to derive from it (EPW §§6, 7R, 38R). What made doctrines philosophical as opposed to empirical was only their formal structure, their organization or systematization (EPW §246R). In this regard it is important to note that Hegel, like Schelling, did not accept the Kantian distinction between a priori and a posteriori judgments, as if the former were the subject matter of metaphysics and the latter the concern of the empirical sciences.[26] The distinction between the a priori and the a posteriori is not between distinct classes of judgments but depends entirely upon the state of our knowledge, on whether a judgment could be given a place in a system. If a judgment could have such a place it was a priori, because it could be demonstrated from other propositions; but if no such place could be provided, the judgment was a posteriori. Thus the neo-Kantian criticism that *Naturphilosophie* confuses the a priori concerns of metaphysics with the a posteriori results of the empirical sciences only begs the question.

Third, a crucial part of Hegel's objection against mechanism, atomism and empiricism is that it presupposed a very crude metaphysics of its own (EPW §§38R, 98R, 270R). Its pretension to avoid metaphysics became a source of dogmatism because it failed to examine its own assumptions. Hegel insisted that metaphysical questions are inevitable in the natural sciences themselves, and that a properly critical methodology would acknowledge and discuss them rather than attempt to conceal them. Once again, the neo-Kantian critique of Hegel for introducing metaphysics into the natural sciences only begs the question.

Five

The Realm of Spirit

LIFE AND SPIRIT

We saw in the last chapter that Hegel's philosophy grew out of his organic vision of the world. Some of his most basic concepts were organicist in meaning; and some of the central tenets of absolute idealism had their source in Hegel's organicism. Furthermore, a major concern of the young Hegel was to defend his organic concept of nature against the challenge of Kant's critique.

It is of the first importance to stress, however, that organicism provides only a necessary, not a sufficient, account of Hegel's philosophy. If we explain Hegel's philosophy entirely in organic terms, we ignore its characteristic feature, its fundamental difference from Schelling's philosophy. During their collaboration in Jena (1801–4), Schelling and Hegel joined in a common cause: to defend absolute idealism. But, even then, there were simmering tensions, growing differences between them. These eventually led to Hegel's ultimate break with Schelling in 1807.

In a brilliant article,[1] Jean Hyppolite suggested that Schelling's Jena system was first and foremost a philosophy of life, whereas Hegel's was primarily a philosophy of spirit. According to his interpretation, the main theme of Schelling's system was the concept of life, which had an essentially naturalistic or biological meaning, whereas the central motif of Hegel's system was the idea of spirit, which had a fundamentally historical or cultural meaning. For Hegel, spirit is not just life but something more: the self-consciousness of life. While the concept of life appears in all the different levels or potencies of nature, the idea of spirit manifests itself in the realms of society, history and the state.

Hyppolite's theory does capture something important about the fundamental differences between Schelling and Hegel during their Jena years (1801–4). One of Schelling's main interests then was to develop and defend the organic concept of nature.[2] This was part of his effort to establish his system of absolute idealism, his so-called 'philosophy of identity', according to which the absolute is the pure identity of subject and object.[3] It is very revealing, however, that in his absolute idealism Schelling gave pride of place to his philosophy of nature, virtually equating the standpoint of absolute identity with nature itself.[4] With Hegel, however, the focus is very different. To be sure, he is still very much concerned with the philosophy of nature, which he develops in several manuscripts of the early Jena years.[5] But, starting in 1802, Hegel shifts much of his energy toward developing a philosophy of spirit. Some of the main works of the Jena period deal with ethics, politics and anthropology.[6] When we compare Hegel's interests with Schelling's in this respect we are indeed struck by the contrast. Schelling gave a very small place to the realms of society and the state in his main exposition of the philosophy of identity, the unpublished 1804 'System of All Philosophy'.

It is indeed significant that, even during their collaboration, Hegel himself began to criticize Schelling along just these lines. In some of his early 1802 manuscripts Hegel had already faulted Schelling's philosophy of identity for not admitting qualitative differences within the absolute standpoint.[7] Such differences were crucial if the philosophy of identity were to take into account the development of spirit, which proceeds through self-differentiation and self-opposition. There is also a striking passage in Hegel's 1802 'Naturrecht' essay where he declares that the realm of spirit is higher than nature, because nature is only the externalization of the absolute, whereas spirit encompasses both its internalization and externalization (W II, 503/111). With some plausibility, this passage has been read as an implicit critique of Schelling, who had virtually equated the absolute standpoint with nature itself.[8] At any rate, some of Schelling's students detected the growing differences between Schelling and Hegel, for they charged Hegel with a lack of feeling for 'the poetry of nature'.[9]

Still, despite their difference in interests, and despite Hegel's growing criticisms of Schelling, it would be unwise to overstate the differences between them. They do not reflect a fundamental difference in principle, only one of interest and emphasis. Hegel never understood spirit as something existing above and beyond nature but as the highest organization and development of its powers; even the self-awareness of life was implicit within life itself. The importance that the realm of spirit had for the later Hegel in no way diminishes the significance of the organic concept that he learned from Schelling; for in developing his account of the realm of spirit Hegel simply applied that organic concept to the realms of society, history and the state. For his part, Schelling acknowledged that the self stood on a higher level than the organic. In his 1802 *Bruno* he admitted that self-awareness, the realm of the ego, was the highest organization and development of the organic powers of nature.[10] In any case, most of Hegel's criticisms of Schelling really only concern one phase of Schelling's development, more specifically the formulation of the philosophy of identity in the 1801 *Presentation of My System*. The differences between them diminish when we consider Schelling's later formulations, especially those of the *Further Presentation from the System of Philosophy*, which he wrote with Hegel.

THE SPIRIT OF LOVE

To understand Hegel's concept of spirit it is necessary to return to the writings of his early Frankfurt period, more specifically the 1797 fragments on religion and love,[11] and the set of manuscripts entitled *The Spirit of Christianity and its Fate*, which were written between 1798 and 1800.[12] It is in these early manuscripts that Hegel first conceives and develops the concept of spirit that will play such a central and characteristic role in his later system. Hegel's concept of spirit grew out of his early attempt to formulate the meaning and structure of love. He was motivated to reflect on the concept of love because, under the influence of Schiller and Hölderlin, he began to see it as the very heart of religion and morality. These early reflections are really the key to unlock the mystery of Hegel's concept of spirit. When we first encounter Hegel's concept of spirit in his mature system it is bound to appear utterly baffling. All its talk about the self going outside itself and returning within itself seems totally obscure and pointless. These features make perfect sense, however, as soon as we take the concept back to its original context: the early reflections on love.

In the early fragments on religion and love, Hegel states that in love there is a unity of subject and object, or what he calls, true to the jargon of his time, pure subject–object identity. According to Fichte, Schelling and Hölderlin, the identity of subject and object is realized only in self-consciousness because only in self-consciousness are the subject and object of consciousness one and the same. Hegel accepts this theory of subject–object identity; but he now adds something new to it that is not found in his contemporaries. Hegel claims that such subject–object identity, such self-consciousness, exists perfectly only in love. What he means is that in love the self (the subject) finds itself in the other (the object) as the other finds itself in the self. In the experience of love subject and object, self and other, realize their natures through one another, and moreover each of them recognizes itself only through the other. Hence there is subject–object identity because there is a *single structure of self-consciousness* holding between self and other: the self knows itself in the other as the other knows itself in the self.

Hegel further explains, however, that love involves not only a moment of identity, but also a moment of difference; it is a unity-in-difference. There is also difference in love because by its very nature it consists in appreciating the other *just because* it is an other; love is possible only through the mutual respect between equal and independent partners. The self does not love the other if it attempts to dominate and subordinate the other to itself (I 394/322). It is noteworthy that Hegel distinguishes the standpoint of love from that of morality where the self attempts to dominate and control the other. Here he was criticizing Fichte, who understood morality as essentially a process of striving by which the self attempts to dominate and control the world. Like Hölderlin, Hegel regarded such an ethic as completely hostile to the spirit of love.

For Hegel, then, the structure of love consists in what he calls – using a redolent term that will become a central theme of his mature system – 'unity-in-difference', 'the unification of unification and non-unification'. It is important to see, however, that for him love is not simply a static structure or form; it is also a living experience, and as such a process. More specifically, love is the paradoxical process whereby the self both loses itself (as an individual) and finds or gains itself (as a part of a wider whole). Love contains therefore the moments of *self-surrender* and also of *self-discovery*. There is a moment of *self-surrender* in love because the self loses itself by renouncing self-interest as its ultimate value, and by ceasing to define itself in opposition to others. There is also a moment of *self-discovery* because in love the self also finds itself in and through the other; it sees that it is no longer something opposed to the other but the unity of itself with the other. Hegel has in mind the common experience of love where one makes oneself richer by giving to the other. In one fragment,[13] he stresses both moments of self-surrender and self-discovery in love by referring to Juliet's lines in *Romeo and Juliet*: 'The more I give to thee the more I have.'

Hegel also describes the experience of love in terms of *externalization* and *internalization*. It is one of *externalization* in so far as the subjective becomes objective, the inner becomes outer; it is also one of *internalization* in so far as the objective becomes subjective, the outer becomes inner. The moment of *externalization* is that whereby the private or individual self loses or surrenders itself in the other, which it once saw as completely outside itself. The moment of *internalization* is that whereby the self now finds or discovers itself in the other, so that the other it once saw as outside itself has now become part of itself. If the moment of externalization is that of *self-negation*, the moment of internalization is that of *self-affirmation*, the negation of self-negation.

In some striking passages from *The Spirit of Christianity* Hegel calls what both produces and results from love, the whole process of self-surrender and self-discovery, of externalization and internalization, *spirit* (*Geist*).[14] He first uses the term in a religious context, in writing about how the spirit of Jesus was present at the Last Supper. He wrote that the spirit of Jesus is the spirit of love, which first makes itself objective, externalizing itself in the bread and wine, and then makes itself subjective, internalizing the bread and wine through the act of eating. Hegel likens the process to that of understanding meaning from a written word; the thought is first objectified in the sign, and it is then resubjectified when the sign is read as having a specific meaning. Whatever the original context of Hegel's use of the term, its introduction would later prove decisive for his philosophy as a whole. When Hegel later writes of spirit it always has the structure and development that he once gave to the experience of love.

It is not only the concept of spirit that emerges from these early reflections on love. Another notorious Hegelian concept also appears, if only implicitly. The opposing movements involved in the experience of love – its externalization and internalization, self-surrender and self-discovery – Hegel will later call '*dialectic*'. Hegel will later use the term in this sense to describe the process of spiritual development. It is important, however, to distinguish at least two meanings of this concept: the *ontological*, whereby it defines something happening in reality; and the *methodological* or *epistemological*, whereby it signifies a method of doing philosophy. While Hegel has the concept in the ontological sense in *Spirit of Christianity and its Fate*, he still does not have it in the methodological or epistemological sense. In this latter sense Hegel will develop his dialectic much later, though there are already anticipations of it in the earlier Frankfurt fragments.

THE METAPHYSICS OF LOVE

The account given so far of Hegel's concept of love leaves out its metaphysical dimension. It seems to describe what could take place between any two people in love. For just this reason it seems to be an insufficient analysis of Hegel's later concept of spirit, which has a clear metaphysical status. The mature Hegel sees spirit as more than the experience of love between two finite individuals. Spirit is when finite selves become conscious of themselves as infinite; and when the infinite becomes self-conscious through finite selves (XII 480).

It is important to see, however, that even in his early Frankfurt writings on love Hegel does give it a mystical and religious significance. Even in this regard, then, the later concept of spirit is already implicit in the early reflections on love. In one early fragment he states that where subject and object are one there is something divine, and that subject–object identity is the ideal of every religion.[15] It is characteristic of religion, he argues, that it unites subject and the object in the bond of love. If the moral or practical standpoint demands that the subject dominate the object, and if the philosophical or theoretical standpoint assumes that the subject and the object are distinct from one another, religion is higher than morals and philosophy because it gives an experience of the identity of subject and object. In another fragment Hegel simply identifies the standpoint of religion with that of love.[16] In love we are at one with the object, which is also at the same time not us. Hegel then cites *Phaedrus* 251a where the lover first sees the ideas through the visible form of beauty. In yet another fragment Hegel states that love is indeed a feeling, but it is more than a single feeling; it is life that finds itself in a totality of feelings. Life manifests itself in love, which is the process by which an original unity becomes many and then returns back into itself as a differentiated unity.[17]

What all these early fragments seem to say is that we must place the experience of love in the context of nature as a whole. Two lovers are parts of the organic unity of nature. Since in an organism the parts are inseparable from the whole and the whole is inherent in each of its parts, the love of one person for another expresses nothing less than the entire universe from his or her point of view. In the *Spirit of Christianity* Hegel is indeed explicit about this premise, stressing how in a living thing the whole is within each of its parts.[18] The organic unity of nature means, therefore, that when the self loves the other that is not only the act of a single individual but also of the whole of nature acting through it. When the self loves the other it also feels – though in a subconscious form – the infinite acting in and through itself. Hence Hegel writes that life finds itself in love, and that it manifests itself as the whole process of internalization and externalization characteristic of love.[19]

It is evident from these early fragments how Hegel's account of the experience of love fits into his general organic concept of nature, which he developed around the same time. Although Hegel's account of love has a religious, and indeed mystical, dimension, it should now be clear why he thinks that it must have this dimension. It would be a false abstraction from the organic whole of nature if we were to separate human experience from it, as if it took place inside some enclosed *sui generis* sphere. This would be very much like the Cartesian or Kantian dualistic view that Hegel was so eager to avoid. But if all human activity and experience must be placed within the whole of nature, and if that whole is an organic unity where the whole appears in each of its parts, then it follows that all forms of human activity and experience will have a cosmic or mystical dimension. If, further, the living power of nature reaches its highest manifestation, organization and development in human experience, then love, as the most intense form of human experience, will be the culmination of the powers of the universe itself. Of course, in our normal experience of love we are not conscious of this cosmic dimension; but this is no argument against it. What Hegel wants us to cultivate through religion is the self-awareness of the universe through the experience of love.

The organic context of Hegel's early reflections on love becomes further apparent from the close analogy between the processes of love and life. The moments of externalization and internalization of love are, not accidently, analogous to the moments of differentiation and re-integration characteristic of life. The moment of differentiation, by which an inchoate unity becomes more concrete and specific, happens when the self externalizes itself in the other; the moment of re-integration, whereby the differentiation is reunified, happens when the self internalizes itself through the other. Since love is an essentially organic process, since the organic powers of the universe come to their highest realization and manifestation in the powers of love, we have to understand the dialectic of love as one of differentiation and re-integration.

Now that we have seen the organic context of Hegel's early reflections on love, it should be clear why both inflationary and deflationary accounts of the concept of spirit are inadequate. Inflationary accounts see spirit as a single entity existing beyond its embodiment in specific individuals; but, true to his organic concept, Hegel will insist that any organism, any living force, exists only in particular individuals, only in its individual embodiments. This does not mean, however, that it is logically reducible to these embodiments, given that an organic whole is prior to its parts and makes them possible. Deflationary accounts go astray, therefore, if they see spirit as nothing more than its embodiments within particular individuals. This not only fails to see how the universal is logically prior to the particular, but it also separates the experience of love from its place in nature, which Hegel would regard as a false abstraction.

THE TRANSFORMATION OF LOVE

Whatever the precise meaning of the concept of spirit, it should be apparent by now how much Hegel's later concepts of spirit and dialectic arose from his early reflections on the experience of love. These concepts, which initially are so obscure, appear to have a perfect meaning and point when we place them in their original context. But now a difficult question arises: What meaning do those concepts have once their original context and purpose disappear? In his later work Hegel continues to use the concepts of spirit and dialectic; but he ceases to give love the importance he gave it in his early writings. Does this mean that the concepts of spirit and dialectic lose their original meaning?

There are at least two basic differences between the early and the mature Hegel regarding the treatment of love. First, in his Frankfurt years Hegel insists that the experience of love is a mystery, indeed a miracle, which cannot be expressed in discursive form.[20] In his later years, however, Hegel will attempt to grasp the experience of love, the process of life, in some discursive form. While he will continue to stress that this experience and process transcend the concepts of the understanding, he will also emphasize that they can be grasped through the dialectic of reason. While the understanding is an analytic faculty that divides and analyzes, failing to grasp objects as wholes, reason is a synthetic faculty that unites parts into a whole, showing how no part exists on its own apart from the whole. In the Frankfurt years, however, Hegel sees all thinking in terms of the understanding; and so anything that is not divisible, anything that has to be understood as an organic whole, transcends the domain of intellectual comprehension. We have to experience it; but we cannot conceive or demonstrate it.

The other basic difference between Hegel's earlier and later treatments of love concerns the significance of love in his later system. Beginning in his early Jena years, Hegel stopped giving love such a central and crucial place in his system. The legal and moral relations of ethical life rapidly gain favor over love, and eventually love is replaced by mutual recognition. Already in his 1802/3 *System of Ethical Life* Hegel states that subject-object identity is realized not in love but in the mutual recognition between citizens in a community.[21] The unity of subject and object cannot be found in love, he argues, since it is only a natural bond between male and female, and these partners are not on an equal footing. The male is rational and represents the universal interests of science, business and the state; the female is emotional and intuitive, and acts only in behalf of the individual interests of her family. The 1805 *Philosophy of Spirit* continues in the same direction. Love is now confined to the family; and it is only a primitive subconscious form of the realm of ethical life.[22] It is no longer love, but only the moral and legal relations of ethical life, Hegel now contends, that give someone self-awareness as a rational or universal being. Although love is indeed a unity in opposition where distinct persons are self-conscious through one another, it is only a primitive form of self-consciousness. Lovers are self-conscious only of their particular personalities, and their bond is created only by their passing natural desires. These developments of the Jena years came to their culmination in Hegel's 1821 *Philosophy of Right* where Hegel confined love to the realm of the family.

The demotion of love in the later system goes hand-in-hand with Hegel's later demand for a rational account of the realm of spirit. As it became the object of reason, spirit became more rational itself. Hegel will later make reason one of the defining characteristics of spirit. By its very nature love is less amenable to rational treatment; its desires, feelings and intuitions are below the threshold of rational comprehension. Ironically, then, this development seems to confirm Hegel's original romantic objections against conceptual thought: in trying to conceive love, reason makes it more rational, and so destroys its very nature.

It is noteworthy that this development too was already incipient in Hegel's early years. In *The Spirit of Christianity and its Fate* Hegel had elevated love into the highest principle of religion and morality. But even during his Berne years, he had his doubts about the Christian ethic (see pp. 126–31), and these resurfaced in the Frankfurt years, even in *The Spirit of Christianity* itself, the very work where Hegel had espoused his romantic gospel. The ethic of love was, of course, the gospel of Jesus. But Hegel saw fatal flaws in that gospel. Such an ethic is suitable more to a sect than the whole community, he argued, because while I can love my brethren, it is hard for me to love everyone, especially those who do not share my faith. It is also hard to square the Christian ethic, which demands that we give away everything, with the property rights so important for a larger community. Worst of all, though, the Christian ethic is simply too beautiful, too good for this world. Rather than fighting to make the world a better place, it attempts to escape from it, promising us salvation in heaven. The Christian does not fight for his rights but simply cedes them, turning the other cheek. In *The Spirit of Christianity and its Fate* Hegel explains how Jesus, embittered by the failure of his teaching to take hold among the Jews, cut himself off from the world, confined himself to his closest followers, and preached that one should render unto Caesar what is Caesar's. Jesus faced a dilemma: enter the world and compromise himself, or keep one's purity and flee from the world (N 328). Jesus chose to maintain his purity, and so he withdrew from life. As a result, though, his ethic became irrelevant to the world. Because he refused to compromise with the world, because he fled from it to maintain his purity, Jesus could find freedom only in a void. Yet Hegel teaches that the man who seeks to save his soul by fleeing from the world only loses it. A heart lifted above all the ties of rights no longer has anything to give or forgive (286). It is clear from Hegel's account of the beautiful soul that he thinks its ethic is noble but flawed: *noble*, because it rises above the moral law, the demands of justice, and dispenses forgiveness and avoids conflict of rights; but *flawed*, because its act of abstracting from legal entanglements and conflict leaves us with nothing to preserve. It is already in the *Spirit of Christianity and its Fate*, then, that we see one of the basic teachings of Hegel's later philosophy: that true independence and freedom come not from fleeing the life of this world but only from learning how to live in a community with others.

It was these doubts about the Christian ethic that later compelled Hegel to demote the role of love in his mature system. Already in the Frankfurt years, then, he had realized that love could not have the supreme significance that he wanted to give it. It was only a matter of thinking this matter through, of dropping the ethic of love and finding an ethic more suitable to the community at large, an ethic more adequate to life in the world. It is to this task that Hegel turns in his early Jena years in the *System of Ethical Life* and the *Philosophy of Spirit*.

Though love loses its significance after the Frankfurt years, it would still be wrong to conclude that Hegel's original reflections on love were of little or no importance for his later concept of spirit. The later concept still shows the same structure and development as love itself: there are moments of self-discovery and self-destruction, of externalization and internalization, and there is the same organic pattern of development: from unity to difference to unity-in-difference. All the characteristics of love are incorporated into the theme of mutual recognition, which Hegel now sees as definitive of spirit. The intersubjective dimension of love is simply made into a defining characteristic of rationality itself.

It would also be a mistake to think that love no longer plays an important role in the later system. Although love ceases to be the culmination of spirit, it remains its original home and starting point. In his later treatments of love the family is made the primitive basis of ethical life, which is the starting point of spirit itself. In the 1821 *Philosophy of Right* Hegel will insist how spirit first actualizes itself in the realm of ethical life (§§156–7), and how the love within the family is the foundation for ethical life itself (§158). To be sure, love is still a primitive form of spirit because it is not yet self-conscious of itself as rational but only in the immediate form of feeling and desire; nevertheless, love does mark 'the immediate substantiality' of spirit (§158).

The main point to see now is that the ultimate difference between Hegel's early and later concept of spirit is really only one of form rather than substance. Spirit remains the same in the early and later Hegel; it is just that in the later Hegel spirit becomes self-conscious of itself, and its self-consciousness involves rational comprehension. To be self-conscious spirit must know itself as subject to a moral and legal realm of rights and duties. Of course, love consists in desires and feelings that are below the threshold of rational comprehension; but Hegel does not think that reflection destroys but actualizes, and culminates in love. Here it is important to note a point that Hegel will later stress in his philosophy of religion: that though rational reflection changes the form of feeling and intuition it does not change its content; indeed, it is the realization and actualization of that content, which exists only in an inchoate and confused form in the realm of sensibility (see pp. 146–52). Rational reflection is therefore not the destruction of love but its highest organization and development. Ultimately, then, the spirit of Hegel's mature philosophy was nothing more than the rationalization and institutionalization of that love he had once celebrated in his Frankfurt years.

Six

The Religious Dimension

THE UNENDING DEBATE

Soon after Hegel's death in 1831, a fierce dispute arose about the religious dimension of his thought.[1] Left-wing Hegelians saw Hegel as a covert atheist or humanist, or at best a pantheist having only nominal affinities with official Christianity. Right-wing Hegelians embraced Hegel as a defender of the Christian faith, and indeed as an apologist for the Prussian Church. In their view, Hegel did for modern Protestantism what Aquinas had once done for medieval Catholicism: he too gave a rational foundation for the faith.[2]

Both sides could mass evidence in their behalf. The left-wing Hegelians could easily demonstrate that Hegel was no orthodox Protestant. His God was not transcendent but immanent; he had no time for miracles and the Bible; and he portrayed Christianity as a form of alienation between self and world. Was it indeed not Hegel who first declared 'the death of God'? For their part, the right-wing Hegelians could stress Hegel's concern to wed knowledge and faith, his attempt to rationalize the trinity and the incarnation, and his eagerness to find reason in the actual institutions of Prussia, first and foremost among them the Church. Indeed, the right had the most telling evidence of all: Hegel's express declaration, on several occasions, that he was a Lutheran.[3]

The dispute continues today. To be sure, it has lost its political urgency; but the fundamental issues remain the same. Some scholars insist that the religious dimension of Hegel's thinking is fundamental for all his thought, because Hegel's basic aim is to rationalize the Christian faith.[4] Others contend that the religious dimension is of negligible significance, a mere mystical gloss for Hegel's essentially humanistic and atheistic agenda.[5] Although they note that Hegel writes about God, they regard this as little more than a pious term for the universe. 'The secret of Hegel' is not that he was a Christian apologist but a covert atheist, 'the precursor of atheistic humanism in German philosophy'.[6]

This dispute concerns much more than Hegel's philosophy of religion. The underlying issue is fundamental for the interpretation of all his thought, for it concerns the very purpose of his philosophy. At stake here is the question whether it was Hegel's purpose to defend or to undermine the Christian legacy. Furthermore, the question about the metaphysical dimension of Hegel's philosophy, which we discussed in Chapter Three, is really derivative, depending on the role religion plays in Hegel's philosophy. If religion is indeed central to Hegel's concerns – if we must take literally his claim that philosophy and religion both have the divine for their subject matter – then all non-metaphysical interpretations of his philosophy will prove untenable.

This dispute extends to every phase of Hegel's intellectual development, both his early writings before 1800 and his mature writings after 1806. It is not possible to limit the dispute to Hegel's mature writings alone, as if his earlier writings are no longer relevant.[7] For advocates of both readings take the early writings as the key to the interpretation of the mature Hegel.

As we shall soon see, both Christian and humanist interpretations are inadequate. The Christian interpretation has never done justice to Hegel's critique of Christianity or his heterodox conception of God. The humanist interpretation has failed to reduce Hegel's God down to the universe, and it has virtually ignored his attempt to rationalize traditional Christian beliefs. Ultimately, the religious dimension of Hegel's thought proves richer than both extremes. For it was Hegel's aim to steer a middle path between them; he wanted to develop a new theology to overcome the weaknesses of both humanism and traditional Christianity.

EARLY CRITIQUE OF CHRISTIANITY

The dispute about the religious dimension of Hegel's philosophy begins with his early manuscripts, those written in Tübingen, Berne and Frankfurt. The chief manuscripts from the Tübingen (1788–93) and Berne periods (1793–7) are the *Tübingen Essay*, *Berne Fragments*, *Life of Jesus* and *The Positivity of the Christian Religion*. The main manuscripts from the Frankfurt period (1797–1800) are the *Sketches on Religion and Love*, *The Spirit of Christianity and its Fate* and the *Fragment of a System*.

Rosenkranz and Haym, who first read these manuscripts, were convinced that Hegel's primary concerns were religious, and indeed theological.[8] According to Dilthey, who made a more thorough study of them decades later, these writings were fundamentally religious and even mystical, revealing Hegel's place in the tradition of mystical pantheism.[9] Herman Nohl, Dilthey's pupil, edited the early writings and first published them under the title *Hegels theologische Jugendschriften* (Tübingen: Mohr, 1907). The title summarized a whole tradition of interpretation; but, to some, it was sheer provocation.

One of the notable champions of the theological or religious interpretation, though from an antipathetic perspective, was Nietzsche. He saw all the progeny of the *Tübinger Stift* – Hegel, Schelling and Hölderlin – as secret apologists for Christianity. He wrote in *Anti-Christ*: 'One only has to say the word "Tübinger Stift" to conceive what German philosophy is at bottom: a cunning theology . . . The Swabians are the best liars in Germany because they lie innocently.'[10]

Other scholars have contended that Hegel's early writings are best described as anti-theological, indeed as anti-Christian, because they severely criticize Christianity.[11] According to Lukács, the so-called 'theological phase' of Hegel's development is 'a reactionary legend'. In his view, Rosenkranz, Dilthey and Haering appropriated Hegel for their own nationalist ends, completely ignoring the radical republicanism that was the basis for his critique of Christianity.[12]

In this debate it is of the first importance to specify which early writings one is talking about.[13] There are great changes in Hegel's attitude toward Christianity from the Tübingen to the Frankfurt period. While the Tübingen and Berne fragments are very critical of Christianity, the Frankfurt writings are more sympathetic to the Christian legacy. Predictably, humanist interpretations are inspired by the Tübingen and Berne fragments, while Christian interpretations are based on the Frankfurt writings.

Regarding the Tübingen and Berne writings, it is misleading to describe them as theological, if 'theology' means the explanation or justification of Christian doctrine. In the *Tübingen Essay*, which sets the agenda for his early thought, Hegel explicitly states that theology is a matter of doctrine, and that he does not want to discuss that (I 16, 17/8, 9). During the Tübingen and Berne years he had remarkably little interest in the basis of religious belief, and he was content to accept Kant's doctrine of moral faith, according to which the beliefs in God, providence and immortality are justified on moral grounds (TE I, 16, 17/8, 9). The reason for this lack of interest is that Hegel's fundamental concern in Tübingen and Berne was to develop his ideal of a civic religion; his interest in doctrine was not in its meaning or truth but in its value for society and state. Yet, precisely because Hegel has little interest in theology, it would also be misleading to describe these early writings as 'anti-theological'; Hegel has no animus against theology but simply brackets it.[14]

It is fair, however, to describe Hegel's interests in these writings as 'religious', as even the most ardent advocates of the anti-Christian reading have conceded.[15] Hegel's religious interests are clear from his distinction between *subjective* and *objective* religion in the *Tübingen Essay*. Objective religion is doctrine and dogma, religion as codified and institutionalized. Subjective religion is religion as it is lived by the individual; it is a matter not of doctrine but of feeling and action (TE I, 13–14/6). Hegel makes it very plain that his main concern is with subjective religion: 'Everything depends on subjective religion; this is what has inherent and true worth. Let the theologians squabble all they like over what belongs to objective religion, over its dogmas and their precise determination . . .' (I 16/8). Since his main interest is in subjective religion, the young Hegel has been described as an existentialist *avant la lettre*.[16] But this is a mistake. Hegel's concern is not Kierkegaard's: he does not seek those beliefs that give meaning to my life and that are necessary to my salvation or self-realization. He has no interest in personal salvation or self-realization but wants only to foster subjective religion so that the citizen plays a more effective role in the state.

Granted that Hegel has no interest in theology, and that his concern with religion is subordinate to politics, is it accurate to maintain that the Tübingen and Berne writings are *anti*-Christian? At first blush, this seems too extreme. It seems possible to defend a Christian reading of these writings. In the tenth of the *Berne Fragments* Hegel asks whether Christianity fulfills the requirements of a civic religion, and he answers in the affirmative (BF I, 90/62). Indeed, for just this reason he writes his *Life of Jesus* where he interprets the gospel of Jesus in terms of Kant's moral philosophy. Although the fundamental concern of the *Positivity Essay* is to expose the positivity of the Christian religion, i.e. its attempt to base belief upon legal authority rather than reason alone, Hegel still argues explicitly that the core of Christianity is rational (P I, 105, 124/153, 166), and that it became positive only as a result of historical accident. Further evidence for the Christian reading comes when Hegel states in the *Berne Fragments* that it is precisely the divinity of Jesus that makes him an exemplar of moral virtue. 'Without the divinity of his person we would have only the man; whereas here we have a truly super-human ideal – an ideal not foreign to the human soul . . .' (BF I, 82/57). Finally, the anti-Christian interpretation has difficulty in explaining *The Life of Jesus*. If this is Hegel's attempt to write the scripture of a folk religion, why does Hegel choose Jesus as his model?[17]

Although there is some evidence for the Christian interpretation of the Tübingen and Berne writings, on balance there is more evidence for the anti-Christian interpretation. Throughout the *Berne Fragments* and the *Positivity Essay* there is a pervasive and passionate critique of Christianity. The critique goes so far that it even undermines Hegel's lukewarm support for the ideas that Christianity has an essentially moral content and that it is suitable as a civic religion. Arguably, if Hegel were more consistent, he would have rejected Christianity as a civic religion, denied the moral value of its teachings, and argued that positivity is the very essence of Christianity.

While Hegel seems to endorse Christianity as a civic religion, the general upshot of his argument both in the *Berne Fragments* and in the *Positivity Essay* is that Christianity is dangerous for the state. Thus he argues in the *Berne Fragments* that Christ's precepts are contrary to the basic principles of the state, such as laws concerning property and self-defense. The Christian would not defend the state but turn the other cheek; and since he preaches charity he would undermine laws to protect private property (BF I, 61–2/41–2). The teachings of Jesus are really only suitable, Hegel contends, for a sect or the family; if we attempt to make them into laws they become 'the most shocking profusion of repressive institutions and ways of deluding mankind' (BF I, 63/42). In the *Positivity Essay* Hegel argued that the Christian concern for personal salvation arose only because of the decline of republican virtue (P I, 206–13/221–4). If the individual worked for the common good, he would find his immortality in the republic.

Hegel also argues that Christianity is not the best religion for the cultivation of morality. Both in the *Berne Fragments* and the *Positivity Essay* Hegel prefers Socrates to Jesus as a teacher of morality (BF I, 50–4/32–5; P 119–20/163). While Socrates respects the freedom of the individual, his right to find the truth for himself, Jesus preaches a prescribed path toward salvation (I 51–2, 54/33, 35). Socrates does not seek disciples; but Christ demands faith in his person, and even wants 'an empire complete with generals and assorted high officials' (I 50/32). Socrates knows he is no better than anyone else; but Christ regards himself as a savior. In the *Berne Fragments* Hegel even argues that Christianity is useless as a virtue religion because it works only if a person is good already (BF I, 60/40). Furthermore, Christianity cannot claim to be preeminent as a virtue religion because the writings of Rousseau, Plato and Xenophon also stress the value of virtue (I 64–5/59).

In the final *Berne Fragments* Hegel attacks the very heart of Christian ethics, its doctrine of eternal salvation. This doctrine makes the condition of salvation belief in Christ and his expatiatory death (BF I, 90/62). Hegel contends that the real purpose of morality is lost sight of in such an ethic (I 84–5/59). Morality demands autonomy, whereas Christianity requires faith in the authority of a single person. The Protestant doctrine of salvation *sola fide* is charged with undermining a fundamental principle of morality: 'that one is worthy of happiness on the basis of a moral life' (I 93/65).

Hegel's critique of Christian ethics also includes the divinity of Christ, a doctrine he initially appears to accept. Although he first states that this belief encourages morality, he soon retracts this by writing that the whole idea of the divinity of Christ rests upon a degrading conception of human nature. We elevate Christ to divine status, as if he alone were the paragon of virtue, only because we believe natural sin makes us incapable of virtue (BF I, 96–7/67). Hegel notes that the characteristic belief of Christianity is the divinity of Christ; yet he rejects this belief because it is part of the whole *ordo salutatis*, which is incompatible with morality (BF I, 97–8/68–9).

There is another powerful reason for thinking that Hegel's Berne writings are essentially anti-Christian. Namely, in the *Positivity Essay* he argues that the idea of the divine will as the source of moral laws is a form of hypostasis, and indeed the source of all heteronomy.

One almost believes one is reading Feuerbach or Marx in the following passage: 'The objectivity of the divinity kept apace with the corruption and slavery of man, and it [the objectivity] is only a revelation, only an appearance, of the spirit of the time' (P I, 211–12/227–8). But the passage is not a fluke, a passing passion. Hegel had already anticipated this thesis in the *Berne Fragments* when he wrote that 'the great principle that duty and virtue are self-sufficient' is undermined by 'the merest association with the idea of God' (BF I, 73–4/50–1).

Hegel's powerful critique of Christianity in the Berne years places him firmly in the tradition of the radical Enlightenment. There are remarkable affinities between Hegel's critique and the radical English free-thinkers, John Toland, Matthew Tindal and Anthony Collins, whose doctrines were well known in Germany.[18] There are many points in common: (1) that the main purpose of Christian doctrine is the propagation of morality; (2) that the clergy are dangerous because they subvert the autonomous action behind morality; (3) that the doctrines of sin, saving faith and the atonement subvert the moral purpose of Christianity by making faith rather than virtue the condition of salvation; (4) that the only essential religious beliefs are in the existence of God, providence and immortality; (5) that the basis of Christian belief cannot rest upon the testimony of history and miracles, because these cannot withstand critical examination; (6) that the divine element in Christ is not unique to him but exists within all humanity. No less important for Hegel's affinity with this tradition is his republicanism.

When it comes to the Berne and Tübingen writings, then, those who have argued the case for Hegel's *anti*-Christian agenda have the weight of evidence in their favor. Whether Hegel was really an atheist in this period is still hardly proven; but, at the very least, his attitude toward Christianity was extremely hostile.

REVERSAL IN FRANKFURT

What was true in Tübingen and Berne was not true in Frankfurt. Indeed, almost the exact contrary is the case. During the Frankfurt years Hegel's thinking about religion underwent a remarkable change, indeed a virtual *volte-face*. Hegel reverses his earlier thinking in several fundamental respects.[19] (1) In the Berne years Hegel saw Kantian morality as the essence and purpose of religion; in the Frankfurt years he sees religion as a standpoint above Kantian morality. The Kantian critic of religion became a religious critic of Kant. (2) In the Berne years Hegel saw the *solution* to positivity in Kantian morality; in the Frankfurt years he sees Kantian morality as part of the *problem* of positivity. (3) In the Berne years Hegel was a critic of some of the fundamental articles of faith of Christianity, such as the incarnation and the trinity; indeed, he saw the very idea of faith as a violation of rational autonomy. In the Frankfurt years Hegel not only defended these articles but also argued that faith is essential to Christianity. (4) In his earlier years Hegel insisted upon the ultimate authority of reason as a sanction for religious faith. In the Frankfurt years he maintained that religious belief is based upon the experience of love, which transcends reason. The Kantian rationalist thus became a religious mystic.

The main writing in which this reversal takes place, *The Spirit of Christianity and its Fate*, is the stumbling block to all anti-metaphysical, atheistic and humanist interpretations of Hegel.[20] This manuscript is fundamentally the work of a religious mystic, of a repentant rationalist who has been newly converted to the higher realms of religious experience, and to some traditional religious dogmas that articulate it. A defense of mysticism pervades the whole work: Hegel stresses that the infinite consists in a divine love that transcends demonstration; and he maintains that the infinite is accessible only to faith, which consists in an inner experience. To be sure, Hegel will later break with this mysticism, insisting that the infinite can be known only through reason (pp. 88–9); but he will not change his more sympathetic attitude toward Christianity that he acquired during the Frankfurt years.

What explains such a dramatic *volte-face*? Perhaps it was due to the influence of Hölderlin, who had already expressed mystical ideas before Hegel's arrival in Frankfurt. But this is somewhat hypothetical, since we know so little about the discussions between Hegel and Hölderlin during the Frankfurt years.[21] In any case, this could not be a sufficient explanation. For, even if there were an influence, there must have been something in Hegel's development that made him receptive to it. Ultimately, the answer lies in the inner tensions of Hegel's intellectual development.

The main problem facing Hegel in his Tübingen and Berne years was how to formulate the doctrines of a modern civil religion. Hegel demanded that these doctrines satisfy three criteria: (1) they had to be founded on reason; (2) they had to appeal to the heart and imagination; and (3) they had to serve all the needs of life, especially public and official transactions (TE I, 33/20). The chief obstacle facing Hegel was the Christian legacy, which clashed violently with these desiderata. Contrary to (1), its fundamental teachings were infected with positivity; and contrary to (3), Christianity valued personal salvation over the common good, and its precepts were more suitable for a sect than a state. On the other hand, Hegel recognized that a civic religion would have to be based on Christianity, which had been the dominating force in the development of Western culture for nearly two millennia. He also realized that it was hopeless trying to revive a pagan mythology in the age of Enlightenment.

So the tension was that Hegel *had to*, but also *could not*, build his civic religion on Christianity. In the Berne years Hegel's solution to this problem was to interpret Christianity so that it seemed – if not to himself at least to the people – to be a religion of reason. Hence he wrote his *Life of Jesus*, a story of Jesus's life, according to which Christ is a preacher of Kantian morality. But the first person who did not believe in this new myth of reason was Hegel himself. For it clashes violently with his belief in the positivity of Christianity. Already in the *Berne Fragments* Hegel had argued that Christ was an inferior teacher to Socrates because Christ demanded surrendering to faith rather than independent thinking. Ideally, Hegel really wanted Socrates to be the guiding spirit behind his civic religion; but he could not make such a move in the context of his time, which remained in the grip of the Christian tradition.

If, then, Hegel were to uphold his ideal of a civic religion, and if he had to base it upon Christianity, he had no other recourse than to *re-interpret* the meaning of Christianity. This is just what happens in the Frankfurt years. The fundamental move forward is that Hegel now has a new and more plausible interpretation of Christianity. He no longer sees Jesus as the spokesman for Kantian morality but as the preacher of love. After all, there was much stronger biblical evidence for such a reading, first and foremost the gospel of John, which Hegel cites often.[22] Such a reading had none of the forced anachronism of making Christ a preacher of Kantian morality. With this reinterpretation Hegel was now in a position to appropriate and explain many of the fundamental doctrines of the Church, such as the incarnation and the trinity. Now even his attitude toward Kant would have to change, given that Kant's ethics remained on the level of duty and had not recognized the higher power of love.

However strategic, the new interpretation of Christianity was still only a temporary solution. For Hegel also realized in the Frankfurt years that the gospel of love was not suitable for his civic religion. While it certainly appealed to the heart and the imagination, it was also an ethic more suitable for a sect than an entire society. While I love my brethren, it is hard to muster any affection for other citizens of a large state. Furthermore, the mystical elements behind love did not satisfy the demands of reason, one of the fundamental desiderata of a civic religion. Paradoxically, the rationalism of Hegel's later theology was already latent in his mysticism, especially the equation of God with the divine *logos* (GC 374/307).

A NEW RELIGION

It was only in the Jena years (1801–7) that Hegel sketched the outlines of his mature philosophy of religion. The most important development of this period was his attempt to reconcile the realms of philosophy and faith. It was during these years that he first conceived his dialectic to ascend the absolute. The mysticism of the Frankfurt years, which had placed faith above reason, disappeared in the face of Hegel's growing recognition of the need to justify the idea of the absolute. The precise stages in which Hegel developed his dialectic, and moved toward his later rationalism, are not our concern here.[23] Our sole interest is to determine the nature of Hegel's religious, and indeed Christian, belief.

The religious dimension of Hegel's thinking in the Jena years is plain, profound and pervasive. In the beginning of his *Differenzschrift*, and in his 1801/2 lectures on logic and metaphysics, Hegel is explicit that the aim of philosophy is to know the absolute (D II, 25/94; GW V, 271). In a short review from the *Critical Journal* he wrote that the idea of God should again be placed at the pinnacle of philosophy, so that it is 'the only ground of everything, the single *principium essendi* and *cognoscendi*' (W II, 195). The program for a reconciliation of faith and reason is declared and defended in most detail in *Faith and Knowledge*, where Hegel criticizes the dualism between reason and faith in Kant, Jacobi and Fichte. What Hegel aspires to is 'a speculative Good Friday' where reason resurrects itself from the ashes of reflection, ascending to the absolute through the negation of the categories of the understanding (GuW II, 432–3/190–1).

But if this is a religious agenda, is it a Christian one? It would be a complete misunderstanding of Hegel to think that he now regards himself, in any orthodox sense, as a Christian philosopher. His new sympathy toward Christianity never amounted to a Christian conversion. It is indeed telling that, although Hegel uses Christian metaphors to describe his philosophy, he refuses to call it Christian; indeed, he is explicit that it involves *transcending* Christianity. This is evident from two important but neglected sources: the conclusion of his *System of Ethical Life*, of which we only have a summary handed down by Rosenkranz;[24] and an essay of the Jena years co-written with Schelling for the *Critical Journal*.[25] In the first writing Hegel states that the task of philosophy is to establish *a new religion* that is neither Protestant nor Catholic. Hegel is so far from identifying himself with Protestantism that he regards it as an expression of extreme alienation of the self from the world, the very problem he wants to overcome. In the second writing Hegel makes it clear that Christianity and paganism are both partial perspectives that should be overcome in the new higher standpoint of philosophy. If it was the essence of Christianity to begin with the infinite and descend to the finite, it was the essence of paganism to begin with the finite and ascend to the infinite. The new higher standpoint of philosophy will unite both perspectives. It will see the divine in nature, to correct paganism; but it will also see nature in the divine, to complement Christianity.

Undoubtedly, the most important text for an understanding of Hegel's attitude toward Christianity in the Jena years is the 'Unhappy Consciousness' chapter of the *Phenomenology*. The mysticism of the Frankfurt years never dulled Hegel's animus against some aspects of Christianity. Some of the anti-Christian spleen of the *Berne Fragments* resurfaces in 'The Unhappy Consciousness'. This chapter is a passionate critique of traditional Christianity, more specifically its transcendent God and its ethic of salvation. Although Hegel never mentions a specific historical figure, his chief target is the Christian view of life on earth as a pilgrimage on the way to heaven, the view articulated most notably by Augustine in Book XIX of *The City of God*. Since the Christian sees his salvation in heaven, he regards himself as a stranger on earth. The highest good cannot be in the earthly city, which is a realm of disease, death and destruction, and it therefore has to be found in the heavenly city. But the Christian also has to wrestle with his own feeling of unworthiness, his consciousness of sin, which makes him deserve only eternal perdition. Hegel argues that the Christian cannot find hope even in the doctrines of trinity and resurrection, at least on their orthodox interpretation. Although these doctrines are supposed to effect a reconciliation between God and man, they only solidify and reinforce their separation. This is because the appearance of Christ is only contingent, a single historical event, and because Christ is only a single individual, the uniquely favored son of God. The death of Christ means that God has withdrawn from the world, and that there are no longer direct mediators between individual and God. Hence the unhappy consciousness, in the depth of despair, concludes that 'God himself is dead'.

The 'Unhappy Consciousness' chapter of the *Phenomenology* shows very clearly why Hegel must reject traditional Christianity: it was the most extreme form of alienation between self and world. But if this chapter is anti-Christian, is it anti-religious? It scarcely follows from its critique of traditional Christianity that Hegel was a secular humanist. On the contrary, just because it was Hegel's aim to overcome the alienation between self and world he still gave a fundamental role to religion. It was religion that would reconcile the individual to his world by showing him the immanence of the divine in nature and history. So if the solution to the problem of alienation was to deny a transcendent God, it was also to affirm an immanent one.

The redolent phrase 'the death of God' in the *Phenomenology* has been taken as the motto and focus for the humanist interpretation of Hegel. The phrase appears often in Hegel's writings: at the close of *Faith and Knowledge*, in the Rosenkranz report on the *System of Ethical Life*, in the 'Revealed Religion' section of the *Phenomenology*, where it refers back to the 'Unhappy Consciousness' section, and finally in the lectures on the philosophy of religion.[26] The phrase does not mean, however, what Feuerbach or Nietzsche later meant by it: the irrelevance of faith in a more secular culture. Instead, Hegel uses it to declare the end of traditional Christianity and the need for a new religion, or at the very least a new understanding of Christianity.

The phrase refers to the death of Christ, the son of God, on the cross. Its origin appears to have been Johann Rist's hymn '*O grosse Not! Gott selbst ist tod. Am Kreuz ist er gestorben*' (Oh, great need! God himself is dead. He has died on the cross).[27] Hegel explains that the death of Christ fills the Christian with 'infinite grief' because God has withdrawn from the world by forsaking his only begotten son (W II, 432–3/190–1). Now that the mediator between God and man has died, it seems that there is no hope of redemption or resurrection. But this death is only one moment in the life of the idea, Hegel reassures us. It is the moment of negativity that is to be negated itself in a new resurrection. We should interpret the death and resurrection of Christ not as an historical event, Hegel suggests, but as a metaphor for the life of the spirit. It expresses the fact that we must lose and discover ourselves in the experience of love and in the development of reason.

Ultimately, Hegel's attitude toward Christianity in the Jena years was ambivalent or Janus-faced. He wanted to unite paganism with Christianity, to divinize nature and to naturalize the divine. Both Christian and humanist readings of Hegel fail to do justice to this attitude because they are one-sided. The Christian does not see that Hegel intends to naturalize the divine; the humanist ignores that he wants to divinize nature. For the same reason, the common statement that Hegel secularizes the Christian tradition is both profoundly correct and profoundly misleading. It is correct because Hegel rationalizes the concept of God, denying its supernatural status and making it immanent in the world, so that God is inseparable from nature and history. But it is also misleading because it suggests that Hegel reduces God down to the level of nature and history, as if he were nothing more than the totality of natural and historical events. This does not see that Hegel wanted to divinize nature and history as much as to naturalize and historicize the divine.

In general, we must avoid inflating or deflating Hegel's concept of the divine. The divine is first in the order of explanation, but not first in the order of existence. If it comes to existence only in nature and history, it also cannot be reduced down to the sum total of all historical and natural events, for it is the whole that makes all these events possible. The Christian interpretation is guilty of inflating Hegel's concept of God, as if it were first not only in essence but also in existence; it then appears as if God denotes a substance that, because it is conceptually prior to the world, also exists prior to it. The humanist interpretation is guilty of deflating Hegel's concept, as if it were secondary in essence because it is so in existence; it then seems as if God were nothing more than the sum total of all particular things, a mere pious term for the universe.

MATURE STANDPOINT

The program of Hegel's Jena years set the agenda for his mature philosophy of religion, which took its final form in his Berlin lectures. Hegel lectured four times on the philosophy of religion, in 1821, 1824, 1827 and in the year of his death, 1831. What is most remarkable is the degree of continuity between his mature philosophy of religion and the Jena years. But there is still one striking difference: Hegel's later confession that he is a Lutheran. If sincere, the confession signals Hegel's self-consciousness as a Christian philosopher; it means the abandonment of the Jena ideal of a new religion.

In the preface to the second edition of his *Encyclopedia* (1827) Hegel made a revealing statement about the purpose of his mature philosophy and its relation to religion. He wrote that the task of philosophy is to find the rational core behind religion and state. Its purpose is 'to recognize, indeed to justify' the 'rational actuality of law and a simple religion and piety' (EPW VIII, 15/5). Hegel wanted to restore the natural harmony between philosophy and its culture that had been broken by the radical criticism of the Enlightenment. There was a happier time, he wrote, when philosophy was in harmony with church and state, when it attempted to justify them through natural law and religion. But this natural harmony was broken through the radical criticism of the Enlightenment. Now it is time, he affirms, to create a new higher synthesis, but one that returns to the original harmony of philosophy and culture through radical criticism. By the same criticism that once undermined state and church, philosophy will 'contradict contradiction itself', so that 'the spirit celebrates its own reconciliation with itself'.

Hegel seems to give philosophy the same conservative agenda in religion that he gave it in politics. The analogy with the preface to the *Philosophy of Right* is unmistakable. Just as in politics the philosopher should not prescribe how we ought to live, so in religion he should not prescribe what we ought to believe. Whether in religion or in politics, the task of philosophy is to find the rationality that is actualized in current practices and institutions. It was indeed on just these grounds that Haym charged Hegel's philosophy of religion with the same reactionary tendencies as his political philosophy. It seemed to Haym that Hegel's philosophy of religion would attempt to rationalize the Prussian Church just as his *Philosophy of Right* defended the Prussian state.[28] Hegel's apparent reactionary tendencies also seem to provide the perfect context to understand his Lutheran confession: if the philosopher rationalizes Prussian institutions, should he not declare his loyalty to them?

But this reading is much too simplistic. The same ambivalence that appears in Hegel's double dictum resurfaces in his philosophy of religion (see pp. 221–3). The double dictum states that the actual is rational – there is reason in the present institutions – and that the rational is actual – the standards of reason will be realized in history. Applying this dictum to the Church, the philosopher has to recognize that, though there is some rationality present in the Church, the Church will also have to change to realize the standards of reason. If there is reason behind ecclesiastical history as much as political history, then the Church must change as much as the state to become fully rational. The same qualification that Hegel made for the rationality of the actual in the case of the state also holds for

the Church: not everything that exists qualifies as actual (§6). With
this crucial qualification – introduced quite pointedly immediately
after announcing his reconciliation program – Hegel introduced all
the critical distance he could desire between his philosophy and the
official Prussian Church.

The ambivalence of the double dictum accounts for what has
been rightly dubbed 'the double-edged sword' of Hegel's philosophy of religion.[29] Hegel's philosophy is at once both an apology
and a critique of traditional Christianity. To be sure, it attempts to
rationalize Christian doctrine; but in doing so it also purges it of
its non-rational elements, many of which belong to traditional
Christianity. It is far too simplistic, therefore, to see Hegel from a
one-sided perspective, as either a left-wing humanist-atheist or a
right-wing apologist for the Prussian State Church. In general,
Hegel's relationship toward traditional Christianity was typical of
his dialectic: it both preserves and negates its subject matter.

The ambivalence of the double dictum also applies to Hegel's
Lutheran confession. It is the reason that Hegel both identifies with,
and distances himself from, Lutheranism. But if this confession was
not the declaration of a reactionary, what are we to make of it? We
could read it as a political ploy, as appeasement of the Prussian
state.[30] After all, it was only prudent of Hegel to declare his Lutheranism before Altenstein, the Prussian minister of culture, when he
had to protect himself against charges of anti-Catholic sentiment in
his lectures. Hegel contended that he had a right to criticize
Catholicism in an officially Protestant university. But the confession
was not only a political stratagem. For it is striking how in his
lectures Hegel defended Luther's conception of the mass.[31] He gave
great importance to the mass, which he saw as 'the central point
of Christian doctrine', from which all other differences followed
(W XVII, 326). He criticized Catholic transubstantiation as well as
the Reformed Church's symbolic conception of the mass; Luther's
conception of the mass – that the spirit and the body of Christ are
present only through the experience of the believer – was 'the

richest in spirit', 'even if it has not fully attained the form of the idea' (W XVII, 327). Not only as a loyal civil servant, then, but also in matters of ecclesiology Hegel could claim to be a Lutheran.

To resolve the question about Hegel's Lutheranism we only have to ask ourselves what Luther meant to Hegel. He was always very clear about Luther's fundamental principle and role in history (GP XX, 49–60/III 146–55). It was Luther who first articulated the principle of subjectivity, so fundamental to the modern world, according to which I should accept no belief that does not agree with my own conscience. When Hegel declared that he was a Lutheran he was affirming first and foremost this principle, which he took to be the very spirit of Luther's teaching. Since this principle plays such a fundamental role in his philosophy (pp. 230–3), he had another good reason to declare himself a Lutheran.

In the end, then, Hegel's Lutheran confession was not mere lip-service. It was a sincere statement of allegiance to a principle and a ritual. But it hardly implied Lutheran orthodoxy; for, as we shall soon see, Hegel departed fundamentally from Luther's theology.

CONCEPT OF GOD

Hegel's ambivalent relationship with traditional Christianity is most apparent from his concept of God. Hegel's concept preserves the traditional definition of God as the infinite; but it negates the traditional interpretation of the infinite as a supernatural entity that exists apart from its creation. In the *Logic* Hegel argues explicitly against any conception of the infinite that would separate it from the finite, or by implication against any conception of the divine that would separate it from the world (WL I, 95–146). If the infinite were conceived in opposition to the finite, he reasons, then it would be finite itself, because it would be limited by the finite. There would then be *per impossibile* a greater reality than the infinite, namely, the unity of the infinite and the finite. The true infinite must therefore include the finite, so that the divine encompasses the entire universe. This concept of the infinite ran counter to the orthodox theistic conception of God, according to which God transcends the world and it makes no difference to God's identity whether it creates the world or not. Against this orthodox concept Hegel bluntly declares: 'Without the world God is not God' (W XVI, 192).

Contrary to traditional Christianity, then, Hegel conceives of God as immanent. God reveals or embodies itself in the finite world, and it is inseparable from its embodiment in nature and history. It is important to stress, however, that it is not reducible to its embodiment, even though it does not transcend it. Precisely because it is the foundation, substance and source of its embodiments, it is something more than them and so irreducible to them. In virtue of God's inseparability from the world, Hegel naturalizes and historicizes the divine; but in virtue of his non-reducibility to the world, he divinizes history and nature.

Some of Hegel's more orthodox contemporaries accused him of pantheism, a serious charge in his day because it was commonly associated with atheism. Since his radical students also interpreted him as a pantheist or atheist, both left and right were in this regard strange bedfellows. Given that Hegel is still often described as a pantheist and interpreted as an atheist, it is important to examine his response to this criticism.[32]

Hegel has two lines of defense against this accusation. His first consists in a *defense* of pantheism. It is a misrepresentation of Hegel's polemic to think that he repudiates pantheism to prove his own orthodoxy.[33] Rather, his strategy is to charge his accusers with having a distorted conception of pantheism. It is a complete misunderstanding, he argues, to equate pantheism with atheism. Such an equation assumes that the pantheist identifies God with the totality of finite things. But, Hegel protests, no one has ever held such a crude position. The pantheist holds that God is the *substance* or *essence* of all finite things, which are only appearances of it. Rather than giving divinity to finite things, the pantheist makes finite things disappear in the divine. It would be better to call such a doctrine 'acosmism', Hegel contends, meaning by that term the disappearance of the finite in the infinite. The main source of misunderstanding about pantheism, he continues, is that people confuse two senses of universality or unity: *abstract* universality or unity, where the parts precede the whole; and *concrete* universality or unity, where the whole precedes its parts by making them possible. What the pantheists or acosmists maintain is that God is the concrete universal or unity behind all things; but their concrete universality or unity is conflated by their enemies with an abstract one, so that it seems as if the pantheists simply identify the divine with the totality of individual things. A simple point, to be sure, but one overlooked by contemporary Hegel scholars, who maintain that Hegel's pantheistic God is only a more pious way of talking about the universe.[34] Assuming for a moment that Hegel's God is pantheistic, there is still a very big difference between equating God with the totality of finite things and making God the source, substance and essence of this totality.

Hegel's second line of defense is that, though pantheism is not atheism, he is not a pantheist after all. Hegel repudiates the charge of pantheism not because he thinks pantheism is false but because he thinks it is incomplete; in other words, pantheism provides a necessary but not sufficient account of God. Hegel agrees with the pantheists that there is a single universal substance that is the essence and source of all finite things; but he disagrees with them in two fundamental respects. First, he does not think that the realm of finitude *disappears* in the absolute; rather, he insists that this very realm *reveals* the absolute, and indeed that the absolute comes into being only through it. Hegel insists that philosophy has to explain the reality of the finite world; and on just this ground, as we have seen, he rejected Spinoza's pantheism (pp. 92–3). Second, he holds that the infinite is not only substance but also subject; to say that it is also subject means that (1) it reveals itself not only in nature, but especially in the sphere of culture and history; and that

(2) it is not only organic but also spiritual, consisting not only in life but also the self-awareness of life.

Hegel's stress on the subjectivity of the absolute was crucial for his attempt to preserve the rationality of Christian beliefs and institutions. Because the pantheistic tradition had not developed the subjective side of the absolute, Hegel argued that it could not uphold some of the fundamental and characteristic beliefs of Christianity, such as the incarnation and the trinity. Hegel held that one could explain such beliefs only in terms of the subjectivity of the absolute. His first attempt to provide such an explanation is in the *Spirit of Christianity*. Here Hegel appeals to the structure of an organism to explain the trinity: the tree is the unity of all its branches yet each branch has its own life while still inseparable from the whole (GC I, 376–7/308–9). Hegel never abandoned this explanation but only elaborated it in his later writings. In the *Encyclopedia* and lectures on the philosophy of religion he explains the three figures of the trinity according to the moments of the concept, the three stages of development characteristic of subjectivity or spirit. The moment of unity is that of the father, the creator of heaven and earth; the moment of difference is that of the son; and the return of difference into unity is the holy spirit (EPW §§567–71). The incarnation and the trinity, Hegel believed, were simply metaphors, intuitions and feelings about this fundamental truth of reason.

It would be rash to conclude, however, that Hegel's deduction of the trinity and the incarnation establish his orthodox status and justify his Lutheran confession. The truth of the matter is that Hegel's theology is the very opposite of Luther's.[35] Hegel's God is rational and acts from the necessity of its own nature alone; Luther's God is mysterious and acts according to free decrees. Hegel's absolute idealism opposes all forms of dualism; Luther's theology is based upon his dualism between the heavenly and earthly. While Luther's faith is based on the Bible, the record of supernatural revelation, Hegel does not believe in miracles and thinks that the Bible is an insufficient foundation for the faith. But these theological differences are minor compared to an even more fundamental one: Hegel's critique of the ethic of salvation. The very heart and soul of Luther's theology was its concern with salvation, its belief that the individual is saved through faith alone. As we have seen, the young Hegel completely rejected this ethic, condemning its obsession with personal fate as a sickness arising from the decline of true republican spirit. The mature Hegel never really abandoned this critique,[36] even if he never explicitly reaffirmed it. When one reads his later lectures on the philosophy of religion Hegel appears to appropriate and reaffirm the Protestant doctrine of salvation.[37] It is as if his early republican spirit has given way to a concern for reconciliation in Christ in the classical Protestant manner. But it is easy to be misled. Hegel accepts the Protestant doctrine only on a symbolic or metaphoric level. Christ's death and resurrection are a symbol for the dialectic of the spirit, for how each individual has to lose his individuality and to find himself in the universality of society and history. To read it in a literal manner creates inconsistencies. For Hegel has undermined the metaphysics that give this doctrine its literal meaning, more specifically its beliefs in the immortality of the soul and the supernatural realm of heaven.[38] These beliefs are incompatible with some of the fundamental tenets of Hegel's metaphysics: that to exist is to be determinate; and that to be determinate is to embody oneself in some place at some time. Hegel has all the classical difficulties Aristotelians have in explaining the Christian belief in the separate existence of the soul; it is this, more than sheer indifference, that explains his curious silence about the immortality of the soul.[39]

THE IDENTITY THESIS

The foundation of Hegel's project to reconcile philosophy and religion is his identity thesis, his claim that both have the same object or subject matter. He could not be more explicit in stating this thesis. He declares that both philosophy and religion have God, and God alone, as their object (EPW §1; VPR I, 63/152). He also says that, in subject matter, there is no fundamental difference between philosophy and theology: 'philosophy is theology' (VPR I, 3–4/84). When philosophy understands itself, he says, it understands religion; and when it understands religion, it understands itself (VPR I, 63/152–3). Philosophy is indeed nothing but a form of worship (VPR I, 63–4/153).

To say that philosophy and religion have the same object does not mean they are identical, however. They are both forms of worship; but they are different kinds of worship. Although they do not differ in content – in what they know – they do differ in form – in how they know their object. Philosophy knows God through the medium of concepts; and religion knows God through the medium of feeling or intuition (EPW §§2–3). Hegel calls the feelings and intuitions of religion 'representations' (Vorstellungen). As a more reflective or self-conscious form of religion, the task of philosophy is to replace representations with concepts. He writes: '. . . philosophy puts thoughts and categories, but more precisely concepts, in the place of representations' (EPW §3R).

The crucial question for Hegel's reconciliation is whether philosophy really can translate the representations of religion into conceptual form. If philosophy distorts these representations by putting them in discursive form, there will be no identity between philosophy and religion after all. So, when philosophy translates feelings and intuitions into concepts there must be no loss of content. Hegel fully realized what was at stake here. In the Encyclopedia he was especially worried about objections that philosophy cannot grasp religion but only distort it (§2R). He insisted that philosophy would have to justify any difference between its own discursive formulations and religious representation (§4).

Hegel knew his claim was very controversial, first and foremost because the romantics held that any translation of intuition and feeling into discursive form must be distortion, not only in form but also in content. In his influential Speeches on Religion Schleiermacher had declared that the intuition of the universe characteristic of religion cannot be formulated in discursive terms.[40] Intuition grasps its object as a whole or unity; but thinking analyzes the object into parts. While intuition sees the object in itself, thinking considers it only in its relations to other things. These points were very familiar to Hegel, who worried greatly about them. Throughout his philosophy of religion, in all its versions, he nervously looked over his shoulder at Schleiermacher, constantly taking issue with him.[41]

This raises the question of how Hegel could justify his translation project, and more specifically his thesis that the conceptual formulations of philosophy are the same in content as the feelings and intuitions of religion. A crucial premise behind Hegel's translation project is his general argument for the possibility of a dialectic (pp. 155–9). If there can be a dialectic, then it would show, against the romantics, that thinking can grasp wholeness and unity after all. Schleiermacher's arguments for the *sui generis* status of intuition and feeling depend on his claim that they alone can grasp unity and wholeness; he simply assumes that all discursive thinking is analytical and conditional. It was just this assumption, though, that Hegel wanted to question with his dialectic. All the resistance to the identity of philosophy and religion, all the insistence on the separation of these realms, he argued, ultimately had its source in a paradigm of thinking as reflection (EPW §§2R, 5).

Yet even if the dialectic were a reality, it still would not be sufficient to support Hegel's general project. For the question remains whether the dialectic *transforms* the object of intuition and feeling in the act of knowing it. Even if the object of thinking is a whole, is it the *same* whole? There are other serious questions about the translation project. How do different forms of consciousness or cognition have the same object? Someone might object that the mode of consciousness or cognition also determines its content, so that each form of awareness has a distinct object. Indeed, Hegel even concedes that thinking of an object *changes* its nature as it is first given in intuition and feeling (EPW §22). But if this is so, how do we know the *original* object?

In the *Encyclopedia* Hegel himself raises this very question (§3). His response to it is very interesting, revealing one of the most important underlying premises of his philosophy of religion. Hegel maintains that intuiting and feeling can have the same object as thinking because they are ultimately only subconscious and inchoate forms of thinking themselves. Reason enters into every characteristic human activity, he maintains, so that all forms of representation are modes of rationality. Hence thinking does not change the object of intuiting or feeling because it only makes explicit what is already implicit in the first place. Hegel questions, therefore, the dualism between thinking and feeling that is so central to the romantic philosophy of religion. It now turns out that the difference between philosophy and religion – the difference in their modes of consciousness or cognition – is not really that much of a difference after all.

The premise behind Hegel's thesis emerges most clearly when he states that 'there is really only *One* thinking' (§2). This was a central theme of German idealism: that there is a unity to theoretical and practical reason, that Kant's three faculties (understanding, will and judgment) are parts of a single system. This idea would have been deeply resisted by Kant himself, who would have regarded it as a relapse into the old dogmatic rationalism of the Leibnizian–Wolffian school, which saw all the powers of the mind as aspects of a single power of representation (*vis representativae*).

Hegel gives another justification for this crucial premise in some later sections in the *Encyclopedia* when he makes a more exact analysis of representation (§§20–3). Hegel's analysis consists in some precise distinctions between sensation, representation and thought (§20R). The distinguishing mark of sensation is that its object is particular; in contrast, the object of thinking is universal. The object of sensation is particular in two senses: first, it is determinate or concrete; and, second, it is isolated, not standing in systematic connection with other particulars. Representation has a middle status between sensation and thinking. Like sensibility, representation might have the particular for its object; but, unlike sensibility, it is universal in form. Where representation differs from sensation is that it transforms its contents into the medium of thinking; even if it has a particular for its object it subsumes it under universals. The distinguishing feature of representation apart from thinking is that, even if it is universal, the content of representation stands isolated, having no systematic connection with other content. Thinking differs from representation not so much in its object – the universal – but in its form – relating the contents to a system. Hence Hegel explains that thinking both preserves and negates the representations of religion through mediation (§12). What he means by mediation is that the representations of religion are related (mediated) to one another or made into parts of a whole (§14R). The representations of religion are negated in their immediacy – their claims to be self-sufficient or independent – but they are preserved in their essential content as parts of the whole.

The main point to see here is that Hegel understands representation as an implicit form of thinking. It is striking that when he first defines representation he refers to Kant's principle of the unity of apperception, according to which a representation is mine only if it is possible for me to be self-conscious of it (§20R). This means for Hegel, as it did indeed for Kant, that representation also involves conceptualization. Hegel endorses Kant's argument in the transcendental deduction that a representation is my own only in so far as I can conceptualize its content and place it in a possible act of judgment. It is through this Kantian point that Hegel secures his claim that representing is ultimately a form of conceptualization. Like Kant, he too thinks that representations are inherently and implicitly universal because they are subconsciously apperceived and categorized. Hence translation of representations into the form of thinking does not distort them; rather, it only makes explicit the universality that is already implicit in them. It was this Kantian point that Hegel would ultimately play off against the romantics, who had so sharply separated feeling from thinking only because they had forgotten the implicit conceptualization necessary to all representation.

Apart from all the problems of its justification, it is also necessary to ask about the implications of the identity thesis. Assuming that the thesis were true, what would follow from it? Not what one might at first think: that philosophy demonstrates all the beliefs held on faith in religion. The translation program does not mean simply having the same beliefs but also having reasons for them. If this were the case, Hegel would have to admit that his program is a failure. For there is significant discrepancy between what his philosophy allows and what traditional religion holds. Hegel frankly admits, for example, that when religion is made rational there is no longer any place for belief in miracles (W XVI, 210–11; XVII, 196–7, 313–20).

It is noteworthy that Hegel does not regard this lack of fit as a refutation for his identity thesis. The reason is that the identity holds not between *beliefs* – the beliefs warranted by philosophy and those held by religion – but between representational *content* – the objects of intuition and feeling and the objects of philosophy. The fact that the thesis holds for intuitions and feeling and not beliefs is crucial, because it gives Hegel room to *interpret* intuitions and feelings. He can still claim that his system provides the best or only rationalization of religious intuition and feeling, even though it is incompatible with many of the beliefs of traditional Christianity. This is because belief is more than intuition and feeling: it also involves an *interpretation* of intuition and feeling. What Hegel rejects in traditional Christianity, he could argue, is not its intuitions and feelings but simply its *interpretations* of them. While it is possible to reject the beliefs on the grounds that they are a false or distorted interpretation of the content, it is possible to affirm the content itself.

At this point one might object that the translation project is something of a sleight-of-hand. For what Hegel is translating into the discourse of philosophy is not the intuition and feeling of religion but really only his *interpretation* of these intuitions and feelings. The starting point of the translation is not what one first thinks – faith as it is historically given, as it is now codified by the Protestant Churches. Rather, it begins only from intuitions and feelings abstracted from their *institutional* interpretation. A successful translation is guaranteed because all that Hegel puts into conceptual terms is his interpretation of the intuitions and feelings.

In response to this objection Hegel could point out that, although he is indeed rationalizing only his interpretation of intuition and feeling, his interpretation is still the only rational one, the only one to give the content of these intuitions and feelings a place in the system of reason. Although there is some discrepancy between his system and traditional beliefs, this is only a discrepancy in the *interpretation* of intuition and feeling and does not involve a rejection of intuition and feeling *per se*.

Part Three
**Epistemological
Foundations**

Seven

The Dialectic

A CRITICAL FOUNDATION FOR METAPHYSICS

Having sketched Hegel's metaphysics in previous chapters (Three–Six), we must now see how he attempted to justify it. The problem of justification was indeed an especially formidable one for Hegel. His absolute idealism, his organicism, his concept of spirit and notion of God, are metaphysics on the grandest scale. Through pure thinking alone Hegel attempts to give us knowledge of reality in itself, the absolute or the universe as a whole. It was in just this sense, however, that Kant had attacked the possibility of metaphysics in the *Critique of Pure Reason*. Hegel had no choice, therefore, but to face the Kantian challenge. After all, as we saw (pp. 54–5), Hegel affirms what Kant denies: that it is possible to have a knowledge through pure reason of the absolute or the unconditioned.

To the neo-Kantians, Hegel failed to address this challenge. His metaphysics was an irresponsible relapse into pre-Kantian 'dogmatism', a self-conscious attempt to revive the tradition of Leibniz, Malebranche and Spinoza, which had uncritically attempted to give us knowledge through pure reason about reality in itself. Hegel himself seemed to encourage this charge when, in the introduction to the *Encyclopedia*, he commended the old rationalism for its attempt to know reality through pure thinking, and even placed it on a higher level than Kantian criticism (§28). It was on these grounds that the neo-Kantians cried: '*Back to Kant!*' They demanded a return to epistemic responsibility, so that philosophy became a handmaiden to the empirical sciences and did little more than examine the limits of knowledge.

But the neo-Kantian interdict against Hegel did him scant justice. It completely ignored the extent to which he endorsed Kantian criticism and distanced himself from the rationalist tradition. This is fully clear from Hegel's retrospective assessment of the old metaphysics and Kantian criticism in the introduction to the *Encyclopedia*. It was one of Kant's great merits, he wrote, to have subjected the old metaphysics to criticism (§41A1). He agreed entirely with Kant that one of the chief failures of past metaphysics was its *dogmatism*, i.e. its failure to investigate the powers and limits of reason (§26). Hence Hegel fully endorsed the demands of Kantian criticism, insisting that 'any future metaphysics that comes forward as a science alone' would first have to pass the test of criticism. The old metaphysics was naive, because it simply assumed that we could know truth through thinking alone without having first investigated this possibility. There were two respects, Hegel further explained, in which the old metaphysics was uncritical: first, it did not examine the meaning of the concepts that it applied to the unconditioned; and, second, it did not investigate the limitations of the traditional forms of judgment in knowing the truth (§28R). Hegel's diagnosis of the chief failing of the old metaphysics is very similar to Kant's: its main problem was that it applied the concepts of the understanding to the infinite or the unconditioned (§28A). Since these concepts are valid only for the finite realm of experience, we cannot apply them to the infinite.

So far was Hegel from resisting Kant's demand for criticism that he insisted that Kant had not gone far enough. In the *Encyclopedia* he argued that Kant's critique of metaphysics had been deficient on several counts (§41A1–2). First, Kant did not investigate the inherent logic of concepts themselves, determining their precise meaning and powers. Rather, he just classified concepts as either subjective or objective according to his presupposed epistemological principles. Second, Kant insisted that we should have a criterion of knowledge before we make claims to knowledge; but this demand created an infinite regress, for the criterion of knowledge too amounts to a claim to knowledge, so that we need another higher criterion to test it. Third, Kant failed to see that we cannot criticize the forms of thinking without first using them. Hegel likened his attempt to know the logic of our concepts before using them to the efforts of the wise Scholasticus to learn to swim before jumping in the water. All these points came together in Hegel's complaint that the method of Kantian criticism is *external*, presupposing the truth of some standard of criticism that does not derive from the concepts themselves. Against Kant, Hegel insisted that the criticism of knowledge must be *internal*, so that the subject matter is evaluated according to its own inherent standards and goals. It is for this reason that the method of the *Phenomenology* would be the *self*-examination or *self*-criticism of consciousness.

It was Hegel's recognition of the rightful demands of Kantian criticism that eventually forced him to abandon the concept of intellectual intuition, which, along with Schelling, he once championed as the organ of absolute knowledge. An intellectual intuition was meant to be a purely experiential, immediate or non-discursive grasp of the absolute. In the late 1790s and early 1800s Hegel advocated intellectual intuition because he shared the common romantic view that reason cannot grasp the unconditioned. Since reason grasps everything according to the principle of sufficient reason, it postulates an infinite series of conditions or causes, so that it is incapable of conceiving what is unconditioned or self-causing. Around 1804, however, Hegel began to realize that the appeal to an intellectual intuition is ultimately dogmatic.[1] If someone contradicts the claims of intellectual intuition, it is impossible to demonstrate them according to the common understanding. What right, then, does the intuition have to our assent? The principle of self-thought of the critical philosophy – a principle that Hegel explicitly reaffirmed – demands that we accept only those beliefs that agree with the critical exercise of our own reason; but the claims of an intellectual intuition pretend to stand above any such exercise.

Hegel's endorsement of Kantian criticism, his critique of the methods of the older rationalism, and his rejection of intellectual intuition, all derived from his deeply held conviction that metaphysics stood in need of a new foundation. Ever since his early Jena years, Hegel's fundamental concern was to provide a critical foundation for metaphysics. This new metaphysics would be critical in the sense that it would begin with a critique of knowledge – an examination of the limits and powers of reason – and then derive metaphysics from it. It would start with the examination of our ordinary experience or the use of our everyday concepts, and then show how the ideas of metaphysics are necessary conditions of such experience or the use of such concepts. In more Kantian terms, Hegel was saying that the conditions of experience involve not only the intuitions of sensibility and concepts of understanding but also the ideas of reason. Such a metaphysics therefore would be immanent in the Kantian sense, remaining within the limits of experience and renouncing speculation beyond it.

Hegel saw his metaphysics not only as a *possibility* but as a *necessity* of the critical philosophy itself. It was only through metaphysics, he argued, that the critical philosophy could resolve its own inherent problems, and more specifically the problem of the possibility of knowledge. As we have already seen (pp. 104–7), during the 1790s many thinkers had argued that Kant's dualisms made it impossible for him to resolve this problem. The possibility of knowledge required some correspondence between the realms of the intellectual and the empirical, the subjective and the objective; but Kant had postulated such a sharp dualism between these realms that any correspondence between them became unintelligible. For Hegel, the necessity of metaphysics therefore derived from the need to explain the single source of Kant's divided faculties. Kant himself had forsworn all speculation about the single source of understanding and sensibility; but, without such speculation, Hegel argued, there could be no resolution of the fundamental problem of the critical philosophy itself.

Once we take into account this point it becomes clear that the neo-Kantian reaction against Hegel's metaphysics really only begged the question against it. For the underlying assumption behind the demand for a return to Kant is that epistemology is autonomous, perfectly capable of resolving its problems on its own without metaphysics. Yet it was just this assumption that had worn so thin, and proven so illusory, to Hegel's generation, the thinkers who came of age in the 1790s. By the late 1790s the dreams of epistemology as a *philosophia prima* had been utterly shattered. After the *Grundsatzkritik* and meta-critical campaign, it had become clear to many not only that epistemology could not be *philosophia prima* but also that it could not resolve its own problems. These developments were completely forgotten by the neo-Kantians, who had fallen into a dogmatic slumber all their own.

MYTHS AND LEGENDS ABOUT DIALECTIC

For Hegel, the problem of justifying metaphysics was essentially one of discovering and following the right philosophical method. It has been wisely said that 'Hegel is the most methodologically self-conscious of all philosophers in the Western tradition'.[2] This statement is especially true of Hegel during his Jena years, when he was in desperate search for the proper methodology to justify his new metaphysics. The eventual fruit of this search was his dialectic.

The very term 'dialectic' is redolent. No aspect of Hegel's philosophy has been more interpreted, more misunderstood, and more controversial. Before we examine its precise structure, it is necessary to correct some misunderstandings and to sort through a few controversies.

The dialectic has been so controversial that some scholars even deny that Hegel had such a method.[3] In the usual sense of the word, a 'method' consists in certain rules, standards and guidelines that one justifies a priori and that one applies to investigate a subject matter. But, in this sense, Hegel utterly opposed having a methodology, and he was critical of philosophers who claimed to have one. Hence he objected to Kant's epistemology because it applied an a priori standard of knowledge to evaluate all claims to knowledge; and he attacked Schelling's *Naturphilosophie* because it mechanically applied a priori schemata to phenomena. Against all such a priori methods, Hegel insisted that the philosopher should bracket his standards, rules and guidelines and simply examine the subject matter for its own sake. The standards, rules and guidelines appropriate to a subject matter should be the result, not the starting point, of the investigation. So, if Hegel has any methodology at all, it appears to be an *anti*-methodology, a method to suspend all methods.

Hegel's term for his own anti-methodology is 'the concept' (*der Begriff*), which designates the inherent form of an object, its inner purpose. It is the purpose of enquiry to grasp this inner form, Hegel argues, and it is for this reason that he demands suspending all preconceptions. If the philosopher simply applies his a priori ideas to the subject matter, he has no guarantee that he grasps its inner form or the object as it is in itself; for all he knows, he sees the object only as it is for him. When Hegel uses the term 'dialectic' it usually designates the 'self-organization' of the subject matter, its 'inner necessity' and 'inherent movement'. The dialectic is what follows from the concept of the thing. It is flatly contrary to Hegel's intention, therefore, to assume that the dialectic is an a priori methodology, or indeed a kind of logic, that one can apply to any subject matter. The dialectic is the very opposite: it is the inner movement of the subject matter, what evolves from it rather than what the philosopher applies to it.

It seems, then, that it would be only in the spirit of Hegel to banish all talk about method, let alone a dialectic. But this too would be only another misconception. Although Hegel thinks that the proper method for a subject matter cannot be determined a priori at the beginning of an enquiry, he still holds that it can be determined a posteriori at its end. When the dialectic of his subject matter ends, he can then abstract from it a general structure, though such a summary will have only a *post facto* validity. On just these grounds there is a detailed discussion of methodology at the end of the *Science of Logic*. Of course, the philosopher can discuss methodology even prior to enquiry – as Hegel himself does in the *Phenomenology* – but he must recognize that his conclusions are only preliminary, a mere assurance of the truth to be assessed by later investigation. Sure enough, Hegel often makes just these caveats in his prefaces and introductions. So we can talk about Hegel's dialectic after all, and we can do so without violating his spirit, provided that we see it as nothing more than an a posteriori summary of the formal structure of his investigations.

Although it is possible to talk about a dialectic, it is advisable to avoid the most popular way of explaining it: in terms of the schema 'thesis–antithesis–synthesis'. Hegel himself never used this terminology, and he criticized the use of all schemata.[4] In the *Phenomenology* Hegel did praise 'the triadic form' that had been rediscovered by Kant, describing it even as 'the concept of science' (PG 41/¶50); but this is a reference to the triadic form of Kant's table of categories, not a method of thesis–antithesis–synthesis. Although Kant's antinomies were the inspiration for Hegel's dialectic, Hegel never used Kant's method of exposition of thesis and antithesis. It has been said that this method was used by Fichte and Schelling, and then by extension wrongly attributed to Hegel; but it corresponds to nothing in Fichte or Schelling, let alone Hegel.[5]

Another common misconception is that the dialectic is some kind of alternative logic, having its own distinctive principles to compete with traditional logic. But Hegel's dialectic was never meant to be a *formal* logic, one that determines the fundamental laws of inference governing all propositions, whatever their content. In its most general form in the *Science of Logic* the dialectic is a metaphysics whose main task is to determine the general structure of being. Such a metaphysics does not compete with formal logic because it has a content all its own, even if a very general one, namely, the most general categories of being. Those who have pronounced the death sentence on Hegel's logic have simply recycled the common misconception that it is a competitor to traditional logic.[6]

Still another popular misconception is that Hegel's dialectic is committed to denying the laws of identity and contradiction. To be sure, Hegel criticized traditional logic for its strict and rigid adherence to the laws of identity, contradiction and excluded middle. There are indeed passages in Hegel where he seems to countenance contradiction itself.[7] His detractors have not been slow in pointing out the disastrous consequences: that it is possible to prove any proposition whatsoever.[8] Still, even if Hegel is confused, his dialectic is not *committed* to a denial of these laws, and its operations really presuppose them. Hegel's criticisms of traditional logic have to be understood in their original context, which shows that Hegel is not rejecting these laws themselves but simply the *metaphysical application* of them. More precisely, he is criticizing a very specific metaphysical doctrine: that we can completely determine substance, reality in itself, through one predicate alone. Hegel rejects this claim because he thinks (on independent metaphysical grounds) that reality in itself is the universe as a whole, which has to be described as both F and -F. Since, however, he holds that F and -F are true of *distinct* parts of the whole, there is no violation of the law of contradiction. Indeed, the point of the dialectic will be *to remove* contradictions by showing how contradictory predicates that seem true of the same thing are really only true of *different* parts or aspects of the same thing. What Hegel is criticizing, then, is not the law of identity as such but the confusion of this law with the metaphysical claim that reality in itself must have one property and not another. We naturally but fallaciously move from 'No single thing is both F and -F at the same time' to 'Reality as a whole cannot be both F and -F at the same time'. Because it is true of each single thing that it cannot be both F and -F, we conclude that reality as a whole cannot be both F and -F. The problem is that we treat reality as a whole as if it were just another entity, another part of the whole.

STRUCTURE OF THE DIALECTIC IN THE *LOGIC*

Hegel's attempt to provide a critical foundation for metaphysics left him with a quandary. Any such foundation would have to recognize the rights of the understanding, and more specifically the right of the common understanding to think for itself and to accept only those beliefs for which it could find sufficient evidence. But there was a fundamental contradiction between the understanding and the subject matter of metaphysics, a contradiction made apparent to him through Kant's and Jacobi's critique of reason. The subject matter of metaphysics is the absolute, which is infinite, unconditioned and indivisible; but, since its concepts are finite, conditioned and divisive, the understanding destroys such an object in the very act of conceiving it.

Kant and Jacobi put forward three arguments for this conclusion. (1) The understanding proceeds according to the principle of sufficient reason, attempting to find the causes for all events, the necessary and sufficient conditions for their occurrence. For any given event, it finds a prior condition or cause, and so on *ad infinitum*. Since, however, the absolute is self-causing or unconditioned, to understand it according to the principle of sufficient reason would be to give a cause for the self-causing, a condition for the unconditioned. (2) The understanding is an analytical power, i.e. it takes a whole and divides it into its parts, each of which it regards as self-sufficient apart from the whole. But the absolute is indivisible, a whole that precedes its parts by making them possible. Hence the attempt to understand the absolute would be to divide the indivisible. (3) All concepts are finite or limited because they have their determinate meaning only through negation; but the infinite is by definition infinite or unlimited, so that to conceive or describe it would be to make it finite.

The dialectic was Hegel's response to these arguments. The basic strategy and idea behind the dialectic is simple, even if its application in specific cases is often very complex. The dialectic arises from an inevitable contradiction in the procedures of the understanding. The understanding contradicts itself because it both *separates* things, as if they were completely independent of one another, and *connects* them, as if neither could exist apart from the other. It separates things when it analyzes them into their parts, each of which is given a self-sufficient status; and it connects them according to the principle of sufficient reason, showing how each event has a cause, or how each part inheres in a still smaller part, and so on *ad infinitum*. Hence the understanding ascribes both independence and dependence to things. The only way to resolve the contradiction, it turns out, is to reinterpret the independent or self-sufficient term as the whole of which all connected or dependent terms are only parts. The mistake of the understanding arose in giving self-sufficient status to a part of the whole; it rectifies its error and resolves its contradiction when it ascends to the standpoint of the whole itself.

The crucial point to see here is that the ascent to the whole comes from within the understanding itself, deriving from its own inherent activity and proceeding according to its own laws. It does not come from any higher act of intuition or conception that abstracts from its activity, and that needs some other kind of justification. Although Hegel often distinguishes between reason (*Vernunft*) and understanding (*Verstand*), these terms do not designate completely independent functions or faculties. Reason is simply the necessary result of the immanent movement of the understanding. Both the contradiction and its resolution proceed strictly according to its own laws and have to be warranted by its own insight. Whether the dialectic is correct can be determined every step along the way by the understanding itself, and there is no reason to think that it cannot appraise the dialectic until its course is finished.[9]

The chief result of the dialectic is that reason is not only a form of mechanical explanation, which shows how one finite thing depends upon another, but also a form of holistic explanation, which shows how all finite things are parts of a wider whole. The fundamental mistake of Jacobi and Kant, in Hegel's view, was that they understood reason according to a mechanical paradigm of explanation, which understands an event by its prior causes and so on *ad infinitum*. Since they believed that reason is limited to such a form of explanation, they had to conclude it could never grasp the unconditioned, which is never given in the series of finite causes. They failed to see, however, that reason also has the power to explain the presence of the entire series of causes, to grasp the reason for which it exists in the first place. The inner logic of the understanding ultimately demands that we see both cause and effect, condition and conditioned, as parts of a single indivisible whole.

There are many ways of explaining Hegel's dialectic, but one of the simplest, and historically most accurate, is to see it as Hegel's response to Kant's antinomies.[10] In the Transcendental Dialectic of the *Critique of Pure Reason* Kant had argued that reason of necessity contradicts itself whenever it transcends the limits of possible experience. On the one hand, reason finds itself compelled to postulate the unconditioned to bring the totality of conditions to completion; there must be some first cause, some ultimate constituents, because otherwise there would be an infinite regress and nothing would come into being. On the other hand, however, reason is forced always to seek the condition for any event or thing, so that for any cause or constituent there must be some prior cause or simpler constituent. Kant discovered four such antinomies, which all have the same basic structure. In the thesis the understanding *must* postulate something unconditioned; and in the antithesis it *cannot* postulate something unconditioned because it must regard everything as conditioned and seek the conditions for it. In sum, the contradiction consists in the fact that the series of explanation *must* and *cannot* end.

What Hegel admired in Kant's antinomies was his insight into the necessity of the contradictions of the understanding (EPW §48R). Kant rightly saw that the understanding of necessity contradicts itself whenever it goes beyond the limits of experience; he also fully recognized that the understanding is compelled to go beyond experience in its attempt to seek the unconditioned cause of all conditions in experience. Hegel agreed with Kant too about the general structure of the antinomies: there is a thesis that postulates something unconditioned, and an antithesis that postulates a condition for everything. When we consider the general structure of the Kantian antinomies – the apparently natural need both to continue and to stop an infinite series of explanation – it is possible to appreciate Hegel's point about the inevitable dialectic of the understanding.

For all his agreement with Kant, Hegel differed from him on several crucial points. First, he criticized Kant for discovering only four antinomies; in his view, there are many such contradictions, which are omnipresent in reason (EPW §48R). Second, Hegel also drew very different lessons from the antinomies. They show not that the understanding must remain within the confines of the finite, but that it must go beyond the finite (EPW §48A). They show that the understanding is *self-transcending*, that it destroys of necessity its own limitations and goes beyond them.

The Hegelian solution to the antinomies is the direct antithesis of the Kantian. For Kant, the solution to the last two antinomies is to divide the world into noumena and phenomena, the realms of the unconditioned and conditioned, where the thesis holds for the noumenal realm and the antithesis for the phenomenal realm. In so dividing the world Kant believed he had given both tendencies of reason their due: if it was possible to postulate the unconditioned for the noumenal realm, it was also possible to postulate the conditioned for the phenomenal realm. But Hegel saw Kant's dualism as part of the problem rather than the solution. The proper solution to the antinomies is not to divide but to unite the noumenal and the phenomenal, unconditioned and conditioned, by showing how both form necessary parts of a single indivisible whole; it was necessary to show, in other words, that the noumenal is within the phenomenal, the unconditioned within the conditioned.

We can have a better understanding of the dialectic if we review its specific stages as outlined by Hegel in the *Encyclopedia* (§§80–2). There Hegel states that there are three stages to the dialectic: the moment of abstraction or the understanding; the dialectical or negatively rational moment; and the speculative or positively rational moment. Each stage deserves separate comment.

The moment of abstraction or the understanding

This moment is the analogue of the Kantian thesis. The understanding postulates something unconditioned or something absolute, which it attempts to conceive in itself, as if it were independent and self-sufficient. This is the moment of the understanding whose specific virtue is to make sharp and fast distinctions between things, each of which it regards as self-sufficient and independent. But, in insisting upon its hard and fast distinctions, the understanding is in fact making a *metaphysical* claim: it holds that something exists in itself, that it can exist on its own without other things.

The dialectical or negatively rational moment

This moment is the correlate of the Kantian antithesis. When the understanding examines one of its terms it finds that it is not self-sufficient after all, but that it is only comprehensible through its relations to other things. It finds that it has to seek the reason for its apparently self-sufficient terms, because it is artificial to stop at any given point.

This stage is dialectical because the understanding is caught in a contradiction: it asserts that the unit is self-sufficient or comprehensible only in itself, because it is the final term of analysis; and that the unit is comprehensible only through its relations or connections to other things, because we can always find some further reason outside itself. The contradiction is that we must affirm both thesis and antithesis: the unit of analysis is both unconditioned and conditioned, both independent and dependent.

The speculative or positively rational moment

This final stage is characteristically Hegelian, whereas the former stages had analogues in Kant. The understanding now finds that the only way to resolve the contradiction is to say that what is absolute or independent is not one thing alone, but the whole of that thing and all others upon which it depends. If we make this move then we can still save the central claim of the thesis – that there is something self-sufficient or unconditioned – and we can also admit the basic thrust of the antithesis – that any particular thing is dependent or conditioned We avoid the contradiction if we ascend a higher level, to the standpoint of the whole, of which the unit and that on which it depends are only parts. While any part of this whole is conditioned and dependent, the whole itself is unconditioned or independent with respect to them.

The problem with the understanding is that it unwittingly sees the unconditioned simply as *one part of the whole*, whereas the only thing that can be unconditioned is the whole, of which the unit and that on which it depends are only parts. This whole is unconditioned relative to its parts since it does not stand in relation to them as they stand in relation to one another. They stand to one another as one thing *outside* or *external* to another; but the parts are internal to the whole. The whole's relation to its parts is a *self-relation*; but the parts, before they are integrated into the whole, stand in relation to an other.

Of course, the dialectic must continue. The same contradiction arises for the whole, of which the unconditioned and conditioned are only parts. It claims to be unconditioned; but there is something else, on the same level, upon which it depends, so that it too is conditioned. The same thesis and antithesis work on the new level. The dialectic will go on until we reach the absolute whole, that which includes everything within itself, and so cannot possibly depend upon anything outside itself. When this happens the system will be complete, and we will have achieved knowledge of the absolute.

TASK OF DIALECTIC IN THE *PHENOMENOLOGY*

Hegel first developed his idea of a dialectic in his 1801 Dif-ferenzschrift in the section entitled 'Reflection as Instrument of Philosophizing'. There Hegel sketched the idea of a dialectic of reflection whereby the concepts of the understanding of necessity contradict themselves and resolve their contradiction by ascending to the level of the infinite whole (II, 25–30/94–7). The earlier sketch of the dialectic in the 1800 *Systemfragment* does not lead to such a positive result: it shows only the contradictions inherent in the understanding, and the infinite remains beyond the scope of reason.[11] Yet in the *Differenzschrift* too Hegel vascillated about the status of his dialectic. Sometimes he wrote as if knowledge of the absolute required an intellectual intuition independent of reflection, or as if the dialectic led only to a negative result, destroying the concepts of reflection in their attempt to know the absolute (II 18, 20, 42, 45/88, 89–90, 110, 112). But at other times he maintained that the ideas of reason are the positive result of the dialectic of reflection, so that they can be deduced from its contradictions (II 25, 44/94, 111). Hegel still held to the need for an intellectual intuition, and shared Schelling's view that there could not be an introduction to the standpoint of philosophy, which was esoteric and mysterious to ordinary consciousness and understanding. As Hegel originally conceived his dialectic, then, it did not fully or unequivocally satisfy the demands of Kantian criticism.

The dialectic first appears in its fully mature form in Hegel's 1807 *Phenomenology of Spirit*. This work grew out of Hegel's rejection of intellectual intuition and his recognition that it is necessary to provide some kind of critical foundation for metaphysics. After

Schelling's departure from Jena in 1803 Hegel became more and more preoccupied with the problem of providing a foundation for his metaphysics.[12] He now realized that it was question-begging to appeal to an intellectual intuition because its fundamental claim – that the subject and object are identical in the absolute – is contradicted by ordinary consciousness, which finds a dualism between subject and object in experience. Ordinary consciousness would now have to discover the truth of the standpoint of philosophy from within, according to its own *self*-examination and *self*-criticism.

Hegel's strategy to resurrect metaphysics on the basis of the Kantian critique of knowledge is most apparent from his original conception of the *Phenomenology*: a 'science of the experience of consciousness' (*Wissenschaft der Erfahrung des Bewusstseins*).[13] This science made experience its fundamental standard of knowledge. 'Consciousness knows and conceives nothing more than what is within its experience . . .', Hegel wrote in the preface (32/¶36).[14] The metaphysician's claim to absolute knowledge therefore has to be tested against, and if true ultimately derived from, the experience of consciousness itself. As Hegel sometimes put it, what is '*in itself*' for the philosopher has to become '*for itself*' through consciousness's own experience. In making experience his standard of knowledge, Hegel was embarking upon nothing less than a *transcendental deduction* of metaphysics. According to Kant, a transcendental deduction is a justification of synthetic a priori principles that shows them to be necessary conditions of possible experience (KrV, B 117, 129). It begins from some undeniable fact that is true of any possible experience (namely, that having representations implies the possibility of awareness of them) and it then discovers the necessary conditions of such a fact, arguing that it cannot hold unless other synthetic a priori principles hold. Now just as Kant argues in the Transcendental Deduction of the first *Critique* that the categories are a necessary condition of any possible experience, so Hegel contends in the *Phenomenology* that the ideas of metaphysics are a necessary condition of actual experience. By embarking upon such a transcendental deduction, Hegel hopes to disarm Kant's fundamental objection to metaphysics: that it transcends the limits of possible experience. The *Phenomenology* aims to establish a strictly *immanent* metaphysics, and it does not tolerate a special source of knowledge transcending experience, such as an intellectual intuition. Hence the absolute knowledge of the *Phenomenology* is nothing more than 'Re-collection' (*Er-innerung*), the recounting of the whole experience of consciousness.

Certainly, to justify metaphysics through experience, Hegel has to extend the sense of 'experience' beyond its narrow Kantian limits, where it applies exclusively to sense perception. But Hegel thinks that Kant has artificially and arbitrarily restricted the meaning of experience, so that it means something as banal as 'Here is my lighter and there is my tobacco tin' (GP XX 352/III, 444–5). Experience is not only sense perception, Hegel insists, but also what is discovered and lived through. This is by no means a stipulative or technical sense of the word '*Erfahrung*', and there is no need to replace it with another synonym, such as *Erleben*.[15] Hegel is only reviving the original sense of the term, according to which '*Erfahrung*' is anything that one learns through experiment, through trial and error, or through enquiry about what appears to be the case.[16] Hegel's term '*Erfahrung*' is therefore to be taken in its literal meaning: a journey or adventure (*fahren*), which arrives at a result (*er-fahren*), so that '*Erfahrung*' is quite literally '*das Ergebnis des Fahrts*'. The journey undertaken by consciousness in the *Phenomenology* is that of its own dialectic, and what it lives through as a result of this dialectic is its experience (73; ¶86).

It is ironic that Hegel criticizes Kant for having a narrow concept of experience. For what allows him to extend the concept of experience beyond its narrow use in the empiricist tradition, where it indicates nothing more than the data of sensation, is his all-too-Kantian insistence that it is not possible to separate what appears in perception from the conditions of its appearance. This Kantian point means that what we perceive is constituted by the conditions under which we perceive it. For Hegel, the empiricist's definition of experience as sense impressions in contrast to abstract ideas simply begs the question, because the concepts by which experience is understood are constitutive of it, conditions of its very appearance. Hence Hegel's decidedly more intellectual concept of experience: it is not just sense perception, which cannot even appear to consciousness on its own, but it is also the laws and concepts that make it appear: 'The empirical is not only mere observing, hearing, feeling, perceiving particulars, but it also essentially consists in finding species, universals and laws' (GP XX 79/ III, 176).

This concept of experience means that it is possible to broaden and deepen one's experience simply by reflecting on the necessary conditions of its appearance. This extension of experience through the progressive discovery of its necessary conditions is in fact characteristic of the entire dialectic of the *Phenomenology*. As it ascends a new stage of consciousness, the self-examining subject learns the conditions of its experience on a previous stage; it discovers that what is apparently given on a lower stage requires the concepts and presuppositions of a higher stage. This discovery or higher-order self-awareness does not stand above experience but it is part of experience itself. Hence in the Introduction to the *Phenomenology* Hegel explains how the experience of consciousness consists in the discovery that the content of knowledge is inseparable from the criteria by which we evaluate claims to knowledge (73; §86). If we change these criteria, the object of knowledge too undergoes change.

Obviously, Hegel's project for a transcendental deduction of metaphysics is of a tall order. It can succeed only if all its arguments leading from the standpoint of ordinary consciousness to that of absolute knowledge prove to be rigorous and necessary. We cannot retrace here the many arguments of the *Phenomenology* that presume to lead to this result. Our only point now is to stress one fundamental aim of the *Phenomenology*: its attempt to provide a critical foundation for metaphysics. At the very least this shows it is a false dilemma to think Hegel is either a dogmatic metaphysician or not a metaphysician at all.

Eight

Solipsism and Intersubjectivity

THE SPECTER OF NIHILISM

Of all the problems Hegel faced in attempting to base metaphysics on the critique of knowledge the most serious was the challenge of 'nihilism'. As we have already seen (pp. 28–9), in the late 1790s and early 1800s in Germany, nihilism was understood as radical doubt about the existence of everything: God, the external world, other minds, and even my own self. Since he doubts the existence of everything, the nihilist believes in nothing at all. Nihilism was therefore closely associated with skepticism; and the paradigm nihilist was David Hume, who, at the close of the first book of the *Treatise of Human Nature*, famously declared that he could find no reason to believe in the existence of anything beyond his own passing impressions. After the publication of Kant's *Critique of Pure Reason* in 1781, there was something of a Hume revival in Germany when Kant's many critics cited Hume to point out the insufficiencies of transcendental idealism. If Kant were only consistent, his critics charged, he would become a nihilist, a Prussian David Hume.[1]

The nihilistic theme gained in urgency and popularity in 1799 when Jacobi, in his *Letter to Fichte*, charged Kant's and Fichte's transcendental idealism with nihilism.[2] Jacobi argued that the fundamental principle of Kant's and Fichte's idealism, 'the principle of subject–object identity', traps the self inside the circle of its own consciousness. According to this principle, the self knows a priori of objects only what it creates, or only what it produces according to its own inherent laws. Since its a priori activity is the condition of all knowlege, the self knows only its own creations, not reality as it exists in itself, prior to the deployment of its knowing activity. Of course, Kant himself acknowledged that we know objects only as appearances; but he sometimes held that these appearances are more than representations because they are appearances of things-in-themselves. But here Jacobi was ready with another objection. For in his *David Hume* he had famously argued that Kant, on his own premises, had no right to postulate the reality of things-in-themselves.[3] Kant held that we know nothing beyond experience, and that things-in-themselves are not within experience. How, then, is it possible to know that things-in-themselves exist? If Kant were only consistent, Jacobi claimed, he would have to admit that appearances are only representations, representations of nothing at all. The Kantian philosophy is therefore 'a philosophy of nothingness'.

No one worried more about nihilism than Hegel himself. The reason for his concern was plain enough. Nihilism seemed to be the inevitable result of epistemology, the very foundation for his new critical metaphysics. Hegel alluded to this very problem in the first paragraph of his Introduction to the *Phenomenology* (63–4/¶73). Epistemology seems to show us that the faculty of knowledge is either an instrument or a medium for knowing the truth, so that it appears we cannot know the object in itself, as it exists prior to the application of the instrument or medium. So if the phenomenology affirms epistemology as an immanent critique of consciousness, how does it avoid trapping consciousness inside the circle of appearances?

Hegel's concern with nihilism appears more explicitly in an early treatise he co-authored with Schelling, the 1802 *Further Presentation from the System of Philosophy*.[4] Here Hegel and Schelling, under the influence of Jacobi, pondered Fichte's dilemma at the close of his 1794 *Wissenschaftslehre* (Doctrine of Science).[5] This dilemma consists in the fact that the Fichtean ego is caught between two impossible extremes: the circle of its own consciousness and an unknowable thing-in-itself. The vocation of the Fichtean ego is infinite striving, a ceaseless struggle to make nature conform to the laws of its own activity. In so far as it conquers nature, the ego knows it; but in so far as nature remains resistant, it is an unknowable thing-in-itself. The dilemma is the inevitable result, Schelling and Hegel argue, of Fichte's principle of subject–object identity.

It was just this dilemma that Schelling and Hegel wanted to overcome with their absolute idealism. But, by 1804, Hegel realized that Schelling did not have a solution to Jacobi's challenge. Schelling had argued that to attain the standpoint of the absolute – to have insight into reality in itself – it was only necessary to abstract from the subjective.[6] But he never fully explained how such abstraction is possible. This only begged the question against Kant and Fichte, who had insisted that the 'I' is a necessary condition of all knowing. We cannot think away the 'I', they argued, without presupposing it in the very attempt. Hegel's dissatisfaction with Schelling's cavalier treatment of the problem appears in his famous damning lines in the preface to the *Phenomenology*: that Schelling had shot absolute knowledge out of a pistol.

Hegel's problem was how to avoid Fichte's dilemma without making Schelling's dogmatic leap. To avoid such a leap he would have to begin with the critique of knowledge; consciousness would have to examine itself according to its own standards, and by its own immanent necessity rise to the standpoint of absolute knowledge. But it was just the critique of knowledge that seemed to lead to nihilism. Somehow, then, Hegel would have to show how criticism, from its own internal dialectic, breaks outside the circle of consciousness so that the self knows a reality independent of itself.

Hegel's essential moves toward achieving this end appear in some of the most celebrated and discussed chapters of the *Phenomenology*, chapters IV and IVA of 'Self-Consciousness', 'The Truth of Self-Certainty' and 'Lordship and Bondage'.[7] It is here that Hegel attempts to break outside the circle of consciousness, leading the self to its intersubjective self-awareness as spirit. The essence of

Hegel's strategy is simple. He argues that self-knowledge as a rational being is possible only through mutual recognition; in other words, the self knows itself as a rational being only if it grants to the other the same status it would have the other grant to itself. This common structure of self-awareness in mutual recognition – that the self knows itself through the other as the other knows itself through the self – Hegel calls 'spirit' (*Geist*).

The central target of Hegel's argument is the claim that there is a privileged realm of subjectivity where the self knows itself independent of others and the world outside itself. Against the Cartesian tradition, Hegel contends that the self knows itself to be a rational being only if it recognizes the equal and independent reality of others, and only if the others recognize its own equal and independent reality. Without the recognition of others the self cannot prove its claim to be a rational being, and so it cannot know itself as rational. Hegel does not deny that the self might be *conscious* of itself without recognizing the equal and independent reality of others; but he does claim that it could not *know* itself without such recognition. Here knowledge is used in the strong sense of a claim that would have to be tested and proved through experience.

Seen from a broader perspective, Hegel's argument is striking because of the connection it forges between realism and intersubjectivity. Apparently paradoxically, Hegel combines realism with an emphasis on the social dimension of knowledge, an emphasis that has been all too often anti-realistic.[8] But, for Hegel, intersubjectivity is not a replacement for realism but its very foundation. What Hegel essentially does in these chapters is to socialize Kant's idealism, so that the 'I' of Kant's 'I think' must be part of a 'We think'.

Chapters IV and IVA of the *Phenomenology* have been some of the most discussed in the entire work. They have been read from many different angles, ethical, existential, anthropological, psychological and political.[9] All these perspectives are interesting, valid and fruitful; but they fail to take into account the original epistemological and metaphysical context of these chapters that are essential for a full understanding of Hegel's meaning. The main problem with most interpretations is that they read into the text, as if it were a given, the very conclusion Hegel intends to prove: the equal and independent reality of the other. Such interpretations do violence to the whole purpose and argument of the *Phenomenology*, for these never permit Hegel to take for granted such a significant conclusion. The context of these chapters, and Hegel's general goal in the *Phenomenology*, make it necessary to read these chapters as a single coherent argument that attempts to break outside the circle of consciousness and to establish the equal and independent reality of the other. Here again, then, it is important to stress the metaphysical dimension of Hegel's general project.

The primary task of the next two sections will be to provide just such an interpretation. Each section will focus on the relevant transitions of chapters IV and IVA. In the reading provided here I take into account Hegel's formulation of the argument in other texts, especially the expositions in the *Nurnberg Propaedeutic* and the *Encyclopedia*.

THE CONTEXT OF THE ARGUMENT

Never in chapters IV and IVA does Hegel mention the word nihilism, nor does he directly and explicitly consider the doctrine that we know only our representations. However, it is significant that Hegel does consider directly and explicitly the view Jacobi charges with nihilism: Fichte's idealism. Hegel's essential concern is to determine whether Fichte's idealism can provide an adequate account of our ordinary knowledge-claims. His allusions in chapter IV leave little doubt that he has Fichte in mind. Thus he refers to the 'ego' or 'I', which is Fichte's central concept, and to the 'I am I', which is his first principle (134/¶167). It is also striking that Hegel treats this 'I' in an active role, just as Fichte had in the third part of his 1794 *Wissenschaftslehre*. Furthermore, Fichte too had treated this active self in terms of drives and feelings, just as Hegel will write of desire. Some of the most difficult transitions are easily explained if we focus on their Fichtean context, and more specifically Hegel's concern to break outside the circle of consciousness of the 1794 *Wissenschaftslehre*.

Hegel's concern with Fichte's idealism is also apparent from the context of chapter IV. After its experience in 'Consciousness', the ego feels justified in assuming that its self-knowledge is absolute, i.e. that to know anything is only to know itself. It has discovered through several stages of experience – 'Sense Certainty' (chapter I), 'Perception' (chapter II), and 'Force and Understanding' (chapter III) – that its knowledge of an object is simply an externalization of its self-knowledge. The ego that begins chapter IV now wants to confirm the result of its previous experience. It aims to establish that everything in its experience is its self-consciousness and not consciousness of an external object (134–5/¶¶166–7). This ego wants to show that it is all reality, and that everything exists only for it (143/¶186).

Although self-consciousness has shown itself to be the truth of consciousness, this truth too must now be put to the test. The self has to prove this thesis against its actual experience. But a problem immediately arises: it does not appear to be self-conscious in its experience since what appears to its senses comes and goes independent of its will and imagination; what is given appears independent of its conscious control. Thus Hegel writes that the ego consists at this stage in two opposing moments: *self-consciousness*, where it is conscious only of itself; and *consciousness*, where it is conscious of something distinct from itself, a manifold of given and contingent representations, which it considers only as an appearance (134–5/¶167). What the ego has to demonstrate now is that, despite the apparent givenness of its sense experience, it is still all reality, that it is still *self*-conscious despite its consciousness in experience. Somehow, it has to show that these representations are also within its conscious control, and that they are not independent of its will and imagination after all.

Hegel poses the problem facing consciousness here in these

terms: How is it possible to establish the identity of identity and non-identity? This is only a more abstract formulation for the idealist's problem of how to explain ordinary experience on the basis of self-knowledge. Self-knowledge is subject–object identity, because the subject and object of knowledge are the same; ordinary experience, however, involves subject–object non-identity because the object is given for the subject, appearing independent of its will and imagination. The dilemma facing the idealist is that there must be *and* cannot be such an identity of identity and non-identity. According to idealist principles, there *must be* such an identity because subject–object identity is the first principle of *all* knowledge, even the awareness of an apparently distinct object in experience; but there also *cannot be* such an identity because the principle of subject–object identity contradicts the subject–object dualism of experience. Hence the problem Hegel considers here is that confronting any idealism: If all reality is only my consciousness, how is it possible to explain the origin of my experience, the fact that there are representations that apparently do not depend on my conscious activity? This was precisely the problem that Fichte tried to solve in his *Wissenschaftslehre*, and that he considers the central problem of his idealism.[10] So in setting forth this problem in chapter IV, Hegel is only asking if and how Fichte comes to terms with his own problem.

With the start of chapter IV, the ego enters into a new realm of experience: it ceases to intuit, perceive or explain, as in chapters I–III, and it begins to act. In short, it moves from the realm of theory into that of practice (134/¶167). The reason for the transition is not hard to fathom when we keep in mind the idealist's fundamental problem. The ego now has to begin acting since action is the decisive test for its thesis that all reality is under its control. If it wants to demonstrate that it is all reality, it has to show that it is so by making the world conform to its will. In making action into the test of the ego's thesis, Hegel almost certainly had in mind Fichte's practical deduction of consciousness in Part III of his 1794

Wissenschaftslehre, where Fichte argues that the ego proves that it is all reality through its infinite striving to control the non-ego. Thus the dialectic of chapter IV is nothing less than an internal critique of Fichte's idealism. Hegel tests the Fichtean ego by its own standard: action.

At this early stage of 'Self-Consciousness', the ego knows itself only through actions directed by desire (*Begierde*). It knows itself through desire rather than through another form of volition, such as choice or love, since its earlier dialectic in 'Force and Under-standing' had only led it to its self-consciousness as life, and the form of volition appropriate for a merely living being, as opposed to a fully rational one, is desire. On this level, then, the ego knows itself only as a sensible being with animal desires, not as a rational being with a will. Hence it is first as a living being, or through its animal desires, that it attempts to establish its claim that it is all reality. This means that it tries to demonstrate its conscious control over objects by *consuming* them.

Although it is not fully self-conscious of its goal at this stage, the end of the ego's actions is what Hegel calls 'absolute independ-ence'.[11] Absolute independence means that the ego does not depend on anything outside itself, and that it has power over its entire world. When the ego attains its absolute independence, it has made all nature submit to the laws of its activity; hence when it is conscious of its object it is really only self-conscious of its own creations. So, when it establishes its thesis that all consciousness of an external object is really only its self-consciousness, the ego will realize its absolute independence.

To appreciate the moves behind the dialectic of chapters IV and IVA, it is important to keep in mind that the ego's constant goal is absolute independence. For what the ego's experience amounts to throughout the dialectic is so many attempts to discover the condi-tions for the fulfillment of its goal. The ego goes through several stages: desire, the life/death struggle, the master/slave conflict; and only in the end with the mutual recognition between equal and independent persons does it learn the conditions for its absolute independence: self-consciousness as spirit. It is only when the ego is self-conscious as spirit that it knows that it is absolute, that it is all reality, and that it is not determined by anything outside itself. And it is only then that it discovers what it has struggled for all along: absolute independence, complete authority where it obeys only self-imposed laws. This has always been known by the philosopher; but only at the end of the dialectic does it become known for consciousness itself. To follow Hegel's dialectic in these chapters, then, it is necessary to follow what experience the ego must go through to attain its absolute independence.

THE DIALECTIC OF DESIRE

The ego's first experience is that it cannot attain absolute independence on the level of animal desire. The aim of desire is 'to negate' its object; desire destroys its object by consuming it, by forcing it to conform to its life-processes (digestion, excretion). The ego feels that it shows control over its experience just as long as it destroys objects through its desires. But it soon recognizes, if only through a glass darkly, that this is not good enough for absolute independence. Desire falls between two uncomfortable extremes. On the one hand, it still depends upon an independent object, an object that is completely alien to itself, for desire by its very nature is the desire for something that one does not have. Of course, desires are sometimes satisfied; but this dependence upon an independent object is inescapable because desire regenerates, and it always requires another object to consume and assimilate. An infinite regress then arises where desire follows upon desire, object upon object. On the other hand, though, the ego does not depend upon an object, for it has consumed it; but it then only returns to its empty self-identity as an individual. It has not shown that it has control over its experience since it has only brought the object inside itself by consuming it. The ego has not demonstrated that it is all reality, for it has only made one object conform to its individual nature. So the ego confronts either something completely alien to itself or only itself: something alien to itself, in that the object is independent of itself and only something to be negated; and only itself, in that the object is destroyed and consumed and it returns to its self-identity. In other words, there is either identity or non-identity but not the required identity of identity and non-identity. The predicament of consciousness here is very much that of Fichte's ego in Part III of the *Wissenschaftslehre*.

After this experience, the philosopher who observes the ego is justified in concluding that there are two conditions for the fulfillment of its absolute independence. The first condition is non-identity: that the object is independent of the individual and that it is not just negated or destroyed by it. This is necessary to avoid the relapse into individual self-identity, a self-identity that is abstract and opposed to all the determinations of experience. The second condition is identity: that the ego sees its identity in its object, so that it is not completely alien to it. This condition is required so that the ego does not lose its absolute independence and depend on something else outside itself; otherwise, a subject–object dualism returns and the ego cannot claim to be all reality. Both these conditions must be joined, so that consciousness seeks the identity of identity and non-identity. Its goal is therefore paradoxical: self-consciousness in an other, or what Hegel calls 'the unity of itself in its otherness' (*die Einheit seiner selbst in seinem Andersein*) (140/¶177).

Surprisingly, at this point Hegel introduces a new factor in the dialectic: another ego, another self-conscious agent (139/¶175). He reaches this result by reflecting on the conditions for unity with oneself in otherness. Since the subject cannot negate the otherness of its object, there can be unity in otherness only if the *object* negates its otherness to the subject (139/¶175). What can negate its otherness to the subject must be another subject, another self-conscious being. Hence Hegel declares: 'Self-consciousness achieves its satisfaction only in another self-consciousness' (139/¶175).

So, it seems at this point as if Hegel has already reached – virtually by a sleight-of-hand – his intended conclusion: the equal and independent reality of something else outside the subject's consciousness. But it is important to see that Hegel's reasoning here is only provisional and from the standpoint of the philosopher. This is a truth that will have to be earned through the experience of consciousness itself in the next chapter.

Still writing from the standpoint of the philosopher, Hegel asks: What fully satisfies the conditions of absolute independence? He answers: Only the mutual recognition between equal and independent persons (139–40/¶175–7). Mutual recognition satisfies the condition of non-identity since both persons are equal to and independent of one another; by its very nature such recognition requires that the self and other accept their equal and independent status. Mutual recognition also fulfills the condition of identity because the self is *self*-conscious only through its other; it sees itself in the other as the other sees itself in the self. This mutual recognition is nothing less than self-consciousness as spirit, for spirit arises from the mutual recognition between equal and independent persons. It is that single act of self-consciousness between two selves where each recognizes itself in the other as the other recognizes itself in it. As Hegel famously put it, it is the 'I that is We and the We that is an I' (**Ich**, *das* **Wir**, *und* **Wir**, *das* **Ich** ist) (140/¶177). Hence Hegel is now in a position to draw the conclusion that the ego realizes its absolute independence only through its self-consciousness as spirit.

There is another argument implicit in the text for self-consciousness as spirit. Only such self-consciousness, Hegel implies, upholds the ideal of independence and remains true to the experience of consciousness. If absolute independence means that the self does not depend upon anything outside itself, and if its experience as an individual is that it does depend upon something else outside itself (the object of desire), then there is one, and only one, way in which its ideal can be consistent with its experience: through self-consciousness as spirit. Self-consciousness as spirit realizes absolute independence since it of necessity incorporates both individual egos within itself, so that, as a whole, it does not have anything outside itself. This keeps to the meaning of absolute independence; and it accommodates the experience of consciousness, since the self recognizes that it depends upon an other that has equal and independent status to its own consciousenss. What the ego learns through this dialectic is that it cannot satisfy its ideal of independence as an isolated individual but only as one part of a whole.

LORDSHIP AND BONDAGE

Hegel's argument in chapter IV is chiefly from the standpoint of the philosopher. Although the self that he observes has had the experience of the futility of desire, and although it has discovered the independence of its object, it has still been left to the philosopher to conclude that the necessary condition of absolute independence is mutual recognition or self-awareness as spirit. What is only for the philosopher in chapter IV, though, must now be confirmed by consciousness itself in chapter IVA. Through its own self-examination, the ego has to discover the necessity of mutual recognition and self-awareness as spirit. So Hegel's task in chapter IVA is to narrate those stages of self-consciousness that emerge from the self's inner experience. What are these stages? And how does their dialectic add up to self-awareness in spirit?

The dialectic in IVA begins from where it left off in IV. The subject aims to prove its absolute independence, its power over the world.[12] It now recognizes, however, that it cannot achieve such control through desire, by compelling objects to satisfy its physical needs. It is now forced to admit that there is something outside itself, something recalcitrant to its efforts at conscious control: all those objects that it cannot consume, all those objects that continue to come and go independent of its will and imagination. These objects first confronted it in the form of other living beings, because these were the kinds of things that it could consume. Still, the subject refuses to give equal and independent status to any other living beings, even those that appear to have the same organic structure and physical appearance as its own; it refuses to acknowledge that among them there are others that have its status as a rational being. To establish its independence, it will attempt to show its control and power over the others; it will attempt to make them obey.

The self's attempt to establish its independence is the mainspring of the forthcoming dialectic. The self will have to pass through several stages of experience – the need for recognition, the life/death struggle, the master/slave conflict – before it discovers in what its real independence consists. Through this dialectic, the self will eventually break outside its solipsistic shell. In the end, it will realize that its independence requires giving equal and independent status to the other, and that its independence consists in the self-awareness of equal and independent beings through one another.

The task now at hand, then, is to reconstruct the stages of the self's experience, seeing how each is necessary for the achievement of absolute independence, and noting how they progressively crack the self's solipsistic shell. Let us take each stage in turn.

The first stage: the need for recognition

If the self is to prove its independence, it must gain the recognition of others, which it regards only as living beings. It can gain its independence only if it has control over the world, and it has such control only if it can make these beings obey its commands. Otherwise, if they refuse, it proves its lack of power.

This need for recognition already seems to presuppose the existence of other rational beings. It is important to see, however, that, at this stage of the argument, the self has still not granted the equal and independent existence of the other. It does not demand recognition from another rational agent that it believes stands on the same footing as itself. What it seeks in its demand for recognition is that the other, whatever it might be, obey its commands, or at the very least that it not interfere with its activity. For all the self knows at this stage, the other could still be a robot or an animal.[13]

To be sure, Hegel has already introduced other rational persons into his argument in chapter IV (139–40/¶175). But, again, this was only from the standpoint of the philosopher; the self now has to discover from its own experience in IVA what the philosopher has already known in IV. Failure to note the precise status of Hegel's argument in IV has blinded some from seeing the argument against solipsism in IVA, since it then seems as if Hegel already presupposes the existence of other minds.[14]

The second stage: the life/death struggle

If the self is to gain the recognition of others, it must enter into a life/death struggle with them. It must struggle against others, for they too attempt to realize their absolute independence. If the self demands obedience from the other, the other demands obedience from the self. The self cannot establish its independence, then, unless it defends itself against the other and prevents the other from dominating it. This struggle has to be a matter of life and death where the self risks its own life, for it is only in risking its life that it demonstrates its rational status, that it has a power over the realm of mere biological life and its animal desires.[15]

This struggle is not Hobbes's war of all against all. The self fights for recognition of itself as a rational being; and, unlike Hobbes's state of nature, it does not compete with others to satisfy its desires or to gain power to satisfy them. For Hegel, right arises from the recognition of a person's rational status; it is not simply the permission to act on my wants. In making the self ready to risk its life to gain its independence, Hegel is taking issue with Hobbes's own analysis of human nature, according to which the dominating drive in human beings is self-preservation. Against Hobbes, Hegel is saying that freedom is a much more vital end than self-preservation, which is proven by the mere fact that a person is willing to risk his life to attain it.

The third stage: mercy to the foe

If the self is to gain recognition through the life/death struggle, then it cannot kill its opponent. For to kill its opponent means that it has no one to recognize it. A corpse cannot salute. Hence it must grant its enemy at least life.[16]

The fourth stage: master versus slave

If, to gain recognition, the victor cannot kill its vanquished foe, and if, to protect itself from further attack, it cannot grant its foe freedom, then the victor has no choice: it must enslave its foe, making it submit to its demands. The victor and the vanquished are now to one another as master and slave. Although the master grants the slave its life, he still does not consider it as his equal or as a rational being. Even though he respects the slave as a living being – for example, he acknowledges the slave's desires by allowing it food – he still cannot respect the slave as another equal rational being, because he uses it as a means to his own ends. The slave is only an animal, an instrument to satisfy his desires. The master has his reason for treating the slave as an animal. After all, the slave prefers his life over death in the struggle for recognition. Hence the slave fails to prove itself a rational being, worthy of the same respect as the master.[17]

The master/slave relationship is a crucial step down the road toward mutual recognition. The master has to recognize the independent life of the slave – his status as a living being – even if he has not granted him a rational status equal to himself. This is a greater experience of an independent reality than that on the stage of desire. Although desire experiences the independence of its object, that is only because it is caught in an infinite regress; there is no definite object that it still cannot consume, although any object is always succeeded by another. Now, though, the self has to restrain its desires – such restraint is a great step forward in its education as a rational being – and admit that there is one definite object that it cannot consume: its vanquished foe, the slave.

The master's recognition of the slave is therefore a decisive step outside the circle of consciousness. What is within that circle is only what is within the self's conscious control. The self now discovers, however, that there is a living being that is outside its conscious control. This is because it cannot kill or consume this creature, making it conform to its desires; rather, it must respect its desires as a living creature. To kill it, or to treat it only as an object of desire, is to undermine the recognition it needs.

The fifth stage: collapse of the master/slave relationship

If the self and other are to one another as master and slave, then the master still does not get the required recognition of himself as autonomous and independent. The master degrades the slave to the status of an animal and reduces him to an instrument for his own ends. The recognition of the slave is therefore of little value, if not worthless, to him. It is not the free recognition of another rational being, but it is only the humbled submission of an animal. Recognition loses all value if it comes from domination or coercion; it is only of value when it derives from the free choice and judgment of another. Since the master despises the slave, he does not get the assurance that he is after.[18]

Not only does the master/slave relationship not give the master the recognition that he demands, but it also degrades his status as a rational being. The master regresses back to the stage of his animal desires. This is for two reasons: (1) he treats the slave only as a means to his own ends, and as an instrument to satisfy his desires; (2) he simply consumes the products of the slave's labor; he does not gain independence over his objects through labor, like the slave who labors for him, but he depends upon the slave's labor for his idle enjoyment. So if the slave is not worthy of giving recognition, the master is not worthy of receiving it.

The sixth stage: liberation of the slave

If the master is to gain recognition as a free being, then he has to recognize the slave as a free being. For the master gains reassurance not from the submissive acknowledgment of an inferior but only from the recognition of an equal. If the master recognizes the slave as a free being, then he also ceases to degrade himself to the level of his animal desires. He proves that he is rational because he recognizes that another person is an end in itself.[19]

There is an implicit Kantian or Rousseauian theme lurking behind this stage of the dialectic: that the self demonstrates that it is rational only when it acts according to self-imposed universal laws that oblige it no less than others. If the self acts according to such laws, there are two reasons why it must be rational: first, because only a rational being acts according to the idea of the law (i.e. its universalizability); and, second, because only a rational being restrains its desires to act for the sake of the law. In the context of the master/slave dialectic, this theme means that the master proves his rationality when he finally recognizes the equal and independent reality of the slave. If he does this, that shows that he acts according to universal laws that grant someone else the same rights as himself. The master proves his freedom not by dominating this slave, then, but by treating him as his equal.[20] Thus Hegel proves the wisdom behind Rousseau's famous lines: 'He who believes himself a master of others is more a slave than they.'[21] The entire dialectic of chapters IV and IVA is really only an elaborate defense of Rousseau's dictum.

This experience brings the dialectic to its conclusion. The self knows that it is rational because another rational being recognizes its autonomy. But it also knows that it is rational because it recognizes the autonomy of another rational being. In other words, the self knows that it is rational only through mutual recognition. This is nothing less than its self-awareness as spirit, though, since spirit is that unifying act of self-awareness that arises from the mutual recognition between free rational beings. The self has now come to the same conclusion as the philosopher at the close of chapter IV.

Now the nihilist takes his final step outside the darkness of the circle of consciousness and into the broad daylight of reality. If, on the stage of desire, he acknowledges the reality of an external object, and if on the stage of the life/death struggle he grants that there is another living being, now after the master/slave dialectic he recognizes the equal and independent reality of another rational being. He finally admits that he is not the only self-conscious being, but that there is another such being. The self acknowledges that the other is not simply its own representations because it sees that the other is outside its conscious control. It cannot consume the other, as if it were an inanimate object; and it cannot treat it as a means to satisfy its desires, as if it were a slave. Rather, it admits that the other is outside its conscious control because it is an end in itself, a being that has a right to live according to its own self-appointed ends, even if they do not agree with the self's own ends. So, for Hegel, to recognize another rational being as an end in itself is the refutation of nihilism. By such recognition, the solipsist has to concede that not all reality is within its conscious control, and that there is another rational being having equal status to itself.

It is important to be clear about the precise status and limits of Hegel's argument. All that he has established is that a rational being *ought to* recognize the equal and independent reality of others, or that the self *should* give the same status to others as it would have them give to itself. In the end, this is more a *moral* than a *metaphysical* refutation of nihilism. The radical nihilist might object that it is still possible for the other to be an automaton. Even though I have to *recognize* its equal status to myself – even though I am obliged to *treat* it as I would have it treat me – it is still possible that it is not really equal. Hegel would have to accept this point. But his main objection to it would be that it is impossible to live according to such nihilism. Even if we forever doubt the reality of the other, we still cannot act on those doubts. We have to grant it equal and independent reality to ourselves; for only then do we confirm our own status as free and rational beings.

Part Four
**Social and
Political Philosophy**

Nine

Freedom and the Foundation of Right

METAPHYSICS AND POLITICS

Although most contemporary scholars have declared Hegel's metaphysics dead, they stress that his social and political philosophy is alive and well. With some justice, they hail Hegel's *Philosophy of Right* as a classic in political thought, a work on a par with Plato's *Republic*, Hobbes's *Leviathan* and Rousseau's *Social Contract*.[1] But, with some embarrassment, they tiptoe around Hegel's metaphysics. Since any connection of Hegel's social and political philosophy with his metaphysics would seem to render it obsolete, most scholars have adopted a non-metaphysical approach.[2]

However tempting, such an approach is flatly contrary to Hegel's own intentions. For, from the very beginning, it was his ambition to provide a metaphysical foundation for social and political philosophy. In his first publication on the topic, his 1802–3 *On the Scientific Ways of Treating Natural Law*, he argued that the main shortcoming of previous systems of natural law is that they had separated natural law from metaphysics. They had failed to recognize that metaphysics is the foundation of the other sciences, and that a discipline has a scientific component only to the degree that it rests on such a foundation. Here Hegel self-consciously set himself in opposition to the positivistic spirit of much modern jurisprudence that attempts to free law from metaphysics. The problem with positivism, Hegel argues, is that metaphysics is inescapable, and that in pretending to be free from it we only beg the most basic questions against it.

Still, there is something to be said for the non-metaphysical approach. If only on a superficial level, it is possible to understand much in Hegel's social and political philosophy without his metaphysics. Much in Hegel's theory is straightforwardly intelligible, as much the result of observation and prudence as speculative logic. Although the architechtonic structure of the *Philosophy of Right* – its routine divisions into the dialectical moments of universality, particularity and individuality – reflects Hegel's speculative logic, this structure is somewhat artificial and arbitrary, more imposed upon than derived from its subject matter. Hegel is indeed often at his best when he lays aside his metaphysics and simply explores his subject matter.

It is also necessary to note a profound ambivalence on Hegel's part regarding the foundation of his social and political philosophy. While he sometimes insists that its foundation lies in his speculative logic, he also stresses that its specific doctrines derive entirely from the immanent logic of its subject matter. If Hegel's method is metaphysical, it is also phenomenological, demanding that we examine each subject for its own sake, apart from all prior principles and preconceived ideas (pp. 159–62). Although each specific science derives its foundation from the system as a whole, it should also be self-sufficient, an organic whole in its own right. So if we stress this phenomenological aspect of Hegel's methodology, it would seem that much in his social and political philosophy should be comprehensible in its own terms.

Yet the question remains: *How comprehensible?* And here the short answer must be: not enough. Whatever the spirit of the phenomenological method, the fact remains that some of the central concepts of Hegel's political philosophy presuppose, and are only fully intelligible in the context of, his metaphysics. We shall soon see that Hegel's concept of right rests upon his Aristotelian metaphysics (pp. 210–14), that his concept of freedom is based upon his notion of spirit (p. 201), and that his theory of reason in history is based on his absolute idealism (pp. 263–4).

THE CONCEPT OF FREEDOM

All scholars agree there is no more important concept in Hegel's political theory than freedom. There are good reasons for such rare unanimity: Hegel regards freedom as the foundation of right, as the essence of spirit, and as the end of history. Unfortunately, however, there is no concept of Hegel's political theory that is more opaque and contentious. Since the concept is so pivotal, obscure and controversial, it is necessary to examine it in a little detail.

Hegel has several distinct but related concepts of freedom, which appear in scattered places in his writings. First and foremost, he understands freedom as *autonomy*, i.e. the power of self-government, the capacity to make and follow one's own laws. Hence he writes in *The Philosophy of World History*: '. . . only that will which obeys the law is free; for it obeys itself and is self-sufficient [*bei sich selbst*] and therefore free' (VG 115/97). Hegel's idea of autonomy pre-supposes that the will's self-imposed laws are rational; I am not free simply by creating and following *any* law, but the law must be worthy of the assent of any intelligent being. Hence freedom consists in acting according to the laws of reason.

Hegel also conceives freedom as *independence* or *self-sufficiency*, i.e. not depending on anyone other than oneself. He defines freedom in these terms when he writes in *The Philosophy of World History*: '. . . spirit is self-sufficient being [*Beisichselbstsein*], and just this is free-dom. For if I am dependent, I relate to something that is not I and I cannot be without this external thing' (VG 55/48). A similar account of freedom appears in the *Philosophy of Right* when Hegel explains that the will is free if 'it relates to nothing but itself, so that every relationship of dependence on something *other* than itself falls away' (§23). This sense of freedom is closely connected with autonomy, for an autonomous being is independent in not depending on anyone else to govern itself.

Finally, in the *Philosophy of Right* Hegel sometimes formulates posi-tive freedom in terms of *self-determination* (§§7, 12R, 21). Self-determination essentially means two things: (1) that the self, and not forces outside itself, determines its actions; and (2) that in determining itself, it makes itself determinate, turning what is merely potential, intended and inchoate into something actual, realized and organized. When Hegel thinks of freedom as self-determination he implies that (1) I have a specific essence or nature, which consists in my rationality, and that (2) the process of self-realization, of developing this essence or nature, is natural and necessary (pp. 74–5). Clearly, self-determination is closely connected with autonomy: self-determination means that the self is autonomous because it determines itself into action according to principles it gives itself. For similar reasons, self-determination is also intimately linked with independence: if the self determines itself into action it is independent of causes external to itself.

Hegel's technical formulation for freedom is the will willing itself, i.e. the will having itself for its own object and end (PR §§22, 27). Such language appears paradoxical, but the main point is simple, resting on two straightforward premises. First, Hegel thinks that the very essence of the self consists in freedom. Like Rousseau and Kant, he maintains that the distinctive feature of a rational being is its freedom, more specifically, its autonomy, its power to act on universalizable principles. Second, Hegel maintains that we become free only if we are *self-conscious* that we are free, having the power to make freedom the goal of our actions; a slave who does not know that it is free will never achieve its freedom. Both points together mean that the self will become free only if it makes freedom itself the object and goal of its activity; in other words, the will must will itself. It is in such self-reflexive willing, Hegel further argues, that true independence and self-determination reside. For if the will wills itself, it relates to itself alone, and so it does not depend on anything outside itself.

In §§5–7 of the *Philosophy of Right* Hegel provides a more detailed account of freedom, specifying three fundamental moments necessary for freedom. These three moments – universality, particularity and individuality – correspond to the structure of the concept in his *Logic*. In this context they specify three conditions under which a person can be completely free in the world. According to the moment of universality, a free person must have the power of self-awareness, the capacity to abstract from all specific situations and to be aware of itself apart from them; it must have the ability to stand back from all courses of actions, to reflect on different options and their consequences. If a person had no such power, they would not be free because they would have no sense of its own agency, and they would have no power to rationally assess what they should do. According to the moment of particularity, to be free, a person must choose a particular option and act in a particular situation. Without choosing and without acting a person cannot be free; and to choose and to act they must choose something specific and do something specific. According to the moment of individuality, the synthesis of the other two moments, a person must, after detaching themselves from and reflecting on all options, eventually commit themselves to, and ultimately identify themselves with, one option; in other words, they must accept one situation as worthy of their effort and commitment. Hegel describes this moment of individuality as one of *self-limitation*: one *limits* oneself because, rather than fleeing all commitments, one accepts one situation in life; and yet one *self*-limits oneself because one chooses the situation as a result of reflection and deliberation.

Whatever its basis in his logic, Hegel's analysis of freedom in the *Philosophy of Right* reflects his fundamental moral teaching that freedom has to be realized in the world, and cannot be attained by flight from it. This is a theme that Hegel had first developed in his *Christianity and its Fate* when he argued that Jesus doomed himself by fleeing from the world and seeking redemption in heaven alone. In the *Phenomenology* Hegel later saw the same problems in stoicism, which preached inner retreat from the vicissitudes of fortune, and in French radicalism, which wreaked destruction because it could not accept any specific constitution. In Hegel's view, Christianity, stoicism and French radicalism were all failed strategies for achieving freedom. Since they attempted to escape the world, they did not struggle against it, and so ultimately succumbed to it. Hegel's theme contains a tragic note: the need to reconcile ourselves with the world, to limit ourselves and to commit ourselves to some specific situation in life. Yet this tragic teaching always went hand-in-hand with a moral about the need to struggle against the world. Hegel saw that the main problem for realizing one's freedom in the world is that one has both to struggle and to yield, both to limit oneself and to detach oneself, both to commit oneself yet to remain critical; true freedom lay in finding the delicate balance between these extremes.

A decisive influence in the development of Hegel's concept of freedom was Kant. We can trace each of Hegel's formulations back to Kant, who had already written about freedom in terms of autonomy, independence and self-determination.[3] It was indeed Kant who first suggested, in the *Foundations of the Metaphysics of Morals*, that the free will wills itself because it must act according to the idea of freedom (GMS IV, 448). The influence of Kant's concept of freedom upon Hegel is not a matter of conjecture but easily detectable. In the early Berne writings Hegel made Kant's principle of autonomy his chief moral ideal, his main weapon in his battle against the positivity of Christianity. And in the *Philosophy of Right* Hegel explicitly endorsed Kant's conception of freedom as acting on moral duty: 'In doing my duty, I am with myself [*bei mir selbst*] and free. It is the merit and exalted standpoint of Kant's philosophy in the practical sphere that it has stressed this significance of duty' (PR §133A).

Still, despite these facts, it would be a serious mistake to conclude that Kant's and Hegel's concepts of freedom are substantially the same.[4] Though they are alike in very general respects, Kant and Hegel give them very different, even conflicting, interpretations. The most important differences are fourfold:

¶ Though Kant and Hegel both see freedom in terms of moral action, and though both think that morality must be founded on reason, they have very different conceptions of reason. Kant's conception of reason is *formal* or *abstract*: the power to determine and act on universalizable principles; Hegel's conception of reason is *material* or *concrete*: the ethos and way of life of a specific community.

¶ Though they both conceive freedom as self-determination, they have very different conceptions of the self. Since Kant's rational self stands above the spheres of society and history, it has its identity *apart from* other rational selves like itself; it is self-conscious in opposition to other such selves. Hegel, however, understands the self in and through the other; his self realizes itself only through internalizing the other and making it part of its very identity. Hence, in the *Philosophy of Right*, Hegel describes self-determination as the entire process by which the self externalizes itself in others and then internalizes them in a wider concept of itself (§7). The proper subject of freedom is therefore *spirit*, the intersubjective self, the I that is a We and the We that is an I.

¶ Kant conceives of self-determination as the power of reason over sensibility; Hegel, however, understands self-determination as acting according to my whole nature, where there is no conflict between reason and sensibility. Following Schiller,[5] Hegel insists that my desires and feelings have to be integrated into the powers of rational self-determination, so that the self does its duty *from* inclination and not apart from it, still less contrary to it. Hegel rejected Kant's more rationalistic and dualistic account of self-determination, because if freedom were acting according to my rationality alone it would be still compatible with a form of constraint: namely, the repression of my desires and feelings. He argued that the sovereignty Kant gave to reason had simply moved the sources of domination inside the self.

¶ Kant conceives of freedom as independence from the causality of nature, so that the self is the sole cause of its own actions and has the power to do otherwise. Hegel thinks that such independence is illusory: freedom is realized only within the realm of nature and it requires acting according to the necessity of one's own nature and the universe as a whole. In his understanding of freedom as a form of necessity, as self-awareness of one's place in the universe as a whole, Hegel's main debt is to Spinoza.

Prima facie it might seem that Hegel abandons the concept of freedom as independence when he stresses that the self must live through others and in the world. This seems to amount to the admission that the self has a *de facto* dependence on others. Hegel indeed thinks that we are dependent on others and the world, and that it is only through such dependence that we become who we are. It is important to see, however, that in recognizing such *de facto* dependence he does not think he is abandoning the ideal of independence but embracing it; for he argues that true independence comes not from abstracting or fleeing from the other and the world but in making them part of myself; for if I truly internalize the other and the world, making them part of myself, then my dependence on the other becomes a form of *self*-dependence. It is ultimately Kant who must abandon his ideal of independence, Hegel argues, because he conceives it completely in abstraction from others and the world, so that it cannot recognize its *de facto* dependence upon them.

A BETRAYER OF LIBERTY?

For better or worse, Hegel has gone down in history as one of the chief champions of a 'positive concept' of freedom. Since the distinction between positive and negative liberty is relatively recent, it is anachronistic to apply it to Hegel. Still, it has become such an endemic way of discussing Hegel – by both defenders and detractors alike – that it cannot be ignored. According to Isaiah Berlin's classical distinction,[6] a negative concept of liberty identifies freedom with lack of constraint or absence of coercion, i.e. with non-interference with *any* of my actions; hence the less constraint, the more free I am. Negative liberty therefore essentially consists in freedom of choice, having a multiplicity of options. On the other hand, a positive concept of liberty identifies freedom with a specific course of action, such as acting on moral principle, obeying divine commands, or realizing my true self. Such liberty is then compatible with limiting my options, and even with compelling me to do the specific action. Positive liberty seems to sanction, therefore, Rousseau's notorious dictum: 'forcing a person to be free'. So, not surprisingly, it has been denounced as a threat to negative liberty, as a rationale for totalitarianism or authoritarianism. Interpreted as a one-sided champion of positive freedom, Hegel has been flayed and flailed by his liberal critics as a potent 'betrayer of liberty'.

The most obvious problem with this interpretation is that it cannot account for one stubborn and incontestable fact: that Hegel himself was an unwavering and unequivocal champion of negative as well as positive liberty. Hegel had a distinction between kinds of freedom that is analogous, though not equivalent, to Berlin's; and he is explicit and emphatic in upholding *both* forms of freedom. Hegel's own distinction is between what he usually calls 'formal' or 'subjective freedom' on the one hand, and 'absolute' or 'objective freedom' on the other hand; uncannily, he sometimes even distinguishes between 'negative' liberty and 'affirmative' or 'positive liberty' (PR §§5, 149A; VG 57/50).[7] Formal, subjective or negative freedom involves the power and right of the individual to reflect upon and choose different courses of action, and to choose that option which best suits its taste, judgment or conscience (PR §§ 121, 185R, 228R, 258R, 273R, 274, 301, 316). On the other hand, absolute, objective or positive freedom involves thinking and acting on rational principle, on laws that are recognized in public life (§§149, 258R). In the *Philosophy of Right* Hegel shows himself to be a staunch advocate of formal and subjective freedom on many occasions, and he fully recognizes and stresses that such freedom requires non-interference by the government (§§185R, 206R, 260). He repeatedly argues that the chief weakness of the classical *polis* is that it did not recognize subjective freedom (§§124R, 138A, 185R, 260R, 261R, 262A, 299R), whereas the main strength of the modern state is that it secures individual rights (§§41, 185R, 206R, 260, 262A, 299R).

It is important to recognize that Hegel's defense of negative liberty was not a late development for him but a constant of his intellectual career, one of the enduring hallmarks of all his political writings. In the *Positivity Essay* of the Berne and Frankfurt periods he argued passionately that the state has the duty to protect the rights of individuals, such as freedom of speech and conscience. And in the *Verfassungsschrift* of the late Frankfurt and early Jena periods he protested strongly against the totalitarian state that attempts to control everything from above, leaving no room for individual liberties and local initiatives. Hence the interpretation of Hegel as a one-sided protagonist of positive liberty ignores not only a central feature of his mature doctrine but also a pivotal theme of his early writings.

There seems to be some justification, however, for reading at least the mature Hegel along these lines. In the *Philosophy of Right* (§§15–17), Hegel mounts an argument to the effect that negative freedom is not really freedom in the proper sense. He contends that freedom understood as 'arbitrariness' (*Willkür*), i.e. the power to abstract from all options and to choose between them, contradicts itself because the will is both independent of and dependent on its object. Whatever the merits of this argument, it seems as if Hegel were entirely rejecting freedom in the negative sense for the sake of positive freedom alone.

When, however, we read these passages more in context, this interpretation proves untenable. It suffers from several difficulties. First, the target of Hegel's argument is not really negative liberty (in Berlin's precise sense) but the formal liberty that attempts to realize freedom in complete abstraction from all commitment. Second, Hegel is not criticizing the value of choice as such but, more specifically, arbitrariness, where an agent cannot or will not give reasons for taking one option over another. Third, though Hegel does not think that freedom in the sense of arbitrariness is freedom in the full and complete sense, he still does not reject it entirely but retains it as one essential aspect or moment of liberty.

Hegel fully realizes that there are some choices that we make that lack objective reasons and that might be based on nothing more than the personal or individual choices, such as my choice of a specific career or mode of dress. But even these choices should be protected by the state, Hegel thinks, because they are part of 'the infinite right' of subjectivity (see pp. 231–3).

Granted that Hegel values negative as well as positive freedom, the question remains whether his use of positive freedom sanctions authoritarianism. The issue here is more complicated than many scholars recognize. At stake is not simply the historical or factual issue whether Hegel acknowledges the value of negative liberty, but two logical or systematic issues: whether Hegel's concept of positive freedom has authoritarian implications, and whether Hegel can unite both forms of freedom into a single coherent philosophy of the state. It is not sufficient to point out that Hegel intends or wants negative liberty to be upheld; for that leaves the question whether it is compatible with his ultimate principles. The issue is not disposed of simply by claiming that, because autonomy involves the capacity of choice, subjective freedom is the precondition of objective freedom.[8] For this begs the question: what if my subjective choice is at odds with the standard of rationality involved in autonomy? The question whether Hegel betrays negative liberty ultimately rests upon whether political institutions, as Hegel envisages them, involve sufficient safeguards for negative liberty. We will consider these troublesome issues in more detail below (pp. 237–43).

THE FOUNDATION OF LAW

It is a telling sign of the difficulty and complexity of Hegel's political thought that it has been subject to such conflicting interpretations. This is especially the case with regard to Hegel's views on the foundation of law. Hegel has sometimes been read as a voluntarist, as someone who bases right on the will rather than reason.[9] In this vein, Hegel has been seen as the last great spokesman in the modern voluntarist tradition, which begins with Hobbes and

Grotius and blossoms in Rousseau and Kant. However, Hegel has also been read as just the opposite: as a rationalist, as someone who derives right from reason and gives it a value independent of the will.[10] Accordingly, some scholars have placed Hegel in the natural law tradition, a tradition which ultimately goes back to Aristotle and Aquinas. Finally, Hegel has also been understood as an historicist, as someone who thinks that law is ultimately based on the history and culture of a people.[11] In this respect Hegel has been placed in the tradition of Montesquieu, Möser and Herder, who saw law as one part of the spirit of a nation.

It is a no less striking sign of the subtlety and sophistication of Hegel's political thought that all these interpretations are both right and wrong, both partially correct and partially incorrect. It was Hegel's grand aim to synthesize all these traditions, to preserve their truths and cancel their errors in a single coherent account of the basis of law. In a phrase, Hegel's doctrine was a rational historicism or an historicist rationalism, a rational voluntarism and a voluntarist rationalism.

But such apparent oxymorons raise the ultimate question: Did Hegel really have a coherent doctrine? Before we can assess this question, we must first examine the strengths and weaknesses of the opposing interpretations, and consider more closely what Hegel accepted and rejected from these conflicting traditions.

There is much evidence in favor of the voluntarist interpretation. Hegel justifies right on the basis of freedom, which he understands as the expression of the will (PR §4A). Furthermore, he defines the good in terms of the will, as the unity of the particular will with the concept of the will (PR §129). Finally, he places himself firmly in the voluntarist tradition when he states that Rousseau was right to make the will the basis of the state (PR §258R). It is indeed of the first importance to see that Hegel denied one of the fundamental premises of the natural law tradition: that value exists within the realm of nature, independent of the will (VRP III, 93). He accepts one of the basic theses of Kant's Copernican revolution in ethics:

that the laws of reason are created by us and and not imposed upon us by nature.

However, there is also much evidence against the voluntarist reading. It is a central thesis of the voluntarist tradition that whatever the will values is good simply because the will values it. But Hegel protests against the purely formal and abstract will chiefly because the will alone cannot be a source of the law (PR §§135–40). It is also a basic premise of the voluntarist tradition that nothing can be good in itself or in nature, independent of human agreements or contracts. But Hegel insists that some things are valuable in themselves, whether they are enshrined into law or recognized by governments (PR §100R). Hegel's distance from the voluntarist tradition could not be greater when he attacks the social contract theory. If we make right depend on the will of the individual, he argues, we undermine all obligation because a person will have the right to quit the contract whenever he dissents from it (PR §§29R, 258R).

There is just as much evidence for the rationalist as the voluntarist interpretation. Hegel seems to endorse the central principle of rationalism when he writes that 'in a political constitution nothing should be recognized as valid unless it agrees with the right of reason' (VVL IV, 506/281).[12] Although Hegel bases right on the will, it is necessary to add that he defines the will in terms of reason, so that it seems to amount to little more than an imperative of practical reason. Hence he stresses that there is no separation between the will and thought because the will is really only 'a special manner of thinking': 'thinking translating itself into existence, thinking as the drive to give itself existence' (PR §4A). It is also noteworthy that Hegel makes a sharp distinction between the objective will and the subjective will, where he virtually identifies the objective will with rational norms. He then stresses that the norms of practical reason have an objective validity whether or not they are recognized by the subjective will, which consists in only individual desires (PR §§126, 131, 258R). When he stresses the objectivity of norms against the formality and particularity of the subjective will he is clear that their objectivity consists in their rationality (PR §§21R, 258R).

Still, there are at least two serious difficulties with the rationalist interpretation. First, Hegel never accepted the natural law doctrine, so central to rationalism, that norms exist in nature or in some eternal realm, independent of human activity. For Hegel, the ultimate basis of the law – and here he shows his voluntarist loyalities – lies in freedom, which cannot be understood apart from the will. Second, although Hegel insists that the will consists in and depends on thinking, he also stresses the converse as well: that thinking consists in and depends on willing (PR §4A). This is not a mere gesture on Hegel's part, a routine recognition of the equality of opposites; rather, it reflects his teaching, which he develops at great length in the *Encyclopedia* (§§440–82), that all the stages in the development of spirit are simply 'the way by which it produces itself as will' (PR §4R). True to the voluntarist tradition, therefore, Hegel assigns primacy to the role of the will in the development of reason. Reason is for him essentially a form of *practical* intelligence.

The historicist interpretation has no less evidence in its behalf than the voluntarist and rationalist readings. In his youth Hegel was deeply influenced by the historicist tradition.[13] He acknowledged that debt in the *Philosophy of Right* when he praised Montesquieu's 'genuinely philosophical viewpoint' that 'legislation in general and its particular determinations should not be considered in isolation and in the abstract but rather as dependent moments within *one* totality, in the context of all the other determinations, which constitute the character of a nation and an age'. It is within such a context, Hegel significantly adds, that laws 'gain their genuine significance and hence also their justification' (PR §3R). In the *Philosophy of Right* Hegel would endorse other central doctrines of historicism. First, that though they can be changed, constitutions cannot be made (§§273R, 298A). Second, that the policies of a government should be in accord with the spirit of a nation, in agreement with its concrete circumstances and way of life, and not imposed from above by some leader or committee (§§272, 274, 298A).

But the historicist interpretation too suffers from fatal problems. Hegel makes a sharp distinction between the historical explanation of a law and its conceptual demonstration, warning us in the firmest tones never to confuse them (PR §3R). To establish the moral validity of a law, he argues, it is not sufficient to show that it arose of necessity from its historical circumstances. Since circumstances are constantly changing, this cannot provide a *general* justification for a law or institution. If we show that a law came from specific circumstances in the past, that is all the more reason to conclude that it is no longer valid under new circumstances in the present. Hegel also could not accept the relativism implicit within historicism. If we attempt to justify a law by showing that it plays a crucial role in a culture, then we have to accept the value of all laws and institutions, no matter how morally reprehensible. It is indeed telling that Hegel points out just this consequence of historicism with regard to slavery (PR §3R). Such a consequence was sufficient for him to reject the doctrine that sanctioned it.

It is one of Hegel's striking departures from historicism – and one of his most telling endorsements of the natural law tradition – that he insisted that there are certain universal and necessary principles of morality and the state. Hence in the *Philosophy of Right* he states that everyone deserves certain basic rights just in so far as they are human beings, regardless of whether they are Catholics, Protestants or Jews (§209); and he is clear that there are some fundamental goods that are inalienable and imprescriptable for all persons in so far as they are free beings, such as the right to have religious beliefs and to own property (§66). Then, in a later essay, Hegel praises the monarch of Württemberg for introducing a rational constitution that comprises 'universal truths of constitutionalism' (VVL, IV, 471/254). Among these truths are equality before the law, the right of the estates to consent to new taxes, and the representation of the people.

The problems with all three readings raise anew the question: Does Hegel really have a single coherent doctrine, one that saves the strengths and cancels the weaknesses of voluntarism, rationalism and historicism? He indeed does have such a doctrine, though it is profoundly metaphysical, resting upon his absolute idealism.

Hegel's theory about the sources of normativity is based on his social and historical conception of reason, which ultimately derives from his Aristotelian view that universals exist only in re or in particular things. The fundamental claim behind this conception is that reason is embodied in the culture and language of a people at a specific place and time. There are two more basic theses behind this claim, both of them deeply Aristotelian. First, the *embodiment thesis*: that reason exists as the specific ways of talking, writing and acting among a specific people at a specific time. This thesis states that to understand reason, we must first ask 'Where is reason?', 'In what does it exist?' It claims that the answer must lie in the language, traditions, laws and history of a specific culture at a specific time and place. Second, a *teleological thesis*: that reason also consists in the *telos* of a nation, the fundamental values or goals that it strives to realize in all its activities. The teleological thesis derives from Hegel's immanent teleology, which he applies to the historical world as well as the natural. Hegel thinks that just as each organism in the natural world has a formal–final cause, so each organism in the social world has such a cause, which consists in its defining values or ideals. In his philosophy of history Hegel will argue that these values and ideals play a decisive role in determining the actions of people in a culture, even if they do not pursue them in an organized and co-ordinated manner, and even if they are not aware of them (pp. 267–70).

True to his immanent teleology, Hegel understands norms and values essentially as the formal–final causes of things. The norm or law for a thing consists in its formal–final cause, which is both its purpose and essence. In Aristotle, the form or essence of a thing and its purpose or end are essentially one and the same, because it is the purpose or end of a thing to realize or develop its inner essence or nature. Hence we determine whether something is good or bad, right or wrong, according to whether it realizes this purpose or essence. The good or right is that which promotes the realization of this end; the bad or wrong is that which prevents its realization.

It is important to see that this formal–final cause has both a normative and an ontological status: a normative status because a thing ought to realize its essence; and an ontological status because this essence exists in things as their underlying cause and potentiality. It is for this reason that norms have an objective status for Hegel: the formal–final causes are in things whether or not we recognize or assent to them. It is also for this reason, however, that norms are not simply to be identified with whatever happens to exist: the norm is what is essential to a thing, and it is not necessary that it is realized in all circumstances. Since the norm has an objective status, existing inherently in things, we cannot understand it, *pace* the voluntarists, as the result of convention or agreement; but since the norm is also the essence of a thing, its ideal or intrinsic nature that it might not realize in its specific circumstances, we also cannot reduce it down to any accidental or incidental facts, such as the present status quo, *pace* the historicists. Hence Hegel breaks decisively with one of the basic premises of the voluntarist tradition: the distinction between 'is' and 'ought', between facts and values. But in doing so he never fell into the historicist camp, which virtually conflated 'ought' and 'is' by identifying the rational with *any* set of social and historical circumstances.

In fundamental respects, Hegel's Aristotelian doctrine places him very firmly in the scholastic branch of the natural law tradition. It was indeed Aristotle's metaphysics that inspired some of the classics of that tradition, such as Hooker's *Lawes of Ecclesiastical Politie* (1597) and Suarez's *De Legibus ac Deo Legislatore* (1612). Hegel was fully aware of his debt to the Aristotelian natural law tradition, which he was intent on preserving and continuing. It is indeed for this reason that he subtitles the *Philosophy of Right* 'Natural Law and Political Science in Outline'. It would be a serious mistake, however, to see Hegel's theory simply as a revival of the traditional scholastic doctrine. For, in two basic respects, Hegel transforms that tradition so that it accords with his modern age. First, Hegel identifies the formal–final cause not with perfection, the traditional concept, but with freedom itself, in accord with the modern definition of humanity given by Rousseau, Kant and Fichte. Second, he applies his immanent teleology on the social and historical plane, so that it applies to the entire spirit of a nation, the whole social and political organism. Thus Hegel took the central concept of the historicists – the *Volksgeist*, the spirit of a nation – and cast it in Aristotelian terms, so that it became the underlying formal–final cause of a nation. When we put both these points together – that the formal–final cause is freedom and that all nations have such a formal–final cause – we get the fundamental thesis of Hegel's philosophy of history: that the goal of world history consists in the self-consciousness of freedom. Armed with this thesis, Hegel believed he could take into account the truth of historicism while still avoiding its relativisitic consequences. Since the self-awareness of freedom is the goal of world history, it provides a single measure or criterion of value. We can now talk about progress, appraising cultures according to whether they promote or hinder the realization of this goal.

Understanding Hegel's normative theory in Aristotelian terms enables us to explain what at first sight seems an irresolvable contra-diction: namely, Hegel's insistence upon the objective status of value and his claim that values are made by human beings. This apparent contradiction is resolved as soon as we recall the Aristotelian distinction between the order of explanation and the order of exist-ence (pp. 56–7). While Hegel thinks that the formal–final cause is first in the order of explanation, he does not think that it is first in the order of existence. It is only through the activity of particular wills, he argues, that it comes into existence. So, although having normative status does not depend on the wills of individuals, these norms are still realized or actualized only in and through these individual wills. The voluntarist then made the classic confusion: he assumed that what is first in order of existence – the particular will – is also first in the order of essence and explanation.

We are now finally in a position to understand, in summary fashion, how Hegel's social-historical teleology preserves the truths and cancels the errors of the rationalist, voluntarist and historicist traditions. The rationalists were correct that values are within nature and that they have an objective status; but they were wrong to see them as eternal norms above history or as static essences within nature; rather, these values are realized only in history and through the activity of particular individuals. The voluntarists were right to stress the central role of freedom, and to emphasize the role of the will in bringing values into existence; but they went astray in thinking that the will alone – rather than reason – is the source of normativity. Finally, the historicists were correct to see norms embodied in the way of life of a people; but they were too indiscriminate, identifying the formal–final cause, the norm of historical change, with any specific set of social and historical circumstances. Since they did not understand history in teleological terms, the historicists confused the historical explanation of values with their conceptual demonstration: the historical explanation focuses on the factual causes, whereas conceptual demonstration accounts for the underlying formal–final cause.

So, ultimately, Hegel's normative doctrine was original, profound and coherent. In a remarkable fashion it fused the rationalist, voluntarist and historicist traditions, preserving their truths and cancelling their errors. But there should also be no doubt that the doctrine was deeply speculative and metaphysical, resting upon Hegel's Aristotelian metaphysics. Hegel made at least three basic metaphysical claims: (1) that universals exist *in re*, (2) that we can apply such formal–final causes to organisms in the natural world, and (3) that we can also apply them to 'organisms' in the social-political world. All these claims added together yield absolute idealism. We have seen Hegel's rationale for the first claim in chapter Three and his justification for the second in chapter Four; we will consider his defense of the third claim in chapter Eleven. Whatever the success of Hegel's arguments, it should be clear that his entire account is intelligible and defensible only as a metaphysics. So if we insist on a non-metaphysical reading of Hegel's social and political theory, we cannot appreciate its foundation.

MACHIAVELLI'S CHALLENGE

For Hegel, the question of right – 'How are we to justify the law?' – was never only a matter of its mode of justification but also one of its application. The rationalist, voluntarist and historicist traditions really only quarrelled about *how* to justify right; but they took it for granted that it had an application to the political world. It was one of Hegel's great merits as a political thinker that he fully recognized and struggled with the issue of its application. Beginning in his later Frankfurt years, Hegel saw the force of Machiavelli's challenge: that moral principles cannot be applied to the political world because if people act according to them they destroy themselves. Some of Hegel's central and characteristic doctrines arose from his attempt to answer Machiavelli.

As an idealistic youth, Hegel had the greatest confidence in the power of moral principles in the political world. In April 1795 he wrote Schelling that he expected a revolution in Germany from the Kantian philosophy.[14] He saw himself as a *Volkserzieher*, an educator of the people, who would promulgate the principles of the Kantian philosophy to the public. If the people were only aware of their natural rights, he believed, they would demand them and overthrow their oppressors. Still, Hegel's early moral idealism was not really as naive as it seemed. It was based on his hope that his native Württemberg would be liberated by invading French armies, which would impose a new modern constitution. The French army had already invaded his homeland in 1796; though it had soon retreated, its return seemed imminent. If the French had already created new republics in Milan, Rome and Switzerland, why should Württemberg not be next? Like many young Swabians, among them Schelling and Hölderlin, Hegel saw himself as '*ein Patriot*', someone who believed that the Swabian constitution should be reformed along modern French lines.[15]

Eventually, these hopes crashed against reality. The rude awakening came with the Congress of Rastatt, a peace conference between the French and German empires, which took place between December 1797 and April 1799. Hegel knew of the proceedings of this conference from inside sources: his friends Hölderlin and Isaak von Sinclair attended the conference and gave him detailed reports about their discussions with the Württemberg delegates. Along with Hölderlin and Sinclair, Hegel became deeply disillusioned by the outcome of the conference. It showed that the French had no interest in exporting their revolution but only in acquiring power for themselves. Furthermore, the states of the German Empire acted only in their self-interest and sacrificed nothing for the empire as a whole. For Hegel and his friends, the congress confirmed a sad reality that everyone knew but no one would admit: there was no longer a Holy Roman Empire.

Rastatt taught Hegel a deeply sobering lesson about the political world: that politicians act not to realize their ideals but to maximize their power. They would make treaties but violate them whenever it suited their self-interest. It was pointless to condemn politicians on moral grounds, Hegel realized. They acted from sheer necessity, for the sake of mere survival. In the political world one was either victor or loser, perpetrator or victim. Since 'ought' implies 'can', moral ideals apply to the political world only if we can act on them; but experience shows we cannot, because if we do act on them we destroy ourselves, and no one has an obligation to allow their self-destruction.

The lesson was pure Machiavelli. It was indeed no accident that Hegel would soon invoke his name in his first major work on political philosophy, his essay on the German constitution, the so-called *Verfassungsschrift*, which he wrote from 1799 to 1800 after the disillusionment of Rastatt.[16] One of the most striking features of Hegel's tract is its outspoken defense of Machiavelli, who still had a terrible reputation in eighteenth-century Germany. If you read Machiavelli's theory in the context of his times, Hegel argued, it shows itself to be 'one of the truest and greatest conceptions of a genuine political head of the greatest and noblest kind' (I, 555/221). Hegel's sympathy for Machiavelli derived not least from the similarity he saw between his own situation and Machiavelli's. Like Italy in the sixteenth century, Germany was now torn asunder by foreign powers; furthermore, the independent states of the empire were like the independent Italian cities, which acted only for their own self-interest and to aggrandize their power. On Hegel's reading, Machiavelli's perfectly legitimate overriding interest was the salvation of Italy, the end of anarchy and the achievement of Italian unity (I, 556/221).

Not surprisingly, given his sympathy for Machiavelli, some scholars have seen Hegel's *Verfassungsschrift* as essentially a defense of *Realpolitik*. *Realpolitik* is the doctrine that politicians always act in their self-interest, that their self-interest consists in acquiring, maintaining or increasing power, and that therefore the principles of morality have no application to the political world. Such was the doctrine ascribed to Hegel by Friedrich Meinecke, the great scholar of German historicism.[17] For Meinecke, there were three great figures in the history of *Realpolitik*: Machiavelli, Friedrich II and Hegel. Though now largely forgotten, Meinecke's interpretation has had some eminent followers, among them Ernst Cassirer, Karl Popper and Isaiah Berlin.[18]

Was Hegel really a champion of *Realpolitik*? This question raises anew the old controversy whether Hegel was a progressive or a reactionary. The consensus of contemporary scholarship is that Hegel was a liberal reformer, and the reactionary interpretation has now been so discredited that it has virtually attained the status of a myth.[19] But many of the more liberal interpretations of Hegel are based upon a consideration of Hegel's later Prussian context. They consider only his later *Philosophy of Right*, virtually ignoring the *Verfassungsschrift*.[20] This still ignores the question whether Hegel was really championing *Realpolitik* in the *Verfassungsschrift*, and if so whether we should read his later work in the light of the earlier one.

A close examination of the *Verfassungsschrift* reveals considerable evidence for Meinecke's interpretation. Four aspects of his theory seem to confirm it conclusively. First, Hegel maintains that the essence of the state, its central and defining characteristic, is having power, the power to enforce and defend its policies and laws (VD I, 472–85/153–64). He excludes religion, culture, the form of government, national identity, from having any necessary role in the concept of the state. Second, Hegel argues that right consists in nothing more than the advantage of the state, as acknowledged and settled by treaties (I, 541/209). He then stresses that no state is bound by its treaties if other states do not act on them (I, 540; 208); and he is explicit that other states will not act on them (I, 565/229). Third, Hegel is convinced that in politics nothing really matters besides power. He stresses that there is no real difference between politics and *Faustrecht*, i.e. the right of the stronger, and that moral idealists delude themselves when they overlook the central fact that in politics 'the truth lies in power' (I, 529/199). Fourth, Hegel apparently identifies right with historical necessity. In the introduction to the *Verfassungsschrift* he attacks moral idealists who tell us about how the political world ought to be and stresses that the way the world must be is the way it ought to be (I, 463/145).

After considering such evidence, it might seem that Hegel is indeed a champion of *Realpolitik*. But a closer examination of the text shows that this conclusion would be premature. There are three mitigating factors. First, although Hegel emphasizes having power as the central feature of the state, he also maintains that there is a purpose to such power: namely, protecting the rights of its citizens (VD I, 481–2, 520/161–2, 192). The objective of state power is 'the immutable maintenance of rights' (I, 543/211), and to prevent the relationships between states degenerating into the rights of the stronger (I, 542/210). Hegel defends a single central state because this is the only means to ensure basic law and order, which is the foundation for freedom, the enjoyment of one's basic rights and property (I, 550, 555, 556/217, 220, 221). Second, Hegel thinks that the powers of the state should be severely limited, so that it does only what is necessary to organizing and maintaining a central authority and administration. He is a severe critic of both the old absolutist state and the modern revolutionary state for attempting to control everything from above. The state should allow room for the freedom and the initiative of its citizens. Hence he writes: 'Nothing should be so sacrosanct to the government as facilitating and protecting the free activity of citizens in matters other than this [organizing and maintaining authority]' (I, 482/161–2). Third, Hegel's defense of Machiavelli is not that he saw the great value of power for its own sake, but that he saw that power is sometimes the only means of eradicating anarchy (I, 556/221). Machiavelli recognized that the first obligation of the state is to maintain law and order, and that to do so it is sometimes necessary to commit immoral actions. Such extreme measures were only justified, Hegel held, in cases of necessity, where the very existence of law and order was threatened (GW VIII, 259).

So, although a closer examination of the *Verfassungsschrift* does not vindicate Meinecke's interpretation, it does show that Hegel was much closer to the tradition of *Realpolitik* than many of his more liberal interpreters allow. If Hegel was still an idealist in politics, he was an idealist of the most realistic kind. He still wanted to overcome the gap between theory and practice; but he recognized that his ideals would have to be achieved through, and not in spite of, the quest for power. We will examine later Hegel's mature attempt to meet Machiavelli's challenge in his philosophy of history (pp. 267–70).

THE IDEALISM OF A REFORMER

Hegel's sympathy for Machiavellianism in the *Verfassungsschrift* seems to leave an insurmountable gap between theory and practice. If politicians act only on their self-interest, if their chief end is to acquire power, then moral ideals seem to have no validity in the political sphere at all – except, of course, as disguises for self-interest. In the preface Hegel himself seemed to draw just this conclusion (I, 461–4/142–5). Here he expressed his contempt for all idealists who presume to teach the world how it ought to be. His main target was the old legal theorists who refused to admit that the empire had collapsed, and who persisted in trying to find some constitution behind the chaos of its three hundred autonomous states.[21] But he also directed his scorn against those radicals and reformers – persons like himself years earlier – who think that they can change the world according to their moral ideals. Against all such idealists Hegel now preached a gospel of bitter resignation, of patient acquiescence. The sole purpose of his tract, he declared, is to know the deeper causes behind the collapse of the empire, and why events must be and cannot be otherwise. If we only knew the necessity behind historical development, he explained, this would promote 'a calmer outlook and a moderate endurance of it'. What makes us resentful is not reality itself but the thought that reality is not as it ought to be. If, however, we recognize that reality is as it must be, then we will accept that it is as it really ought to be. Here Hegel anticipated his later statement in the preface to the *Philosophy of Right* that the purpose of philosophy is not to prescribe how the world ought to be but only to reconcile us to why it must be.

Nevertheless, despite such resignation, Hegel does not reject idealism as such. What he criticizes is a specific kind of idealism: that which preaches how things ought to be, or that which ignores the real motivations of human action. But he still upholds another kind of idealism: that which perceives the goals behind historical development. When he gives historical necessity his normative sanction he does not mean to approve any form of historical development at all; he has a very definite idea of where history is going and why it ought to be as it must be. Already in the *Verfassungsschrift* he suggests a central theme of his later philosophy of history: that the end of history is the realization of freedom, and more specifically the principle that the people should have some definite share in government. The modern principle of representation – that each individual should participate in the state – grew out of the forests of Germany and will eventually dominate the entire modern world (VD I, 533/203).

Ultimately, then, Hegel never really renounced his ideals; he simply read them into history itself. He could accept the realities of history only because he believed that they were stepping-stones toward progress, means of the realization of the higher ends of reason. The great lesson he learned from the post-revolutionary era is that reason is not an eternal norm above history but the immanent purpose and inner necessity of history itself. Hegel's famous thesis of the cunning of reason was his reaffirmation of idealism in the face of the harsh realities of the political world. This thesis states that even if politicians act only for their self-interest, they are still the unwitting instruments for the higher purpose of reason, of which they have only a vague presentiment. Hegel's message was that reason is more cunning than the most cunning political tactician, cleverer than all the wily snares of *Realpolitik* (pp. 267–70).

Hegel's grand theme of reason in history grew out of not only the disillusionment of Rastatt, but also his attempt to resolve the famous theory–practice dispute of the late 1790s (pp. 31–3). It was his attempt to find a middle path between the extremes of rationalism and empiricism. The rationalists (Kant and Fichte) held that practice should follow theory, or that we ought to change the world to conform to the moral ideals of reason; the empiricists (Möser, A.W. Rehberg, Friedrich Gentz) countered that theory should follow practice, or that we should determine our political principles by following tradition, precedent and historical experience. Hegel agrees with the rationalists that the principles of the state should be founded on reason; but he disagrees with them that they should be imposed on history. He concurs with the empiricists that good laws and policies should arise from history and adapt to local circumstances; but he parts company with them in their emphasis upon precedent, privilege and tradition as the basis for the law. In short, the main problem for the rationalist is that he emphasizes reason at the expense of history; and the chief difficulty of the empiricist is that he stresses history at the expense of reason. The middle path between these extremes is that there is reason within history. The fundamental principles of the Revolution – liberty, equality and fraternity – are really the ends of history itself. The faulty premise behind the false antithesis between rationalism and empiricism is that history consists in nothing more than an accumulation of facts. This gives the rationalist his motive for neglecting history, and the empiricist his excuse for neglecting reason. What both failed to see is that there is reason in history, that its final purpose is the realization of freedom, the self-awareness that man as such is free.

We are now in a better position to understand Hegel's famous 'double dictum' (*Doppelsatz*) in the preface to the *Philosophy of Right*. The double dictum declares: 'What is rational is actual; what is actual is rational.' There is probably no other statement of Hegel's that has created more commentary and controversy; but its basic meaning becomes clear as long as we remember Hegel's middle path between rationalism and empiricism. The first dictum – that the rational is the actual – means that reason is a self-actualizing end, a purpose that of necessity realizes itself. The rational is not just an ideal about what ought to be but an end that must be. This dictum is directed against conservatives, who tend to dismiss ideals as unrealizable, quixotic or utopian. The second dictum – that the actual is the rational – states that the actual embodies, realizes and develops the idea. It is directed against radicals, who want to sweep away the past for their moral ideals. It is important to note, however, how Hegel explicitly qualified the second half of the dictum in his *Enzyklopädie* (§6). Anxious to avoid the objection that he was sanctioning all forms of the status quo in saying that the actual is rational, he explained that we have to distinguish *actuality* (*Wirklichkeit*) from *reality* (*Dasein*) or *existence* (*Existenz*). Actuality is what of necessity realizes the essence of a thing, and so it is not mere reality or existence, which is contingent. Hence Hegel does not mean to endorse every aspect of the existing social and political world as rational. Crime, poverty and tyranny might be real or exist but they are not actual because they do not realize any ideal of reason.

When understood in its historical context, Hegel's dictum shows itself to be neither radical nor reactionary. It is not radical because it demands that the statesman build on the historical past; and it is not reactionary because it forces him to recognize the progressive forces of history. Hegel's dictum therefore advises the statesman to seek the middle path of reform. This is indeed just what we expect Hegel to say when we place him in his Prussian context. Although Hegel has often been seen as a spokesman for the Prussian Restoration, several basic facts refute this interpretation. (1) Hegel's connections in Prussia were not with reactionary court circles, but with the reforming administration of Stein, Hardenberg and Altenstein. It was indeed Altenstein who called Hegel to Prussia because he was attracted to his reformist views.[22] Rather than siding with the reactionaries, Hegel criticized them sharply in his correspondence and in the *Philosophy of Right*.[23] For their part, the reactionary circles in the Prussian court under Count von Wittgenstein harrassed and spied upon Hegel and his pupils.[24] (2) Hegel developed the outlines, and even the details, of his organic conception of the state before his association with Prussia in 1818.[25] Until 1805, when the foundation of his views had already been laid down, he regarded not Prussia but Austria as the major hope for reform in Germany.[26] (3) Rather than glorifying the status quo, most aspects of Hegel's ideal state were far from a reality in the Prussia of 1820. Indeed, Hegel's demands for a constitutional monarchy, an elected assembly, local self-government, and a powerful civil service were all defeated by the Prussian reactionaries in 1819. (4) Hegel's organic state closely resembles the ideals for the reform of the Prussian state put forward by Stein and Hardenberg. Like Hegel, Stein and Hardenberg advocated (a) a bi-cameral estates assembly, (b) more local self-government, (c) more freedom of trade and the abolition of feudal privileges, (d) a constitution ensuring funda-mental rights to all citizens and placing limits upon the powers of the monarchy, (e) greater equality of opportunity, so that positions in the army and civil service were open to anyone with sufficient talent, and (f) a more powerful bureaucracy, which did not simply execute the orders of the king and cabinet but which actively formulated government policy.

Given all its affinities with the Prussian Reformation, and all its tensions with the Prussian Restoration, it is tempting to regard Hegel's theory of the state as the philosophy of the Prussian Reform Movement. This is indeed a more accurate characterization of Hegel's position. It is important to remember, however, that Hegel developed almost all his ideas *before* the formation of this move-ment, so that they are at best only an *ex post facto* rationalization of it.[27]

Ten

Hegel's Theory of the State

HEGEL'S POLITICAL PROJECT

In one of his few arresting metaphors Hegel wrote in the Preface to his *Philosophy of Right* that the owl of Minerva only flies at dusk. In a sombre tone he explained that philosophy always arrives too late on the scene, painting its 'gray upon gray' only when a form of life has grown old. If we apply these lines to Hegel's own political philosophy, we might well wonder what relevance it has for us today. After all, if Hegel's philosophy was already obsolete for his age, what value can it possibly have for our own?

Although much in Hegel's political philosophy is indeed dated, philosophers today still value it for raising important questions and for posing alternatives to the dominant liberalism of contemporary political thought. Usually, Hegel is seen as the great modern spokesman for communitarianism and as the pioneering critic of liberalism. Some historians regard his political philosophy as the major conceptual alternative to the liberal tradition, and they explain its historical significance in just such terms.[1]

But this common picture of Hegel distorts his true historical position. It is misleading to cast Hegel in such a role for the simple reason that it had already been played so well by so many of his predecessors and contemporaries. If we limit ourselves to the German tradition alone, we quickly find thinkers who criticized liberalism and defended communitarianism before, or around the same time as, Hegel. Among them were Justus Möser, A.W. Rehberg, Novalis, Schleiermacher, Friedrich Schlegel and Adam Müller. Many of Hegel's criticisms of liberalism, and many of his communitarian ideals, were part of the common heritage of his generation. Purely for the sake of convenience, we might consider Hegel *the chief representative* of this wider tradition. We should not conclude, however, that these ideas are original to, or characteristic of, him.

This picture of Hegel is inaccurate for another reason: it falsifies his intentions. For it was never Hegel's aim to reject the liberal tradition for the sake of communitarianism. Unlike some of the more conservative critics of liberalism, such as Möser and Haller, Hegel continued to uphold fundamental liberal values, such as freedom of conscience, equality of opportunity and the right of dissent. While these conservatives denied liberal values for the sake of community, Hegel insisted upon preserving them within the community. Hegel's significance as a political thinker lies less in his defense of communitarianism or his critique of liberalism than in his attempt *to synthesize* communitarianism with liberalism in a single coherent conception of the modern state. It is chiefly in this regard that Hegel remains relevant to contemporary social and political thought.

Here again, though, it is important to recognize that such a project was not unique to Hegel. It was indeed the general program of the early romantic generation. There was, however, something new to *how* Hegel would attempt this synthesis: he would try to unite the individual to the state according to the bonds of reason rather than those of sentiment and imagination. Contrary to the romantics, Hegel insisted that the individual could identify with the state only if the state somehow satisfied the demands of critical reason. He rejected, therefore, Novalis's famous thesis that the bonds of the state should be based upon 'faith and love'.[2]

Hegel's project for a synthesis of the liberal and communitarian traditions seems to propose a virtual squaring of the circle, given that these traditions seem to be so fundamentally at odds with one another. Already in the 1790s, the battle-lines between these traditions were beginning to appear.[3] They were opposed in at least four respects. First, the liberals held that the chief purpose of the state is to protect liberty, the rights of citizens to pursue happiness in their own manner. The communitarians claimed, however, that the main end of the state is to ensure the common good, which is more than the sum of private interests but those basic goods essential to everyone as a human being. Second, liberals contended that the state is an aggregate that arises from the sum of individuals, each of which is a self-sufficient unit; communitarians, however, held that the state is an organic whole that determines the identity of the individuals that compose it. Third, liberals maintained that there should be a clear distinction between legality and the sphere of morality and religion: the law regulates only external actions whereas morality and religion concern the realm of inner conscience and choice. Since the communitarian held that the state is sustained only by the patriotic virtues and beliefs of its citizens, and since he stressed that it is the role of the state to educate its citizens to have these virtues and beliefs, he denied a sharp separation between these spheres. Fourth, the liberals adopted a negative concept of liberty, according to which freedom consists in the absence of coercion and constraint; the communitarians had a positive concept of liberty, according to which freedom consists in performing definite actions, such as participating in public life.

Already in his early Berne and Frankfurt years, Hegel had come under the influence of both the liberal and communitarian currents of thought. The communitarian influence is apparent in three respects. First, from his admiration for the Greek and Roman republics, which he praises because their citizens lived and died for the common good.[4] Second, from his organic conception of society, according to which its history, religion and politics form an indissoluble unity (TE I, 42/56). Third, from his attempt to develop a civil religion, a religion for every citizen of a state that would serve as a source of social, political and cultural solidarity. The liberal influence is especially apparent from Hegel's early defense of religious freedom. The young Hegel became especially preoccupied with 'positivity' – the enforcement of religious belief by the state – because he saw it as a betrayal of the spirit of Christianity, which consisted in moral autonomy. To counter this danger, Hegel defended in his *Positivity Essay* an essentially liberal conception of the state, according to which the essential purpose of the state is to protect my rights, among which are freedom of speech and conscience as well as security of person and property (N 173, 183). All that the state should require from me is legality, the conformity of my *actions* with the law; but it does not have the right to demand morality, that my *will* should conform to the law (175). On these grounds Hegel insisted upon a separation between church and state.

The tensions between these traditions surfaced in some contradictions in Hegel's own early political thought. It became very difficult for him, for example, to square his ideal of a civil religion with his defense of religious liberty in the *Positivity Essay*. It was the attempt to solve difficulties such as these that eventually led to Hegel's general project for a synthesis of liberalism and communitarianism. His *Philosophy of Right* was his final attempt to resolve these traditions into a single coherent philosophy of the state.

The task of this chapter will be to explain Hegel's attempt to synthesize liberalism with communitarianism in the *Philosophy of Right*. To understand his project, we must first examine what he redeemed, and what he rejected, in each tradition.

THE CRITIQUE OF LIBERALISM AND COMMUNITARIANISM

We can best gauge Hegel's attitude toward communitarianism by considering his views on the ancient republics of Greece and Rome, which were for him the model of complete communal life. Hegel admired the ancient republics for several reasons. First, they gave priority to the public good over self-interest. Like Machiavelli, Montesquieu, Rousseau and Ferguson, Hegel praised the virtue of the ancient republics, the citizen's devotion to the common welfare, his willingness to put the interests of the republic before his private interests. The ancient republics rightly recognized that, in cases of public danger, the citizen must sacrifice his life and property for the state. Second, the ancient republics saw that the highest good – the end of life – is to be achieved only by life in the state. Following Rousseau and Machiavelli, Hegel criticized the Christian tradition for placing the highest good beyond the earthly realm in eternal salvation in heaven. The ancient Greeks and Romans did not need personal salvation, he argued, because they found the meaning of their lives in devotion to the state. Third, the ancient republics were democratic, giving each citizen the right to participate in the affairs of the state. It is important to see that Hegel, like most thinkers in late eighteenth-century Germany, associates democracy more with communitarianism than liberalism. Liberal democracy was a much later nineteenth-century development; and some liberals of Hegel's day, most notably Jacobi and Humboldt, were defenders of constitutional monarchy rather than republicanism. While Hegel, again like most of his contemporaries, doubted that the direct democracy of the ancient republics was practicable in the modern world, he still insisted that the modern state could not survive if the people did not have some share in government, some right, even if indirect, to govern their own affairs (§301A). It was indeed precisely through public participation in the affairs of state that the individual would identify with the state and regard itself as part of the community (§261A).

Despite his admiration for the ancient republics, Hegel still taught that they suffered from two fundamental defects, which he explicitly identifies in the *Philosophy of Right*. First, they gave no place to individual rights, especially the right of the individual to dissent from the government (§§124R,138A,185R, 260R, 261R, 299A). Second, the ancient republics did not expect the citizen to seek his own self-interest in the market place and to find his own path toward happiness (§§46R, 185R, 262A). The citizen was expected to have sufficient means and independence so that he could deliberate about the affairs of state; but, now that slavery was abolished in the modern world, this was no longer a reasonable expectation.

Hegel's partiality for liberalism was no less strong than his sympathy for communitarianism. Although it is implausible to regard Hegel as a liberal,[5] it is certainly the case that he upheld some fundamental liberal values. Not least among these was a free market economy where everyone had the right to pursue their self-interest and to find happiness in their own manner (§§185, 206). Although Hegel held that complete *laissez-faire* was untenable, he still warned against excessive regulation of the market place. One of the guiding goals behind the *Philosophy of Right* was indeed to integrate the freedoms of civil society into the modern state. Another crucial liberal value supported by Hegel was human rights, the doctrine that all people have fundamental rights simply as human beings. He explicitly affirmed this principle in the *Philosophy of Right*: '*A human being counts as such because he is a human being*, not because he is a Jew, Catholic, Protestant, German, Italian, etc. This consciousness, which is the aim of thought, is of infinite importance' (§209R). No less than Locke, Rousseau or Kant, Hegel maintains that some rights are inalienable or imprescriptable, such as the security of my person, the right to own property or to hold religious beliefs (§66R). True to his respect for such rights, Hegel strongly endorsed some classical liberal freedoms: freedom of conscience, association and press. While he still affirmed the value of a single state Church in Prussia, he held that the state should tolerate a diversity of sects, be they Quakers, Jews or Catholics (H 225). Although the state should encourage everyone to belong to some Church, it should leave it entirely to the individual to choose which one (§270R). While Hegel denied that freedom of press should give one the license to print whatever one wanted – for libel was always a problem (§319R) – he still stressed the role of a free press in forming public opinion and in gaining knowledge of the common good (§315).

For all his liberal values, Hegel took exception to liberalism in fundamental ways. First of all, for reasons we shall soon see (pp. 247–51), Hegel questioned the classical liberal economic doctrine that the free workings of market forces naturally work out for the benefit of everyone alike. He contended that the only way to ensure the liberties of civil society was for the government to control market forces (§§185A, 201A, 243). Second, he could not accept the common liberal doctrine that the purpose of the state is only to protect natural rights and the freedoms of the market place (§258R). Such a doctrine seemed to sanction the dissolution of society into a multitude of isolated and self-seeking atoms, having no sense of belonging or responsibility for the common good. Third, Hegel disputed the social contract theory, according to which the state arises from the agreement between independent self-interested parties. Hegel questioned this doctrine on several grounds. (1) There are no such independent agents in the state of nature, since the very identity of a person rests upon society and the state. (2) If the obligation to enter the state depends on the will of the individual, then membership in the state becomes arbitrary or optional; the individual will have the right to leave the state when it is contrary to his self-interest, making all government impossible (§§258R, 281R). Fourth, Hegel did not accept the liberal's strictly negative conception of freedom, according to which freedom consists simply in the absence of constraint and the multiplicity of options. While, as we have seen, Hegel does not dispute the importance and value of such negative freedom, he does not think that it provides an exhaustive or complete account of freedom. His own more positive conception identifies freedom with self-determination or autonomy, the power to act on rational laws that I would impose on myself as a rational being.

Hegel's ambivalent attitude toward liberalism – the source of all its strengths and weaknesses for him – centers around a single fundamental principle, which he calls 'the right of subjectivity' or 'the right of subjective freedom' (§124R). In general, this principle states that every individual has a right to accept only those beliefs or commands, or to do only those actions, that agree with its own judgment (§132R). It means too that every individual is an end in itself, and that it should never be treated simply as a means to the purposes of others (VG 82/70). Hegel gave several more precise formulations to the principle, none of them synonymous or even coextensive. (1) It is 'the right to recognize nothing that I do not perceive as rational' (§132R). (2) 'Whatever it [the subjective will] is to recognize as valid should be *perceived* by it as *good*' (§132). (3) It is '. . . the right of the *subject* to find its *satisfaction* in [its] action' (§121;VG 82/70). (4) '[T]he will can *recognize* something or *be* something only in so far as that thing is *its own* . . .' (§107). (5) '. . . [F]or a content to be accepted and held to be true, man must himself be actively involved with it, more precisely, he must find any such content to be at one and in unity with *the certainty of his own self*' (EPW §7R).

Whatever its precise formulation, Hegel regards this principle as inescapable, as fundamental to and characteristic of the modern world. He traces its roots back to Christianity (§124R), and finds it quintessentially embodied in Protestantism (PR VII, 27/22). This principle is for him central to the modern state, which somehow must incorporate and satisfy its just demands. The main reason for the demise of the ancient *polis* is that it could not accommodate this right (§§138A, 124R, 185R, 260R, 261R, 299R).

Nothing better reveals the liberal side of Hegel's political philosophy than the constant use he makes of the principle of subjectivity throughout the *Philosophy of Right*. Hegel appeals to it to justify several classical political values. (1) The individual is bound by only those laws or policies to which he consents (§§4, 258R). (2) The individual should have the right to participate in government, or at least to have his interests represented in it (§301R). (3) The individual should have moral, intellectual and religious liberty, the right to express his opinion and to exercise his conscience (§§270R, 316, 317A, 319). (4) The individual should have the right to pursue self-interest in a market economy, or he should have the freedom of choice characteristic of civil society (§§185R, 187). (5) The laws and constitution of a country must be clear and coherent, intelligible to the understanding of everyone alike (§211R).

Although Hegel strongly endorses the principle of subjectivity, and although he uses it to justify all these liberal values, he still regards it as deeply problematic. The chief problem with the principle in his view is that it is too abstract, i.e. it does not give an effective criterion or concrete guidelines about which beliefs or actions to endorse. The principle is 'purely formal' because it is compatible with any content; *any* law or belief could satisfy it (PR §§136–8, 140). It does not tell us, therefore, which laws or beliefs to accept, only that whatever laws or beliefs we accept should agree with our reason or conscience. In other words, the problem with subjectivity is that it can be false or wrong. We know that a decision or belief is right or wrong, Hegel argues, only from its content, from *what* it decides or *what* it believes (§137). For this reason, Hegel argues, it is also necessary to recognize the complementary right, which Hegel calls the '*right of objectivity*' (§132). The right of objectivity claims that the decisions and opinions of subjectivity must be correct, i.e. they must have the right content. Just how we determine the content of the right of objectivity we will determine in the next section.

Such are, in very condensed outline, Hegel's basic agreements and disagreements with both liberalism and communitarianism. But the most important question remains: Is it possible to unite into a single coherent conception those aspects of liberalism and communitarianism that Hegel wants to preserve? There is an obvious point of friction: What if the state's concept of the common good is not acceptable to some individuals, or even the great majority of them? If the synthesis rests upon force alone, the right of the state *to compel* the individual to obey, then it will be artificial and contrived.

There are two strategies to resolve this problem. One is to say that there is really no possibility of a conflict between the state's conception of liberty and that of its citizens if the state is sufficiently democratic; then the state's conception of the common good will represent nothing more than the will of its citizens. Another is to reduce the conception of the common good down to nothing more than the self-interest of the individuals who compose it. Since the aim of the state is to guarantee the freedoms of the market place, and since it does nothing more than ensure the *opportunity* for everyone to share in the goods of civil society, there is no real conflict between the state and liberty after all.

Both strategies suffer from serious shortcomings. The chief problem with the first, as we shall soon see, is that Hegel's state is not entirely democratic. The main difficulty with the second is that Hegel's conception of the common good is much more substantial than the totality of the interests of the individuals who compose it. Hence Hegel holds that for its security, the state must sometimes ask the individual to act contrary to his private interest (§324); and he maintains that the unregulated pursuit of private interest can in some cases undermine the common good, which it is the purpose of the government to define (§232). Furthermore, his objective conception of the good means that something has validity regardless of whether people assent to it or not (§§126R, 258R).

Whether or not Hegel's synthesis is successful ultimately depends on how he attempts to satisfy and balance the rights both of objectivity and of subjectivity. To understand his attempt, we must take a closer look at his theory of the institutions and powers of the modern state. Before we do this, however, we must consider one of Hegel's central and characteristic concepts: ethical life (*Sittlichkeit*).

ETHICAL LIFE

The concept of ethical life plays a pivotal role in the *Philosophy of Right*. The exposition of this concept comprises more than half of the work, overshadowing the parallel parts on abstract right and morality. The concept is so crucial because it formulates Hegel's fundamental social and political ideal: the synthesis of the community with the individual.

But if the concept is important, it is also obscure. The problems begin with translation. The German word '*Sittlichkeit*' has no exact English counterpart. It sometimes has the connotation of morality; but its meaning can be broader, including all aspects of human conduct. The term has a specific reference to manners, to standards of politeness and decency, as well as to what is customary and traditional (as in the adage '*Andere Länder, andere Sitten*'). The term can refer to the whole way of living and acting of a person or people. It is in this broader sense that Hegel uses it. He first conceived of *Sittlichkeit* as a translation for the ancient Greek '*ethos*', which connotes the manners, morals and whole way of life of a nation or people (II, 504/159).

Although Hegel intends his concept of ethical life to include moral actions, he makes a technical distinction between ethical life and morality (*Moralität*). Morality concerns the *inner* sphere of the individual, his moral intentions and religious conscience; it is distinguished from the sphere of abstract right or legality, which deals only with *external* actions, their bare conformity to law, regardless of an agent's intentions (§§104A, 105). Both morality and abstract right deal with a person's rights and duties as an individual. They differ from ethical life because they treat each individual on its own, apart from its place in society and the state. By contrast, ethical life considers the individual as an integral part of the social and political whole.

The distinction between ethical life and morality ultimately involves a more fundamental distinction between two different ways of viewing the relationship between the individual and social whole. Morality is an abstract universal: it makes the part prior to the whole, as if each individual were self-sufficient or independent. Ethical life is a concrete universal: it makes the whole prior to the part, such that the very identity of the individual depends on its place in the whole. Hegel therefore thinks that the standpoint of morality is one-sided and abstract because it separates the individual from his place in the social whole, which gives the individual his very identity.

Although the concept of ethical life is essentially holistic, Hegel stresses that it also includes the interests and rights of individuals. While the whole is prior to its parts, it also cannot function apart from them; indeed, it realizes itself only through each of them individually, only if each of them retains its own separate identity as a necessary part of the whole. In his opening account of ethical life in the *Philosophy of Right* (§§142–57), Hegel stresses how whole and part, community and individual, are reconciled and interdependent. If the individuals find their self-consciousness and self-identity in the community, the ideals of the community are also actualized only through the actions and inner dispositions of specific individuals (§142). When Hegel states that the social whole is realized only through individuals he does not mean that they are only necessary *means* for the realization of collective ends; rather, each individual is an end in itself, and its thriving as an individual is also the *end* of the social organism itself (VG 82/70). A well-functioning social whole must take into account the rights of each of its individual members, so that their autonomy and independence are respected.

In ethical life Hegel attempted to synthesize the rights both of subjectivity and of objectivity. Hence he explains that in ethical life the laws and customs of a people are both objective and subjective. They are objective because they seem to exist in their own right, being independent of the wills of individuals; in this regard, they are sources of authority to which the individual conforms or submits (§§144, 146). They are also subjective, however, because they have been internalized in the individual, who acts according to the customs and laws of his people as if they were his own 'second nature' (§§147, 151). They are his second nature not only because he has been educated and habituated to do them, Hegel stresses, but because they have also satisfied his own inner conviction and reflection. While ethical life negates morality in so far as morality attempts to separate the individual from the whole, it also attempts to preserve the fundamental principle of morality, the right of subjectivity (§154). If the individual is to become one with the community, he must do so from within, according to his own critical reflection. Hence Hegel insists that the synthesis of the community with the individual in ethical life is not based on trust or faith alone (§147).

As explained so far, the concept of ethical life seems to be a straightforward contradiction. On the one hand, Hegel states that ethical life establishes the right of objectivity, so that the individual recognizes the higher authority of its laws and customs and no longer questions them. On the other hand, however, he also stresses that in ethical life the individual becomes one with his community not on the naive level of trust and faith but on the higher level of critical reflection. Hence ethical life seems both to satisfy and to suspend the right of subjectivity. How does Hegel resolve this apparent contradiction?

Hegel could resolve this contradiction by invoking a distinction he often uses in the *Philosophy of Right*: that between the objective and subjective will of the individual. The subjective will involves the individual's power of choice, his interests and needs; the objective will expresses the norms of reason, which are realized in the laws, customs and morality of social life. The contradiction then disappears if we claim that the subjective will is suspended while the objective will is reinstated.

But such a distinction seems to exclude the very right of subjectivity that it was Hegel's purpose to honor. For the question remains: What if the individual, through his critical reflection, does not endorse the laws, customs and morality of the state? Hegel seems to assume that the individual's self-reflection will eventually teach him to lay aside his own personal interests and opinions, so that he will find his higher freedom and self-awareness in the community. But what is to ensure this? Like Plato and Aristotle,

Hegel assigns great importance to education in binding the individual to the community. It is only through education, he argues,
that we acquire our second nature and become rational beings
(§§151A, 187R). Education will perfectly tie the individual to the
state, however, only if, like Plato's system in the *Republic*, it becomes
so detailed, rigorous and comprehensive that the individual is
trained never to question the state. But Hegel himself had doubts
about Plato's system precisely because it was too totalitarian
(§185R).

The main suspicion against Hegel's concept of ethical life is that
it achieves its synthesis of the individual with the community only
by its implicit authoritarianism, only by favoring the right of
objectivity over subjectivity. Hegel's original argument in behalf of
ethical life, and against the one-sidedness of morality, only seems
to confirm how much it is slanted in favor of the right of objectivity. To overcome the abstractness of the principle of subjectivity, he
argues, we must supplement it with the communitarian ideal. We
can give content to our reason, an *objective* norm to our conscience,
only if we place them within the ethos of the community (§§146,
148). Hegel then writes as if we should simply accept and follow
what the community tells us to do:

> In an ethical community it is easy to say *what* someone must do and
> *what* the duties are which he has to fulfill in order to be virtuous. He
> must simply do what is prescribed, expressly stated, and known to
> him in the situation.
>
> (§150)

The danger here is not simply that the laws and customs of
ethical life could be imposed on the individual; the problem runs
deeper because the individual also has no standards or principles
outside of those that are given to him by ethical life. He has no
higher moral standards or principles to criticize the practices and
institutions of the community. After all, apart from the content of
ethical life, the right of subjectivity is purely formal, the sheer

activity of reflecting. But what worth does this have on its own, especially if it is incorrect and wrong?

The suspicion of authoritarianism only grows when we recognize that, whenever there is a conflict between the rights of subjectivity and objectivity, Hegel unhesitantly and emphatically gives clear priority to the right of objectivity. Thus he declares that, however important the right of subjectivity, 'the right of the rational – as the objective – over the subject remains firmly established' (§132R). He also maintains that 'the subjective will has worth and dignity only in so far as its insight and intention are in conformity with the good' (§131). He further holds that 'since the good . . . is the [i.e. the particular will's] substance, it has an *absolute right* as distinct from the abstract right of property and the particular ends of welfare' (§130). Hegel argues that we must never declare the right of subjectivity against the state. My particularity is only a right at all in so far as I am free; and therefore I cannot assert it in contradiction to 'the substantial basis on which it rests [i.e. ethical life]' (§126). He explains that it is 'one of the commonest errors of abstraction to insist on private rights and private welfare as *valid in and for themselves* in opposition to the universality of the state' (§126R).

The problem of authoritarianism can also be seen from this angle: that Hegel, like Kant,[6] does not take actual, but only possible, consent as a sufficient criterion of a person's acceptance of the laws. What is decisive is not any kind of assent but *rational* assent (§§4A, 29R, 258R). So if a person *could* assent to the laws, even if he in fact happens to dissent from them, the laws are still legitimate. A person can be regarded as having given his assent to laws provided that they are rational. But then the question remains: rational according to whom? We are still left with Locke's decisive question: *Who shall be judge?* Hegel's answer seems to be perfectly clear: that it should not be the people but the government. He never had much confidence in the judgment of the common man to determine whether the laws are rational, or even to know his best interests (§§301R, 308R, 317R). He maintains that it is the universal estate alone, the government bureaucracy, which knows the best interests of the estates, even if they have not been articulated by them (§§289, 301R).

Yet all these suspicions are still premature and inconclusive. For we cannot resolve the question of authoritarianism – and the whole issue of whether Hegel has a successful synthesis of communitarianism and liberalism – unless we first examine his general theory of the state. Although Hegel does give the bureaucracy great power, his account of its power is embedded in a much larger theory of the division of powers, of the checks and balances, between the branches of government. The question would then be: Does Hegel impose sufficient limits on the bureaucracy's power to prevent it from becoming tyrannical or authoritarian? It is important to recognize that the general concept of ethical life by itself is only abstract; it *postulates* an identity of the individual and the social; but it still does not show us how to realize it. But Hegel does have a much more complex account of how ethical life is to be realized in the structure of the modern state. It is to this account that we must now turn.

THE ORGANIC STATE

Hegel's account of the structure of the state explains it in essentially organic terms. Throughout the *Philosophy of Right* Hegel constantly refers to the state as an organism, using this concept to define his view of the state in opposition to others.[7] What Hegel means by 'the concept' or 'the idea' of the state is indeed its organic structure. To explain the state according to its concept or idea, as opposed to explaining its historical origins, is to demonstrate its organic structure, showing how all its parts play a necessary role in the whole. The organic concept of the state was widespread in the 1790s, however, and virtually a mainstay of the republican and romantic traditions. Since there is no definite meaning to the concept as such, and since its specific sense depends on the thinker, we have to be more precise to capture the meaning Hegel gave to it.

Hegel attributes three fundamental and general features to the organic state. First, the whole exists for each of the parts as much as each of the parts exists for the whole; in other words, the individual is as much a means as an end for the state (§§269–70). Second, that there must be life in each part of the state, so that each has some degree of autonomy or independence (§§272, 303R). Third, each part, in maintaining itself and seeking its own self-interest, also promotes the interest of the whole (§§184, 286).

Hegel read a more specific political meaning into each of these general features. The first feature means that there should be no dispute between liberalism and communitarianism regarding the purpose of the state. Since the whole exists for the parts, the liberal is right that the state should promote the rights and interests of everyone as an individual; but since the parts also exist for the whole, the communitarian is correct that the individual should devote himself to affairs of state since doing so is ultimately in his self-interest. The second feature means that the state must respect the rights of individuals as individuals, and that there should be some autonomous groups within the state, independent of central administration and control, which represent economic interests and engage in local government. The third feature means that there should be no conflict between self-interest and the public good. The great strength of the modern state over that of antiquity, Hegel argued, is that the individual is tied to the state not through virtue but through self-interest. The individual can recognize that his own private interest depends upon his participation in public life, and that he does not have to sacrifice himself for the public good (§§260–1).

As stated so far, the organic concept is still too abstract to determine how Hegel attempted to fuse liberal freedoms with communitarian values. All that the organic concept seems to provide is some desiderata for a synthesis but no real means of resolving it. We still do not know the precise constitutional or institutional mechanisms that would tie self-interest to the good of the community. We shall consider some of these mechanisms in more detail in later sections. Right now, however, we should stress one general feature that was crucial for Hegel's synthesis: its pluralism.

For Hegel, like all the romantics, the organic concept meant primarily a state having a unified but differentiated structure (§§269–71). In Hegel's jargon, the state must possess 'unity-in-difference'. The moment of unity is a single centralized authority, which consists in a monarch, a parliament, and a civil service or administration. The moment of difference stands for the whole realm of civil society, where individuals compete against one another in the market place, and where they have rights against one another to protect their property and freedom. What holds these moments of unity and difference together – the unity of unity and difference – is the plurality of independent bodies, such as local councils, trade groups, community associations, guilds, and so on. Hegel gave a decisive role to the corporations and the legislative assembly in his state, and they are indeed crucial in reconciling the conflicting claims of community and liberty (§§289, 290A). On the one hand, they answer to the need for community because they provide sources of belonging, becoming a 'second family' (§252); but, on the other hand, they also respond to the demand for liberty because they are independent of central control and represent local and popular interests.

Like many of the romantics, Hegel believed that the absence of independent groups within the modern state was the common failing of both the absolutist state of the *ancien régime* and the revolutionary state of modern France (§290; VD I 481–5/161–4). Both absolutism and Jacobinism went astray in not providing for sufficient self-government within the state. They reduced the state down to a single centralized power and the masses, abolishing all the intermediate groups between them. This was a source of constant instability, because the masses were easily manipulated by the rulers, and the rulers were easily deposed by the masses. The only way to prevent such instability – the extremes of tyranny and ochlocracy – is for the state to have intermediate groups, since they organize and control the people yet serve as a bulwark against central oppression.

With its pluralistic structure, Hegel's organic state is reminiscent of the corporate society of the Middle Ages, with all its guilds, estates and self-governing cities.[8] Like many of the romantics and the Hanoverian Whigs, Hegel believed that some of the old medieval institutions of Germany, if they were only properly reformed, could provide the stable basis for political change in the post-revolutionary era. Though it is a commonplace of Marxist historiography that the romantic longing for the Middle Ages is reactionary, Hegel and the romantics valued aspects of the medieval constitution as a safeguard of liberty and a bulwark against tyranny. 'Never was there so much liberty, equality and fraternity as in the Middle Ages', Friedrich Schlegel once wrote.[9] Hegel too believed that the medieval world was the source of all the ideas about liberty that shook the modern world. That the Revolution was a break with the medieval past was for him 'one of the silliest of notions'.[10]

Still, there was a difference between Hegel and the romantics regarding the extent to which the modern state should be modeled on its medieval past. Hegel was emphatic that the modern state could not be based simply upon the principles of government of the Middle Ages. He criticized the medieval political order for its lack of a firm central power, for its inherited privileges, and for its failure to recognize the basic freedoms of civil society.[11] If he wished to return to the old medieval guilds, he also insisted that they be reformed by abolishing restrictive trade practices and hereditary privileges.[12]

Given the pluralistic structure of Hegel's state – its inclusion of intermediate groups and the whole realm of civil society – it should be clear that the common liberal criticisms of Hegel as a defender of absolutism, or as a forerunner of modern totalitarianism, are very wide of the mark. What is so unfair about these criticisms is that Hegel shares the liberal's hatred of totalitarianism and develops his organic model of the state to prevent it. It was one of the chief aims of his organic state to avoid the 'machine state' of Prussian absolutism or French Jacobinism, where everything is controlled from above, leaving no room for local self-government or autonomous corporations. No less than the liberal, Hegel would have disapproved of socialism as a cure for the ills of modern civil society. If we are determined to find twentieth-century analogues to Hegel's view of the state, we can do no better than to look at modern defenders of pluralism, such as de Tocqueville and Durkheim.

CIVIL SOCIETY

One of the most important aspects of Hegel's political theory is his extensive treatment of civil society (*bürgerliche Gesellschaft*) in the *Philosophy of Right* (§§182–256). Hegel's analysis of civil society has been much celebrated, the focus of much recent scholarship.[13] Scholars have pointed out the importance of the Scottish political economists – Adam Ferguson, James Steuart and Adam Smith – for the development of Hegel's historical and political views. They have praised Hegel for his thorough understanding, and trenchant criticisms, of the emerging industrial society in Germany. In this respect, they see Hegel as far ahead of his time, and indeed as one of the most important forerunners of Marx. Supposedly, Hegel was the first thinker of the modern German tradition to recognize the importance of economics for social, political and cultural life.[14]

Unfortunately, such a generous assessment evaporates with a broader historical perspective. Hegel was not the first in his generation to perceive, or even to analyze, the problems of modern civil society. The young romantics did this in the late 1790s, so that in this respect too Hegel was only typical of his generation.[15] Furthermore, Hegel did not provide a detailed account of the laws of modern political economy, and in this regard was even behind some of his contemporaries. The treatment of money, labor and exchange in Adam Müller's *Elemente der Staatskunst* (Elements of the Art of State) (1809), for example, surpasses anything in Hegel's published works or surviving manuscripts.[16]

Still, these points do not diminish the significance of Hegel's treatment of civil society. Although it is not original in recognizing the importance of civil society, and although it does not give a detailed analysis of its economic laws, it does contain an interesting attempt to reconcile the values of civil society with the demands of community. The chapter 'Civil Society' is one of the most important to assess the full meaning of Hegel's program of wedding liberal principles with communitarian ideals. What is most striking about Hegel's treatment of civil society is his balanced appraisal of it, his attempt both to preserve and to negate it. Hegel was as critical of radical utopians who would banish civil society as of extreme liberals who would remove all restrictions from it. In this regard, the *Philosophy of Right* still remains relevant and topical.

In the early modern era the term 'civil society' had a very general meaning. It referred to society in so far as it is governed by laws; civil society was therefore contrasted to the state of nature. By the late eighteenth century, however, the term began to acquire its more narrow contemporary meaning. It now refers to one aspect of modern society, namely a capitalist economy, society in so far as it is based on private enterprise, free markets and modern forms of production and exchange. It is in this more narrow and modern sense that Hegel uses the term.

According to Hegel's system, civil society is subsumed under the category of ethical life. Ethical life consists in three fundamental moments: the family (immediate unity); civil society (difference); and the state (unity-in-difference), where all the differences of civil society are retained within a more integrated and organized whole (§157). What is so significant about this apparently perfunctory and artificial classification is that it shows how much Hegel wants both to preserve and to limit civil society within the modern state. On the one hand, Hegel finds fault with ancient political philosophy, especially Plato, for failing to give economic activity a significant role in the state (§185R). On the other hand, however, he is also critical of modern liberalism, which makes the sole purpose of the state the protection of civil society (§258R). In placing civil society under the category of ethical life Hegel means to say that it is on its own an artificial abstraction that presupposes the more substantial unity of ethical life (§182A).

Hegel begins his treatment of civil society by baldly stating its two leading principles (§182). The first is the pursuit of self-interest. In civil society everyone seeks their own good, regarding everyone else simply as a means for their own ends. The second principle is that everyone satisfies his self-interest only if he also works to satisfy the self-interest of others (§199). Hence people relate to one another strictly on the basis of mutual self-interest. Since they see public life only as a means to satisfy their own ends, Hegel describes civil society as the stage of 'the alienation of ethical life' (*Entfremdung der Sittlichkeit*) (H 149).

Hegel placed great value on civil society chiefly because it was a necessary stage in the development of freedom. He saw civil society as another manifestation of the fundamental principle of the modern world: the right of subjectivity or individual freedom (§185R). Hence he praised its many liberties: equality of opportunity, the right to pursue one's self-interest, and the freedom to buy and sell goods in the market place. It was the main failing of the ancient *polis*, he argued, that it could not permit these liberties and eventually succumbed to them (§§185R, 260R, 261R, 299R). Still, the freedom of civil society is not freedom in the full and positive sense; it is only a form of negative liberty, i.e. the right to pursue my interests independent of the interference of others (H 150). Hegel sometimes describes the freedom of civil society as purely formal and abstract, because the content of our ends is still given to us by our desires and inclinations (§195). It is therefore unlike the positive freedom of the state, where the content of our ends – the laws and ways of life of the state – is determined by reason.

Hegel's defense of civil society in the *Philosophy of Right* made it necessary for him to reckon with his old master, Jean-Jacques Rousseau. Throughout the opening section of 'Civil Society'

(§§182–208), Hegel takes issue, more or less implicitly (§§187, 194), with Rousseau. Notoriously, in his *Second Discourse* Rousseau had argued that civil society destroys freedom because we lose the power to satisfy our natural needs by ourselves; instead, we acquire new artificial needs and depend upon others to satisfy even our natural ones. Flatly contrary to Rousseau, Hegel maintains that we do not lose but gain freedom through civil society. Hegel sees a false premise behind Rousseau's argument: that freedom consists in natural independence, the power to satisfy our natural needs by ourselves. He insists *per contra* that freedom involves the power to *liberate ourselves* from our natural needs and to act according to rational principles (§187R). While this higher freedom is present only in the ethical life of the state, civil society is an important part of our education toward it. In civil society we begin to liberate ourselves from nature through work, which gives us the power to form objects according to our own concepts (§194). Since we have to make ourselves useful to others to satisfy our own needs, we are forced to develop talents and skills (§§195, 197). Rousseau condemned artificial needs because they undermine our natural independence; but Hegel celebrated them because they are the product of our own free activity rather than nature (§194). Where Rousseau deplored imitation and competition as the workings of *amour-propre*, Hegel saw them as an important stage in the education of the self into a more rational being (§193; VNS §§95–6).

In his defense of civil society Hegel had to confront Rousseau regarding another troubling issue: inequality. Rousseau attacked civil society for its inequality, because it marked a fall from the paradise of the state of nature, where everyone was equal in their power to satisfy their natural desires. Hegel disputed the existence of such a state of primal equality. He maintains against Rousseau that nature is the source of *inequality* because of the natural differences in talents between people (§200R). What makes people equal is not nature but freedom, their power to attain habits and virtues through their own activity. Still, Hegel, like Rousseau, realized that perfect equality could never be achieved in civil society, even if we gave everyone maximal opportunity to develop their talents. The problem was that there are natural physical and intellectual inequalities between people, which result in inequalities in the skills and resources they bring into civil society (§200). What people receive from civil society is then in direct proportion to what they bring into the market place.

Hegel's acceptance of inequality in civil society is most apparent from his theory of estates or classes (*Stände*). In the *Philosophy of Right* he held that society must be stratified into three different estates: the agricultural estate or peasantry, the commercial estate or bourgeoisie, and the universal estate or bureaucracy (§§201–5). Hegel attempts to base this classification upon the structure of the concept (§202). The peasantry is the natural estate because it lives in an immediate unity with and dependence upon nature; the bourgeoisie is the reflective estate because it uses its powers of reflection in the market place and in fashioning nature into commodities; and the universal estate is the most comprehensive where our rational powers are used for the sake of the common good. Though it appears very traditional, Hegel's classification departs radically from the old division of society into clergy, nobility and aristocracy. What is most striking about it is that it is wholly functional or economic. Hegel excludes the clergy entirely because they are not productive within civil society (H 265); and he admits the aristocracy into the universal class only in so far as they play a productive role in the government (H 270). The inequalities and stratification of estate society were tolerable to Hegel essentially because he strongly affirmed the ideal of equality of opportunity (§206; VNS §106). True to his belief in the equalizing powers of freedom, he believed that a person's social role and place were ultimately determined by their choice, effort and ability. Caste or hereditary privileges were utterly repellent to Hegel, who regarded them as one of the worst forms of oppression (VNS §106R).

For all his willingness to countenance inequality, Hegel too had his limits. No less than Rousseau, he deplored extremes of wealth and poverty, which he saw as a danger to the communal values of ethical life. He is somewhat pessimistic about poverty, holding that it arises inevitably from laws of the market place (H 193). The laws of supply and demand are sometimes such that the need for certain goods disappears, destroying whole branches of industry and impoverishing masses of people. The great danger of poverty is that it creates a rabble, whose income does not provide them with the means of subsistence (§244). What makes a rabble is not only poverty but also an attitude of rebellion (§244A). The rabble loses that 'feeling of right, integrity and honour that comes from sup-porting oneself by one's own activity' (§244). The problem with this is that it deprives a person of his or her freedom, their right to enjoy the liberties of civil society (§243).

Hegel's greatest reservations about civil society concern its methods of production. In the first drafts of his philosophy of spirit in Jena,[17] he treated some of the disturbing effects of the modern division of labor. Whole masses of people were 'damned' to work-ing in unhealthy, insecure and deadening conditions in modern factories and mines (VIII, 244). While the division of labor had made work much more productive, it also made it much more mechanical, tiring and spiritless (VIII, 243; VI, 321). The whole purpose of technology was to liberate mankind by freeing it from the bondage of nature; but nature had revenged herself by making man the slave of the machine (VI, 321). Rather than working less, people had to work more in dull routine tasks to keep pace with competition. Hegel also noted how the modern worker had become estranged from his own needs: he does not work to satisfy his own needs but only to get the means of satisfying them; work is therefore only a means of creating a means (the acquisition of money) to one's own ends. The worker had to create a surplus of goods of a very specialized kind, so that he produced what he did not need and needed what he did not produce (VI, 321–2). Work had also become very insecure: one learned very specialized skills, which could become superfluous with changes in the market place (VIII, 244; VI, 2). Though Hegel does not directly apply the term 'alienation' (*Entfremdung*) to modern labor, his own analysis anticipates in crucial respects Marx's own account in the 1844 *Manuscripts*.

Although Hegel writes as if civil society consists in only an assemblage of independent self-seeking atoms connected merely by ties of self-interest, it is important to see that he also thinks that civil society presupposes the more concrete unity of the state (§184A). This is the basis for Hegel's criticism of *laissez-faire* liberalism: the order of civil society is not self-sufficient and self-governing but requires the active intervention of the state in order to function at all. Hegel contests the standard liberal view that the common good will emerge naturally and necessarily from the play of economic forces in civil society. Although he agrees with Adam Smith that the pursuit of self-interest naturally creates some social order and interdependence (§§184R, 187, 189), he denies that this order is for the common good of all. To achieve such a good, Hegel argues that the market forces of civil society must be controlled and regulated by the state (§§185A, 201A, 236, 243, 246). Civil society was 'a wild beast that needs a constant and strict taming and mastery' (GW VI, 324).

Hegel gives several arguments for intervention. (1) Actions that are in accord with abstract right can still be harmful for the public at large (§232). (2) The interests of producers and consumers can come into conflict with one another, so that there must be an external agency to regulate their affairs that stands above both sides (§236). He gives as an example that the public has a right to inspect commodities and not to be cheated. (3) Large branches of industry are dependent on circumstances outside their control and their actions often have consequences for public health that they cannot foresee (§236). (4) Fluctuations in supply and demand can destroy whole branches of trade and industry, forcing many people into poverty (§244).

It is striking that Hegel's arguments for intervention are entirely immanent, evaluating the workings of the market place according to the standards of civil society itself. In pointing out the problems of an unregulated market place, he argues not that they erode community but that they undermine individual liberty and the pursuit of self-interest. Hence he complains that though civil society increases our needs it leaves their satisfaction to chance (§185); and he attacks poverty because it deprives a person of their right to enjoy the liberties of civil society (§243).

To address the ills of civil society, Hegel proposed all kinds of measures for the state: that it should tax, or even limit, profits;[18] that it should help the poor through public work projects (§241); that it provide for the education of the poor so that they can compete for jobs (§239); that it predict cycles of supply and demand to help the planning of industry;[19] and that it create new markets for industry through colonization (§§246–8). Besides regulating market forces, Hegel thinks that the state should promote the public good in areas not benefited by the market, namely, public health, street lighting, bridge- and road-building, and so on (§236A).

It was clearly crucial to Hegel's general attempt to fuse the liberal and communitarian traditions that he strike some balance between regulation and liberty in the market place. If too little regulation would undermine community, too much would throttle liberty. Aware of this very problem, Hegel stresses the need to find some middle path between controlling everything and nothing (§236A). Hegel denies, however, that there is some general rule that can be formulated about where to draw the boundary line between intervention and liberty (§234). He argues that this boundary line will be per necessitatem moving, depending upon circumstances. Whatever regulation the state undertakes, Hegel thinks that it should strive to ensure fairness and stability in the market place. Left on its own, the market place could be very unfair and unstable, impoverishing people so that they are in no position to compete for scarce jobs and resources. The task of the state was then to guarantee that everyone should have at least the opportunity to work and to provide for themselves through their own labor. Thus Hegel states unequivocally that if civil society has certain rights it also has certain duties (§§238A, 240A). It has the duty to ensure that all have the right to work, and that they are able to feed themselves (§240A). Above all, it has the duty to ensure that everyone be able to enjoy its advantages and liberties (§243).

So far it seems as if Hegel, in arguing for the right of the state to control industry, is a proto-socialist. It is crucial to see, however, that his solution to the problems of civil society does not lie with the state alone. As much as he believes that the state has to control the market place, he also fears granting it too much power. In keeping with his pluralistic vision, Hegel proposes his own non-socialist solution to the problems of the market economy: the corporation (*Korporation, Genossenschaft*). The corporation is a group of people sharing the same trade or profession, officially recognized by the state though independent of it. Like the medieval guilds, on which it is clearly modeled, the corporation would organize, support and recognize all individuals who had become competent in their trade or profession (§252). It would address the problem of social alienation since it would become the individual's 'second family', aiding him in times of need and providing him with a sense of belonging. And it would address the problem of political alienation, because it would organize and represent the interests of the individual in the Estates Assembly.

THE STRUCTURE AND POWERS OF THE STATE

In the *Philosophy of Right* (§§283–329), Hegel provides a detailed theory of the structure of his ideal state. The central thesis of Hegel's theory is that the rational form of the state is a *constitutional monarchy* (§273R; H 238). *Prima facie* such a claim seems reactionary, and it has been interpreted along just these lines.[20] However, in the early 1800s such a claim was standard reformist doctrine. It was the view of the Hanoverian Whigs and the Prussian Reformers, indeed of all those who wanted to reform the state of the *ancien régime* from above so that it could adapt to the revolutionary currents of the age. This reformist faith in constitutional monarchy has to be contrasted against the reactionary defense of *absolute monarchy*, which attempted to free the monarch from constitutional safeguards and make his will alone the source of law. The main Prussian spokesman for absolute monarchy was K.L. von Haller, whose *Restaurations der Staats-Wissenschaft* (Restoration of State Science) became the chief manifesto of the reactionary cause. Hegel's distance from the reactionary cause is evident not least from his lengthy polemical broadsides against Haller in the *Philosophy of Right* (§§219R, 258R).

Still, Hegel's strong claim in behalf of constitutional monarchy is somewhat surprising, given that he disdains disputes about the ideal constitution, and given that he endorses Montesquieu's doctrine that the proper constitution for a nation depends on its specific culture, history, climate and geography (§§3R, 273R). Hegel does not simply hold that constitutional monarchy is the best constitution for Prussia, or that it alone is suitable for its stage of historical development. Rather, he maintains that constitutional monarchy is the rational form of the state because it, more than any other form of government, realizes the ideal of freedom (H 238). Hegel's claim becomes more comprehensible when we consider his view, expressed most clearly in his Heidelberg lectures, that constitutional monarchy alone guarantees the rights of individuality so characteristic of the modern world (VNS §§135R, 137R). Like Kant, Humboldt, Jacobi, Schiller and many others, Hegel feared that radical democracy, which gave limitless power to the will of the people, does not necessarily respect the fundamental rights of everyone alike. The crucial case in point was Athens's persecution of Socrates.

The great strength of constitutional monarchy for Hegel is that it is a mixed constitution, incorporating the advantages of all three forms of government. He maintains that constitutional monarchy is a synthesis of monarchy, aristocracy and democracy (§273R). A constitutional monarchy consists in three fundamental powers: the *sovereign*, which formally enacts the laws; the *executive*, which applies and enforces the laws; and the *legislative*, which creates the laws (§273). Since the sovereign is *one* individual, since the executive consists in *several* individuals, and since the legislative consists in *many* individuals, each power represents one form of government: monarchy, aristocracy and democracy (respectively) (§273R).

The main virtue of mixed government for Hegel resides in its division of powers. Since this prevents any single power from dominating others, it provides the best institutional guarantee for freedom. In this regard it is noteworthy that Hegel reaffirmed Montesquieu's famous doctrine of the division of powers because, 'understood in its true sense, [it] could rightly be regarded as the guarantee of public freedom' (§272R). While Hegel warns that an extreme separation of powers will undermine the unity of the state (§§272R, 300A), he still thinks that the modern state realizes freedom only if it involves a differentiation of function and separation into distinct spheres of government (VNS §132; H 231).

Hegel makes a much more systematic or metaphysical claim in behalf of constitutional monarchy: that it alone realizes the very idea of the state (§§272–3). Each power of constitutional monarchy represents one of the moments of the concept: since it enacts general laws, the legislative is universality; since it applies laws to specific cases, the executive is particularity; and since it is incorporates in a single person both the legislative and executive, the monarch is individuality. While Hegel gives more weight to his systematic argument than any prudential consideration about the best form of government (§272), the fact remains that his systematic argument is best understood in the light of his claim that constitutional monarchy provides the best institutional safeguards for freedom. Since the idea of the state is based on freedom, and since constitutional monarchy realizes freedom more than any other form of government, it follows that constitutional monarchy is the highest realization of the idea of the state.

To understand Hegel's political values, to assess the authoritarian charges against him, and to appreciate exactly how he attempts to wed liberalism and communitarianism, it is necessary to know in some detail something about the structure of his ideal state. We should examine more closely each of the powers of a constitutional monarchy.

The sovereign

The sovereign power is the monarch. Hegel defends monarchy as a necessary part of the rational constitution because it provides the state with a single source of sovereignty. Since the monarch is one person, he or she is an indivisible power, and so better represents and executes sovereignty than an assembly, which could be divided within itself (§279). He maintains that a single source of sovereignty is a necessity of the modern state. The problem with the medieval constitution is that its many independent corporations and communities lacked a single source of sovereignty, and so could not act coherently even to defend itself (§278).

Hegel advocates *hereditary* monarchy on the grounds that it ensures a stable succession and stands above all conflict of factions (§281; VNS §138). Since the monarch is the highest authority, Hegel denies that he is only the highest official of the state, as if he were somehow accountable to the people and bound by a contract with them (VNS §139). He denies that the monarch can be held responsible for his actions, fixing all responsibility for them on his ministers (§284; W §140). Such is the exalted status he attributes to the monarch that he even expounds his own speculative form of the divine right doctrine, according to which the monarch represents the divine on earth (§279R).

Although Hegel's defense of divine right doctrine seems to give the monarch absolute power, he is very far from defending the old absolutism. Instead, his chief concern is to bind the monarch to the constitution. He stresses that in a rational state the personality of the monarch should be irrelevant, and that it is in the insignificance of the monarch's person that the rationality of the constitution lies (VNS §138). The only real powers that he permits the monarch are the right to pardon criminals and to appoint and dismiss ministers (§§282–3). He insists that the monarch possesses sovereignty only in so far as he is bound by the constitution (§278R). The monarch must follow the advice that he receives from his ministers, so that he can do nothing more than say 'yes' and sign his name to the measures placed before him (§§279R, 280A). It is for this reason alone that Hegel says that the monarch cannot be held accountable as a person (§284); for in the end, all real responsibility falls on his ministers. Ultimately, the monarch plays essentially a formal role in the Hegelian state, serving as 'the highest instance of formal decision'. Yet this symbolic role is of the greatest significance for Hegel, because it represents the unity, sovereignty and culture of the people (§§279–80).

The executive

The purpose of the executive power is to implement and enforce the decisions of the sovereign (§287). The executive power consists in the police, judiciary and civil service (§287). The cornerstone of the executive is the civil service or bureaucracy, whose main task is to mediate the particular interests of the corporations with the universal interests of the state (§289). The bureaucracy possesses great power in Hegel's state: its advice not only binds the monarch (§279A), but it also knows the true interests of the corporations, even if these have not been voiced directly by them (§§289, 301R). Nevertheless, Hegel should not be cast as an uncritical advocate of mandarinism or the bureaucratic state. He is also aware of the dangers of corruption in the bureaucracy (§295), and of the bureaucracy becoming the dominant power in the state. Hence he stresses that its powers should be limited and its activities monitored by the monarch from above and the corporations from below (§§295, 297; VNS §145). He recommends that the opposition within the legislative have the right to question ministers because this will make them accountable to the public (VNS §149).

The legislative

The legislative power consists in a bi-cameral Estates Assembly on the English model (§312). There is an upper house composed of the nobility, who inherit their office; and a lower house composed of commoners, who are elected to office. Hegel thinks that such a two-tiered assembly, by creating several levels of deliberation, provides a guarantee for mature decisions and reduces chances of collision with the executive (§313). The Estates Assembly represents the two estates of civil society: the agricultural estate or the landed aristocracy, and the estate of trade and industry or the *bourgeoisie* (§§303–4). Although members of the lower house are elected through their corporations and communities, they do not receive a mandate from them (§309A). The chief role of the Estates Assembly is to develop public consciousness of political issues, and to create a link between people and the sovereign (§§301–2). They also provide an important buffer between government and people. While they protect the people from tyranny by organizing and representing their interests, they shield the government from the 'mob' by controlling, directing and channeling the interests and energies of the people.

How democratic was Hegel's constitutional monarchy? There can be no question about Hegel's support for the democratic element of a constitutional monarchy. The very possibility of a common ethical life (*Sittlichkeit*) or community, he often argued, depends upon popular participation, for only when the people participate in the state do they identify with it and care about it (§§261, 308R).[21] Accordingly, the Hegelian state provides for some truly democratic procedures. Hegel envisages not only elected representatives in the lower house but also competing parties in the Estates Assembly (VNS §156R). These are not parties in the modern sense because they do not compete for popular votes; but they do represent opposing viewpoints that increase accountability. Hegel envisages three parties: one for the people, one for the government, and another neutral one to mediate between them. He further stresses that the government should have the support of the majority party in the Estates (VNS §156R).

Nevertheless, it is important to recognize that Hegel does not advocate democracy in the modern sense of universal suffrage. All his life he was skeptical of direct democracy because he doubted the wisdom of the people, who did not have sufficient knowledge to determine their best interests.[22] Like many of his contemporaries, Hegel insisted upon a limited franchise, which excluded workers, servants and women. Furthermore, he argued against the radical view that any male of a certain age and income should be given the right to vote.[23] He put forward two arguments against this view: first, the individual does not know his best interests simply in virtue of his age and wealth; and, second, it leads to voter apathy, because the individual will feel his vote is meaningless when it is only one in millions, and when he votes for only one person in a large assembly. Instead of voting according to universal suffrage and geographic districts, Hegel advocates voting according to group affiliation or vocational interests; in other words, he thinks that a person should vote not directly as an abstract individual but indirectly as a member of a group. Hence it is the corporations, not a mass of individual votes, who elect a delegate to the Estates Assembly. Such a system, Hegel contends, has several advantages: it organizes, directs and controls the interests of the people, who could otherwise turn into a violent mob; and it prevents indifference because the individual feels his vote matters as a member of a group that has much greater powers of representation than a single individual (§§302A, 303R, 311R).

Although Hegel's constitutional democracy did have some genuine democratic elements, one might well ask if these were sufficient for Hegel's ideal of ethical life. That ideal requires that everyone should identify with the state, that everyone should find their sense of purpose and belonging in life in it. Hegel himself had stressed that developing such an identification, such a sense of purpose and belonging, required participation in the affairs of state. But Hegel's limited conception of the franchise, his reservations about complete democracy, had the effect of excluding large groups of the population from participation in public life. The peasants of the agricultural estate were virtually unrepresented in the Estates Assembly; if they were represented at all it was through the nobility, who were not elected (§307). Hegel also had his doubts that the businessmen of the commercial estate were sufficiently free and knowledgeable to devote themselves to affairs of state (§§308, 310A). Although he stressed the importance of corporations to develop a sense of belonging, he had excluded day laborers from them, thereby disenfranchising them.[24] Thus he denied integration into society to the very group that needed it most, leaving the prospects for *Sittlichkeit* in jeopardy.[25]

So even if Hegel's political philosophy was not guilty of the worst charges of authoritarianism thrown against it, even if it did uphold basic liberal values, the question remained whether he satisfied his own ideal of community. So, oddly, it is really communitarians rather than liberals who should file complaints against Hegel. Ultimately, Hegel's grand synthesis failed not because he did too little for community and not enough for liberty, but because he did too much for liberty and not enough for community.

Part Five
Philosophy of Culture

Eleven

HEGEL AND HISTORICISM

In his 1830 *Encyclopedia*, the mature exposition of his system, Hegel gave perfunctory treatment to world history, assigning it only five paragraphs (§§548–52), the longest of which was really a discussion about the relationship of church to state (§552). A reader might infer from this that history was not that important for Hegel. But here, as always, it would be naive to equate the importance of a topic with the length of its treatment. Though Hegel gave it short shrift in the *Encyclopedia*, history played a crucial role in his philosophy. For the characteristic theme of his philosophy is spirit (pp. 110–12), whose chief domain is history. The distinguishing feature of spirit over life, Hegel maintains, consists in freedom; but freedom realizes itself only in history.

So important was the philosophy of history for Hegel that he lectured on the subject five times in Berlin. We now know his philosophy of history almost entirely from a few fragments and student lecture notes. Because they are readable, these lectures have been the most popular introduction to his philosophy. The popularity of these lectures, and Hegel's influence in the 1820s, helped to spread his reputation as the philosopher of historicism. Some scholars have even seen historicism as Hegel's central contribution to philosophy. Supposedly, it was Hegel who first historicized reason, and who introduced the idea of development into philosophy itself.[1]

Hegel's reputation as the philosopher of historicism demands careful reassessment. Much here depends on the precise meaning given to 'historicism', a very vague and ambiguous term. We have already defined the original and general sense of the term (pp. 29–31): the doctrine that everything in the human world has a history, that society has an organic structure, and that all human beliefs and practices derive of necessity from their specific historical context. In its original form, historicism did not have the meaning that has often been later associated with it: the thesis that historical development is inevitable and progressive. Wary of generalizations about society and history as a whole, Montesquieu, Hamann and Möser, the fathers of historicism, always insisted upon the individuality and uniqueness of historical context, so that it was impossible to determine a single measure of progress for all cultures. Already in the late eighteenth century, however, there were clear traces of this later historicist doctrine. Lessing, Kant, Schelling, Herder and Schlegel maintained that there are laws of history, and that there is progress in its development. Schelling, Herder and Schlegel extended the organic analogy to history, so that each culture had its own birth, childhood, maturity and decline.

If historicism is understood in both the above senses, then Hegel was indeed an historicist. He not only subscribes to the general doctrine, but also advances the thesis that history is progressive. We cannot say that Hegel was the *founder* of historicism in these senses, because the doctrine had such a long history before him; but we can say that, due to his influence, he was a central *propagator* or *transmitter*. Hence, if only in this modest sense, Hegel's reputation as an historicist is deserved.

There is, however, another meaning to the term 'historicism' in this period, one in which it denotes a very specific moral and legal doctrine. According to this doctrine, there are no universal moral laws or legal codes, because the only rationale for morals and laws must be within their specific historical and cultural context. Such a relativistic doctrine seemed to be the inevitable result of historicism in the general sense: if all laws are the product of a specific social and historical context, they are inseparable from it and adapted to it; hence they have no validity beyond it. If we universalize these laws, as if they held for all mankind, we are guilty of ethno-centrism, the fallacy of judging all cultures by the standards of our own. This moral and legal doctrine was developed by Möser, Hamann and Herder, who used it to undermine the rationalism of the Enlightenment. It eventually blossomed into the historical school of law of the early nineteenth century, whose main proponents were F.K. Savigny and K.F. Eichhorn.

It is important to see that, in this sense, Hegel was not an histori-cist, and that he was indeed a central figure in the reaction against it. It was one of the central aims of Hegel's philosophy to uphold the authority of reason against the relativism of historicism. Hence his epistemology would attempt to restore rational criticism, and his philosophy of right would re-attempt to re-establish natural law, in the face of historicism. What makes Hegel's reputation as the historicist *par excellence* so misleading is that the central thesis of his philosophy of history – that there is reason in history – was partly a reaction against emerging historicism.

In sum, Hegel's role in the development of historicism was ambivalent. He was both its defender and critic: a defender of the doctrines that all human activities are the product of history and that history conforms to laws; but a critic of its relativism, its attempt to undermine the universal authority of reason. In this ambivalence we can again discern Hegel's attempt to preserve and reform the legacy of the Enlightenment.

REASON IN HISTORY

In the introduction to his lectures on the philosophy of world history Hegel states that the fundamental idea that philosophy brings to history is that of reason, and more specifically the idea that 'reason governs the world, and that world history is therefore a rational process' (VG 28/27). This thesis follows straightforwardly from his absolute idealism, according to which everything is an appearance of the absolute idea. The philosophy of history is essentially the application of absolute idealism to history itself. This basic point is the stumbling-block to all those who wish to separate Hegel's social and political philosophy from his metaphysics.

What, more precisely, does Hegel mean by reason in history? On the most basic level he means that history conforms to laws, or that everything within it acts according to necessity. Hence Hegel identifies the form of reason with necessity (EPW §§1, 9); and he opposes his thesis that reason governs history with the Epicurean tradition, according to which everything happens by chance (VG 37/34).

Of course, Hegel's thesis means more than just that history is governed by laws. For Hegel has in mind a specific kind of laws. These laws are not only mechanical, explaining events by their immediate context, but also teleological, accounting for them by their purpose or end. To say that there there is reason in history therefore means for Hegel that events conform to some purpose or design, or that they happen of necessity to realize a purpose (VG 50/44). Thus Hegel stresses that the philosopher of history must not rest content with *external* necessity, 'a necessity that originates in causes that are themselves no more than external circumstances' (VG 29/28), and that he should strive to explain the *internal* necessity of things, why they happen from their underlying purpose or inherent form.

In his *Logic* Hegel has a very specific account of mechanical and teleological explanation, which is important for his philosophy of history. Mechanical explanation makes the reasons for events prior causes in time; it is hypothetical or conditional: if one earlier event occurs another later event must also occur. Teleological explanation, however, assumes that the reason for an event is some purpose, which is not prior in time. Like Aristotle, Hegel identifies the purpose with the inherent form or essence of the thing, its 'formal–final cause'. He too stresses that this formal–final cause is first only in order of explanation, not order of existence; and that it is realized, or comes into existence, only through the activity of particular agents:

> The first thing that we must observe is this: that what we have called a principle, final end, or vocation, or what is spirit *in itself,* its nature or concept, – is only something *universal* or *abstract*. A principle, so too a fundamental proposition or law, is something universal or inner, that as such, however true in itself, is still not completely actualized . . . For its actuality another moment has to be added, and this is the enactment, actualization, whose principle is the will, the activity of men in the world. It is only through this activity that those concepts, implicit determinations, are actualized.
>
> (VG 81/69–70)

In stressing the importance of teleological explanation in history, Hegel does not mean to exclude mechanical explanation. He thinks that mechanical explanation is perfectly valid of all parts within a whole; but it is inadequate from the standpoint of the whole itself. When we consider the standpoint of the whole we must take into account its purpose or design. We require teleological explanation, Hegel thinks, to explain why all the parts are present in the first place. The workings of mechanical causality are simply the means or instruments by which the purposes of history are realized.

When Hegel claims that history conforms to teleological laws he means, on the most basic level, that it follows the same laws of organic development as nature itself. He treats the objects of history – nations, cultures, and states – as organisms, which are subject to the same process of organic growth as anything in nature. 'The national spirit is a natural individual; as such it blossoms, grows strong, fades away and dies' (VG 67/58). Like any organism, historical development is dialectical, consisting in three movements: inchoate unity, differentiation, and reintegration or unity-in-difference.

Hegel is careful to add, however, that history conforms to not only organic laws but also more specific laws distinctive of spirit alone. It is because history involves laws of spiritual development, Hegel maintains, that it is possible to speak of *progress* in history, of something higher than the cyclical development characteristic of life itself (VG 70, 149–55/61, 124–31). Since spirit is not only life but the self-awareness of life, the laws of history must concern the development of its self-awareness. These laws involve the dialectic of externalization and reinternalization, of self-loss and self-discovery, by which the self becomes aware of itself as a rational being (pp. 114–15).

Since the laws of history concern self-awareness of spirit, and since the distinguishing characteristic of spirit is freedom, the laws of history concern the self-awareness of freedom. Such self-awareness is indeed the purpose or end of history itself (VG 63/54). It is in terms of this goal that Hegel measures progress. He divides world history into three major epochs, which are specific stages in the development of the self-awareness of freedom. There is the *Oriental* epoch, which understands that only *one* person is free, the ruler or despot; the *Greek* epoch, which holds that *some* persons (citizens) are free; and the *Germanic* epoch, which knows that *all* persons, or humanity as such, are free. As simplistic as this schema appears, it was obligatory for Hegel, who held that one, some and all were the three categories of quantity. Since history is governed by reason, it must exhibit all three categories.

It is important to see that there is a double meaning to Hegel's phrase 'reason in history'. The phrase refers to not only the form of history – that it conforms to laws or ends – but also its *content* – the specific purpose of history. Since the self-awareness of freedom is the goal of history, and since freedom is the distinguishing characteristic of rationality, the goal of history is also the self-awareness of reason itself. Hence history is governed by reason both in *that* it has a purpose and in *what* this purpose is. To say that there is reason in history means both that it conforms to some purpose or design, and that the purpose or design is the self-realization of reason.

THE CUNNING OF REASON

As stated so far, Hegel's grand theme of reason in history seems vulnerable to two objections. First, it seems to assume, naively and implausibly, that people act from ideals or principles, as if their explicit and self-conscious aim were to realize freedom. Second, it does not give any place to freedom, for if everything happens of necessity, what choice do we have? Although Hegel thinks that the end of history is the self-awareness of freedom, he also stresses that history conforms to laws, so that the realization of this end is necessary. But a freedom that is realized of necessity seems to be no freedom at all.

Of course, Hegel was aware of these problems, and his response to them is one of the most provocative and controversial ideas of his philosophy of history: the cunning of reason (*List der Vernunft*). Stated most simply, the cunning of reason means that reason uses the self-interests of individuals to realize its ends (VG 84–8, 105/ 71–4, 89). Even if there is no coordinated and collective action among individuals, and even if they do not intentionally or self-consciously formulate these ends to themselves, they still realize them subconsciously in pursuing their private interests. So, from the chaos of private interests, the order and common ends of reason still emerge.

Such a thesis seems to resolve both difficulties. First, it does not assume that people act from moral principle; for, even if they follow their self-interest, they still realize the ends of reason. Second, although a person acts from necessity for the sake of reason, he or she does so by following self-interest; hence it is not some higher fate acting outside him or her that compels the person to do what he or she does not want or prevents him or her doing what they do want.

It is one of the great ironies of Hegel's philosophy of history that, though it makes ideals the governing powers of history, it is really not idealistic at all. For the cunning of reason means that the chief motives of human action – and the primary instruments for the realization of reason – are self-interest rather than moral principle. Hegel is indeed explicit that moral idealism should play no role in the realization of reason in history. He flatly declares: '. . . there is no room in living reality for empty notions like that of pursuing goodness for its own sake.' (VG 94/80). He also warns against measuring historical necessity against our ideals of right and wrong, because this only leads to discontentment (VG 107–8/91). More fundamentally, he states that world history works on a higher plane than morality:

> For world history moves on a higher plane than that to which morality properly belongs, which is that of private convictions, the conscience of individuals, and their own particular will and mode of action . . . What is required and achieved by the ultimate purpose of spirit, what is done by providence, lies above the obligations, liability and responsibility which fall to individuality with respect to its ethical life.
>
> (VG 171/141)

It is another irony of Hegel's philosophy of history that, for all its rationalism, it makes the driving force behind history passion rather than reason. The cunning of reason assigns a fundamental role to passion in the realization of the ends of history. Since reason is realized through self-interest, and since the passions are most active in the pursuit of self-interest, passion proves to be crucial in realizing the ends of reason. Hence Hegel preaches that passion is the most potent force in human action: '. . . the natural force of passion has a more immediate hold over man than that artificial and laboriously acquired discipline of order and moderation, justice and morality' (VG 79/68). We seem to read a romantic when Hegel says: '. . . nothing great in the world has been accomplished without passion' (VG 85–6/73). Yet there is nothing really romantic about these lines, since Hegel's concept of passion came more from self-interest than moral idealism. Thus he explains that he uses the term passion in a broad sense: 'Passion is not quite the right word for what I am trying to express. I use it here to denote any human activity that is governed by particular interests, special aims, or, if you will, by selfish intentions . . .' (VG 85/72).

Hegel's demotion of moral idealism, and his promotion of self-interest, raise the inevitable question: When and how do individuals become conscious of the goals of history? Surely, they must be conscious of them at some point, because Hegel insists that the ends of reason are realized only through individuals, and they could hardly be said to realize them if they were never aware of them at all. It is in answering this question that Hegel states that other notorious theme of his philosophy of history: the world-historical individual (VG 97–103/82–9). These are men like Socrates, Luther, Caesar and Napoleon. They alone have the rare power to rise above the limited horizon of their own age, to see where history is heading, and to realize a higher stage in the self-awareness of freedom. They are the leaders of others, who have no power to resist them and who rally around their banner (VG 99/84). Although they do not have the precise knowledge of the philosopher because they are men of action, they still have the power to grasp the new needs of the age and to see what has to be done to satisfy them (VG 98/83).

It is only in the case of world-historical individuals that Hegel seems to allow some degree of moral idealism in the realization of history. For he says that these individuals identify themselves with their causes: '. . . what they want is the universal; this is their pathos . . .' (VG 101/86). He objects to those who would reduce their motives to something purely self-interested or personal, such as honor and glory. Thus to Goethe's famous maxim 'No one is a hero to his valet' he adds the explanation that this is because the valet is a valet and not because the hero is not really a hero (VG 103/87–8). But even here we are warned not to regard these heroes as moral idealists; for they too still act more from passion than principle, and they do not let moral scruples stand in the path of their mission: 'Great men want to satisfy themselves, not the well-meaning intentions of others' (VG 104/89).

If these doctrines seem to remove some of the difficulties with Hegel's philosophy of history, they seem to create others all their own. The cunning of reason seems to encourage fatalism. For if reason realizes itself through self-interest, why should I attempt to be moral at all? If reason realizes itself through all my actions, why should I be a responsible citizen? Both doctrines seem to support an almost brutal *Realpolitik*, undermining the claims of morality in the political sphere. Thus Hegel tells us that world history operates on a higher plane than morality, that we should not measure historical necessity by moral ideals, and that reason uses people as mere means for its ends. There are several passages in his lectures where Hegel acknowledges the 'infinite right' of subjectivity, the value of each and every individual life; but these ring hollow in the face of his callous statement that the world-historical individual 'must trample many an innocent flower underfoot, and destroy much that lies in its path' (VG 105/89).

Yet for all its fatalism and amoralism, there is still a sense in which the cunning of reason is still profoundly moralistic. The whole purpose of the concept is to show that reason ultimately triumphs over moral cynicism after all, for it states that reason is more cunning than the most clever practitioner of *Realpolitik* (p. 220). Even in pursuing *raison d'état* the statesman will be the vehicle of the highest end of reason: the self-awareness that man as such is free.

THE PROBLEM OF EVIL

In his lectures on world history Hegel identifies his central thesis that reason governs the world with the traditional Christian idea of providence (VG 77/67). He likens the reason that rules history to the divine plan behind it, as if reason arose from the will of God. The fundamental task of the philosophy of world history, he explains, is to comprehend that 'God governs the world'. For world history consists in nothing more than 'the content of his government and the execution of [the divine] plan' (VG 77/67).

Although Hegel attempts to reinstate the traditional idea of providence, he also gives it an entirely immanent or this-worldly meaning. According to the Christian tradition, life on earth is only a means toward a higher end: eternal salvation. History is only a pilgrimage, a trial of passage, on the road toward the city of God. True to his immanent theology, Hegel denies that there is a supernatural realm lying beyond history that gives it purpose, meaning or value. Since the end of history does not lie beyond it, redemption has to be achieved in history itself.

The fundamental problem for any belief in providence – whether immanent or transcendent – is the existence of evil. If evil exists, how can there be providence? For why would God, who is infinite and good, create, or even allow for, evil? One of Hegel's main ambitions in his philosophy of history was to resolve this thorny issue. Hence he described it as a *theodicy*, as an attempt to justify the ways of God to human beings (VG 48/42). After pondering the tragedies of history, he explicitly poses the problem of evil by asking '. . . to whom, to what ultimate end . . . have these monstrous sacrifices been made' (VG 80/69). Hegel had to face the problem of evil because he stated explicitly and emphatically the two central premises that sustain it. First, he insisted that God is essentially good, not only in the design he makes for the world but also in the power with which he executes it (VG 77/67). Second, he also fully admitted the reality of evil. In some memorable lines he declared that history is a 'slaughter bench' (*Schlachtbank*) on which tremendous sacrifices have been made (VG 80/69). The periods of happiness are empty pages in the book of history (VG 92/79).

Although the problem of evil arises for any belief in God – for theism and deism as well as absolute idealism – it is for two reasons an especially acute problem for absolute idealism. First, absolute idealism connects the divine with the world, making everything in nature and history a manifestation of the divine; hence the evil deeds of history will not only be allowed by the divine but they will be part of its very nature. Second, absolute idealism seems to make evil, like all events in nature and history, inevitable, a necessary manifestation of the laws of reason. Whatever a man or woman does is done by God acting through him or her, and so by the necessity of the divine nature. This poses the danger of fatalism, because it seems impossible to do otherwise.

How did Hegel attempt to deal with these problems? What was his explanation for the existence of evil? True to his this-worldly conception of providence, Hegel's theodicy attempts to explain evil and to redeem suffering within the realm of history itself. His explanation for evil is that it is necessary to historical progress, a regrettable but essential stage on the road toward the self-awareness of freedom. Like Kant, Schiller and Herder, Hegel explained history according to a secularized version of the Christian innocence–fall–redemption scenario.[2] He understood each of these stages in terms of specific historical epochs: innocence was the Greek world where man lived in unity with himself, others and nature; the fall came with the onset of Christianity, where the individual gave himself supreme significance apart from the community and nature; and redemption – still to be achieved in the Germanic world – came when mankind restored its unity on a higher level that would preserve the rights of individuality. Evil came with the fall, the lapse from the paradise of unity. The fall was necessary because, to realize its freedom, mankind had to develop its powers of reflection, its capacity to think for itself. But in developing such a capacity it had separated itself from its original unity and no longer felt at home in the world.

The heart of Hegel's theodicy ultimately lies with his concept of spirit. In the passage of spirit toward self-realization, evil appears during the moment of difference, of inner division, when the spirit is alienated from itself. We have seen how spirit realizes itself only when it incorporates the other into itself, and that to do this it must first oppose itself to the other (pp. 114–15). More specifically, the stage of division has two aspects: first, the self opposes itself to the other; second, the self still depends on the other. The self fights the other to assert its independence, not realizing that it finds its true independence only in and through the other. Since the self fights the other when its higher identity comes only from incorporating the other, it is divided within itself. This is the moment of evil because, in attempting to destroy what is really essential to itself, the self suffers torment and agony; it is its own worst enemy, though it still does not fully understand why. If we understand evil as the inner division of spirit, which is a necessary stage in the self-realization of spirit, then we can grasp the necessity of evil itself. We can also understand, however, how evil can be justified and redeemed, for the stage of division is overcome when the self finally incorporates the other within itself and makes itself whole again.

In attempting to incorporate evil into his philosophy of history, Hegel develops a distinctive concept of progress. He contrasts his concept with that of the Enlightenment, according to which history consists in gradual improvement, the increasing refinement of culture (VG 150/125–6). This merely *quantitative* notion of progress fails to grasp, he believes, the necessity of conflict and struggle for the development of spirituality itself. If, however, we have a *qualitative* notion of progress, according to which struggle and conflict are necessary for spiritual development, then we begin to see the necessity of evil itself. In Hegel's fundamentally optimistic account, nothing is lost or done in vain in the realm of history. All struggles in the past are preserved as necessary moments toward the self-awareness of freedom. Once we see the necessity of evil, and the necessity of its overcoming, Hegel hopes, we will finally reconcile ourselves to history (VG 67/78). We fail to reconcile ourselves only when we stand outside it and judge it by extrinsic moral standards. All our indignation at the evil of history will collapse, however, once we recognize the necessity of its intrinsic ends, which are realized through both evil and its redemption.

Such is, in its crudest outline, Hegel's theodicy. Though a self-conscious Christian project, it was highly original, departing radically from the Christian tradition in at least three respects. First, it attempts to redeem evil within this world alone, avoiding all appeal to a transcendent realm. Second, it is not dualistic, because it sees good and evil as two sides of the same spiritual development. Third, it stresses not only the reality but the necessity of evil. Hegel's theory is very far from that so often ascribed to him: that the reality of evil is illusory, disappearing when we grasp the universe as a whole.

But, for all its originality, Hegel's theodicy suffers from problems all its own. It is noteworthy that the theory works on different levels, individual and cosmic, which involve incompatible explanations for the existence of evil. On the individual level, the explanation of evil arises from human choice alone. Hegel explains that evil arises when the will chooses to act on its natural desires rather than according to the moral law of reason. The self has the power to choose good over evil; still it chooses evil, even when it has the power to do otherwise. Hegel stresses this point when he attempts to avoid imputing evil to God and to devolve responsibility for evil on the human will alone (VPR III 298/222; PR §139R + A). On the cosmic level, the explanation for evil arises from the divine nature. It holds that evil consists in the inner division of the divine nature. Hegel stresses that this moment of negation is not something contingent that merely happens; rather, it is essential to the divine nature itself, being necessary to its self-realization (PG ¶¶775–6; VPR III 306/229). The problem is that these explanations are incompatible with one another: the first sees the human will as the sole source of evil, whereas the second makes it an essential moment of the divine nature. The first sees evil as something contingent, depending on an act of choice that could be otherwise; the second views it as something necessary, the indispensable condition for the self-realization of spirit.

Apart from these problems, there are other reasons to question Hegel's theodicy. First, we can ask, with Ivan Karamazov, whether any goal, and any amount of progress toward it, can redeem the suffering of the innocent. Is it not better to renounce these goals, and this progress, if their realization requires such evil? Second, Hegel's concept of evil as self-negation seems to account for only one kind of evil, that which arises from inner struggle; but there are other kinds of evil that are not forms of inner struggle; for example, all forms of crime, such as murder, abuse, genocide. It is precisely the existence of wanton and brutal forms of crime that makes the problem of evil so apparently insolvable. Third, Hegel's theory seems to encourage acquiescence in the face of evil. Rather than demanding that people fight evil, absolute idealism tranquilizes its believers into accepting it, because they become convinced of its necessity. The result of believing in such a doctrine, William James contends, is that we accept finite evil 'as if it were potentially the eternal', and so we abrogate ourselves from all responsibility to combat it.[3]

In the light of all the horrors of the twentieth century the optimism of Hegel's theodicy appears dated and naive. The issue has been put in the most forceful terms by Emile Fackenheim:

> Hegel's actuality of the rational leaves room only for world-historically insignificant evils to be disposed of as relapses into tribalism or barbarism. In their post-Enlightenment optimism all but a few modern philosophers have ignored or denied the demonic. Hegel's philosophy . . . is the most radical and hence most serious expression of this modern tendency . . . Any inquiry into [the] truth [of Hegel's philosophy] must confront its claims with the gas chambers of Auschwitz.[4]

Given Hegel's qualitative concept of progress, we might question Fackenheim's claim that the evils of history will be only minor relapses. Still, Fackenheim's main point stands unimpugned: for what could ever redeem such a horror? We might put Fackenheim's point like this: Auschwitz negates double negation, the power of spirit to transcend itself.

THE MEANING OF LIFE

Hegel was intent on reviving the traditional concept of providence not least because he saw it as the only viable solution to the grand existential question about the meaning or purpose of life. That concept had always provided a ready and comforting answer to that fraught question. According to the Christian tradition, the meaning of life is to fulfill the purpose of God in creating us. God had a reason in creating each and every one of us, a reason for making us here and now, even if it is almost impossible for us to fathom it. We still know, however, that God intends us to fulfill our roles in society and state, because society and state, and all specific roles within them, are part of providence. Acting according to our station and its duties therefore has a divine sanction.

Although Hegel purged the Christian concept of providence of its traditional transcendent meaning, he still retained its underlying thesis that the purpose or meaning of life came from fulfilling my place in the divine order. He did not accept the doctrine of modern existentialists that life could have a value or meaning even if existence were absurd, or even if there were no purpose to life.[5] In his view, no individual had by himself the power to give his life meaning, to create the values by which he lived. The purpose of his life had to be made for him by the greater wholes of society, state and history, which give the individual a specific role to perform. Hegel held that his immanent theology could give our lives on earth a much greater meaning and significance than they ever had in the Christian tradition. Since God does not exist apart from history, and since he realizes himself only through it, our deeds and struggles become necessary for the realization of the divine nature itself. Our lives on earth not only prepare us for the kingdom of God, as in the traditional Christian conception: they create that very kingdom. Hegel was perfectly explicit about the point:

> The province of the spirit is created by man himself; and whatever ideas we may form of the kingdom of God, it must always remain a

spiritual kingdom that is realized in man and that man is expected
to translate into actuality.

(VG 50/44)

The inspiration for Hegel's immanent theodicy lay as much in
the pagan as the Christian tradition. If the Christian tradition gave
Hegel his concept of providence, the pagan tradition made him
turn this concept to this-worldly political ends. True to the pagan
tradition, Hegel maintains that the purpose of life is to be found
within one specific form of life on earth: its political form, the state.
Like Plato and Aristotle, Hegel thinks that the highest good – the
supreme value of life – can be achieved only within the state, which
shapes not only the identity of each individual but the very purpose
and meaning of his life. Hence he declares: 'Man owes his entire
existence to the state, and has his being within it alone. Whatever
worth and spiritual reality he possesses are his solely by virtue of
the state' (VG 111/94). Each individual should find the meaning of
his life, therefore, by participating in the affairs of the state, by
becoming a good citizen who fulfills his station and its duties. His
worth and value as an individual depend entirely on what he con-
tributes to society and state as the whole. 'The worth of individuals
is measured by the extent to which they reflect and represent the
national spirit, and have adopted a particular station within the
affairs of the state as a whole' (VG 94/80). The idea that our lives
could have any meaning or purpose apart from the state, Hegel
believes, rests on a false abstraction, on assuming that the individual
has some identity apart from the social and political whole of
which he is a part. We are not existential heroes who give our lives
meaning through individual acts of choice, apart from our specific
place in society and the state.

The proper meaning of these statements becomes apparent only
when we read them in the context of Hegel's development. They
reflect his critique of traditional Christian ethics, a critique that
derives from the republican tradition of Machiavelli and Rousseau.

In his *Berne Fragments* and *Positivity Essay* he argued that in the ancient Roman republic and the Greek city-state the individual found the entire purpose of his life in serving the state. The citizen would find meaning only by helping to create and administer the laws, and by being ready to die for the republic. The thought never occurred to the citizen, Hegel wrote, that his life could have some meaning, let alone existence, apart from the state. The Christian ethic of salvation arose, he argued, only after the decline of the ancient republics. When the state no longer served the common good but was taken over by private interests, the individual sought the highest good outside the earthly sphere altogether in his eternal salvation. The mature Hegel never departed from his critique of the traditional doctrine of salvation, and remained true to his early belief that the purpose of life had to be found within the state. He did, however, give this doctrine a new religious significance by seeing life within the state as an essential part of providence.

HEGEL VERSUS THE EXISTENTIALISTS

Because of Hegel's influence and reputation, his philosophy of history eventually became the central target of two of his most influential critics, Søren Kierkegaard and Friedrich Nietzsche. Kierkegaard in his *Concluding Unscientific Postscript*, and Nietzsche in his *Untimely Meditations*, reacted against Hegel because of the central role he gave to history in understanding the self and in answering the question of the purpose of life. They objected to Hegel's conception of the self as an essentially social and political animal, and they protested against his claim that the purpose of life lay in performing one's role in state and history. It is in their critique of Hegel's historicism that we can detect the glimmerings of later existentialism.[6]

For all their differences as thinkers, Kierkegaard and Nietzsche have a remarkably similar critique of Hegel. Both see the same basic danger in Hegel's emphasis on history: that one loses oneself in the past and forfeits one's existence as an individual. In their view, Hegel's historicism undermines our individual autonomy, the need for each of us to think for ourselves about the fundamental questions of life. For determining our place in society and history teaches us only what *others* have thought long ago; it should not determine what each of us should think for ourselves right now. Hegel assumes that we find ourselves by determining our place in society and history; but the very opposite is the case: we only *lose* ourselves, because who we are is ultimately determined by our sheer individuality, which resists reduction to social and historical roles. It is only by abstracting from society and history, Kierkegaard and Nietzsche argue, that we can finally face the eternal existential questions of life that each individual must ultimately resolve for himself. To settle these questions, Nietzsche advises us to find a '*suprahistorical*' standpoint where values are eternal and not marred by the interests and injustices of history.[7]

Are Kierkegaard and Nietzsche justified in their complaint that Hegel's historicism neglects, and even undermines, the value of individuality? There are many passages in Hegel's *Philosophy of History* that seem to vindicate them. We have already seen how he thinks that the worth of the individual consists in the performance of his duties in society and state. But this is scarcely the end of the matter. Hegel also sometimes writes as if the individual were simply a means for social and historical ends: 'Reason cannot stop to consider the injuries sustained by single individuals, for particular ends are submerged in the universal end' (VG 48–9/43). He seems to commit the very mistake Kierkegaard and Nietzsche impute to him when he states that the individual should be subordinated to the universal and that he should be regarded 'under the category of means rather than ends' (VG 106/90). He insists that, apart from an elite few, 'individuals fade into insignificance beside the universal substance' (VG 60/52). The only individuals that really matter for Hegel are the few world-historical individuals; and they are perfectly justified in treating other individuals as means toward their ends (VG 105/89).

The issue is more complicated, however, because there are

other passages where Hegel does seem to give great importance to individuality, and where he even emphasizes that individuality has 'an infinite right' to be satisfied in history. As if he wishes to parry the very objection that Kierkegaard and Nietzsche hurl against him, he insists that individuality has an intrinsic worth, and that we must regard each individual as an end in himself (VG 106/90). At this point Hegel reasserts the 'right of subjectivity', which claims that individuality has an infinite worth (pp. 230–1). Whenever he acts for social, political or historical ends, each individual has 'an infinite right to be satisfied' in the sense that his own personal interests and needs must also be fulfilled. Since their own individuality must be satisfied in acting for universal ends, they are never simply means toward these ends but part of the ends themselves. It would seem, then, that Nietzsche's and Kierkegaard's criticism ultimately rests on a misreading of Hegel: it fails to see how Hegel attempts to integrate the right of subjectivity or individuality within history.

It is important to see, however, that Hegel equivocates on this crucial question. If in some respects he attempts to incorporate individuality *inside* history, in others he admits that it falls *outside* history. The more he stresses the right of subjectivity, the more he places individuality outside the whole realm of history. Thus he concedes that even the religion and morals of 'a restricted sphere of life', such as that of shepherd or peasant, have an 'infinite worth' apart from their role in history (VG 109/92). He recognizes that 'the inner centre, the personal source of morality and religion', 'remains untouched and protected from the noisy clamour of world history' (VG 109/92). And he stresses that world history operates on a plane so much higher than individual morality that it should ignore the realm of individuality entirely (VG 171/141). These seem to be fatal concessions on Hegel's part, for they basically take the fundamental question of the purpose and value of life outside the realm of society and history, just as Nietzsche and Kierkegaard insist.

Apart from these concessions, Hegel still has a powerful reply to Kierkegaard's and Nietzsche's critique. He could claim that his critics have an implausible asocial and ahistorical conception of individuality. They assume that a person's individuality were somehow separable from its specific place in society and history; but such a conception is a false abstraction, he could argue, because the identity of a person ultimately depends upon its place in society and history. If we attempt to abstract the individual from this place, we are not even left with a human being but a mere cipher. Furthermore, there is no set of eternal problems and concerns that hold for an individual just in so far as he or she is an individual; for these depend entirely upon the individual's social and political context. It is indeed striking that when Kierkegaard lists the questions that should concern every concrete existing individual they turn out to be historically and culturally conditioned. The questions 'What does it mean to be immortal?', 'What does it mean to thank God?' are questions that would interest only someone who believes in the Christian doctrine of salvation – a doctrine that Hegel questions and situates in the culture of the decline of Rome. Hegel could then pose Kierkegaard and Nietzsche with a dilemma: it seems that the more concrete we make the individual, the more it turns out to be a social and historical animal; and that the more we deal with the individual as such, the more it turns into a mere abstraction.

Arguably, the existentialist tradition never really freed itself from the ethic of salvation, which Hegel had subjected to such severe criticism. Both Kierkegaard and Nietzsche, for example, saw the highest good as a form of personal redemption, as an ideal to be achieved by the individual alone apart from the community. In Hegel's view, such a conception of the highest good was only the result of social and political breakdown, and it arose from the false abstraction of a human being from its concrete context in society and history. No doubt, against his later critics Hegel would have cited Aristotle's famous remark: 'Apart from the *polis*, man is either a beast or god.' It was no accident that Zarathustra's sole companions were a serpent and an eagle.

Twelve

Aesthetics

THE PARADOX OF HEGEL'S AESTHETICS

Of all Hegel's works, his Lectures on Aesthetics has been the most popular. Both its subject matter and exposition have made it more accessible than his other works. Since it is a composite of lecture notes and student transcripts, the exposition is more informal and fluent than Hegel's published writings. The text captures some of the liveliness and openness of Hegel's oral delivery, his attempt to communicate to a wide audience. Not surprisingly, the *Aesthetics* has also been Hegel's most influential work.[1] Hegel has been a seminal figure in art history, and indeed he has been seen as the father of modern art history.[2] Remarkably, though, his influence has been greatest among literary critics and art historians, not among Hegel scholars, who until recently gave the *Aesthetics* scant attention.[3]

Karl Rosenkranz, Hegel's first biographer, attests to Hegel's passionate devotion to the arts.[4] It is a myth, he claims, that Hegel's abstruse thinking blunted his aesthetic sensitivity. Of all the great systematic philosophers, he judged, Hegel was alone in penetrating the entire domain of the arts. We know how much he loved music, drama, poetry, painting and sculpture. Whenever he arrived in a new city during his travels, he would take every opportunity to visit museums, operas, concerts and theaters. He adored some singers and actresses, whom he went to great pains to meet. Many of Hegel's contemporaries were deeply impressed by his aesthetic sensitivity, powers of interpretation and critical discernment.

The *Aesthetics* provides more than ample evidence for Hegel's devotion to the arts. The sheer size of the work would seem to make it the most important part of Hegel's system. In most editions of Hegel's works it comprises three volumes, one more than any other part of the system, including even the *Science of Logic*. The *Aesthetics* is even larger than the *Encyclopedia*, the exposition of the system as a whole. In the *Werkausgabe* edition it extends to more than 1500 pages, making it more than 200 pages longer than the *Encyclopedia*. We might attribute the length of the work to the vagaries of Hegel's editors; but, apart from its size, the content of the work leaves no doubt about Hegel's extraordinary devotion to, and knowledge of, the arts. The work has an almost astonishing breadth and depth. The first half is a survey of the history of art, which encompasses every culture from the beginning of history; the second half is an intensive discussion of specific arts, a detailed account of poetry, painting, drama, sculpture and music. Without a doubt, the *Aesthetics* is one of the great works in its field, on at least an equal footing with Kant's *Critique of Judgment* and Schiller's *Aesthetic Letters*.

But if Hegel's devotion to the arts is incontestable, it is also very puzzling. Any reader of the *Aesthetics* eventually has to come to terms with a remarkable fact: Hegel's pervasive and persistent effort to diminish the significance of the arts. Such, at any rate, is the unmistakable purport of two of Hegel's central theses. First, Hegel contends that art as a medium of knowledge is inferior to philosophy; what art glimpses through the obscure medium of the senses philosophy captures through the transparent medium of thought. Second, Hegel holds that art has no future, that it has lost its traditional importance and has no role to play in modern culture. Once he ponders these theses, the reader confronts a paradox: Why does Hegel devote so much space and effort to the arts if he is so intent on diminishing them? Why indeed write a three-volume work on them if they are inferior to philosophy and doomed to obsolescence? Of course, this paradox is not unique in the history of philosophy. Plato banished the artists from his state in the *Republic* only to praise beauty in the *Phaedrus*; Rousseau attacked the arts in his *First Discourse* and *Letter to D'Alembert*, though he was a famous composer and wrote one of the most beautiful novels of the eighteenth century, *The New Heloise*. Still, to put Hegel in such company does not diminish the paradox; it shows only that it applies to him as much as to the others.

One strategy to resolve the paradox is to focus on the polemical intent and context behind the *Aesthetics*. In his later Berlin years Hegel's anti-romantic animus only grew in intensity. He targeted Friedrich Savigny in several places of the *Philosophy of Right*.[5] He had a famous quarrel with Schleiermacher, with whom he would often engage in heated polemics.[6] Hegel never liked Friedrich Schlegel, and his aversion grew into a deep loathing over the years, so that he would sometimes go out of his way to criticize him.[7] All this animus came to a climax in the *Aesthetics*, which was a subtle and sustained polemic against the romantics. The anti-romantic aspects of the *Aesthetics* are profound and pervasive. Both Hegel's theses are directed against the romantic faith in the supremacy of the arts. The first targets the romantic claim that art stands above philosophy as a medium of truth; the second strikes against the romantic doctrine that artists should replace priests and philosophers in forming the ideology of modern culture. Apart from these theses, the whole structure of the first half of the work seems slanted against the romantics. The structure revolves around Hegel's classification of the epochs of art history, which seems specifically designed to prove two anti-romantic points: first, that the height of artistic achievement was in classical Greece; second, that modern romantic art amounts to the dissolution of art. According to this explanation, then, Hegel's devotion to the arts in the *Aesthetics* is really only apparent; it was only his anti-romantic animus that made him spend so much time and energy on art.

Though this explanation has some truth, it is not entirely correct. There were not only negative but also positive reasons for Hegel's preoccupation with the arts. Ultimately, his attitude toward the arts was ambivalent: if he heartily despised the inflated claims made in their behalf, he deeply admired the activity behind them. The arts had indeed a crucial place in the system. Art, religion and philosophy were the three modes of absolute knowledge, one of the three media by which spirit attains its self-awareness. Although art was the lowest of the hierarchy, it was surely significant that it was on the hierarchy at all, and indeed at the very base of the pyramid where it would support religion and philosophy. Art was the first medium in which spirit came to its self-awareness, the first level in which it transcended the spheres of nature and history and returned into itself. For all his polemics against the romantics, Hegel accepted the common romantic doctrine that artists were the first teachers of mankind, and that poetry was the mother tongue of the human race. In general, Hegel grants great significance to works of art as media of cultural self-awareness, as manifestations and expressions of the spirit of an entire age. Here we only need to remind ourselves of the crucial role he assigned to literary works in the *Phenomenology*: to Sophocles' *Antigone* for revealing the Greek *Volksgeist* and to Diderot's *Rameau's Nephew* for disclosing the mentality of pre-revolutionary France.

If we were to explain in a few words the historical significance of the *Aesthetics*, we would have to stress Hegel's role in reviving the legacy of Winckelmann in a post-Kantian and post-romantic age.[8] Throughout the *Aesthetics* the influence of Winckelmann is evident: in Hegel's uncompromising classicism, in his belief in the metaphysical significance of art, and in his attempt to situate art in its cultural context. When we read Hegel's description of classical beauty we can hear clear echoes of Winckelmann.[9] Although he was by no means uncritical of Winckelmann,[10] Hegel also paid handsome tribute to him. It was Winckelmann, he said, who had created a completely new organ for seeing art, a totally new perspective from which to understand it (W, XIII, 92/63). It was Hegel's mission to reaffirm Winckelmann's legacy against Kant and the romantics, who had attacked it in the 1790s. Against the romantics, Hegel reasserted Winckelmann's classicism, which the romantics had rejected as inappropriate for the modern age. While Hegel agreed with the romantics against Winckelmann that classical values could not be restored in the modern age, he still believed with Winckelmann against the romantics that classicism was the epitome of artistic achievement; Hegel's end of art thesis was simply Winckelmann's classicism without his doctrine of imitation. Against Kant, Hegel reinstated Winckelmann's method of placing art in its cultural context, a method that Kant had undermined by placing aesthetic experience in a transcendental realm beyond society and history.

THE SUBORDINATION THESIS

One of the most controversial aspects of Hegel's aesthetics is his subordination thesis, his doctrine that art is inferior to religion and philosophy as a medium of truth. This doctrine has been attacked chiefly on the grounds that it is unduly reductionist, showing a lack of appreciation for the *sui generis* stature of the arts. It has seemed to many as if Hegel wants to reduce poetry down to prose, as if everything that can be said in the media of art could be better said in philosophy.[11] The doctrine has therefore been condemned as a giant step backward in aesthetics, a relapse from Kant's thesis of the autonomy of art, which seems to provide a better basis for the understanding of modern art.[12] It has seemed to some as if Hegel wants to take aesthetics back to bad old pre-Baumgartian days, where aesthetic experience amounted to nothing more than 'a confused representation of understanding'.[13] One might defend Hegel by pointing out that he too explicitly affirmed the Kantian principle of autonomy; but this has not helped him against his critics, who claim that this principle is incompatible with the subordination thesis. After all, they argue, how is art autonomous if it is explicable in the terms of religion and philosophy? Hegel's affirmation of the subordination thesis *and* the principle of autonomy has been regarded as one of the fundamental tensions of his aesthetics.[14]

Whether these objections are well founded can only be determined by a closer examination of Hegel's subordination thesis. We have already examined this thesis in the case of religion (pp. 146–52). It is now necessary to consider it in the case of art, which poses its own special problems.

Hegel's official account of the place of art in his system appears in several dense and obscure paragraphs of the 1830 *Encyclopedia* (§§556–63). Art, religion and philosophy are the three stages of absolute spirit, the three forms of its self-awareness. These stages should be understood primarily as conceptual, as an epistemological classification of levels of self-knowledge. However, Hegel complicates matters by also conceiving these stages in historical terms, so that each stage represents a specific historical epoch. Hence the age of art is classical Greece; the age of religion is the Middle Ages; and the age of philosophy is modernity. This mixture of the conceptual and historical has been regarded as a confusion.[15] But the objection only begs the question, given that Hegel would never have accepted a strict distinction between epistemology and history.

If we follow the *Encyclopedia* account, Hegel thinks that art is subordinate to religion and philosophy because it stands on a lower level of self-consciousness. So we now must ask: Why is art a lower form of self-consciousness than religion and philosophy? Hegel's explanation in the *Aesthetics* follows his general theory of spirit.[16] According to that theory, spirit comes to its self-awareness first through externalization, from going outside itself and into its other, and then through reinternalization, going back inside itself from its other (pp. 114–15). Hegel explains that art belongs to the first stage of self-externalization, primarily because its medium appears to the senses, and secondly because its object exists outside the artist. Although the object is external to the artist, it also embodies his creative activity, and so the artist sees himself in his object, which therefore marks a stage of self-consciousness. Religion and philosophy, however, belong to the later stage of re-internalization because their media are universal and owe their existence to the activity of thinking alone. When the spirit deals with such media it is within a realm entirely created by itself, and so it enjoys greater independence and a higher level of self-consciousness. Part of Hegel's argument here is that aesthetic experience does not involve the structure of identity-in-difference characteristic of spirit. That structure requires that self and its other, subject and object, have the same status; but in the case of art the object is something dead and external, and so not on the same footing as the subject itself. Hence Hegel explains how the artist can distance himself from his object, ridiculing and even destroying it (VPR XVI, 137). Turning the romantic concept of irony against itself, he suggests that if the artist can alienate himself from his work, he cannot attain perfect self-awareness through it.

Hegel's best account of the systematic place of art in his system appears not in the dense and obscure exposition of the *Encyclopedia* but in his 1827 and 1831 lectures on the philosophy of religion.[17] Here the distinction between art, religion and philosophy is not in terms of self-consciousness but in terms of kinds of knowledge or degrees of comprehension. Hegel now explains that art, religion and philosophy all have the same object, the absolute or truth itself; but they consist in different forms of knowledge of it. Art presents the absolute in the form of immediate intuition (*Anschauung*); religion presents it in the form of representation (*Vorstellung*); and philosophy presents it in the form of concepts (*Begriffe*).

Each form of consciousness requires explication (pp. 147–8). In choosing the term 'intuition' to describe the stage of art, Hegel was only keeping with the usage of the romantics, who referred to aesthetic experience as an intuition. Like Kant and the romantics, Hegel understands intuition as the direct or *immediate* representation of a particular in sense experience; it is contrasted to a concept which is a *mediate* representation of a particular because it is a universal representation of many individual representations. Since intuition is a form of sense perception, and as such involved in all acts of seeing, hearing or touching, its medium of expression will be an image, some concrete shape or form in the sensible world.

Hence the medium of the arts will be images; in the case of music these will be sounds, in the case of sculpture they will be shapes, and in the case of painting they will be colours and shapes, and so on. Unlike the intuitions of art, whose objects are particular, the representations of religion are already universal, and so they involve a primitive form of abstraction. In religion we already begin to express the divine in determinate terms that exclude their opposites; for example, we refer to the divine as the infinite as opposed to the finite. Finally, the concepts of philosophy are not only universal but also concrete; they are not abstract like the representations of religion because they do not simply distinguish one thing from another but also involve knowing how each thing depends on another in a complete system.

It is important to see that art, religion and philosophy are all forms of *concrete* universality. In other words, they know their object as a whole or unity that precedes its parts; and they are therefore unlike the purely intellectual activity of the understanding (*Verstand*), which analyzes the whole into independent parts. They differ from one another, however, in the degree of their comprehension of this whole or unity. Intuition sees its object as a whole or unity; but it does not have an articulate grasp of the whole because it does not distinctly see each of its parts. Representation sees the parts of the whole distinctly; when it forms a universal it abstracts some aspect or feature of the whole; however, it has a dim grasp of how all these parts together form the whole. Philosophy stands higher than both art and religion because it grasps the whole within each of its parts; it sees not only the whole but how each individual part depends on it. Hence Hegel's hierarchy reflects perfectly the three stages of the concept: universality, particularity and individuality.[18]

Once we understand the hierarchy in these terms, it should be clear that the charge of reductivism against Hegel begs the question. For Hegel maintains that the conceptual comprehension of philosophy does not analyze but reconstitutes the whole of aesthetic intuition. It is not a form of abstract understanding, which attempts to reduce the whole into its separate parts; rather, it is an attempt to explain more distinctly each part of the whole, and how each part depends on the whole, forming an indivisible unity. The crucial point to see here is that Hegel's form of conceptual comprehension should respect – not reduce – the integrity and individuality of the aesthetic whole. Whether Hegel's own interpretative practice conforms to this ideal is another question; but in principle we cannot accuse Hegel of wanting to destroy or reduce the unity of aesthetic experience. Those who complain about Hegel's excessively intellectualist and rationalist view of art fail to observe his distinction between abstract and concrete universality.

Whether we understand Hegel's hierarchy in terms of self-awareness or degrees of comprehension, it should be clear that it is compatible with his affirmation of the principle of autonomy, at least as he understands it. As Hegel explains this principle in the *Aesthetic*, it means two things. First, that art should not serve ends outside itself. Hence Hegel rejects the old thesis of Gottsched that the purpose of art is moral instruction (XIII, 75–7/50–1). Second, that the media of the various arts have their own intrinsic qualities, which should be enjoyed for their own sake. Thus Hegel warns us against making the message of a poem or play so explicit or direct that the medium becomes superfluous (XIII, 77/51). Hegel's subordination thesis is really about the content of a work of art, which it claims can be reconstructed in conceptual terms. It does not claim that the work of art should serve extrinsic ends, still less that its form or medium does not have its own intrinsic qualities. That each artistic medium has its own unique qualities was a point that Hegel would stress time and again in his treatment of the specific arts.

Although, as stated so far, the objections to Hegel's subordination thesis are rather weak, they could be reformulated in stronger terms. Their chief target is Hegel's assumption that art, religion and philosophy all have the same object; it is only on these grounds that Hegel can grade them in a hierarchy. But one could question this assumption by claiming that each form of consciousness has a distinct object. If art involves unity of form and content, how indeed can we separate the content from its form? Hegel himself admits this very possibility (EPW §3), and it is not clear how he tries to avoid it. He even claims that the different stages of art involve completely different conceptions of their object, leaving the question how they are conceptions of the same thing (XIII, 105/74). So, it seems that one could reject the subordination thesis – and still hold that art is a form of cognition – simply by stressing that each art has its own object that it knows in its own distinct way.

Yet this is still not the end of the matter. For Hegel could defend his subordination thesis with his rationalist doctrine that intuition and representation are simply subconscious and inchoate forms of thinking. We have already seen how Hegel gave this old Leibnizian doctrine a new powerful rationale through Kant's epistemology (pp. 150–1).[19] Whether this doctrine is really true, however, is a thorny issue that we cannot pursue here.

ART AS COGNITION

Although Hegel subordinated art to religion and philosophy, and although he even declared the obsolescence of art, the fact remains that he still gave it fundamental importance. Art was the first medium of knowledge of the absolute. As such, Hegel rated its cognitive powers above the empirical sciences and history (XIII, 20–2/7–9). While they remained confined to the finite world, art could grasp the infinite, glimpsing the eternal within the passing events of nature and history. Indeed, Hegel gave art a higher cognitive status than the understanding. While the understanding is stuck in mere abstractions and opposed to sensibility, art could grasp the concrete universal and reconcile understanding with sensibility (XIII, 21/8, 82/55). Furthermore, the understanding had no power to grasp the true infinite, which art could fathom, even if through the dark glass of sensible images.

In bestowing such cognitive status upon art, Hegel reaffirmed the romantic legacy, despite his many disagreements with it. He agreed with Schelling, Friedrich Schlegel, Schleiermacher and Hölderlin that art was a higher form of knowledge than the understanding. He too held that the insights of art are irreducible to what we can know or explain purely discursively, according to abstract concepts, judgments and syllogisms. However, where the romantics went astray, in Hegel's view, is in placing art above philosophy. They could do this, he argued, only because they had limited philosophy to the abstract concepts of the understanding. They did not have a proper appreciation, therefore, of the dialectical form of reason. For two reasons, Hegel held that the dialectic is a more adequate form of concrete universality than art. First, it grasps explicitly and self-consciously what art sees only implicitly and subconsciously. Second, although the intuitions of art see the unity of the whole, the dialectic also grasps unity-in-difference, i.e. it sees each part of the whole and how they depend upon it.

Whatever Hegel's reasons for departing from the romantics, the basic question remains why he remained loyal to them at all. In other words: why did Hegel continue to uphold the cognitive status of art, its power to grasp the absolute? In the early 1800s the position was still a controversial one. After all, the general trend of eighteenth-century aesthetics had been toward subjectivism, according to which art simply expressed the feelings of the artist or pleased the senses of the observer. The most important representative of this trend was Kant, who had argued in the *Critique of Judgment* that aesthetic judgments have only a subjective validity about what objects are pleasing to the perceiver; though these judgments have a universal validity, they still concern only feelings of pleasure that refer to no qualities in the object itself. Of course, the challenge to the cognitive status of art is even more venerable, going back at least to Plato, who had banished artists from his republic on the grounds that their works could only trade in illusion. When we consider such potent challenges to Hegel's position, we have to ask how he responded to them.

In the introduction to his *Aesthetics* Hegel does have an interesting response to these issues, a defense of the cognitive status of art against its critics. His account is not developed in great detail, however, partly because its epistemological and metaphysical premises are laid down in his other works. Because Hegel's treatment is not sustained or systematic, it has been regarded as derivative, as really resting upon the foundation that Schelling gave it in his *System of transcendental Idealism* and in his *Philosophy of Art*.[20] But this is a mistake. While Hegel indeed had debts to Schelling, the premises behind his position rest on his own epistemology and metaphysics, which involve substantial differences with Schelling. Our task now will be to reconstruct Hegel's position on the cognitive status of art by placing it in the wider context of his epistemology and metaphysics.

Hegel's thesis of the cognitive status of art has its most general and explicit formulation in his definition of beauty: 'the sensible appearing [*Scheinen*] of the idea' (XIII, 151/111). The most significant claim behind this formula is its reevaluation of the concept of appearance. Appearance could be the realm of illusion, in which the truth is disguised or concealed; but it could also be the realm of revelation, where the truth is manifested or disclosed. Notoriously, Plato understood appearances in the former sense, and it was for just this reason that he had banished art from his republic. He distinguished sharply between the intellectual realm of the forms and the sphere of the senses; and since the artist could only imitate objects of the senses, his work amounted to an appearance of an appearance, so that it is two steps removed from the truth. In the introduction to his *Aesthetics* Hegel counters Plato's argument by flatly declaring his opposing concept of appearance. 'Appearance is essential to essence; the truth would not be, if it did not shine and appear . . .' (XIII, 21/8). Hegel agrees with Plato that we cannot take the objects of the senses on their own as reality; and he admits that art would be indeed removed from reality if all it could do is imitate these objects. However, art is significant, Hegel argues, precisely because its sensible forms indicate a more substantial reality lying behind them.

What justification did Hegel have for his revaluation of the realm of appearance? Its basis lay with his organicist metaphysics, and more specifically his Aristotelian conception of universals, which we have already examined above (pp. 56–7). According to that conception, the universal is not merely an abstract term, a collective name for a number of distinct but similar particulars, as it is in the nominalist tradition; still less is it an archetype or eternal form, which is completely beyond the passing world of sense particulars, as in the Platonic tradition.[21] Rather, the universal is concrete, the immanent form of an object, its formal and final cause. This means that sense particulars embody or manifest the universal; they are part of the very process by which the universal comes into being, the specific form in which it realizes itself in the world. Hence the appearances of the sensible world are not illusory but revelatory, because they embody and realize the substantial form of an object. So, in so far as art deals with sensible appearances, it has the power to reveal the immanent form of an object.

Hegel's most concerted effort to explain the cognitive status of art appears in his account of the standpoint of aesthetic contemplation (XIII, 58–9, 152–4/36–7, 113). Here again his Aristotelian metaphysics plays a pivotal role. Like Kant, Hegel distinguishes aesthetic contemplation from the practical and theoretical standpoints. In the practical standpoint we make an object conform to our ends; and in the theoretical standpoint we see the object as an instance of some universal or general laws. Both standpoints see the universal as external to the object: the universal of the practical standpoint is some end that we impose on the object; the universal of the theoretical standpoint lies solely in the understanding or reflection of the observer. In aesthetic contemplation, however, we see the universal as inherent in the object, as deriving from its inner nature (XIII, 154/113). What is characteristic of aesthetic contemplation, Hegel maintains, is that we regard the object as autonomous, as realizing its own intrinsic ends and as acting according to the necessity of its own nature alone.

Here we see the basis for Hegel's departure from Kant. Since aesthetic contemplation gives us insight into the inherent form of the object, it gives us knowledge of that object, of what that object is in itself. In the *Critique of Judgment* Kant had distinguished aesthetic from teleological judgment, and he had insisted that both forms of judgment are strictly regulative, i.e. we must treat them only as if they were true of the object itself. In granting aesthetic experience the power to grasp the inherent form of an object, Hegel went against the grain of both these Kantian points. Aesthetic experience is a species of teleology, and it gives us knowledge of the object, because it grasps its intrinsic purpose, its formal–final cause. Hence the ultimate basis for Hegel's departure from Kant − for his going beyond the Kantian limits and ascribing cognitive status to art − resides in his defense of the constitutive status of teleology (see pp. 100–7).

Hegel's theory of the cognitive status of art has to be placed in the context of his complex attitude toward the doctrine of imitation, which for centuries had been the main theory about the objective status of art. Given his attempt to defend the objectivity of art, one would expect Hegel to be sympathetic toward the theory of imitation. But the very opposite is the case. He sometimes writes about it as if it were completely obsolete, surpassed by modern doctrines that stress the creative activity of the subject. He decisively rejects one version of the doctrine, according to which imitation consists in 'the aptitude to copy natural forms as they are present to us', as if the artist should simply duplicate what is given to the senses. Hegel fires off a whole battery of objections against this version of the doctrine (XIII, 65–9/41–4). He first points out that it makes art superfluous: Why simply duplicate what is already given to us? He then adds that it also makes art absurdly ambitious; for we cannot ever recreate through artistic means all the richness and particularity of nature, given that art recreates with one sensual medium what is given to all our different senses in nature. After pointing out these problems, Hegel complains that imitation reduces art to something purely formal; since what matters is how something is imitated, not what is imitated, even the ugly and trival could be the subject matter for art. Finally, Hegel notes that imitation does not apply to all the arts; architecture and poetry, for example, are hardly imitative.

Yet Hegel's attitude toward imitation was much more complex than some of his polemics suggest. The complexities emerge when he discusses the question, very topical in his day, whether art should idealize nature or imitate it (XIII, 212/160). Here Hegel seems to take the side of those who hold the modern theory that the artist should idealize nature, and he has indeed been read as a one-sided partisan of that approach.[22] But a closer reading of the text shows that he wants to do full justice to both sides of this dispute, and that he endorses one version of imitation after all.

Hegel seems to side with those who insist that art should idealize nature when he stresses the creative activity of the artist, and when he insists that aesthetic objects please us because their form is made rather than given (XIII, 216/164). He argues that it is the task of the artist to grasp his subject matter in its universality, which he cannot achieve simply by copying all the extrinsic and accidental features given to the senses. It soon becomes apparent, however, that Hegel regards such idealization not as a kind of fiction but as a deeper and more adequate representation of reality itself. What the artist represents is not the object in its particularity, externality and contingency but its inherent substantial form. Since this form is not given to the senses, it has to be recreated by the intellect itself (XIII, 221, 227/167, 172). In his account of art in his lectures on the philosophy of religion Hegel explains two different senses in which art can be true of its object. Truth can consist in *correctness* (*Richtigkeit*) where the work is an accurate to the features of the object given in sense; and it can consist in the *correspondence* of the work with the inherent concept of the object (VPR III, 144/I, 235). It is only in this latter sense that Hegel thinks art can have a claim to truth; but it is also in this sense that he could be said to accept one version of imitation.

But Hegel's critique of the traditional doctrine of imitation, and his insistence on the creative powers of the artist, leave a troubling question. How can art give us knowledge of reality if (1) the artist must create his object, and if (2) he should not imitate his object as it is given to him? On just these grounds many aestheticians dismiss the cognitive status of art entirely, maintaining instead that its purpose is to do nothing more than to please our senses or to express feelings. As usual, Hegel seems to want both to have his cake and eat it. He gives the artist license to express his creativity and imagination, and yet confers a metaphysical significance on him for doing so.

To understand Hegel's solution to this problem, we must again place it in the context of his metaphysics. Hegel conceives the artist as one part of the organic whole of nature and history, a whole that is inseparable from each of its parts and that reveals itself entirely in each of them. Furthermore, the artist, as a vehicle of human self-awareness, is one of the highest forms of organization and development of all the powers within this organic whole. This means that the activity of the artist is simply one of the highest manifestations and developments of all the organic powers at work in nature and history, so that what he creates is what nature or history creates through him. It is for just this reason that the artist's work amounts to a stage in the self-awareness of spirit; the artist is not only aware of himself through his work but the spirit of all of history and nature is aware of itself through him. If we assume the contrary, a Cartesian metaphysics according to which the mind of the artist is a *res cogitans* and nature is a *res extensa*, then it is impossible to understand how the artist knows anything in nature at all; for how could two such distinct substances correspond with one another in an act of knowledge? According to a Cartesian metaphysics, then, art must have entirely subjective status, revealing nothing more than the feelings and fantasies of a disembodied mind. If, however, we adopt the opposing organic view of nature, according to which the activities of the mind are simply the highest degree of organization and development of the vital powers of nature, then the representations of the artist manifest, embody and reveal these powers. They do not simply copy or mirror these powers from some external standpoint; rather, they *are* the manifestation or expression of these powers, their highest organization and development. What the artist creates is what nature creates through him, so that the artist's representation of nature is nature's representation of itself through the artist.

It is the same metaphysics that allows Hegel to resolve the apparent tension between the cognitive status of art and the principle of aesthetic autonomy. *Prima facie* these doctrines seem incompatible, because if art represents a reality outside itself, it has a standard outside itself, and so loses its autonomy. Indeed, on just these grounds, Hegel's doctrine of representation has been seen as the *antipode* of the Kantian doctrine of autonomy.[23] Hegel's metaphysics allows him to combine these doctrines, however, since it implies that the representational or cognitive status of the work simply resides in the work itself. The work does not represent or mirror some prototype that lies outside itself. Rather, it simply *is* how the creative activity of the absolute appears to itself, so that its meaning lies within itself.

DEATH OF ART

The most controversial aspect of Hegel's aesthetics has been his notorious theory about 'the end of art'. In the introduction to his lectures on aesthetics Hegel shocked his first listeners, and all his readers ever since, by flatly announcing the obsolescence of art. Art, he seemed to say, had exhausted itself. It had no future, no significant role to play in modern culture. What art had once been in the classical and medieval eras – the representation of its highest aspirations and fundamental values – could now be better achieved by philosophy.

Since 1828, Hegel's announcement has lost none of its power to disturb. It continues to find defenders and detractors to this day.[24] Hegel's theory has indeed become something of a lightning rod for disputes about modern art.[25] Those who think that modern art has exhausted itself often claim Hegel as their seer; but those who think that modern art has a promising future make Hegel their *bête noire*.

Since the doctrine has been so controversial, and since it has been so often misunderstood, it is important to consider exactly what Hegel says and what follows from it.

It is noteworthy that Hegel himself does not use the phrase 'the death of art', which has so often been ascribed to him.[26] Furthermore, he does not even talk about 'the end of art'. He does state explicitly, however, that art is now something past for us (XIII, 25/10), and that it has been 'surpassed' (*überflügelt*) by philosophy (XIII, 24/10). Art no longer addresses, he explains, 'our highest needs' (XIII, 24, 142/10, 103). Whatever the precise wording, Hegel's main point is simple: that art has ceased to have the central importance in the modern age that it once had in the classical and medieval eras. Art played a pivotal role in those cultures because it was the main medium for the representation of their religion, ethics and worldview. Since the modern age is much more rationalistic, the traditional function of the arts is now better performed by philosophy.

It is also noteworthy that Hegel's point is still compatible with the future of the arts. To say that art no longer plays a central role in modern culture is not to say that it should or will end. Hegel never makes such a rash statement; indeed, he expresses the hope that artists will continue to create and strive for greater perfection in their work (XIII, 142/103). He also says that there comes a time in the development of every nation when art surpasses itself (XIII, 142/103), which suggests that the decline of art in modern culture might be a transitory phenomenon, perhaps to be succeeded by a renaissance of the arts in some other epoch.

But if one should not overstate the implications of Hegel's theory, neither should one understate them. Many scholars have attempted to soften its implications, as if Hegel did not really mean what he said.[27] They maintain that, even though Hegel gives more status to philosophy than art, he still thinks that art is one medium for the cognition of the absolute, so that it should have an important role in modern culture. Basing their argument upon the general structure of the dialectic, they point out that Hegel uses his technical term 'aufheben', which means that something has been preserved as well as cancelled in a higher synthesis. Since art is preserved in the dialectic, they infer that it should persist in the modern era, and indeed continue to have its old function as one form of representing the absolute.

A closer examination shows, however, that Hegel's theory has harsher implications than these scholars admit. The general principles of the dialectic establish nothing about the enduring presence of art, still less its significance, in modern society. While the dialectic indeed preserves its preceding stages, their preservation does not imply their continual existence, only that they have shaped the present. It is perfectly compatible with the structure of the dialectic, therefore, for art to disappear entirely. More importantly, however, Hegel does not think that art will perform a central role in the modern world. For, as we shall soon see, he maintains that the modern artist is so alienated from society, culture and state that he has lost irredeemably his role as a spokesman for its fundamental beliefs and values. While art will indeed continue, it will do so in a greatly reduced role: it will be nothing more than a form of individual self-expression.

Granted that Hegel's theory has such severe implications, why does he state it in the first place? What reasons does he have for thinking that art would be obsolete in the modern world? The premises behind Hegel's theory are complex and interleaving. Some are historical, others epistemological, still others cultural. While some are more powerful than his detractors assume, others are weaker than his defenders admit.

Hegel's belief in the obsolescence of the arts was already built into his general classification of the epochs of art history, which structures the entire first half of the *Aesthetics*. He saw three fundamental epochs of art history, each of them corresponding to one moment in the development of the idea. (1) The first epoch, which appeared in ancient Persian, Indian and Egyptian culture, was the symbolic. This era had for its object the idea in itself, the idea in its undeveloped and inchoate stage, the infinite that has not yet embodied itself in the finite world. This stage of the idea was represented in the pantheistic religions of the Orient. Because the idea at this stage is still abstract and indeterminate, it cannot be adequately or fully represented through the sensual media of art, which are concrete and determinate. Hence there could be no match, and indeed only a gulf, between the idea and its sensual representation in symbolic art. The medium of symbolic art was the symbol, an image that had some of the qualities of its object; but since the image had other qualities irrelevant to the object it symbolized, it was never a perfect representation of its object. Because of the poor match between a symbol and its object, Hegel regarded symbolic art as really a form of 'pre-art', which did not realize the ideal of all art, the perfect unity of form and content. (2) The second epoch, which appeared in ancient Greece, was the classical. This era had for its object the idea in the stage of its externalization, as it manifested itself in the finite world. This stage of the idea was represented in the anthropomorphic religions of the classical world. Since the idea is now in the stage of its externalization, manifesting itself in concrete form, it is perfectly represented through the sensual media of art. The object of art is not simply a symbol of the divine; but it is the manifestation and appearance of the divine. Hence Hegel thinks that classical art fully realized the ideal of beauty: a perfect unity of form and content. (3) The third epoch, which is marked by the Christian era, is the romantic. The idea has now created a realm of spiritual inwardness. It has returned into itself after manifesting itself in the world of sense. Since the Christian God is purely spiritual, and since the media of art are sensual, it cannot be represented in artistic form. The gulf between aesthetic media and their object in symbolic art now returns. All that romantic art can express is the Christian ethic of love, since love does have a sensual appearance and embodiment.

The dialectic behind Hegel's classification is unique, showing none of the growth and progression typical of its structure. The shape of this dialectic is parabolic, marked by the gradual ascent, climax and eventual descent of the representative powers of art. Hegel himself characterizes the three stages in such parabolic terms. As he puts it, the symbolic stage marks a *striving* toward the ideal of beauty; the classical stage marks the *achievement* of this ideal; and the romantic marks the *surpassing* of this ideal (XIII, 114/81).

However uncharacteristic, the immediate implication of Hegel's dialectic is plain: that art has no future. The basic problem with art in the modern world is that it cannot represent the fundamental truths behind its characteristic religion: Christianity. Since Christianity remains the dominant religion of the modern world, since its spiritual truths resist sensible representation, art is not an adequate medium to express our fundamental beliefs and aspirations. If we are to comprehend the spiritual truths of Christianity, we need the purely intellectual medium of thought, and so philosophy should replace art in the modern world.

Obviously, Hegel's classification of the epochs of art history betrays his classical taste. For Hegel, art essentially revolves around the ideal of beauty, which consists in the perfect unity of form and content, the appearance of the idea in sensual form. Like Winckelmann, Hegel held that this ideal had been perfectly realized in classical Greek art. The Greeks were able to attain this ideal, Hegel explains, chiefly because of their religion. There was no gulf between the ideal and its sensual form in Greek art because Greek religion was fundamentally anthropomorphic (XIII, 102, 111/72, 79). Since the Greeks conceived of divinity in human form, they could express the divine perfectly through the human body. Hence for Hegel, as for Winckelmann, Greek sculpture represents the pinnacle of its aesthetic achievement (XIV, 87, 92/486, 490). After Greek sculpture, it was impossible for art to achieve anything more; art had effectively reached its end. And so Hegel declares: 'The classical art form had reached the highest that can be achieved through the sensualization of art; and if there is something deficient about it, that is only because of art itself and the limits of the sphere of art' (XIII, 111/72; XIV, 127–8/517).

Given such a declaration, Hegel's theory about the obsolescence of art comes as no surprise. This theory was his lament for the loss of the classical ideal. Art had no future simply because its glory lay in the past, and its past was unrecoverable. Unlike Winckelmann and the neo-classicists, Hegel did not believe that it was possible to imitate Greek art. Any attempt to revive Greek art would be doomed to artificiality and affectation, because Greek art was the unique product of its time and place, which was now gone for ever. Since the achievement of Greek art rested upon its anthropomorphic religion, it would be impossible to revive it in a more enlightened age. For who nowadays, Hegel asks, believes in the gods (XIV, 233/603)? The modern era is so critical that it would never accept the beautiful myths that had been the heart of Greek religion. Hence Hegel rejected the romantic dream of a new mythology.

As explained so far, Hegel's theory seems to rest upon some dubious premises. It assumes that classical art is the epitome of artistic achievement, that art must have a religious vocation, and that Christianity will remain the dominant ideological force of the modern world. It is striking that all these premises were questioned by Schiller and the early romantics, who argued that art was of enduring importance in the modern world precisely because of the decline of Christianity. Since Christianity had fallen victim to the criticism of the Enlightenment, art should replace religion, because it alone could support morality in a popular manner appealing to the heart and the imagination. Philosophy, with all its abstract concepts and abstruse reasoning, could never play this role.

But, however questionable these premises might be, they are not essential to Hegel's theory, which is independent of his classicism and his classification of artistic epochs. The deeper rationale for his theory lies in his diagnosis of the trends and values of modern culture and society (pp. 231–3). In his opening account of the obsolescence of art in the introduction to his lectures, Hegel explains that art has lost its place in modern culture because that culture is so fundamentally rationalistic. Hegel calls it Reflexionskultur, where 'reflection' means our power of critical and abstract thinking. Such a culture is not conducive to art, he explains, because art addresses our sensibility, but we want to express truth in abstract form, in terms of laws, rules and maxims (XIII, 24–5/10). The whole of modern culture is more appropriate to aesthetics, to thinking about art rather than artistic production itself. If philosophy arises only when an age has grown old, then aesthetics, the philosophy of art, should arise only when art too has had its day.

When we examine Hegel's argument more closely, however, it becomes clear that the problem with modern culture is not its rationalism as such, but the effect such rationalism has had on the artist. Since rationalism demands that the individual always think critically and independently, it alienates him or her from the community. Rather than identifying with its customs, laws and religion, the modern individual constantly questions them, accepting and rejecting them strictly according to whether they satisfy the demands of his or her own conscience and reason. The happy harmony between the individual and society, which was the precondition for art in the classical age, has been destroyed in modern society. Since the Greek artist was not alienated from the religion and culture of his people, he became their spokesman, indeed their priest (XIV, 25–6, 232/437, 603). While the content of classical art was given to the artist by the culture and religion of his people, the modern artist must create his or her content, so that it has only an individual significance. They simply play with the content of their art, treating it with complete indifference, much like a dramatist treats the characters in a play (XIV, 235/605–6).

The epitome of the artist's alienation from his community, in Hegel's view, is contemporary romantic art. The aesthetic of artistic alienation is romantic irony. Since he had developed his critical powers to their fullest, the romantic artist remained distanced from everything. His irony expressed his detachment, his eagerness to stand back from and criticize any content whatsoever. Nothing stood above his own creative powers, which could make anything into a work of art. The result was that art had lost its subject matter – the fundamental values and beliefs of a culture – and so ceased to address its fundamental needs and aspirations. Art had now degenerated into little more than self-expression, and it assumed as many different forms as there are individuals to express themselves. If, however, art were only self-expression, then it had ceased to play a role in culture or history. To be sure, art was not dead, and it would continue as long as artists continued to express themselves. But the crucial question is whether art is still important, whether it had any significance beyond individual self-expression. And here Hegel's answer was a decisive 'No'.

Hence Hegel's theory of the obsolescence of art ultimately rested upon his diagnosis of the alienation endemic to modern politics and culture. As such his theory was independent of his classicism, and indeed his belief in the enduring vitality of Christianity. The fundamental challenge facing art in the modern world was the same as that confronting the state: the powerful alienating force of the right of subjectivity. Just as that right had separated the individual from the state, so it did the same to the artist and the culture of his age. The source of the problem was irremovable, since the right of subjectivity was fundamental to and characteristic of the modern world.

One might ask: Why did Hegel not think there could be a reconciliation between the modern artist and his age, just as there could be one for the modern individual and the state? Why not a new higher synthesis, where the artist expresses the fundamental beliefs and values of his culture on a higher level? But it is just in raising this question that we can see the deeper reasons for Hegel's pessimism about art. For he had always insisted that the reconciliation of the modern individual with society and state could take place only on the level of reflection. The structure of modern society and the state would have to satisfy the demands of critical rationality; and it was just these demands that could not be satisfied by art. Art appealed to the senses and feeling, not to a detached critical reason. What the modern individual ultimately needed was an explanation, a reason, not an allegory, a novel or a play.

Hegel's famous dictum in the preface to the *Philosophy of Right* that every philosophy is the self-awareness of its age is, of course, intentionally self-reflexive, applying to his own philosophy. With this dictum Hegel confessed that his own philosophy was really little more than the self-awareness of his age, the articulation of its highest ideals and aspirations. His age was that of the Prussian Reform Movement, which had dominated Prussian political life during the reign of Friedrich Wilhelm III from 1797 to 1840. Although many of its ideals were far from reality, and although hopes for reform were disappointed time and again in the 1820s and 1830s, these hopes and ideals were at least alive in the minds and hearts of the young. Throughout these decades they fervently hoped that their monarch would finally deliver on his promises for reform. As long as that hope remained, the Hegelian philosophy could claim to represent its age, at least in aspiration if not in reality.

Thus Hegel's philosophy reigned supreme in Prussia for most of the Reform era, chiefly from 1818 to 1840. Its rise to prominence began in 1818 with Hegel's appointment to the University of Berlin. Hegel and his disciples received strong official backing from the Prussian Ministry of Culture, especially from two powerful ministers, Baron von Altenstein and Johannes Schulze. They supported Hegel's philosophy largely because they saw it as the medium to support their own reformist views against reactionary court circles. In 1827 Hegel's students began to organize themselves, forming their own society, the *Berliner kritische Association*, and editing a common journal, *Jahrbücher für wissenschaftliche Kritik*. When Hegel died in 1831, a group of his most intimate students prepared a complete edition of his works.

What did these students see in Hegel's philosophy? Why did they regard themselves as Hegelians? Almost all of Hegel's early disciples saw his philosophy as the rationalization of the Prussian Reform Movement, whose ideals they shared. For the most part,[1] they viewed themselves as loyal Prussians, not out of any sense of unconditional obedience, but because they were confident that the Prussian state would eventually realize some of the main ideals of the Revolution through gradual reform. They were proud of the political traditions of the Prussian state, which seemed to embody all the progressive trends of the Reformation and *Aufklärung*.[2] Like Hegel, most of the young Hegelians believed in the virtues of constitutional monarchy and the necessity of reform from above.[3] The radicalization of the Hegelian movement would not begin until after the accession of Friedrich Wilhelm IV and the 1840s. For almost all the Hegelians before 1840, however, Hegel's philosophy represented the genuine *via media* between reaction and revolution. It seemed to be the only alternative for those who could not accept the reactionaries' appeal to tradition or the romantic revolutionaries' call for a sentimental patriotism. To the delight of his converts, Hegel saw the ideals of ethical life embodied in the constitution of the modern state rather than in the traditions of the *ancien régime* or the emotional bonds of the *Volk*.[4]

Despite their shared sympathies, there were deep tensions among Hegel's followers from the very beginning. These became fully public and self-conscious, however, only in the 1830s. When, in 1835, David Friedrich Strauss published his *Das Leben Jesu*, which argued that the biblical story of Jesus was essentially mythical, battle-lines began to form. Some regarded Strauss's argument as a betrayal of Hegel's legacy, while others saw it as its fulfillment. The basic issue at dispute concerned the proper relationship of Hegel's philosophy to religion.[5] To what extent can Hegel's philosophy rationalize the traditional Christian faith, the beliefs in immortality, the divinity of Christ and a personal God? If these beliefs were incorporated into the Hegelian system, would their traditional meaning be preserved or negated? The opposing answers to these questions gave rise to the famous division of the Hegelian school into right-wing, left-wing and centre. This distinction is not anachronistic since it was made by the Hegelians themselves. According to Strauss, there were three possible positions regarding this issue: either all, some or none of the traditional Christian beliefs could be incorporated into the Hegelian system.[6] He then applied a political metaphor to describe these positions. The right wing held that all, the centre that some, and the left that none, could be accommodated by Hegel's system. Among the chief right-wing Hegelians were Henrich Hotho (1802–73), Leopold von Henning (1791–1866), Friedrich Förster (1791–1868), Hermann Ninrichs (1794–1861), Karl Daub (1765–1836), Kasimir Conradi (1784–1849), Phillip Marheineke (1780–1846) and Julius Schaller (1810–68). Among the moderate or centre Hegelians were Karl Michelet (1801–93) and Karl Rosenkranz (1805–79). And among the prominent left-wing Hegelians were Ludwig Feuerbach (1804–72), Arnold Ruge (1802–80), David Friedrich Strauss (1808–74), Max Stirner (1806–56) and, in his later years, Bruno Bauer (1808–82). The second generation of left-wing Hegelians included Karl Marx, Friedrich Engels and Mikhail Bakunin.

Although the battle-lines between the Hegelians first became explicit and self-conscious over a theological issue, their religious differences were ultimately a reflection of their deeper political ones. These political tensions had been present in the early 1820s, but they became more apparent in the 1830s.[7] The basic question at issue concerned the extent to which existing conditions in Prussia realized Hegel's ideals. Here again the Straussian metaphor proved useful to describe the various positions in the debate. The right held that most, if not all, conditions in Prussia fulfilled Hegel's ideals; the centre claimed that some did; and the left believed that few, if any, did. Although there was an apparent chasm between right and left, the dispute between them still took place within the broad confines of Hegel's reformism. All parties remained true to Hegel's basic principles and ideals; they simply quarrelled over the extent to which these were now realized in Prussia. Despite all their disillusionment, the left Hegelians continued to uphold their belief in the unity of theory and practice throughout the 1830s. They were still confident that, even if the present conditions were in conflict with Hegel's ideals, they would not remain so because of the dialectic of history.

These religious and political controversies within the Hegelian school were not so easily resolvable because they involved an apparently intractable problem in the interpretation of Hegel's metaphysics.[8] Namely, what is the nature of Hegel's concrete universal, his synthesis of the ideal and real, the universal and particular? Both left and right could point to some aspects of Hegel's teaching to support their case. For their part, the right argued that Hegel maintains that the universal exists only in the particular, that theory must conform to practice, and that the real is rational or ideal. This side of Hegel's philosophy seemed to show that the historical facts of Christianity, and the present conditions in Prussia, were indeed the realization of Hegel's ideals. They accused the left of creating an abstract universal, a gap between theory and practice, by too rigidly distinguishing between ideals and facts. On the other hand, the left contended that Hegel holds that the universal, the ideal or the rational, is the very purpose of history, to which everything eventually must conform. It is a mistake to assume, they replied to the right, that the ideal must exist in just these particulars when it is realized only through the whole historical process. These issues had indeed troubled Hegel himself ever since his early Jena years. The extent to which a philosophical system can explain or incorporate all the contingencies or particularities of experience proved to be an intractable problem. It seemed as if a system must include all particularities, because only then is it concrete and comprehensive; but it also seemed as if it must *exclude* at least some of them, since reason could never derive all the particular facts of experience. Hence, notoriously, Hegel distinguished between actuality (*Wirklichkeit*) and existence (*Existenz*), where actuality conformed to the necessity of reason but existence did not.[9] But how do we distinguish between actuality and existence? Hegel left his disciples little concrete guidance; hence the disputes among them.

This account of the disputes within the Hegelian school seems to follow, or at least confirm, Engels's famous statement in his *Ludwig Feuerbach und der Ausgang der klassischen deutschen Philosophie*.[10] According to that statement, the division between right and left Hegelians was essentially a split between radicals and reactionaries. While the radicals adopted Hegel's method and his dictum that the rational is the real, the reactionaries embraced his system and his dictum that the real is rational. Engels's account does contain some important germs of truth: that the fundamental split in the movement arose from an ambiguity in Hegel's philosophy, and that it concerned the question of the rationality of present conditions in Prussia. However, it is important not to take it too literally or to draw broader conclusions from it. It is misleading in several respects. (1) Throughout the 1820s and 1830s, the division between right and left was not between radicals and reactionaries, but between opposing wings of a broad reformist politics. The radical currents of left-wing Hegelianism developed only in the 1840s, after the accession of Friedrich Wilhelm IV; and even then there was not that much of a split between radicals and conservatives because right-wing Hegelianism virtually disappeared.[11] (2) The distinction between method and system is not only artificial, but also insufficient to distinguish between right and left Hegelians. After the 1840s the left rejected the method as much as the system because they lost all their faith in the dialectic of history.[12] (3) Engels interprets the division in *narrow* political terms, though religious differences occasioned the split in the first place.[13]

What finally shattered and dissolved Hegelianism was not its internal disputes, its centrifugal tendencies alone. For, as we have seen, the debates of the 1830s continued within a Hegelian framework, never renouncing the grand Hegelian ideal of the unity of theory and practice. What did defeat Hegelianism was the very card its master most loved to play: history. In 1840 the Prussian Reform Movement came to its end. In that fateful year both Altenstein and Friedrich Wilhelm III died. Hopes for reform were raised again with the accession of Friedrich Wilhelm IV. And, indeed, he began his reign with some popular liberal measures: amnesty for political prisoners, the publication of the proceedings of provincial estates, and the relaxation of press censorship. It did not bode well, however, that the new king's personal politics were very reactionary. He advocated government by the old aristocratic estates, disapproved of the plans for a new constitution, insisted upon protecting the state religion, and even defended the divine right of kings. Sure enough, there were some very ominous developments. In 1841, Friedrich Wilhelm showed his true political colors by inviting Schelling to Berlin 'to combat the dragonseed of Hegelianism'. Then, in 1842, the government began to impose censorship, forcing the Hegelians to publish their main journal, the *Hallische Jahrbücher*, outside Prussia. For any Hegelian in the 1840s, then, this course of events could be only profoundly discouraging. Rather than marching forward, as Hegel assumed, history seemed to be moving backward.

Once the forces of reaction began to assert themselves, it was inevitable that Hegel's philosophy would collapse. After all, the very essence of Hegel's teaching made him vulnerable to historical refutation. The great strength of Hegel's system lay in its bold syntheses – of theory and practice, of rationalism and historicism, of radicalism and conservatism – for these seemed to transcend the partisan spirit, granting every standpoint a necessary, if limited, place in the whole. But the great strength of Hegel's philosophy was also its great weakness, its tragic flaw, For, as we have seen (pp. 219–23), all these syntheses rested upon a single optimistic premise: that reason is inherent in history, that the laws and trends of history will inevitably realize the ideals of the Revolution. It was just this optimism, though, that seemed to be refuted by the disillusioning events of the early 1840s. Hegel had bet his whole system on history; and he had lost.

It is not surprising to find, then, that the neo-Hegelian debates of the 1840s take on a new dimension. The question is no longer how to praise and interpret Hegel but how to transform and bury him. The publication of Feuerbach's *Das Wesen des Christenthums* in 1841 convinced many of the need to go beyond Hegel. In 1842, Arnold Ruge, a leading left Hegelian, published his first criticism of Hegel.[14] And in 1843 Marx and Engels would begin their 'settling of accounts' with their Hegelian heritage in *Die deutsche Ideologie*. Internal feuding lost its former energy and meaning. Many of the right-wing Hegelians became disillusioned with the course of events and joined their brothers on the left to form a common front against their reactionary enemies.[15] The common framework for the debates of the 1830s also quickly disappeared. Rather than reaffirming the ideal of the unity of theory and practice, many Hegelians asserted the rights of theory over practice. It seemed to Bruno Bauer, for example, that the growing gap between ideal and reality in Friedrich Wilhelm's Prussia could be overcome only by 'the terrorism of pure theory'.

By the close of the 1840s, Hegelianism was rapidly becoming a fading memory. Having been the ideology for a reform movement that had failed, it could not be the ideology for the Revolution of 1848. Thus the grandest philosophical system of the nineteenth century, and one of its most influential philosophical movements, disappeared into history. The owl of Minerva flew from her roost over Hegel's grave.

Glossary of Hegelian Terms

Contrary to the tradition of German academic philosophy from Wolff to Kant, Hegel rarely gives technical definitions of his terms. He uses them in a variety of senses where the precise meaning depends on the specific context. There is no perfect definition of a Hegelian term that fits every context.

This is not a complete glossary. It provides only a brief account of some meanings of some salient terms. I define terms only that are used frequently and have a special Hegelian meaning. For a more detailed glossary, the reader does well to consult Michael Inwood, *A Hegel Dictionary* (Oxford: Blackwell, 1992). To note the many contexts and passages in which Hegel uses a word, it is very helpful to use the *Register* for *Werke in zwanzig Bänden*, ed. Helmut Reinicke (Frankfurt: Suhrkamp, 1979).

Absolute (*das Absolute*): 'The Absolute' is Hegel's technical term for the subject matter of philosophy. More loosely, he sometimes uses it as a synonym for 'God' or 'truth'. More precisely, the absolute is that which has a self-sufficient or independent existence and essence; it does not depend on anything else to exist or have its essence or nature. In this sense the absolute is Hegel's term for the traditional concept of substance, which has been the subject matter of metaphysics since Aristotle.

Alienation (*Entfremdung, Entäußerung*): this term refers to the stage of the development of spirit when it subconsciously externalizes, alienates or objectifies some aspect of itself, which it consciously sees as alien or hostile to itself. Alienation is the paradoxical phenomenon of self-enslavement, the problem posed by Rousseau's famous dictum 'man is born free; everywhere he is in chains'. The source of alienation lies in hypostasis or reification, i.e., seeing our own creations as if they were things independent of us and to which we must submit.

Appearance (*Erscheinung*):   Hegel uses this term not in the sense of illusion, and not in the sense of how reality in itself appears to *any* consciousness. Rather, by the appearance of a thing he means is its actualization, its coming into being from potentiality. The appearance of a thing does not conceal or mask, but reveals or manifests its essence or nature. Appearances need not exist only for some consciousness, as in *subjective idealism*.

Concept (*Begriff*):   the inherent form or inner purpose of an object, its formal and final cause. The formal cause is the essence or nature of a thing insofar as it is the cause or reason for its activity; the final cause, is its purpose, the goal of its development. Hegel thinks that these are forms of causality are linked in the concept, since the final cause of a thing is to realize its inner nature or essence. Hegel insists that the concept is a *concrete* universal because it is internal to the thing, and not an *abstract* universal, which is external to the thing and true only for the consciousness that attempts to explain it.

In older English translations this term is often rendered as 'Notion', because 'Concept' seems to have connotations of abstractness. But Christian Wolff, who regularized German philosophical terminology in the eighteenth century, used *Begriff* to translate the Latin term *"conceptus"*. Kant followed Wolff's usage. What makes the older translation especially misleading is that Hegel intends the connotations of discursivity implied by concept. He contrasts thinking by concepts (*das begreifende Denken*) with the claims made for immediate knowledge.

Concrete (*konkret*):   Hegel contrasts the concrete with the abstract in two senses. First, the concrete is something understood in the context of a whole; the abstract is something taken on its own outside its context. Second, the concrete is a universal or whole that precedes its parts or makes them possible; the abstract is a universal or whole that succeeds its parts, which make it possible. The distinction between a concrete or abstract universal is the traditional scholastic distinction between a composite (*compositum*) or totality (*totum*). Kant introduced this distinction in §77 of the *Critique of Judgment* as the distinction between an analytic and synthetic universal.

Cunning of Reason (*List der Vernunft*):   One of the most famous phrases of Hegel's philosophy of history, this refers to how the reason that governs history uses individual's for its own ends even when they are not aware of it. There is an anti-Machiavellian point behind the concept: that political cunning, i.e., the struggle for power in politics, still serves the higher ends of reason. So reason is even more cunning than all the forces of *Realpolitik*.

Dialectic (*Dialektik*):   This term designates Hegel's characteristic methodology, his attempt to show that artificial abstractions contradict themselves and that their contradictions are resolvable only when they are placed within a system or whole. Hegel uses this term in two more specific senses, one logical and another metaphysical. In the logical sense it refers to an antinomy, i.e., a contradiction where both thesis and antithesis are necessary; in the metaphysical sense it refers to a process of development involving conflicting tendencies or forces.

Experience (*Erfahrung*):   Hegel uses this term in a broad sense to designate not only whatever we learn through sense perception but also whatever we learn through enquiry and life. It refers to anything that one learns through trial and error, through inquiry and examination, whether it is through theory or practice. The term should be taken in its literal sense: It is a journey or adventure (*fahren*) that arrives at a result (*er-fahren*). Hegel calls his *Phenomenology* a *Science of Experience* because it describes what consciousness lives through and learns through its self-examination.

For itself (*für sich*):   Something is for itself when it is self-directing and self-conscious, fully aware of its activity and ends and striving to realize them. It is contrasted with something that is only in itself, which is only potential and not self-conscious.

Idealism: *Absolute idealism* is for Hegel the doctrine that everything is an appearance of the universal, divine idea. The idea is not simply a Platonic form or archetype but an Aristotelian purpose or final cause. Absolute idealism is then the doctrine that everything in nature and history conforms to a purpose. *Subjective idealism* is for Hegel the thesis that all rationality, all conformity to law, has its source in the creative activity of the subject. *Objective idealism* is the thesis that rationality is not imposed on the world by the subject but exists in objects themselves as their inherent purpose or form.

Immediacy (*Unmittelbarkeit*):   Hegel uses this work in an ontological and epistemological context. In the ontological context it means what is taken in itself, apart from its relations to other things; in the epistemological context it signifies a direct intuition of a particular without the mediation of concepts. Here Hegel follows Kant's usage: Kant defines an intuition as a direct representation of a particular; and a concept as an indirect or mediate representation of a particular because it is a representation abstracted from many representations of particulars, and so knows one particular only through its relations with others. Hegel denies that there is pure immediacy in either of these senses: all objects are constituted by their relations to others; and all awareness of things involves the application of concepts.

In itself (*an sich*):   This phrase has two meanings: something taken by itself, apart from its relations to other things; and something potential, inchoate and undeveloped, which is not self-conscious and completely self-directing. In this latter sense it is contrasted with something *for itself,* which is not only actual, organized and developed but also self-conscious.

Infinite (*das Unendliche*) : The infinite is that which has no limits, or that which contains no negation, i.e., we cannot conceive it by what it is not but only by what it is. Hegel thinks that there is only one thing that could satisfy this requirement: the universe as a whole; for anything less than the whole is still conceivable only against what it is not, only against that which is not contained within itself. There are two senses of the *bad* infinite: that which is beyond the finite or the negation of the finite; and an infinite series that never ends. The first sense is bad because the infinite is still affected by negation, the finite outside itself; the second sense is bad because it is not a complete or self-sufficient whole.

Life (*Leben*) : Hegel uses this term in the normal sense to designate organic nature. But it has a special metaphyiscal significance for him, because it refers to the single living force throughout all of nature. Life was the central concept of Hegel's early organic metaphysics; it later lost some of its importance and was replaced by the concept of spirit, which includes life but stands higher than it as the self-awareness of life. The concept of life signified a specific process of development for Hegel: that of externalization of something internal, and the internalization of something external.

Mediation (*Unmittelbarkeit*) : Like 'Immediacy', this term has both an ontological and epistemological sense. In the ontological sense it means something as it exists in and through its relations to other things; in the epistemological sense it refers to a representation that has been related to others and placed in context.

Phenomenology (*Phänomenologie*) : Hegel defines phenomenology as the science of the experience of consciousness. The phenomenology considers something as it comes into appearance, as it manifests its inner nature. The philosopher refrains from all preconceived ideas and standards and simply observes and describes the appearances of the object.

Representation (*Vorstellung*):   Hegel does not use representation in the broad sense common to much eighteenth century philosophy, where it is equivalent to any kind of awareness, whether that of sensations, concepts or thoughts. He uses it in a more narrow sense where it designates a specific kind of consciousness, one distinct from both sensation and concept. A representation is more abstract than a sensation, which is the awareness of something particular; but it less abstract than a concept, because it contains an image or pictorial content which limits its range of applicability. A representation is aware of things discretely, outside their general context, whereas a concept grasps things as a whole, inside their general context.

Reason (*Vernunft*):   Hegel uses this term in both an metaphysical sense and epistemological sense. In the metaphysical sense it refers to the teleological laws governing the universe, the purpose or end of all nature and history. In the epistemological sense it refers to that faculty that grasps something as a whole or in context; he contrasts it with the understanding or intellect (*Verstand*) that analyzes or divides a thing into its parts. This distinction is often regarded as distinctly Hegelian but it was a commonplace in the eighteenth century, a legacy of Wolff's metaphysics.

Spirit (*Geist*):   This is the central concept of Hegel's philosophy, though he uses it in a variety of senses. The most simple synonym for the most common use would be simply the self. Since Hegel thinks that selfhood is constituted by interpersonal relations and has an intersubjective structure, he calls it 'An I that is a We, a We that is an I'. Hegel sometimes uses spirit to designate the realm of subjectivity in contrast to objectivity or organic nature. In this case spirit refers to the defining characteristics of rationality or subjectivity, namely self-consciousenss and freedom. He also uses the term to refer to the unique and distinctive characteristics of an *entire* nation, culture or state, a sense that has its origins on Montesquieu's *Spirit of the Laws*.

Substance (*Substanz*):   The basic meaning of this term follows Spinoza's definition in the *Ethics*: 'that which is in itself and conceived through itself' (Part I, def. 3). But Hegel also places the concept in the context of his organic metaphysics, where it designates one stage of development of the absolute: the universal whole in its potentiality, before its actualization. More loosely and generally, it refers to the whole apart from its parts, the universal apart from its particulars.

Subjekt (Subject):   Hegel thinks that there are two defining characteristics of subjectivity or rational agency: self-awareness and freedom. Both these characteristics come together: subjects realize themselves when they are self-conscious of their freedom. Hence the end of history is the self-awareness of freedom.

Unhappy Consciousness (*Unglückliches Bewußtsein*):   This famous phrase is the title of a chapter of the *Phenomenology*. Hegel uses it to designinate the alienation of Christianity, the belief that there is no meaning to life on earth and that all redemption lies in another life. More specifically, Hegel uses to designate Christ's feeling on the cross that he had been forsaken by God.

Notes

INTRODUCTION

1 Arthur Schopenhauer, *Parerga und Paralipomena* §295, in *Sämtliche Werke* V, 635.
2 Attributed to Rosenzweig by Emile Fackenheim (1989), p. 72.
3 I have chiefly in mind the work of John McDowell (1996) and Robert Brandom (2002).
4 Attributed to the late Paul Kristeller in a conversation with Bonnie Kent.
5 Rosenkranz (1844), p. 21.
6 On the influence of Württemberg Protestantism on Hegel, see the interesting studies by Dickey (1987) and Magee (2001), pp. 51–83.
7 Rosenkranz (1844), p. 10.
8 See Harris (1972), p. 35.
9 Harris (1972), pp. 58, 64.
10 Haering (1929), I, pp. 49–51, contends that Hegel was not so unhappy at the Stift, and that the Stift was much more liberal than its reputation allowed. Although Haering has a point – it is important not to exaggerate the negative aspects of Hegel's life there – the evidence cited by Harris (1972), pp. 57–95, Fuhrmanns (1962), I, pp. 9–40, and Pinkard (2000), pp. 19–44, shows overwhelmingly that Hegel was not happy with the institution. It is surely compelling that Hegel tried to leave it, and that his illnesses and furloughs were understood as attempts to avoid it. See Harris (1972), pp. 69–70.
11 For the details of the curriculum, see Harris (1972), pp. 73–4.
12 Ibid., p. 83.
13 Ibid., p. 89.
14 On Hegel's study of Kant in the Stift, see Pinkard (2000), pp. 33–8.
15 Rosenkranz (1844), p. 29.
16 GW I/1, 57–72, and *Studien*, Texts nos. 2–16, GW I, 114.
17 GW I/1, 83–115.
18 *Studien*, Texts nos. 17–26, GW I/1, 115–164.

19 The *Positivity Essay* is the name given to three fragments: '. . . *man mag die widersprechendste Betrachtungen* . . .', GW I/1, 281–351; '*Ein positiver Glaube* . . .', GW I/1, 352–8; and '*Jedes Volk* . . .', GW I/1, 359–78. See p, trans. Knox, pp. 67–181.

20 It was published under the title *Vertrauliche Briefe über das Vormalige staatrechtliche Verhältnis des Wadtslandes (Paus de Vaud) zur Stadt Bern* (Frankfurt: Jäger, 1798). For the details of Hegel's notes and introduction, see Pelczynski (1964), pp. 9–12; Rosenzweig (1920), I, pp. 47–54.

21 On this tension in Hegel's early political thought, see Rosenzweig (1920), I, pp. 29, 34, 45.

22 On Hegel's lectures in Jena, see Kimmerle (1967), pp. 53–9, 76–81.

23 These are now known as *Jenaer Systementwürfe I, II* and *III*, and comprise volumes VI, VI and VIII (respectively) of the *Gesammelte Werke*.

ONE CULTURAL CONTEXT

1 Reinhold (1923), I, 24.

2 VI. Spirit, B. II, 'The Enlightenment', PG 383–413/328–55.

3 On this movement, see Frank (1997).

4 *Pace* Forster (1989), it is much too narrow to see Hegel's epistemology as chiefly a response to ancient skepticism.

5 Thus Frank (1997), pp. 502, 617, 715.

6 On the background to this dispute, see Beiser (1987), pp. 44–75.

7 First in his *Glauben und Wissen, in Werke* II, 333–93; then in a 1817 review of Jacobi's *Werke, in Werke* IV, 429–61; then again in the 'Vorbegriff' to the *Enzyklopädie der philosophischen Wissenschaften, in Werke* VIII, 148–67, where Jacobi represents one of the main 'attitudes of thought toward objectivity'; and finally in his *Geschichte der Philosophie, in Werke* XX, 315–29. In all the versions of his lectures on the philosophy of religion Hegel would consider Jacobi, though usually not by name.

8 Nietzsche, *Nachgelassene Fragmente, in Sämtliche Werke* XII, 125.

9 On these writings, see the bibliography.

10 See anonymous (1971), p. 206. The authorship has been much disputed. For a useful summary of its contents, see Blackall (1983), pp. 209–20.

11 On the role of Herder and Möser in the development of historicism, see the classic treatment of Meinecke (1965), pp. 303–444.

12 See Beiser (1993), pp. 270–300.

13 There is no English translation of these important writings. Some of them were collected and published by Henrich (1968). On Rehberg's, Gentz's and Möser's position in this dispute, see Beiser (1992), pp. 288–309, 317–26. For

a more general treatment of Rehberg and Möser, see Epstein (1966), pp. 297–340, 547–94.

TWO EARLY IDEALS

1 Regarding the periodization of German romanticism, see Kluckhohn (1953), pp. 8–9; and Behler (1992), pp. 9–29.

2 See Lukács (1973), I, pp. 34–5, 37; Kaufmann (1972), pp. 64–5, 77; and Avineri (1972), pp. 21–2, 33, 239. The tradition continues with Pinkard (2000), p. 77, who claims that Hegel had only 'a brief self-conscious dalliance' with romanticism at Frankfurt, and that he quickly and permanently abandoned every trace of it in Jena.

3 On this enterprise, see Beiser (2003), pp. 131–52.

4 Aristotle, Nicomachean Ethics, Book I, chapters 1 and 5, 1094a and 1997b. Kant made a similar distinction in his own analysis of the concept. See KpV, V, 110–113.

5 See Locke, Essay, Book II, chap. xxi, §41, §53; Hobbes, Leviathan (1968), pp. 120, 160, 490–1.

6 See, for example, Schleiermacher, Über das höchste Gut, and Über den Wert des Lebens, in KGA I/1, 81–125 and I/1, 391–471. And Schlegel, Transcendentalphilosophie, 'Theil II: Theorie des Menschen', KA XII, 44–90. 'Theil II' is devoted to characterizing 'die Bestimmung des Menschen' (45; cf. 47). Hegel's concern with the question is apparent from the Berne Fragment, 'Jetzt braucht die Menge . . .', W I, 99–101/70–1; and the Frankfurt fragment, 'Jedes Volk hatte ihm eigene Gegenstände . . .', W I, 202–15/219–29. The 1831 lectures on the philosophy of religion explicitly discuss the question, W XVII, 251–99.

7 Taylor (1975), pp. 13–29 and (1979), pp. 1–14 finds the source of this ideal in Herder, and more specifically in his concept of 'expressivism'. But Herder was only one transmitter of an ideal whose origins are ultimately Greek. While there is only indirect evidence for Herder's influence, there is direct evidence of the Greek influence, which came from a reading of Plato and Aristotle in the original. As Taylor himself notes (1975), p. 15, the concept of expressivism has debts to the Aristotelian analysis of human action.

8 Rosenkranz (1844), p. 11.

9 Plato, Timeus, 30d–31a (translation of N.D.P. Lee).

10 Schiller, Philosophische Briefe, NA XX, 119–122; Anmut und Würde, NA XX, 302–4.

11 See, for example, PR §207A, 252R. On Hegel's views on individuality, see Wood (1990), pp. 200–2.

12 In the Spirit of Christianity he already states that love is more the ethic for a sect than a state (W I, 410/336). In his 1802/3 System of Ethical Life he holds that

unity is realized not in love but in the mutual recognition between citizens of a political community (GW V, 289).

13 See the sources cited in note 6 above.

14 This famous aphorism occurs in Novalis, *Fragmente und Studien II*, no. 562, HKA III, 651.

15 Schleiermacher, *Über die Religion*, KGA II/1, 213.

16 Heine, *Schriften* V, 571.

17 W XX, 165/III 257. Cf. *Vorlesungen über die Philosophie der Religion*, W XVI, 109.

18 Schiller, *Aesthetische Briefe*, XX, 323.

19 See Sheehan (1989), pp. 120–3.

20 See the fragment 'Der immer sich vergrößernde Widerspruch . . .', W I, 457–60, which was probably written in Frankfurt in late 1799 or early 1800. This manuscript was first published by Rosenkranz (1844), pp. 88–90; its significance was first fully fathomed by Haym (1857), pp. 79–83; there is a detailed paraphrase and discussion of its contents in Harris (1972), pp. 440–5. This fragment will be discussed in chapter Four (pp. 87–90).

THREE   ABSOLUTE IDEALISM

1 This was an essential aspect of Hegel's critique of empiricism, both in physics and ethics. Empiricism eschewed metaphysics yet presupposed a metaphysics all its own, which it failed to investigate. See EPW §§38R, 270; WBN II, 434–440.

2 Such were the interpretations of Haym (1857), Dilthey (1921), Haering (1929), Findlay (1958), and Taylor (1975).

3 For the theory of categories interpretation, see Hartmann (1972) and White (1983); for the neo-Kantian interpretation, see Pippin (1989); for the proto-hermeneutical interpretation, see Redding (1996); for the social epistemology interpretation, see Pinkard (1994); and for the humanist interpretation, see Solomon (1983), pp. 8–9. I have criticized some of these deflationary interpretations in an earlier review article: Beiser (1995).

4 See Aristotle, *Metaphysics*, Book V, 11, 1018b, 30–6; Book IX, 8, 1050a, 3–20.

5 See Friedrich Schlegel's *Philosophische Lehrjahre*, KA XVIII, 33 (no. 151), 65 (no. 449), 80 (no. 606), 85 (no. 658), 90 (no. 736), 282 (no. 1046), 396 (no. 908).

6 See Schelling, *Fernere Darstellung aus dem System der Philosophie*, Sämtliche Werke IV, 404; 'Ueber das Verhältnis der Naturphilosophie zur Philosophie überhaupt', *Sämtliche Werke* V, 112; 'Zusatz zur Einleitung' to the *Ideen zu einer Philosophie der Natur*, *Sämtliche Werke* II, 67, 68; and *Bruno*, *Sämtliche Werke* IV, 257, 322. The first two works were co-authored with Hegel.

7 EPW §45A, §160Z and §337Z.

8 See WL I, 145; and GuW, W II, 302–3/68.

9 Hegel often uses the terms as if they were synonyms. See, for example, Encyclopedia §12 and §194A. In the 1824 lectures on the philosophy of religion he explains that God and the absolute have the same content or logical meaning, but that God has a more explicit connotation of the absolute having come to its self-awareness (VPR I, 35–6/I, 118–19). Usually, he uses 'God' in the context of the philosophy of religion.

10 See Schelling's System der gesammten Philosophie, Sämtliche Werke VI, 148, §7.

11 Ibid., VI, 198, §41.

12 That Hegel's philosophy was a metaphysics in the classical sense was stressed by Heidegger in his 'Hegels Begriff der Erfahrung' (1972). According to Heidegger, Hegel's conception of philosophy is entirely in the tradition of Aristotle. The purpose of philosophy is to contemplate being as being, or to grasp what is present as such or in itself (das Anwesende in seinem Anwesen). The basis for Heidegger's interpretation had already been laid down in Sein und Zeit (1972), p. 171. Although Heidegger rightly places Hegel in the Aristotelian tradition, he goes astray in assimilating Hegel's concept of experience to intuition or contemplation in the Aristotelian sense. This is virtually to attribute an intellectual intuition to Hegel. For a criticism of Heidegger along similar lines, see Adorno (1969), pp. 45–8, 69.

13 Aristotle, Metaphysics, Book III, 2, 996b14; Book IV, 1, 1003a18–24; Book IV, 2, 1003b17–21; Book VII, 1, 1028b3–4.

14 Schelling, Darstellung meines Systems, Sämtliche Werke IV, 115, §1. Cf. Aphorismen zur Einleitung in die Naturphilosophie, Werke VII, 181, §199.

15 See Schelling's and Hegel's joint work Fernere Darstellungen aus dem System der Philosophie, in Schelling, Sämtliche Werke IV, 393–4.

16 See 'Über das Verhältniß der Naturphilosophie zur Philosophie überhaupt', Sämtliche Werke V, 112; and Ideen, Werke II, 717.

17 Thus Pippin (1989), pp. 16–41.

18 This is the argument of two co-authored writings: Fernere Darstellung aus dem System der Philosophie, in Schelling, Werke IV, 353–61, and 'Ueber das Verhältniß der Naturphilosophie zur Philosophie überhaupt', in Schelling, Werke V, 108–15.

19 Spinoza, Ethica, Part I, Props 15, 25.

20 Ibid., Part II, Props 1–7.

21 Ethica, Part I, definition IV, whose Latin is no clearer: 'Per attributum intelligo id, quod intellectus de substantia percipit, tanquam ejusdem essentiam constituens.'

22 Hegel, Werke II, 52, 96/119, 156.

23 See GuW, Werke II, 345–8/107–9.

24 See, for example, Hegel's statements in EPW §24A, and in VG 85/72.
25 KU V, 192.
26 On this distinction see EPW §§24A1, 24R, 25, 32A, 45A.
27 This is not seen by Wood (1990), pp. 18, 43, 45, who wrongly thinks that Hegel follows Fichte.
28 See Hegel, *Enzyklopädie* §158Z and the *Rechtsphilosophie* §66. In *Rechtsphilosophie* §15 Hegel argues that the classical concept of freedom as choice involves a contradiction.
29 Thus Henrich (1971), pp. 157–86; Taylor (1975), pp. 94, 266; di Giovanni (1993), pp. 41–59; and Burbidge (1993), pp. 60–75.
30 Thus Stewart (1996), pp. 16, 306.
31 See Schelling's critique of Hegel in his *Zur Geschichte der neueren Philosophie*, *Werke* X, 126–64; and in his *Philosophie der Offenbarung*, *Werke* XIII, 57–93.
32 Thus Taylor (1975), p. 94.
33 Ibid., p. 206; and di Giovanni (1993), pp. 51–4.
34 *Wie der gemeine Menschenverstand die Philosophie nehme, – dargestellt an den Werken des Herrn Krug's*, GW IV, 174–87.

FOUR   THE ORGANIC WORLDVIEW

1 See, for example, Pippin (1989), pp. 4, 6, 39, 61–2, 66, 69.
2 On the influence of *Timaeus* on Hegel, see Harris (1972), pp. 102–3, 126 n.; on its influence on Schelling, see Baum (2000), pp. 199–215 and Franz (1996), pp. 237–82. On the influence of Plato on Hölderlin, see Franz (1992). Schelling's early commentary on the *Timaeus* has been published by Buchner (1994).
3 See the *Fragment on Love*, *Werke* I, 246, 248–9 (N 379, 380–1); *Spirit of Christianity and its Fate*, *Werke* I, 370–1 (N 303); and the *Systemfragment*, *Werke* I, 419–23 (N 345–51).
4 See Kielmeyer (1930). Although never published in his lifetime, Kielmeyer's lectures were very influential; notes from them were disseminated in many parts of Germany. He was an important influence on the young Schelling. See Durner (1991), pp. 95–9.
5 For an account of Schelling's organic view of nature, see Beiser (2002), pp. 515–19, 538–50.
6 That Hegel's organicism has a religious origin was pointed out by Haering (1929), I, pp. 510, 520–1, 523, 525, 534.
7 See *Spirit of Christianity and its Fate*, *Werke* I, 373–5 (Nohl, 308–9).
8 See the *Fragment on Love*, *Werke* I, 246 (Nohl, 379); *Spirit of Christianity and its Fate*, *Werke* I, 370, 372 (Nohl, 302, 304–5); and the *Systemfragment*, *Werke* I, 421–442 (Nohl, 347–8).

9 See *Systemfragment*, *Werke* I, 422–3 (Nohl, 348).

10 Hegel, *Briefe*, I, pp. 59–60.

11 See the fragment 'Der immer sich vergrößernde Widerspruch . . .', *Werke* I, 457–60, which was probably written in Frankfurt in late 1799 or early 1800. This manuscript was first published by Rosenkranz (1844), pp. 88–90; its significance was first fully fathomed by Haym (1857), pp. 79–83; there is a detailed paraphrase and discussion of its contents in Harris (1972), pp. 440–5.

12 Harris (1972), pp. 98–101, 103.

13 In the *Tübingen Essay* Hegel appealed to Kant's moral postulates as the basis for a rational religion; he insisted that knowledge of God and immortality had to be based on 'the demands of practical reason' (I 16, 17/8, 9). The text '*Die transcendentale Idee* . . .' from around April 1795 contends that only practical reason can suffice to prove the existence of God. See GW I, 195. Also see Hegel's April 1795 letter to Schelling, *Briefe*, I, p. 24. Hegel began to criticize this doctrine in the fragment '*Ein positiver Glaube* . . .', GW I, pp. 357–8.

14 See Spinoza to Ludivocus Meyer, 20 April 1663, Spinoza (1966), p. 118.

15 On the influence of Hegel on Schelling, see Düsing (1969).

16 According to Rosenkranz (1844), p. 188, Hegel specifically criticized Schelling's theory of the fall in his Winter Semester lectures 1804/5.

17 On Kant's distinction, see KrV A 438; Inaugural Dissertation, *De mundi sensibilis atque intelligibilis forma et principiis*, §15, Corollarium, II, 405; Reflexionen 3789, XVII, 293 and Reflexionen 6178, XVIII, 481.

18 *Über den Gebrauch teleologischer Prinzipien in der Philosophie*, *Werke* VIII, 161–84.

19 See the preface to the second edition of KrV, B xviii. Cf. the first preface A xx.

20 See Schelling's *Von der Weltseele*, in *Sämtliche Werke* II, 496–505, and his *Erster Entwurf eines Systems der Naturphilosophie*, in *Sämtliche Werke* III, 74–8.

21 For a brief and useful survey, see Roe (1981), pp. 1–20; Hankins (1985), pp. 113–57; and Richards (1992), pp. 5–16.

22 See Roe (1981) pp. 80–3, 86.

23 This is documented fully by Larson (1979).

24 See Ameriks (2000), pp. 118–19; and Guyer (2000), pp. 37–56. Ameriks and Guyer fail to appreciate that the monistic aspirations of post-Kantian philosophy arose from an *internal* critique of Kant and not from any prior metaphysical commitments.

25 Fortunately, since the 1980s there has been a concerted attempt to correct the old prejudices against Hegel's *Naturphilosophie*. See the anthologies by Cohen and Wartofsky (1984), Horstmann and Petry (1986), Houlgate (1998), and Petry (1987, 1993).

26 See Schelling, *Einleitung zu dem Entwurf eines Systems der Naturphilosophie*, in *Sämtliche Werke* III, 278.

FIVE   THE REALM OF SPIRIT

1 See Hyppolite (1969a), pp. 3–21.

2 Among these works were the *Erster Entwurf eines Systems der Naturphilosophie* (1799), *Allgemeine Deduktion des dynamischen Prozesses oder der Kategorien der Physik* (1800), *Ueber den wahren Begriff der Naturphilosophie und die richtige Art, ihre Probleme aufzulösen* (1801), *Ueber das Verhältniß der Naturphilosophie zur Philosophie überhaupt* (1802).

3 This was the main concern of five works of the Jena years: *Darstellung meines Systems der Philosophie* (1801), *Bruno oder über das göttliche und natürliche Princip der Dinge* (1802), *Fernere Darstellungen aus dem System der Philosophie* (1802), which he co-wrote with Hegel, *Vorlesungen über die Methode des akademischen Studiums* (1803), and *System der gesammten Philosophie und der Naturphilosophie insbesondere* (1804).

4 This move is clear in Schelling's 1800 *Allgemeine Deduktion des dynamischen Prozesses* §63, *Sämtliche Werke* IV, 76; and in his 'Über den wahren Begriff der Naturphilosophie und die richtige Art ihre Probleme aufzulösen', *Sämtliche Werke* IV, 86–7. On the priority of *Naturphilosophie* in the philosophy of identity, see Beiser (2002), pp. 488–90.

5 See the 1803/4 lectures, *Jenaer Systementwürfe I*, GW VI, 3–265; the 1804/5 lectures, *Jenaer Systementwürfe II*, GW VII, 179–338; and the 1805/6 lectures, *Jenaer Systementwürfe III*, GW VIII, 3–184.

6 Among these works were the *System der Sittlichkeit*, which was written in 1803/4, GW V, 277–362; the *Philosophie des Geistes*, which was Part III of the *System der spekulativen Philosophie* of 1803/4, GW VI, 265–326; and the 1805/6 *Philosophie des Geistes*, which was part of the *Vorlesungsmanuskript zur Realphilosophie*, GW VIII, 185–288.

7 See *Jenaer Systementwürfe II*, GW VII, 15–16. Although Hegel does not mention Schelling by name, the doctrine he criticizes in this passage is Schellingian, and more specifically the view that Schelling had outlined in his 1801 *Darstellung meines Systems der Philosophie*.

8 Rosenkranz (1844), p. 177. Rosenkranz's reading is rendered plausible from another passage he cites from Hegel's 1803/4 Winter Semester lectures. Here Hegel complains that Schelling does not fully develop the speculative idea and too quickly proceeds to its manifestation in the philosophy of nature (ibid., p. 189).

9 Ibid., p. 187.

10 Schelling, *Sämtliche Werke* IV, 288.

11 These fragments are '*Positiv wird ein Glaube genannt . . .*', which was written before

July 1797, W I, 239–43 (Nohl, 374–7); '*. . . so wie sie mehrere Gattungen kennlernen . . .*', W I, 243–4 (Nohl, 377–8), which was written in the summer of 1797; '*. . . welchem Zwecke denn alles Übrige dient . . .*', W I, 244–50, whose first draft was written around November 1797, and whose second draft was written around autumn–winter 1798, W I, 245–50 (Nohl, 378–82). This last fragment is sometimes called the 'Fragment on Love', and it appears in Knox, 302–8. (The dating in the Knox edition is false.)

12 These comprise the fragments '*Mit Abraham, dem wahren Stammvater . . .*', W I, 274–7 (Nohl, 243–5; Knox 182–5), which was written in the autumn of 1798; '*Abraham in Chaldaä geboren hatte schon . . .*', which was written in late 1798 or early 1799, W I, 277–97 (Nohl, 245–61; Knox 185–205); and '*Jesus trat nicht lange . . .*', which was written in the summer of 1799 and not finished before early 1800, W I, 317–418 (Nohl, 262–342; Knox 204–301). There is also an outline of the work, the so-called *Grundkonzept*, which was written in the autumn of 1798, W I, 297–316. (Nohl, 385–98; not in Knox).

13 Autumn/Winter 1798 fragment '*. . . welchem Zwecke denn alles Übrige dient . . .*', Nohl, 380; W I, 248. Hegel refers to the play but does not cite the specific passage.

14 W I, 367/299; W I, 389–90/318.

15 '*Positiv wird ein Glauben genannt . . .*', July 1797, W I, 242.

16 '*. . . so wie mehrere Gattungen kennenlernen . . .*', W I, 244.

17 '*. . . welchem Zwecke denn alles Übrige dient . . .*', W I, 246.

18 See W I, 376/308. See also the so-called *Systemfragment*, '*absolute Entgegensetzung gilt . . .*', where Hegel maintains that a person is an individual life only in so far as he is one with the infinite outside himself (W I, 420/346).

19 See '*. . . welchem Zwecke denn alles Übrige dient . . .*', W I, 246.

20 See W I, 378/309–10; W I, 372/303–5.

21 GW V, 289/110.

22 GW VIII, 210/107.

SIX THE RELIGIOUS DIMENSION

1 For helpful surveys of this dispute, see Jaeschke (1990), pp. 349–421, and Toews (1980), pp. 71–140.

2 The source of this analogy is Kroner (1921), II, p. 259. It is often falsely ascribed to Karl Barth.

3 See GP XVIII, 94/I, 73; Hegel to Tholuck, 3 July 1826, B IV, 28–9/520; Hegel to von Altenstein, 3 April 1826, BS 572–4/531–2.

4 Among this group we could place Stirling (1898), McTaggart (1901), Kroner

(1921), Fackenheim (1967), Findlay (1958), Houlgate (1991), and Olson (1992).

5 Among this group one could find Kaufmann (1966, 1972), Lukács (1973), Garaudy (1966), Marcuse (1967), Kojève (1969) and Solomon (1983).

6 Solomon (1983), p. 582.

7 Solomon rightly objects to Fackenheim's attempt to exclude the early writings from the whole dispute. Cf. Solomon (1983), p. 591 n. 35 and Fackenheim (1967), pp. 5, 7, 156.

8 See, for example, Rosenkranz (1844), p. 48; and Haym (1857), pp. 40–1, 63.

9 Dilthey (1921), pp. 43–60, 138–58.

10 See *Der Antichrist*, SW VI, 176, §10.

11 See Kaufmann (1972), pp. 63, 66–71; and Lukács (1973), I, pp. 34–56.

12 Lukács (1973), I, pp. 7–56.

13 One of the reasons this distinction was not made earlier is because of a false dating of Hegel's early manuscripts. Both Rosenkranz and Haym assigned *Der Geist des Christenthums* to Hegel's Berne period; hence the more religious dimension of this writing seemed to characterize the earlier period as well.

14 *Pace* Kaufmann (1972), p. 63.

15 Ibid., p. 63.

16 See Müller (1959), pp. 52–3; and Kroner (1971), p. 46.

17 See Pöggeler (1990), p. 70, who rightly criticizes Lukács on these grounds.

18 See Hettner (1979), I, pp. 350–1.

19 Both Haering and Harris dispute this break and stress the continuity of Hegel's development. See Haering (1929), I, p. 306, and Harris (1972), p. 259. However, they do not sufficiently explain away the basic tensions stated here. Harris's attempts to do so are labored and artificial, and tend more to prove the contrary (pp. 311, 325).

20 The inability of left-wing Hegelians to explain this manuscript is blatant and embarrassing. Solomon (1983), p. 590, admits that it reveals 'a new tone of conciliation' to Christianity and that Hegel attempts to salvage what is rational in it. Yet he contradicts this assessment in the same paragraph. Completely ignoring Hegel's defense of mysticism, he writes of his abiding 'confidence in reason'; and closing his eyes to Hegel's appropriation of the Johannine *logos*, trinity and incarnation, he writes that Hegel has now debunked 'virtually the whole of Christian theology'. Kaufmann (1972), p. 90, admits that the manuscript is 'a turning point in Hegel's development'. But he insists that the change is essentially a move away from Kant's ethics to Goethe's holistic humanism (pp. 92–4). When Hegel talks of faith it is only 'the love and trust between two free spirits' (p. 93). But this does no justice to Hegel's religious language, his

frequent references to the infinite and the Christian *logos*. Rightly, Kaufmann argues that Hegel does not defend faith in a transcendent God; but this hardly disposes of his immanent God. Lukács (1973), I, pp. 167–8, 171, admits that there is a sharp reversal in the Frankfurt period, and that it involves mysticism and an appropriation of Christianity. He deals with this period by demoting it to a mere transitional phase in Hegel's development, as if Hegel did not later rationalize the concepts of love, life and dialectic he formulated in Frankfurt.

21 On these discussions, see Henrich (1971), pp. 9–40, and Jamme (1983), pp. 141–316.

22 John, 3.16; 13.35; 15.10–12.

23 For a more detailed account of the Jena years, see Jaeschke (1990), pp. 123–207.

24 Rosenkranz (1844), pp. 131–41; there is a translation of this passage in the Harris and Cerf translation of the *System der Sittlichkeit*, pp. 178–86.

25 'Über das Verhältniß der Naturphilosophie zur Philosophie überhaupt', in Schelling, *Sämtliche Werke* V, pp. 106–24 and in GW IV, 265–76. The essay has been translated by George di Giovanni and H.S. Harris in *Between Kant and Hegel* (Albany: SUNY, 1985), pp. 363–82. The authorship of this essay is disputed because both Schelling and Hegel claimed they *alone* wrote it. See 'Editorischer Bericht', GW IV, 543–6. Fortunately, the question of authorship does not have to be settled; the mere fact that both claimed authorship shows that both accepted its contents.

26 W II, 432–3/190–1; Rosenkranz (1844), p. 138; PG 546/§787; W XVII, 291–3, 297.

27 On the exact source, see Burbidge (1992), pp. 97, 107. Hegel refers to the hymn in W XVII, 297.

28 Haym (1857), pp. 424–7.

29 Jaeschke (1990), p. 357.

30 Solomon (1983), p. 582.

31 Nor was this only a tactic, for Hegel had already held something like the Lutheran view of the mass in *The Spirit of Christianity*, W I, 364–9/297–301.

32 Hegel's response to the criticism is in EPW §573R; in the 1831 lectures on the philosophy of religion in W I, 97–101; in the 1824 lectures in VPR I, 246–7/I, 346–7; in the 1827 lectures in VPR I, 272–7/I, 374–80; and in a review in W XVIII, 390–466.

33 This point is ignored by Jaeschke (1990), p. 362, and Solomon (1983), p. 633, who misrepresent Hegel's entire polemic. They maintain that Hegel rejects pantheism because he equates it with the view that the divine is the totality of finite things. But in the 1827 and 1831 lectures, and in *Enzyklopädie* §573, Hegel argues explicitly and emphatically that this is a *misrepresentation* of pantheism.

Only in one passage in the 1824 lectures does Hegel seem to endorse this as an account of pantheism, VPR I 246–7/I 346. But his final expositions are very critical of this interpretation. In general, it is important to see that Hegel is criticizing not the bad concept of pantheism but a bad concept of pantheism.

34 Solomon (1983), p. 62, notes Hegel's distinction but regards it as 'a small technical point' which does not prove him a theist (p. 633). But the point is central to Hegel's whole philosophy; it also shows he is not an atheist.

35 For opposing views, see Houlgate (1991), pp. 189–228, and Burbidge (1992), pp. 93–108.

36 See VBG 36–41.

37 See especially W I, XVII, 251–99; VPR V 45–69/III 109–33.

38 In a few places Hegel does pay lip-service to the dogma of immortality. See W XVII, 303. But he seems to interpret it in moral terms, as an affirmation of the infinite worth of subjectivity.

39 *Pace* McTaggart (1901), pp. 5–6.

40 Schleiermacher, KGA I/2, 215–16/106–7.

41 On Hegel's dispute with Schleiermacher, see Crouter (1980).

SEVEN THE DIALECTIC

1 See the important short fragment '*Anmerkungen: Die Philosophie* . . .', which was probably written in the summer of 1804, GW VII, 343–7.

2 Wood (1990), p. 1.

3 See Solomon (1983), pp. 21–2; Dove (1974) and Simpson (1998).

4 On the origins and problems of this interpretation, see Müller (1958).

5 *Pace* Kaufmann (1965), pp. 75–6.

6 Wood (1990), pp. 4–5.

7 See VSP II, 230/325; EPW §48R, §119A2; WL 58–62.

8 See Popper (1940), pp. 403–10.

9 *Pace* Rosen (1982), p. 24.

10 The role of the Kantian antinomies in the development of Hegel's logic is most apparent in the *Nürnberger Schriften*, W IV, 90–6, 184–92.

11 '. . . absolute Entgegensetzung gilt' (before 14 September 1800), W I, 422–3.

12 Rosenkranz (1844), p. 188.

13 Although Hegel originally conceived the *Phenomenology* as a 'science of experience of consciousness', during the printing of the work he replaced this title with another, 'Science of the Phenomenology of Spirit' (*Wissenschaft der Phänomenologie des Geistes*). On the circumstances surrounding Hegel's decision to change the title, see Nicolin (1967).

14 Cf. PG 558/¶802; and EPW §38R, VIII, 108.

15 This is the suggestion of Kroner (1921), II, p. 374.

16 According to Hoffmeister (1955), p. 209, Paracelsus was the first to use the term 'Erfahrung', where it was the synonym for the Latin 'experientia', a trial or experiment or the knowledge gained by such means.

EIGHT SOLIPSISM AND INTERSUBJECTIVITY

1 On these early critics and criticisms of Kant, see Beiser (1987), pp. 165–88, and Beiser (2002), pp. 48–60.

2 Jacobi, *Werke* III, 3–57/*Main Philosophical Writings*, pp. 497–536.

3 Ibid., II, 291–310/pp. 331–8.

4 Schelling, *Sämtliche Werke* IV, 353–61.

5 Fichte, *Grundlage der gesammten Wissenschaftslehre*, *Sämtliche Werke* I, 278–85.

6 Schelling, *Darstellung meines Systems der Philosophie*, *Sämtliche Werke* IV, 114–15, §1.

7 Arguably, Hegel makes his case against solipsism or skeptical idealism later in the text, only in the section on 'Skepticism' in chapter IVB. Though it is indeed explicit and self-conscious at this stage, it is still implicit in the earlier texts. The problem of solipsism is explicit at IV and IVA for the philosopher; but it is only implicit for consciousness itself. Skepticism is an explicit philosophy, a self-conscious and theoretical attitude toward the world. Although consciousness has not reached this level at the beginning of chapter IV, IVB only brings to self-consciousness what has been implicit and subconscious in the earlier stages. It is of the first importance to see that desire, stoicism and skepticism all adopt the same attitude toward their object: they are failed strategies to reduce it to nothingness, to demonstrate that the self is the only essential and independent object.

8 As Kenneth Westphal (1989) has argued, p. 1.

9 For the ethical approach, see Williams (1997), pp. 46–68; for the existential interpretation, see Hyppolite (1969b), pp. 22–35; for the anthropological reading, see Kojève (1969); for the psychological reading, see Plamenatz (1963), II, pp. 188–92 and Kelly (1972); for a hermeneutical reading, see Redding (1996), pp. 119–43; and for a political reading, see Findlay (1958), p. 96, and Shklar (1976), pp. 58–62. The only commentator to recognize the metaphysical problem is Gadamer (1976), pp. 54–74, though he does not provide a detailed reading of how Hegel resolves this problem. Richard Norman (1976), pp. 45–56, realizes that the problem of solipsism is at stake but does not discuss it.

10 See *Erste Einleitung in die Wissenschaftslehre*, *Werke* I, 422–5.

11 The other versions of this dialectic confirm that absolute independence is at stake. See the version in *Nürnberger Schriften*, *Werke* IV, 120, and that in the 1830

Enzyklopädie, Werke X, 226, §436. Hegel takes the term from Fichte, who describes this ideal in two works: his 1794 *Vorlesungen über die Bestimmung des Gelehrten, Sämtliche Werke* VI, 293–301; and his 1798 *Sittenlehre, Sämtliche Werke* IV, 220–4.

12 See PG 144/¶187. Cf EPW §431A.

13 PG 143–4/¶186. Cf. EPW §§430–1.

14 For example, Soll (1969), pp. 15–16, assumes that Hegel simply dogmatically introduces other minds in chapter IV to discuss aspects of interpersonal action in IVA. Findlay (1958), pp. 96–7, also thinks that the argument against solipsism is already made in chapter IV.

15 PG 144/¶187. Cf. EPW §431.

16 PG 145/¶188–9. Cf. EPW §432.

17 PG 145–6/¶189. Cf. EPW §§433–5.

18 PG 147/¶191. Cf. EPW §§435–6.

19 PG 146–50/¶190–6. Cf. EPW §435–6.

20 This theme appears in the *Encyclopedia* version of the master/slave dialectic, where Hegel comments on the failure of the ancients to achieve true freedom. See §433A.

21 *Social Contract*, Book I, chapter 1.

NINE   FREEDOM AND THE FOUNDATION OF RIGHT

1 Thus Houlgate (1991), p. 77 and Franco (1999), pp. 1–2.

2 For the non-metaphysical approach to Hegel's social and political philosophy, see Plamenatz (1963), II, pp. 129–32; Pelczynski (1971), pp. 1–2; Smith (1989), p. xi; Wood (1990), pp. 4–6; Tunick (1992), pp. 14, 17, 86, 99; Hardimon (1994), p. 8; Patten (1999), pp. 16–27; Franco (1999), pp. 83–4, 126, 135–6, 140, 143, 151–2, 360–1 n. 4; and Rawls (2000), p. 330. For some recent protests against this approach, see Yovel (1996), pp. 26–41 and Peperzak (2001), pp. 5–19.

3 Wood (1990), p. 39, argues that there is an important difference between Kant and Hegel regarding the concept of autonomy because Kant identifies freedom with the capacity for autonomy, which I might or might not execute, whereas Hegel equates it with moral action itself. But Kant's texts do not confirm Wood's contention. See GMS IV, 412, 413, 447; KpV V, 29.

4 *Pace* Patten (1999), pp. 47–63.

5 The importance of Schiller for Hegel is evident from the *Spirit of Christianity* and Hegel's 16 April 1795 letter to Schelling. Schiller's influence on Hegel's concept of freedom is decisive but it has not been appreciated by contemporary Anglophone scholars, who might concede the relevance of the *Aesthetic Letters*

but only to ignore the equally important *Grace and Dignity* and *Philosophical Letters*. Kaufmann (1966), pp. 18–31, rightly stresses Schiller's influence on Hegel but does not spell out its importance for his concept of freedom.

6 See Berlin (1969), pp. 118–72. In this essay Berlin mentions Hegel mostly *en passant*, pp. 146, 150, 168. Berlin's critique of Hegel is better found in *Freedom and its Betrayal* (2002), pp. 74–104.

7 On this distinction, see Patten (1999), pp. 44–5, and Wood (1990), pp. 37–40.

8 *Pace* Wood (1990), p. 41.

9 See Plamenatz (1963), pp. 31–3, 37–8; Franco (1999), pp. 178–87; and Riedel (1973), pp. 96–120.

10 See Foster (1935), pp. 125–41, 167–79, 180–204; Riley (1982), pp. 163–99; Pelczynski (1964), pp. 29, 54; Pippin (1997), pp. 417–50; and Patten (1999), pp. 63–81.

11 See Meinecke (1924), pp. 427–60; Heller (1921), pp. 32–131; Cassirer (1946), pp. 265–8; Popper (1945), II, pp. 62–3; Sabine (1963), pp. 627, 645, 648; Hallowell (1950), pp. 265, 275–6; and Berlin (2002), pp. 94–5, 97–8.

12 Cf. PR §132R.

13 See, for example, his early Stuttgart 1787 essay '*Über die Religion der Griechen und Römer*' (1787), GW I, 42–5, where Hegel argues that history shows us the danger of generalizing about the principles of reason from our own time and place. In his 1793 *Tübingen Essay*, Hegel alluded to Montesquieu's idea of the 'spirit of a nation', and stressed how a culture is a unity, its religion, politics and history forming a living whole (W I, 42/27). Hegel's early interest in history is still very much in the Enlightenment tradition, however. He still believes in a universal human nature behind all the different manifestations of history, and he criticizes past religions from the standpoint of a universal reason. Hegel became aware of the tension between historicism and his allegiance to the Enlightenment only much later; see the 1800 revision of the *Positivity Essay*, the fragment '*Der Begriff der Positivität . . .*', W I, 217–29/139–51.

14 See Hegel to Schelling, 16 April 1795, *Briefe* I, 24.

15 On the political background, see Pinkard (2000), pp. 72–5.

16 Hegel never lost his admiration for Machiavelli. See his 1819/20 Heidelberg lectures on the *Philosophie des Rechts* (H 255–6); and his Berlin lectures on the philosophy of history (W XII, 482–3). His longest later discussion of Machiavelli is in his 1805/6 *Jenaer Geistesphilosophie* (GW VIII, 258–60).

17 See Meinecke (1924), pp. 427–60. See also Heller (1921), pp. 32–131.

18 Cassirer (1946), pp. 265–8; Popper (1945), II, pp. 62–3; and Berlin (2002), pp. 94–5, 97–8.

19 See Stewart (1996), pp. 10–11, and 53–130.

20 Wood (1990), otherwise so admirably thorough, does not discuss the topic. It is also not treated in Kaufmann (1970).

21 On this context, see Rosenzweig (1920), I, pp. 104–7.

22 D'Hondt (1968b), pp. 39–41.

23 See Hegel to Niethammer, 29 April 1814 and 5 July 1816, *Briefe* II, 28, 85. Also see PR §§219, 258R, where Hegel attacks Haller, and §§33, 211, where he criticizes Savigny.

24 D'Hondt (1968b), pp. 90–7.

25 Rosenzweig (1920), II, pp. 161–7.

26 Ibid., II, pp. 62–7.

27 Thus Rosenzweig (ibid.), pp. 161–7, argues that the only respect in which Hegel's doctrine derives from Prussian practice is with regard to the constitution of the army.

TEN HEGEL'S THEORY OF THE STATE

1 For this image of Hegel, see Popper (1945), II, pp. 29, 58; Sabine (1961), pp. 620–68; Plamenatz (1963), II, pp. 129–268; and Hallowell (1950), pp. 254–77.

2 See Novalis's essay 'Faith and Love', in Beiser (1996b), pp. 33–50.

3 Admittedly, these generalizations are anachronistic. Liberalism would become a self-conscious and organized political movement only in the 1830s. Although there were many thinkers who anticipated, and indeed laid the foundation for, later liberalism (F.H. Jacobi, Christian Dohm, Friedrich Schiller, Wilhelm von Humboldt and Kant) they did not regard themselves as liberals. Furthermore, there was no single school of thinkers who would regard themselves self-consciously as communitarian. In the 1790s communitarian views were repre-sented by three very different schools: those who were inspired by the ancient republican tradition (the romantics), those who defended the old paternalist state of enlightened absolutism (the Berlin *Aufklärer*), and those who cham-pioned government by the estates (Friedrich Moser, and the Hanoverian Whigs, Justus Möser, A.W. Rehberg, Ernst Brandes). On the classification of the political movements of the 1790s, see Beiser (1992), pp. 15–22, 222–7, 281–8.

4 See 'Jetzt braucht die Menge . . .', *Werke* I, 99–100/101–2; and 'Jedes Volk . . .', *Werke* I, 204–8/N 221–3.

5 *Pace* Rawls (2000), p. 330.

6 See Kant, TP, VIII, 297/79.

7 See, for example, §§258R, 263A, 267, 269, 271, 276A, 286.

8 VD I, 479/159, I 524/195, and I 535/204; and VVL IV, 483–5/263–5.

9 KA XVIII, no. 1255.

10 VD I, 536/206.

11 See VD I, 516/189, I, 524/195, I, 523–4/201–2; and PR §290A.

12 See PR §§206, 252, and VVL IV, 483–5/263–5.

13 See Lukács (1973), I, pp. 273–91, II, pp. 495–618; Plant (1973), pp. 56–76; Avineri (1972), pp. 81–114, 132–54; Dickey (1987), pp. 186–204; and Chamley (1963). See also Pelczynski (1984).

14 See, for example, Avineri (1972), p. 5; and Dickey (1999), p. 291 n. 58.

15 See Beiser (1992), pp. 232–6.

16 According to Rosenkranz (1844), p. 86, Hegel wrote a detailed commentary on Stewart's 'Staatswissenschaft' in 1799. Since the manuscript has been lost, it is impossible to determine conclusively the full extent of Hegel's treatment of political economy.

17 See the 1803/4 Geistesphilosophie, GW VI, 319–26; the 1805/6 Philosophie des Geistes, GW VIII, 243–5. The importance of these fragments was first stressed by Avineri (1972), pp. 87–98. Although the 1820 Philosophy of Right does not contain a detailed critique of modern forms of production, it is noteworthy that a similar, though shorter and less graphic, analysis can be found in the 1817/18 Heidelberg lectures (VNS §104) and in 1819/20 lectures on Philosophie des Rechts (H 158–61). In Hotho's 1822/3 Vorlesungsnachschrift there is a more detailed account of the damaging effects of the division of labor (VRP III, 609–13).

18 System der Sittlichkeit in GW V (277–362), 354–6/170–3; and GW VIII, 244.

19 System der Sittlichkeit in GW V, 351–2/168.

20 Thus Haym (1857), pp. 365–8; Popper (1945), II, pp. 27, 53–4.

21 Cf. VD I, 576–7/237–8; and ER XI, 111–12/318.

22 PR §301R. Cf. ER XI, 110–11/ 317.

23 PR §§303R, 308R. Cf. ER XI, 110–13/317–19 and VVL IV, 482–4/263–4.

24 PR §253R. Cf. System der Sittlichkeit in GW V, 354/171.

25 This point has been forcefully argued by Avineri (1972), pp. 98–9, 109, 148, 151–3.

ELEVEN PHILOSOPHY OF HISTORY

1 See, for example, Berlin (2002), pp. 99–100.

2 Hegel's interpretation of the Genesis myth is chiefly to be found in his lectures on the philosophy of religion, VPR V, 134–9, 220–9/VPR III, 202–6, 296–305. See also EPW §24A3 and PG ¶¶775–8.

3 James (1907), pp. 73–4.

4 See Fackenheim (1996), p. 171.

5 Camus (1955), p. 15.

6 In the 1950s some scholars tried to legitimate Hegel by interpreting his philosophy as a proto-existentialism. See, for example, Müller (1959), pp.

52–3; Hyppolite (1969b); and Wahl (1951), p. 7. It will be clear from this section, however, that there is good reason for the traditional interpretation of Hegel as an *anti*-existentialist.

7 Nietzsche (1980), I, pp. 254–5.

TWELVE AESTHETICS

1 On its reception and influence, see Bubner (1980), Koepsel (1975) and Gombrich (1965).

2 See Gombrich (1977).

3 For reactions against this neglect, see Moran (1981) and Desmond (2000). There are significant signs of improvement; see the important collections edited by Otto Pöggeler and Annemarie Gethmann-Siefert (1983, 1986).

4 Rosenkranz (1844), pp. 347–52.

5 See, for example, PR §§3, 211R, 212R. Hegel does not mention Savigny by name.

6 On the quarrel with Schleiermacher, see Crouter (1980), and Pinkard (2000), pp. 445–7, 501.

7 See, for example, Hegel's nasty aside in his preface to Hinrichs, *Religionsphilosophie*, *Werke* XI, 61. See also some of the personal swipes at Schlegel in the *Aesthetics*, *Werke* XIII, 383/296, XIV, 116/508, XIV, 180/423.

8 For other accounts of Winckelmann's significance for Hegel, see Gombrich (1977) and Baur (1997).

9 For example, XIII, 232/176–7; XIV, 82/481–2, 83–4/483, 87/486.

10 See, for example, Hegel's skeptical account of Winckelmann's enthusiasm for the Apollo Belvedere, XIV, 431/766.

11 Thus Glockner (1965), pp. 438–9; Croce (1978), pp. 301–3; Knox (1980), pp. 5–6; Bungay (1984), p. 83; and Bowie (1990), p. 131.

12 Bubner (1980), p. 31.

13 Bowie (1990), p. 135.

14 Houlgate (1991), p. 140.

15 Bungay (1984), p. 31.

16 XIII, 143/104; XIV, 127–8/517–18.

17 See VPR III, 143–5/I, 234–6. Cf. *Werke* XVI, 135–40.

18 *Pace* Bungay (1984), pp. 31–2.

19 Bungay (1984), p. 83, fails to see Hegel's rationale for this doctrine, which he dismisses as 'a subtle *non sequitur*' in the theory.

20 Thus Kuhn (1931), pp. 34, 38–9.

21 For this reason it is misleading to write about Hegel's debts to the neo-Platonic tradition, as Brocker (1965) does (pp. 40, 49).

22 Thus Bungay (1984), p. 15, maintains that Hegel 'bans the concept of mimesis from aesthetics'.

23 See Bubner (1980), p. 30.

24 See the defense of Hegel's theory by Rapp (2000), Hofstadter (1974), Danto (1984) and Harries (1974). For a defense of romanticism against Hegel's critique, see Bowie (1990) and Norman (2000).

25 See the interesting collection of essays edited by Lang (1984).

26 The origin of this phrase seems to have been Croce, who in his influential *Aesthetica* wrote that Hegel 'proclaimed the morality, nay, the very death, of art'. See Croce (1978), p. 302. Carter (1980), p. 94, suggests that one reason for the prevalence of the death of art interpretation was that the early Osmaton translation of the *Aesthetics* translated '*Kunst sich selbst aufhebt*' as 'art commits an act of suicide'.

27 Bosanquet (1919–20), pp. 280–8; d'Hondt (1972); Carter (1980), pp. 83–98; Desmond (1986), p. 13; Etter (2000), pp. 39–40; and Müller (1946), p. 51.

EPILOGUE   THE RISE AND FALL OF THE HEGELIAN SCHOOL

1 See Toews (1980), pp. 232–4 and McLellan (1969), pp. 15–16, 22–4, 25.

2 This becomes most visible in Karl Köppen's tract *Friedrich der Grosse* (Leipzig: 1840). See McLellan (1969), p. 16.

3 See Toews (1980), p. 233; and McLellan (1969), p. 15.

4 Toews (1980), pp. 95–140, esp. p. 84.

5 For a further exploration of some of these religious issues, see Toews (1980), pp. 141–202, and Brazill, *The Young Hegelians* (1970), pp. 48–70.

6 D.F. Strauss, *Streitschriften* (Tübingen, 1841), III, p. 95.

7 See Toews (1992), pp. 387–91.

8 Brazill (1970), pp. 17–18, seems to me to be incorrect in arguing that the divisions between the Hegelian school did not result from any ambiguity in Hegel's philosophy. This underrates the interpretative problems regarding Hegel's dictum about the rationality of the real.

9 The distinction is in *Enzyklopädie* §6.

10 MEGA, XXI, 266–8.

11 Toews (1980), pp. 223–4, 234–5.

12 Ibid., p. 235.

13 McLellan (1969), pp. 3, 6; and Brazill (1970), pp. 7, 53.

14 McLellan (1969), p. 24. The new critical developments of the 1840s are well summarized by Stepelvich (1983), pp. 12–15.

15 Toews (1980), pp. 223–4.

Further Reading

These suggestions for further reading are very selective and made with a beginning student in mind. For obvious reasons, they focus on English sources; I mention German and French ones only when it is important to know about them. Students who are interested in a general bibliography should consult Steinhauer (1980) and Weiss (1973), though they are now out of date.

GENERAL INTRODUCTIONS

There are several good general introductions to Hegel in English. The best comprehensive treatment, though it is very lengthy, is Charles Taylor's *Hegel* (1975). An excellent shorter introduction is Stephen Houlgate's *Freedom, Truth and History: An Introduction to Hegel's Philosophy* (1991). Raymond Plant's *Hegel* (1973) is also an admirable general introduction from the perspective of Hegel's social and political concerns. Ivan Soll's *An Introduction to Hegel's Metaphysics* (1969) provides a very clear but brief introduction to some aspects of Hegel's metaphysics.

CULTURE AND CONTEXT

Indispensable for the general historical background is Sheehan (1989), and for the general cultural context Bruford (1935). The political developments of the period are treated by Aris (1936), Epstein (1966) and Beiser (1992). The pantheism controversy and nihilism are treated in Beiser (1987). For the development of German idealism before Hegel, see Royce (1919), Kroner (1921), Ameriks (2000a), Beiser (2002) and Pinkard (2002).

INTELLECTUAL DEVELOPMENT

Unfortunately, the best studies of Hegel's intellectual development are in German and untranslated. Kaufmann (1966) is very uneven and dated; Nauen (1971) is illuminating but very brief. The older German treatments – Rosenkranz (1844), Haym (1857), Dilthey (1921), Haering (1929) and Lukács (1973) – are still very much worth reading. Rosenkranz and Haym are especially valuable because they had access to manuscript sources that have since been lost; however, it is necessary to use them with caution because they wrongly dated many of the early writings. The modern chronology of Hegel's early writings, indispensable for all study of Hegel's intellectual development, is Gisela Schüler's 'Zur Chronologie von Hegels Jugendschriften', *Hegel-Studien* 2 (1963): 111–59.

The classic studies in English of Hegel's early intellectual development are Henry Harris's *Hegel's Development: Toward the Sunlight, 1770–1801* (1972) and *Hegel's Development: Night Thoughts (Jena 1801–1806)* (1983). Because of their detail and close scholarship, Harris's studies are best read directly in conjunction with Hegel's texts. They do not serve well as introductions to Hegel's development. Unfortunately, Harris tends to get lost in the details and does not clearly establish or defend his own general viewpoint.

The best biography of Hegel – in any language – is Terry Pinkard's *Hegel: A Biography* (2000). This situates Hegel firmly in his historical context and also provides an illuminating introduction to all aspects of his philosophy.

PHENOMENOLOGY

There are many good commentaries in English on the *Phenomenology of Spirit*. The beginner would do well to start with Richard Norman (1976) or Harris (1995). The more detailed studies by Merold Westphal (1979), Solomon (1983), Lauer (1993 [1976]), Pinkard (1994b) and Stern (2002) all contain instructive points and illuminating readings. The political themes of the book are treated brilliantly by Shklar (1976). The commentary by Jean Hyppolite (1974), while sometimes obscure, is still worthwhile. Jon Stewart (2000) and Michael Forster (1998) have written excellent accounts of the unity and general structure of the book. Kenneth Westphal (1989 and 2003) closely examines the epistemological ideas in the *Phenomenology*. Since one commentary often illuminates what another neglects, the student is advised to consult as many as he or she can and to use them selectively.

The famous study of Kojève (1969) is historically important in its own right, having been an important influence on French philosophy in the post-war years. It was also crucial for the later Hegel renaissance of the 1970s. While sometimes illuminating, Kojève's reading of the text is partisan and limited; and he had little appreciation of its metaphysical dimension.

The monumental work on the *Phenomenology* is Harris's *Hegel's Ladder* (1997), two volumes. While all scholars will want to consult this work, it is not definitive or authoritative (as often said). It would not have surprised Harris to know that his readings can be easily challenged.

LOGIC

The *Phenomenology* has now surpassed the *Logic* as the text of choice among Anglophone Hegel scholars. There has been no complete commentary on the *Logic* for generations, though I suspect this will soon change when the prejudices against Hegel's work are finally exposed. The older studies of McTaggart (1910, 1912) are still useful, though they should be used cautiously because they view Hegel very much through the lenses of British idealism. W.T. Stace's *The Philosophy of Hegel* (New York: Dover, 1955), which focusses on the *Logic*, is still useful here and there. Serious students need to consult the studies by John Burbidge (1981, 1992), Robert Stern (1990) and Clark Butler (1996). The anthology by di Giovanni (1990) contains many interesting articles. Two short introductory articles on Hegel's conception of logic are provided by Houlgate (1991), pp. 5–40 and Burbidge (1993). Houlgate has written a detailed commentary on the Greater Logic, *The Opening of Hegel's Logic: Greater Logic from Being to Infinity* (Lafayette: Purdue University Press, 2005).

SOCIAL AND POLITICAL PHILOSOPHY

The best study of Hegel's political philosophy is Franz Rosenzweig's *Hegel und der Staat* (1920), two volumes. Unfortunately, it has not been translated and remains sadly neglected in the Anglophone world. A very helpful introduction is Cullen (1979); some good general surveys are Avineri (1972) and Franco (1999). A very illuminating account of Hegel's concept of *Sittlichkeit* is Neuhouser (2000). Wood (1990) is indispensable for Hegel's ethics. Hegel's concept of freedom is treated admirably by Tunick (1992) and Patten (1999). On Hegel's attitude toward liberalism, see Smith (1989). A useful introduction to the *Philosophy of Right* is provided by Knowles (2002). For a detailed commentary, the reader will want to consult Peperzak (2001).

PHILOSOPHY OF RELIGION

The best study on Hegel's philosophy of religion is Fackenheim (1967). On the development of Hegel's religious views, see Jaeschke (1990) and Crites (1998). On Hegel's concept of God see Lauer (1962) and Olson (1992). O'Regan (1994), Magee (2001) and Dickey (1987) provide detailed studies of Hegel's appropriation of religious traditions. Two anthologies are recommended: Christensen (1970) and Kolb (1992).

PHILOSOPHY OF HISTORY

Considering its historical importance and frequent use as an introduction to Hegel's philosophy, the dearth of solid secondary sources on Hegel's *Philosophy of*

History is remarkable. The genesis, context and content of the work remain unexplored. The treatments by O'Brian (1975) and Wilkins (1974), though still useful, focus almost entirely on Hegel's methodology and belief in historical necessity. For starters, the reader should read the essays by Forbes (1975) and Walsh (1971), the introduction by Hyppolite (1996) and the general study by McCarney (2000).

AESTHETICS

A first-time reader who wants some orientation would do well to read the chapter on aesthetics in Houlgate (1991), pp. 126–75, the article by Wicks (1993), and that by Moran (1981).

Unfortunately, there are not many books on Hegel's aesthetics in English. The early study by Kaminsky (1962) is very dated and limited in its coverage. The study by Bungay (1984) is more comprehensive but marred by its failure to understand Hegel's metaphysics. The study by Desmond (1986) is a notable and noble attempt to restore the metaphysical dimension of Hegel's aesthetics, which had been read out of it by Kaminsky, Bungay and Gombrich (1965). The anthology by Steinkraus (1980) contains a useful bibliography; and the anthology by Maker (2000) has some helpful articles. Students interested in Hegel's end-of-art thesis should read Bungay (1984), pp. 71–89 and the articles by Harries (1974) and Rapp (2000). The anthology by Lang (1984) contains several stimulating articles.

Bibliography

PRIMARY SOURCES

Anonymous (1971) *Die Nachtwachen des Bonaventura*, trans. Gerald Gillespie. Austin: University of Texas Press; Edinburgh: Bilingual Library, no. 6.

—— (1972) *Nachtwachen – Von Bonaventura*, ed. Wolfgang Paulsen. Stuttgart: Reclam.

Arnauld, Antoine (1964) *The Art of Thinking*, trans. James Dickoff and Patricia James. Indianapolis: Bobbs-Merrill.

Fichte, J.G. (1845–6) *Sämtliche Werke*, ed. I.H. Fichte. Berlin: Veit, 8 vols.

Heidegger, Martin (1972) *Sein und Zeit*. Tübingen: Niemeyer.

Heine, Heinrich (1981) *Sämtliche Schriften*, ed. Klaus Briegleb. Frankfurt: Ullstein, 12 vols.

Herder, J.G. (1881–1913) *Sämtliche Werke*, ed. B. Suphan. Berlin: Weidmann, 33 vols.

Hobbes, Thomas (1968) *Leviathan*, ed. C.B. Macpherson. Harmondsworth: Penguin.

Hölderlin, Friedrich (1943–85) *Sämtliche Werke. Grosse Stutgarter Ausgabe*, ed. Friedrich Beißner *et al.* Stuttgart: Cotta Nachfolger.

Hume, David (1958) *A Treatise of Human Nature*, ed. L.A. Selby-Bigge. Oxford: Oxford University Press.

Jacobi, F.H. (1812) *Werke*. Leipzig: Fleischer, 6 vols.

—— (1994) *The Main Philosophical Writings and the Novel Allwill*, trans. George di Giovanni. Montreal: McGill-Queen's University Press.

Kant, Immanuel (1902 *et seq.*) *Gesammelte Schriften*, ed. Preußischen Akademie der Wissenschaften. Berlin: de Gruyter.

Kielmeyer, C.F. (1930) '*Über die Verhältnisse der organischen Kräfte untereinander in der Reihe der verschiedenen Organization, die Gesetze und Folgen dieser Verhältnisse*', *Sudhoffs Archiv für Geschichte der Medizin* 23: 247–67.

Kierkegaard, Søren (1992) *Concluding Unscientific Postscript to Philosophical Fragments*, ed. and trans. H.V. and E.H. Hong. Princeton, NJ: Princeton University Press.

Locke, John (1959) *An Essay concerning Human Understanding*, ed. A.C. Fraser. New York: Dover.

Maimon, Solomon (1965) *Gesammelte Werke*, ed. Valerio Verra. Hildesheim: Olms.

Marx, Karl (1982) *Marx-Engels Gesamtausgabe*, ed. Institut für Marxismus-Leninismus. Berlin: Dietz.

Nietzsche, Friedrich (1980) *Sämtliche Werke*, ed. G. Colli and M. Montinari. Berlin: de Gruyter.

Obereit, J.H. (1787a) *Die verzweifelte Metaphysik zwischen Kant und Wizenmann*. [No place of publication given]

—— (1787b) *Die wiederkommenete Lebensgeist der verzweifelten Metaphysik, Ein kritisches Drama zur neuen Grundkritik vom Geist des Cebes*. Berlin: Decker & Sohn.

—— (1791) *Beobachtungen über die Quelle der Metaphysik vom alten Zuschauern, veranlasst durch Kants Kritik der reinen Vernunft*. Meiningen: Hanisch.

Reinhold, Karl Leonhard (1923) *Briefe über die kantische Philosophie*, ed. Raymond Schmidt. Leipzig: Meiner.

Rink, F.T. (1800) *Mancherley zur Geschichte der metacriticischen Invasion*. Königsberg: Nicolovius.

Schelling, F.W.J. (1856–61) *Sämtliche Werke*, ed. K.F.A. Schelling. Stuttgart: Cotta, 14 vols.

Schiller, Friedrich (1943) *Werke. Nationalausgabe*, ed. Benno von Wiese *et al.* Weimar: Böhlaus Nachfolger, 42 vols.

Schlegel, Friedrich (1958 et seq.) *Kritische Friedrich Schlegel Augabe*, ed. Ernst Behler *et al.* Paderborn: Schöningh.

Schleiermacher, Friedrich (1980 et seq.) *Kritische Gesamtausgabe*, ed. H. Birkner *et al.* Berlin: de Gruyter.

Schopenhauer, Arthur (1968) *Sämtliche Werke*. Darmstadt: Wissenschaftliche Buchgesellschaft.

Spinoza, Benedict (1924) *Opera*, ed. C. Gebhardt. Heidelberg: Winter, 4 vols.

—— (1966) *The Correspondence of Spinoza*, ed. A. Wolf. London: Frank Cass.

SECONDARY SOURCES

Adorno, Theodor (1969) *Drei Studien zu Hegel*. Frankfurt: Suhrkamp.

Ameriks, Karl, ed. (2000a) *The Cambridge Companion to German Idealism*. Cambridge: Cambridge University Press.

—— (2000b) 'The Practical Foundation of Philosophy in Kant, Fichte, and After', in *The Reception of Kant's Critical Philosophy*, ed. Sally Sedgwick. Cambridge: Cambridge University Press, pp. 109–29.

Aris, Reinhold (1936) *History of Political Thought in Germany, From 1789 to 1815*. London: Frank Cass.

Avineri, Shlomo (1972) *Hegel's Theory of the Modern State*. Cambridge: Cambridge University Press.

Baum, Manfred (2000) 'The Beginnings of Schelling's Philosophy of Nature', in *The Reception of Kant's Critical Philosophy*, ed. Sally Sedgwick. Cambridge: Cambridge University Press, pp. 199–215.

Baur, Michael (1997) 'Winckelmann and Hegel on the Imitation of the Greeks', in *Hegel and the Tradition*, ed. Michael Baur and John Russon. Toronto: University of Toronto Press, pp. 93–110.

Behler, Ernst (1992) *Fruetomantik*. Berlin: de Gruyetr.

Beiser, Frederick (1987) *The Fate of Reason: German Philosophy from Kant to Fichte*. Cambridge, MA: Harvard University Press.

—— (1992) *Enlightenment, Revolution & Romanticism: The Genesis of Modern German Political Thought, 1790–1800*. Cambridge, MA: Harvard University Press.

—— (1993) 'Hegel's Historicism', in *The Cambridge Companion to Hegel*. Cambridge: Cambridge University Press, pp. 270–300.

—— (1995) 'Hegel, a Non-Metaphysician! A Polemic', *Bulletin of the Hegel Society of Great Britain* 32: 1–13.

—— (1996a) *The Sovereignty of Reason: The Defense of Rationality in the Early English Enlightenment*. Princeton, NJ: Princeton University Press.

—— (1996b) *The Early Political Writings of the German Romantics*. Cambridge: Cambridge University Press.

—— (2002) *German Idealism: The Struggle Against Subjectivism, 1781–1801*. Cambridge, MA: Harvard University Press.

—— (2003) *The Romantic Imperative: The Concept of Early German Romanticism*. Cambridge, MA: Harvard University Press.

Berlin, Isaiah (1969) *Four Essays on Liberty*. Oxford: Oxford University Press.

—— (2002) *Freedom and its Betrayal*. Princeton, NJ: Princeton University Press.

Blackall, Eric (1983) *The Novels of the German Romantics*. Ithaca, NY: Cornell University Press.

Bosanquet, Bernard (1919–20) 'Appendix on Croce's Conception of the "Death of Art" in Hegel', *Proceedings of the British Academy* IX: 280–8.

Bowie, Andrew (1990) *Aesthetics and Subjectivity*. Manchester: University of Manchester Press.

Brandom, Robert (2002) *Tales of the Mighty Dead*. Cambridge, MA: Harvard University Press.

Brazill, William (1970) *The Young Hegelians*. New Haven, CT: Yale University Press.

Brocker, Walter (1965) *Auseinandersetzungen mit Hegel*. Frankfurt: Klostermann.

Bruford, W.H. (1935) *Germany in the Eighteenth Century*. Cambridge, MA: Cambridge University Press.

Bubner, Rüdiger (1980) 'Hegel's Aesthetics – Yesterday and Today', in *Art and Logic* in *Hegel's Philosophy*, ed W. Steinkraus and K. Schmitz. Atlantic Highlands, NJ: Humanities Press, pp. 15–30.

Büchner, Hartmut (1965) 'Hegel und das Kritische Journal der Philosophie', *Hegel-Studien* 3: 98–115.

—— (1994) *Friedrich Wilhelm Joseph Schelling. Timaeus (1794)*. Stuttgart: Frommann-Holzboog.

Bungay, Stephen (1984) *Beauty and Truth: A Study of Hegel's Aesthetics*. Oxford: Oxford University Press.

Burbidge, John (1981) *On Hegel's Logic: Fragments of a Commentary*. Atlantic Highlands, NJ: Humanities Press.

—— (1992) *Hegel on Logic and Religion*. Albany, NY: SUNY Press.

—— (1993) 'The Necessity of Contingency: An Analysis of Hegel's Chapter on "Actuality" in the *Science of Logic*', in Lawrence Stepelvich (ed.) *Selected Essays on G.W.F. Hegel*. Atlantic Highlands, NJ: Humanities Press, pp. 60–75.

Butler, Clark (1996) *Hegel's Logic: Between Dialectic and History*. Evanston, IL: Northwestern University Press.

Camus, Albert (1955) *The Myth of Sisyphus*, trans. Justin O'Brian. London: Hamish Hamilton.

Carter, Curtius (1980) 'A Re-examination of the "Death of Art" Interpretation of Hegel's Aesthetics', in *Art and Logic in Hegel's Philosophy*, ed. Warren Steinkraus and Kenneth Schmitz. Atlantic Highlands, NJ: Humanities Press.

Cassirer, Ernst (1946) *The Myth of the State*. New Haven, CT: Yale University Press.

Chamley, Paul (1963) *Economie politique chez Stuart et Hegel*. Paris: Dalloz.

Christensen, Darrel, ed. (1970) *Hegel and the Philosophy of Religion*. The Hague: Martinus Nijhoff.

Cohen, Robert and Wartofsky, Marx, eds (1984) *Hegel and the Sciences*, Dordrecht: Reidel. Volume 64 in Boston Studies in the Philosophy of Science.

Collingwood, R.G. (1993) *The Idea of History*, rev. edn. Oxford: Clarendon Press.

Crites, Stephen (1998) *Dialectic and Gospel in the Development of Hegel's Thinking*. University Park: Penn State Press.

Croce, Benedetto (1915) *What is Living and What is Dead in the Philosophy of Hegel*, trans. Douglas Ainslee. New York: Russell & Russell.

—— (1978) *Aesthetic*. Boston, MA: Nonpareil.

Crouter, Richard (1980) 'Hegel and Schleiermacher at Berlin: A Many-Sided Debate', *Journal of the American Academy of Religion* 48: 19–43.

Cullen, Bernard (1979) *Hegel's Social and Political Thought*. New York: St Martin's Press.

Danto, Arthur (1984) 'The Death of Art', in *The Death of Art*, ed. Berel Lang. New York: Haven, pp. 5–38.

Desmond, William (1986) *Art and the Absolute: A Study of Hegel's Aesthetics*. Albany: SUNY Press.

—— (2000) 'Art and the Absolute Revisited: The Neglect of Hegel's Aesthetics', in *Hegel and Aesthetics*, ed. William Maker. Albany: SUNY Press, pp. 1–13.

D'Hondt, Jacques (1968a) *Hegel secret*. Paris: Presses Universitaires de France.

—— (1968b) *Hegel en son temps (Berlin 1818–1831)*. Paris: Éditions Sociales.

—— (1972) 'La Mort de l'Art', *Bulletin International d'Esthetique*, 17.

—— (1988) *Hegel in his Time*, trans. John Burbidge. Lewiston: Broadview.

Dickey, Laurence (1987) *Hegel: Religion, Economics, and Politics of Spirit, 1770–1807*. Cambridge: Cambridge University Press.

—— (1999) *Hegel, Political Writings*. Cambridge, MA: Cambridge University Press.

Di Giovanni, George (1983) 'On the Impotence of Spirit', in Robert Perkins (ed.) *History and System: Hegel's Philosophy of History*. Albany: SUNY Press, pp. 195–212.

—— ed. (1990) *Essays on Hegel's Logic*. Albany: SUNY Press.

—— (1993) 'The Category of Contingency in the Hegelian Logic', in Lawrence Stepelvich (ed.) *Selected Essays on G.W.F. Hegel*. Atlantic Highlands, NJ: Humanities Press, pp. 60–75.

Dilthey, Wilhelm (1921) *Die Jugendgeschichte Hegels*. Leipzig: Tuebner. Volume 4 of *Wilhelm Diltheys Gesammelte Schriften*.

Dove, Kenley Royce (1974) 'Hegel's Phenomenological Method', in *New Studies in Hegel's Philosophy*, ed. Warren Steinkraus. New York: Holt, Rinehart & Winston, pp. 34–56.

Durner, Manfred (1991) 'Die Naturphilosophie im 18. Jahrhundert und der naturwissenschaftlichen Unterricht in Tübingen', *Archiv für Geschichte der Philosophie* LXXVIII: 72–103.

Düsing, Klaus (1969) 'Spekulation und Reflexion: Zur Zusammenarbeit Schellings und Hegels in Jena', *Hegel-Studien* 5: 95–128.

—— (1973) 'Die Rezeption der kantischen Postulaten lehre in den frühen philosophischen Entwürfe Schellings und Hegels', *Hegel-Studien* 9: 53–90.

—— (1999) 'The Reception of Kant's Doctrine of Postulates in Schelling's and Hegel's Early Philosophical Projects', trans. Daniel Dahlstrom, in *The Emergence of German Idealism*, ed. Michael Baur and Daniel Dahlstrom. Washington: Catholic University of American Press. Volume 34 in Studies in Philosophy and the History of Philosophy, pp. 201–41.

Epstein, Klaus (1966) *The Genesis of German Conservatism*. Princeton, NJ: Princeton University Press.

Etter, Brian (2000) 'Hegel's Aesthetic and the Possibility of Art Criticism', in *Hegel and Aesthetics*, ed. William Maker. Albany: SUNY Press, pp. 13–30.

Fackenheim, Emil (1967) *The Religious Dimension in Hegel's Thought*. Chicago: University of Chicago Press.

—— (1989) *To Mend the World*. New York: Schocken.

—— (1996) *The God Within: Kant, Schelling and Historicity*. Toronto: University of Toronto Press.

Ferrarin, Alfredo (2001) *Hegel and Aristotle*. Cambridge: Cambridge University Press.

Findlay, John (1958) *Hegel: A Re-Examination*. London: Allen & Unwin.

Forbes, Duncan (1975) 'Introduction', in *Lectures on the Philosophy of World History*. Cambridge: Cambridge University Press, pp. vii–xxxv.

Forster, Michael (1989) *Hegel and Skepticism*. Cambridge, MA: Harvard University Press.

—— (1993) 'Hegel's Dialectical Method', in *The Cambridge Companion to Hegel*. Cambridge: Cambridge University Press, pp. 130–70.

—— (1998) *Hegel's Idea of a Phenomenology of Spirit*. Chicago: University of Chicago Press.

Foster, Michael (1935) *The Political Philosophies of Plato and Hegel*. Oxford: Clarendon Press.

Franco, Paul (1999) *Hegel's Philosophy of Freedom*. New Haven, CT: Yale University Press.

Frank, Manfred (1997) *Unendliche Annäherung: Die Anfänge der philosophischen Frühromantik*. Frankfurt: Suhrkamp.

Franz, Michael (1992) ' "Platons frommer Garten". Hölderlins Platonlektüre von Tübingen bis Jena', *Hölderlin Jahrbuch* 28: 111–27.

—— (1996) *Schellings Tübinger Platon-Studien*. Göttingen: Vandenhoeck & Ruprecht.

Fuhrmanns, Horst (1962–75) 'Schelling in Tuebinger Stift Herbst 1790–95', in *Briefe und Dokumente*. Bonn: Bouvier, 2 vols.

Gadamer, Hans-Georg (1976) *Hegel's Dialectic: Five Hermeneutical Studies*, trans. Christopher Smith. New Haven, CT: Yale University Press.

—— (1990) *Wahrheit und Methode*. Tübingen: J.C.B. Mohr. Volume 1 of *Gesammelte Werke*.

Garaudy, Roger (1966) *Pour connaître la pensée de Hegel*. Paris: Bordas.

Glockner, Hermann (1965) 'Die Ästhetik in Hegels System', *Hegel-Studien, Beiheft* 2: 443–53.

Gombrich, Ernst (1965) *In Search of Cultural History*. Oxford: Clarendon Press.

—— (1977) 'Hegel und die Kunstgeschichte', *Die Neue Rundschau* 88: 202–19.

Guyer, Paul (2000) 'Absolute Idealism and the Rejection of Kantian Dualism', in *The Cambridge Companion to German Idealism*, ed. Karl Ameriks. Cambridge: Cambridge University Press, pp. 37–56.

Haakonssen, Knud (1996) *Natural Law and Moral Philosophy: From Grotius to the Scottish Enlightenment*. Cambridge: Cambridge University Press.

Haering, Theodor (1929) *Hegel, sein Wollen und sein Werk*. Leipzig: Teubner, 1929, 2 vols.

Hallowell, John (1950) *Main Currents in Political Thought*. New York: Henry Holt.

Hankins, Thomas (1985) *Science and the Enlightenment*. Cambridge: Cambridge University Press.

Hardimon, Michael (1994) *Hegel's Social Philosophy*. Cambridge: Cambridge University Press.

Harries, Kartsen (1974) 'Hegel on the Future of Art', *Review of Metaphysics* 27: 677–96.

Harris, H.S. (1972) *Hegel's Development: Toward the Sunlight, 1770–1801*. Oxford: Clarendon Press.

—— (1983) *Hegel's Development: Night Thoughts (Jena 1801–1806)*. Oxford: Clarendon Press.

—— (1995) *Hegel: Phenomenology and System*. Indianapolis: Hackett.

—— (1997) *Hegel's Ladder I: The Pilgrimage of Reason*. Indianapolis: Hackett.

—— (1997) *Hegel's Ladder II: The Odyssey of Spirit*. Indianapolis: Hackett.

Hartmann, Klaus (1972) 'Hegel: A Non-Metaphysical View', in *Hegel*, ed. A. MacIntyre. New York: Doubleday, pp. 101–24.

Haym, Rudolf (1857) *Hegel und seine Zeit*. Berlin: Gaertner.

Heidegger, Martin (1972) 'Hegels Begriff der Erfahrung' in *Holzwege*. Frankfurt: Klostermann, pp. 105–92.

Heller, Hermann (1921) *Hegel und der nationale Machtstaatsgedanke in Deutschland*. Leipzig: Tuebner.

Henrich, Dieter (1968) *Kant, Gentz, Rehberg: Über Theorie und Praxis*. Frankfurt: Suhrkamp.

—— (1969) 'Kunst und Natur in der Idealistischen Ästhetik', in *Nachahmung und Illusion*, ed. H.R. Jauß. Munich: Fink.

—— (1971) *Hegel im Kontext*. Frankfurt: Suhrkamp.

—— (1979) 'Art and Philosophy Today: Reflections with Reference to Hegel', in *New Perspectives in German Literary Criticism*, ed. Richard Amcher and Victor Lange. Princeton, NJ: Princeton University Press, pp. 107–33.

—— (1985) 'The Contemporary Relevance of Hegel's Aesthetics', in *Hegel*, ed. Michael Inwood. Oxford: Oxford University Press.

Hettner, Hermann (1979) *Geschichte der deutschen Literatur im Achtzehnten Jahrhundert*. Berlin: Aufbau, 2 vols.

Hirsch, Emmanuel (1973) 'Die Beisetzung der Romantiker in Hegels Phänomenologie', in *Materialien zu Hegels Phänomenologie des Geistes*, ed. Hans Friedrich Fulda and Dieter Henrich. Frankfurt: Suhrkamp, pp. 245–75.

Hochstrasser, Timothy (2000) *Natural Law Theories in the Early Enlightenment.* Cambridge: Cambridge University Press.

Hoffmeister, Johannes (1955) *Wörterbuch der philosophischen Begriffe.* Hamburg: Meiner.

Hofstadter, Albert (1974) 'Die Kunst: Tod und Verklärung. Überlegungen zu Hegels Lehre von dem Romantik', *Hegel-Studien, Beiheft* 11: 271–85.

Horstmann, Rolf-Peter and Petry, Michael John, eds (1986) *Hegels Philosophie der Natur: Beziehungen zwischen empirischer und spekulativer Naturerkenntnis.* Stuttgart: Klett-Cotta. Volume 15 in Veröffentlichungen der Internationalen Hegel-Vereinigung.

Houlgate, Stephen (1991) *Freedom, Truth and History: An Introduction to Hegel's Philosophy.* London: Routledge 2nd edn, Oxford: Blackwell, 1994.

—— (1998) *Hegel and the Philosophy of Nature.* Albany: SUNY Press.

Hyppolite, Jean (1969a) 'The Concept of Life and Consciousness of Life in Hegel's Jena Philosophy', in *Studies on Marx and Hegel,* trans. John O'Neill. London: Heinemann, pp. 3–21.

—— (1969b) 'The Concept of Existence in the Hegelian Phenomenology', in *Studies on Marx and Hegel,* trans. John O'Neill. London: Heinemann, pp. 22–32.

—— (1974) *Genesis and Structure of Hegel's Phenomenology of Spirit,* trans. Samuel Cherniak and John Heckman. Evanston, IL: Northwestern University Press.

—— (1996) *Introduction to Hegel's Philosophy of History,* trans. Bond Harris and Jacqueline Spurlock. Gainesville: University of Florida Press.

Jaeschke, Walter (1990) *Reason in Religion: The Foundations of Hegel's Philosophy of Religion,* trans. J. M. Stewart and Peter Hodgson. Berkeley: University of California Press.

James, William (1907) *Pragmatism.* New York: Longmans.

—— (1909) *A Pluralistic Universe.* New York: Longmans, Green.

Jamme, Christoph (1983) ' "Ein Ungelehrtes Buch", *Die philosophische Gemeinschaft zwischen Hölderlin und Hegel in Frankfurt 1797–1800*', in *Hegel-Studien, Beiheft* 23. Bonn: Bouvier.

Kaminsky, Jack (1962) *Hegel on Art.* New York: SUNY Press.

Kaufmann, Walter (1965) *Hegel: Texts and Commentary.* Garden City: Doubleday.

—— (1966) *Hegel: A Re-interpretation.* Garden City: Doubleday.

—— ed. (1970) *Hegel's Political Philosophy.* New York: Atherton Press.

—— (1972) 'The Young Hegel and Religion', in *Hegel,* ed. Alasdair MacIntyre. Garden City: Doubleday, pp. 61–100.

Kelly, George (1972) 'Notes on "Hegel's Lordship and Bondage" ', in *Hegel: A Collection of Critical Essays,* ed. Alasdair MacIntyre. New York: Anchor, pp. 189–218.

Kimmerle, Heinz (1967) 'Dokumente zu Hegels Jenaet DozenentatigKeit 1801–1807', *Hegel-Studien* 4: 21–100.

Kluckhohn, Paul (1953) *Das Ideengut der deutschen Romantik,* 3rd edn. Tübingen: Niemeyet.

Knowles, Dudley (2002) *Hegel and the Philosophy of Right*. London: Routledge.

Knox, T.M. (1980) 'The Puzzle of Hegel's Aesthetics', in *Art and Logic in Hegel's Philosophy*, ed. W. Steinkraus and K. Schmitz. Atlantic Highlands, NJ: Humanities Press, pp. 1–10.

Koepsel, Werner (1975) *Die Rezeption der Hegelschen Ästhetik im 20. Jahrhundert*. Bonn: Bouvier.

Kojève, Alexandre (1969) *Introduction to the Reading of Hegel*, trans. James Nichols. New York: Basic Books.

Kolb, David (1986) *The Critique of Pure Modernity: Hegel, Heidegger and After*. Chicago: University of Chicago Press.

—— ed. (1992) *New Perspectives on Hegel's Philosophy of Religion*. Albany: SUNY Press.

Koselleck, Reinhart (1992) *Kritik und Krise*. Frankfurt: Suhrkamp.

Kroner, Richard (1921) *Von Kant bis Hegel*. Tübingen: Mohr, 2 vols.

—— (1971) 'Introduction: Hegel's Philosophical Development', in *Hegel's Early Theological Writings*, trans. T.M. Knox. Philadelphia: University of Pennsylvania Press.

Kuhn, Helmut (1931) *Die Vollendung der klassischen deutschen Ästhetik durch Hegel*. Berlin: Junker & Dünnhaupt.

—— (1974) 'Die Gegenwärtigkeit der Kunst nach Hegels Vorlesungen über Ästhetik', *Hegel-Studien, Beiheft* 11: 251–69.

Lang, Berol, ed. (1984) *The Death of Art*. New York: Haven.

Larson, James (1979) 'Vital Forces: Regulative Principles of Constitutive Agents? A Strategy in German Physiology, 1786–1802', *Isis* 70: 235–49.

Lauer, Quentin (1962) *Hegel's Concept of God*. Albany: SUNY Press.

—— (1993[1976]) *A Reading of Hegel's Phenomenology of Spirit*. New York: Fordham University Press.

Löwith, Karl (1949) *Von Hegel zu Nietzsche: Der revolutionäre Bruch im Denken des 19. Jahrhunderts*. Zurich: Europa Verlag.

Lukács, Georg (1973) *Der junge Hegel*. Frankfurt: Suhrkamp, 2 vols.

Magee, Glenn (2001) *Hegel and the Hermetic Tradition*. Ithaca, NY: Cornell University Press.

Maker, William, ed. (2000) *Hegel and Aesthetics*. Albany: SUNY Press.

Marcuse, Herbert (1967) *Reason and Revolution: Hegel and the Rise of Social Theory*, 2nd edn. London: Routledge & Kegan Paul.

McCarney, Joseph (2000) *Hegel on History*. London: Routledge.

McDowell, John (1996[1994]) *Mind and World*, Cambridge, MA: Harvard University Press.

McLellan, David (1969) *The Young Hegelians and Karl Marx*. London: Macmillan.

McTaggart, John (1901) *Studies in Hegelian Cosmology*. Cambridge: Cambridge University Press.

—— (1910) *A Commentary on Hegel's Logic*. New York: Russell & Russell.

—— (1912) *Studies in the Hegelian Dialectic*, 2nd edn. New York: Russell & Russell.

Meinecke, Friedrich (1924) *Die Idee der Staatsräson in der neueren Geschichte*. Munich: Oldenbourg.

—— (1965) *Die Entstehung des Historismus*. Munich: Oldenbourg.

Moran, Michael (1981) 'On the Continuing Significance of Hegel's *Aesthetics*', *British Journal of Aesthetics* 21: 214–39.

Müller, Gustav (1958) 'The Hegel Legend of "Thesis-Antithesis-Synthesis"', *Journal of the History of Ideas* XIX: 411–14.

—— (1959) *Hegel: Denkgeschichte eines Lebendigen*. Berne: Francke.

—— (1946) 'The Function of Aesthetics in Hegel's Philosophy', *Journal of Aesthetics and Art Criticism* V: 49–53.

Nauen, Franz (1971) *Revolution, Idealism and Human Freedom: Schelling, Hölderlin and Hegel and the Crisis of Early German Idealism*. The Hague: Nijhoff. Internationales Archives of the History of Ideas, no. 45.

Neuhouset, Frederick (2000) *Foundations of Hegel's Social Theory*. Cambridge, MA: Harvard University Press.

Nicolin, Friedrich (1967) 'Zum Titelproblem der Phänomenologie des Geistes', *Hegel-Studien* 4: 113–23.

Norman, Judith (2000), 'Squaring the Romantic Circle: Hegel's Critique of Romantic Theories of Art', in *Hegel and Aesthetics*, ed. William Maker. Albany: SUNY Press, pp. 131–44.

Norman, Richard (1976) *Hegel's Phenomenology*. London: Chatto & Windus.

O'Brian, George (1975) *Hegel on Reason and History*. Chicago: University of Chicago Press.

Olson, Alan (1992) *Hegel and the Spirit*. Princeton, NJ: Princeton University Press.

O'Regan, Cyril (1994) *The Heterodox Hegel*. Albany: SUNY Press.

Patten, Alan (1999) *Hegel's Idea of Freedom*. Oxford: Oxford University Press.

Pelczynski, Z.A. (1964) 'An Introductory Essay', in *Hegel's Political Writings*, trans. T.M. Knox. Oxford: Clarendon Press.

—— (1971) 'The Hegelian Conception of the State', in his *Hegel's Political Philosophy: Problems & Perspectives*. Cambridge: Cambridge University Press.

—— (1984) *Hegel and Civil Society*. Cambridge: Cambridge University Press.

Peperzak, Adrian (1969) *La jeune Hegel et la vision morale du monde*. The Hague: Nijhoff.

—— (2001) *Modern Freedom: Hegel's Legal, Moral, and Political Philosophy*. Dordrecht: Kluwer.

Petry, Michael, ed. (1987) *Hegel und die Naturwissenschaften*. Stuttgart Bad-Cannstatt: Frommann. Volume 2 in Texte und Untersuchungen zum Deutschen Idealismus, Abteilung II: Untersuchungen.

—— (1993) *Hegel and Newtonianism*. Dordrecht: Kluwer. Volume 136 in International Archives of the History of Ideas.

Pinkard, Terry (1988) *Hegel's Dialectic*. Philadelphia, PA: Temple University Press.

—— (1994a) *Hegel Reconsidered*. Dordrecht: Kluwer.

—— (1994b) *Hegel's Phenomenology: The Sociality of Reason*. Cambridge: Cambridge University Press.

—— (2000) *Hegel: A Biography*. Cambridge: Cambridge University Press.

—— (2002) *German Philosophy 1760–1860: The Legacy of Idealism*. Cambridge: Cambridge University Press.

Pippin, Robert (1989) *Hegel's Idealism*. Cambridge: Cambridge University Press.

—— (1997), 'Hegel's Ethical Rationalism', in *Idealism as Modernism*. Cambridge: Cambridge University Press, pp. 417–50.

Plamenatz, John (1963) *Man and Society*. London: Longman, 2 vols.

Plant, Raymond (1973) *Hegel*. London: Allen & Unwin.

Pöggeler, Otto (1990) 'Hegels philosophische Anfänge', in *Der Weg zum System*, ed. Christoph Jamme and Helmut Schneider. Frankfurt: Suhrkamp.

—— (1999) *Hegels Kritik der Romantik*. Munich: Fink.

Pöggeler, Otto and Gethmann-Siefert, Annemarie, eds (1983) *Kunsterfahrung und Kulturpolitik im Berlin Hegels*, Hegel-Studien, Beiheft 22. Bonn: Bouvier.

—— (1986) *Welt und Wirkung von Hegels Ästhetik*. Hegel-Studien Beiheft 27. Bonn: Bouvier.

Popper, Karl (1940) 'What is Dialectic', *Mind* 49: 403–10.

—— (1945) *The Open Society and its Enemies*. London: Routledge, 2 vols.

Rapp, Carl (2000) 'Hegel's Concept of the Dissolution of Art', in *Hegel and Aesthetics*, ed. William Maker. Albany: SUNY Press, pp. 13–30.

Rawls, John (2000) *Lectures on the History of Moral Philosophy*. Cambridge, MA: Harvard University Press.

Redding, Paul (1996) *Hegel's Hermeneutics*. Ithaca, NY: Cornell University Press.

Richards, Robert (1992) *The Meaning of Evolution*. Chicago: University of Chicago Press.

—— (2002) *The Romantic Conception of Life: Science and Philosophy in the Age of Goethe*. Chicago: University of Chicago Press.

Riedel, Manfred (1973) *System und Geschichte: Studien zum historischen Standort von Hegels Philosophie*. Frankfurt: Suhrkamp.

Riley, Patrick (1982) *Will and Political Legitimacy*. Cambridge, MA: Harvard University Press.

Ritter, Joachim (1965) *Hegel und die franzöische Revolution*. Frankfurt: Suhrkamp.

Roe, Shirley (1981) *Matter, Life and Generation: 18th Century Embryology and the Haller-Wolff Debate*. Cambridge: Cambridge University Press.

Rosen, Michael (1982) *Hegel's Dialectic and its Criticism*. Cambridge: Cambridge University Press.

Rosenkranz, Karl (1844) *G.W.F. Hegels Leben*. Berlin: Duncker & Humboldt. New edn, Darmstadt: Wissenschaftlicher Buchgesellschaft, 1972.

—— (1870) *Hegel als deutscher Nationalphilosoph*. Leipzig: Duncker & Humblot.

Rosenzweig, Franz (1920) *Hegel und der Staat*. Munich: Oldenbourg Verlag, 2 vols. New edn, Aalen: Scientia Verlag, 1982.

Royce, Josiah (1919) *Lectures on Modern Idealism*. New Haven, CT: Yale University Press.

Sabine, George (1963) *A History of Political Theory*, 3rd edn. London: Harrap.

Schmidt, James, ed. (1996) *What is Enlightenment? Eighteenth-Century Answers and Twentieth-Century Questions*. Berkeley: University of California Press.

Sheehan, James (1989) *German History, 1770–1866*. Oxford: Oxford University Press.

Shklar, Judith (1976) *Freedom & Independence. A Study of the Political Ideas of Hegel's Phenomenology of Mind*. Cambridge: Cambridge University Press.

Simpson, Peter (1998) *Hegel's Transcendental Induction*. Albany: SUNY Press.

Smith, Steven (1989) *Hegel's Critique of Liberalism*. Chicago: University of Chicago Press.

Soll, Ivan (1969) *An Introduction to Hegel's Metaphysics*. Chicago: University of Chicago Press.

Solomon, Robert (1983) *In the Spirit of Hegel*. Oxford: Oxford University Press.

Steinhauer, Kurt (1980) *Hegel Bibliographie*. Munich: Sauer.

Steinkraus, Warren, ed. (1980) *Art and Logic in Hegel's Philosophy*. Atlantic Highlands, NJ: Humanities Press.

Stepelevich, Lawrence (1983) *The Young Hegelians*. Cambridge: Cambridge University Press.

Stern, Robert (1990) *Hegel, Kant and the Structure of the Object*. London: Routledge.

—— (2002) *Hegel and the Phenomenology of Spirit*. London: Routledge.

Stewart, Jon (1996) 'Hegel and the Myth of Reason', in Jon Stewart (ed.) *The Hegel Myths and Legends*. Evanston, IL: Northwestern University Press, pp. 306–18.

—— (2000) *The Unity of Hegel's Phenomenology of Spirit*. Evanston, IL: Northwestern University Press.

Stirling, James (1898) *The Secret of Hegel*. Edinburgh: Oliver & Boyd.

Taylor, Charles (1975), *Hegel*. Cambridge: Cambridge University Press.

—— (1979) *Hegel and Modern Society*. Cambridge: Cambridge University Press.

Timm, Hermann (1974) *Gott und die Freiheit. Studien zur Religionsphilosophie der Goethezeit*. Frankfurt: Klostermann. Volume 22 in Studien zur Philosophie und Literatur des neunzehnten Jahrhunderts.

Toews, John (1980) *Hegelianism: The Path toward Dialectical Humanism, 1805–1841*. Cambridge: Cambridge University Press.

—— (1992) 'Transformations of Hegelianism', in *The Cambridge Companion to Hegel*, ed. Frederick C. Beiset. Cambridge: Cambridge University Press, pp. 378–413.

Tuck, Richard (1979) *Natural Rights Theories: Their Origin and Development*. Cambridge: Cambridge University Press.

Tunick, Mark (1992) *Hegel's Political Philosophy*. Princeton, NJ: Princeton University Press.

Wahl, Jean (1951) *La Malheur de la conscience dans la philosophie de Hegel*. Paris: Presses Universitaires de France.

Walsh, W.H. (1971) 'Principle and Prejudice in Hegel's Philosophy of History', in Z.A. Pelczynski, *Hegel's Political Philosophy: Problems & Perspectives*. Cambridge: Cambridge University Press, pp. 181–98.

Weil, Eric (1950) *Hegel et l'État*. Paris: Vrin.

Weiss, Frederick (1973) 'A Bibliography of Books on Hegel in English', in J. O'Malley, (ed.) *The Legacy of Hegel*. The Hague: Nijhoff, pp. 298–308.

Westphal, Kenneth (1989) *Hegel's Epistemological Realism*. Dordrecht: Kluwer.

—— (2003) *Hegel's Epistemology*. Indianapolis: Hackett.

Westphal, Merold (1979) *History and Truth in Hegel's Phenomenology*. Atlantic Highlands, NJ: Humanities Press.

—— (1992) *Hegel, Freedom, and Modernity*. Albany: SUNY Press.

White, Alan (1983) *Absolute Knowledge: Hegel and the Problem of Metaphysics*. Athens: Ohio University Press.

Wicks, Robert (1993) 'Hegel's Aesthetics: An Overview', in *The Cambridge Companion to Hegel*, ed. Frederick C. Beiser. Cambridge: Cambridge University Press, pp. 348–78.

Williams, Robert (1997) *Hegel's Ethic of Recognition*. Berkeley: University of California Press.

——(1987) 'Hegel's Concept of *Geist*', in Peter Stillman (ed.) *Hegel's Philosophy of Spirit*. Albany: SUNY Press, pp. 1–20.

Wilkins, Burleigh (1974) *Hegel's Philosophy of History*. Ithaca, NY: Cornell University Press.

Winfield, Richard (1988) *Reason and Justice*. Albany: SUNY Press.

—— (1991) *Freedom and Modernity*. Albany: SUNY Press.

Wood, Allen (1990) *Hegel's Ethical Thought*. Cambridge: Cambridge University Press.

Wolff, Hans (1949) *Die Weltanschauung der deutschen Aufklärung*. Berne: Francke.

Yerkes, James (1983) *The Christology of Hegel*. Albany: SUNY Press.

Yovel, Yirmiahu (1996) 'Hegel's Dictum that the Rational is the Actual and the Actual is the Rational: Its Ontological Content and its Function in Discourse', in *The Hegel Myths and Legends*, ed. Jon Stewart. Evanston, IL: Northwestern University Press, pp. 26–41.

Index

Routledge Philosophy GuideBook to Hegel on *History*

Joseph McCarney, South Bank University, UK

'Excellent, clearly written introduction. I cannot recommend it more highly to people who want to increase their understanding on Hegel's ideas.'

– Philosophers' Magazine

198x129: 400pp
Hb: 0-415-11695-3
Pb: 0-415-11696-1

Philosophical Romanticism

Edited by **Nikolas Kompridis**, York University, Toronto, Canada

This collection of specially-written articles by world-class philosophers explores the contribution of romantic thought to topics such as freedom, autonomy, and subjectivity; memory and imagination; art and ethics.

234x156: 352pp
Hb: 0-415-25643-7
Pb: 0-415-25644-5

Routledge Philosophy GuideBook to Hegel and the *Phenomenology of Spirit*

Robert Stern, University of Sheffield, UK

'Stern provides an excellent study of the Phenomenology of Spirit ... It will be extremely helpful for students.'
- *International Journal of Philosophical Studies*

'Robert Stern has added another valuable volume to the Routledge Philosophy GuideBook series. This is a clear, thoughtful, very erudite and successfully didactic work. Its reading is careful and its adjudications of secondary literature very acute.' - *Journal of the British Society for Phenomenology*

198x129: 256pp
Hb: 0-415-21787-3
Pb: 0-415-21788-1

Routledge Philosophy GuideBook to Hegel and the *Philosophy of Right*

Dudley Knowles, University of Glasgow, UK

'Presents clearly and accurately the main ideas of the *Philosophy of Right* ... a most useful aid for readers not familiar with Hegel's thought and terminology. It provides direct, yet intelligent, access into his moral, legal, social and political theory.'
– *Jean-Philippe Deranty, Australian Journal of Political Science*

198x129: 400pp
Hb: 0-415-16577-6
Pb: 0-415-16578-4

Printed in Great Britain
by Amazon

57209798R00220